OXFORD PRIVATE INTERNATIONAL LAW SERIES

GENERAL EDITORS:

JONATHAN HARRIS QC

Barrister, Serle Court;
Professor of International Commercial Law,
King's College, London

&

ANDREW DICKINSON

Fellow and Tutor, St Catherine's College and
Professor of Law, University of Oxford;
Solicitor (England and Wales)

SOVEREIGN DEFAULTS BEFORE DOMESTIC COURTS

OXFORD PRIVATE INTERNATIONAL LAW SERIES

General Editors: Jonathan Harris QC & Andrew Dickinson

The aim of this series is to publish works of quality and originality in a number of important areas of private international law. The series is intended for both scholarly and practitioner readers.

ALSO IN THIS SERIES

Intellectual Property and Private International Law (Second Edition)
JAMES J FAWCETT AND PAUL TORREMANS

The Anti-Suit Injunction
THOMAS RAPHAEL

Cross-Border Divorce Law: Brussels II *bis*
MÁIRE NÍ SHÚILLEABHÁIN

The Rome II Regulation: The Law Applicable to Non-Contractual Obligations
ANDREW DICKINSON

Cross-Border Consumer Contracts
JONATHAN HILL

Agreements on Jurisdiction and Choice of Law
ADRIAN BRIGGS

Civil Jurisdiction Rules of the EU and their Impact on Third States
THALIA KRUGER

Conflict of Laws within the UK
KIRSTY J HOOD

Insolvency in Private International Law (Second Edition)
IAN F FLETCHER

The Transfer of Property in the Conflict of Laws
JANEEN M CARRUTHERS

International Sale of Goods in the Conflict of Laws
JAMES J FAWCETT, JONATHAN HARRIS, AND MICHAEL BRIDGE

Choice of Law for Equitable Doctrines
T M YEO

Procedural Law in International Arbitration
GEORGIOS PETROCHILOS

Foreign Law in English Courts
RICHARD FENTIMAN

Declining Jurisdiction in Private International Law
JAMES J FAWCETT

SOVEREIGN DEFAULTS BEFORE DOMESTIC COURTS

HAYK KUPELYANTS

OXFORD
UNIVERSITY PRESS

OXFORD
UNIVERSITY PRESS

Great Clarendon Street, Oxford, OX2 6DP,
United Kingdom

Oxford University Press is a department of the University of Oxford.
It furthers the University's objective of excellence in research, scholarship,
and education by publishing worldwide. Oxford is a registered trade mark of
Oxford University Press in the UK and in certain other countries

First Edition published in 2018

Impression: 1

Published in the United States of America by Oxford University Press
198 Madison Avenue, New York, NY 10016, United States of America

British Library Cataloguing in Publication Data
Data available

Library of Congress Control Number: 2017960265

ISBN 978–0–19–880723–0

Printed and bound by
CPI Group (UK) Ltd, Croydon, CR0 4YY

General Editors' Preface

In the general editor's preface to the first book published in this series in 1995, Peter Carter QC stated that "the aim of the series is to publish works of originality and quality on a number of important and developing areas of private international law". Over the next twenty years and more, those aims have been admirably fulfilled under the general editorship of Peter Carter and his successor, Professor James Fawcett. We are delighted and honoured to follow in their footsteps as general editors of the series, and will strive to maintain the standards that our predecessors have set.

Of course, the series can only ever be as good as the work of its authors. In this respect, we are pleased that the first book published under out editorship is Dr Hayk Kupelyants's book on *Sovereign Defaults before Domestic Courts*. It is a thorough and original analysis of a subject of great contemporary importance. The author points out that, in 2014, sovereign debt obligations accounted for more than 25 per cent of the world's global debt, amounting to about US$58 trillion. Bondholders have shown increasing tenacity and ingenuity in pursuing claims and seeking to enforce judgments against sovereign debtors. Yet, there remains considerable uncertainty as to the law, and the legal analysis, of many aspects of sovereign defaults and restructurings. For instance, Dr Kupelyants considers whether restructuring should be treated as purely a question of contractual renegotiation, or subject to something analogous to an insolvency regime. As he points out, the absence of clear legal regulation in this area has, in turn, helped to stimulate the market in distressed debt and aggressive holdout claims.

Although the author's primary focus is on sovereign debt disputes in the English courts, he also draws upon extensive comparative research, especially as to the position before the New York courts. He focuses particularly on the litigation options available to bondholders and sovereign debtors. Dr Kupelyants analyses both the domestic and international markets for sovereign bonds. He examines the contractual context within which sovereign debt disputes fall to be determined, the ability of the State unilaterally to modify domestic bonds and defences to repayment. He also considers in detail the myriad of cross-border problems arising in applying the rules of jurisdiction, choice of law (particularly in the absence of choice) and enforcement to sovereign debt claims, including issues of state immunity. A particularly important part of Dr Kupelyants's work is his taxonomy of the challenges to sovereign debt restructurings.

Dr Kupelyants examines the legal problems created by sovereign defaults against the wider political and economic landscape and considerations of public policy. He considers the practical issues and challenges facing bondholders and the State when a default occurs. The author has also conducted empirical research and interviews, as well as examining a large sample of bond documentation. The result is a book that ably integrates rigorous legal analysis and practical context.

Sovereign Defaults before Domestic Courts is an important work and one that is likely to be influential in the further development of the law in this area.

Professor Jonathan Harris QC
London

Professor Andrew Dickinson
Oxford

11 December 2017

Preface

Sovereign defaults are perhaps unavoidable in the current international financial system. While efficient debt management practices and mechanisms for reducing overborrowing need to be conceived, it would border upon ignorance to shut one's eyes to the realities of sovereign debt litigation. Active bondholders do not shun litigation, principally before English and New York courts, and their attempts to enforce judgments against sovereign debtors have often been met with success.

What the book seeks to achieve is to provide guidance on and fill the gaps in the many stages of sovereign debt litigation. Sovereign debt litigation is an area of law where much is yet to be discovered and where many rules are still inchoate. The entire practice of sovereign debt litigation is further confused by the fact that sovereign defaults conflate issues of positive private law, public-law thinking, policy-fuelled reasoning, and emotional reactions. The task of any commercial judge hearing a sovereign debt dispute is all the more exacerbated by the lack of any sovereign insolvency regime proper.

This book is an expanded and revised doctoral thesis written at the University of Cambridge. Many people contributed to my research. First and foremost, I am greatly indebted to my supervisors Richard Fentiman and Michael Waibel. They provided invaluable assistance and support throughout the three years of my research. They were role models for academic rigour and integrity.

I further owe special thanks to the examiners of my PhD: Philip Wood QC and Jonathan Harris QC. Their constructive critique helped transform a PhD thesis into a more well-rounded monograph. Coincidentally, Jonathan Harris QC is, together with Andrew Dickinson, the General Editor of the Oxford Private International Law Series, and their support and encouragement were critical. I wish to record my special thanks to Andrew Dickinson who, in addition to his role as the General Editor of the Series, had a much earlier and decisive role in the writing of this monograph: he first sparked my interest in sovereign debt litigation.

The monograph would not have been possible without the generosity and support of the Luys Foundation, Sidney Sussex College and the Insolvency Lawyers' Association. Sidney Sussex College and the Squire Law Library where the PhD thesis was written provided a stimulating and congenial environment for my research. My colleagues at the Faculty of Law at Cambridge have been nothing but supportive and encouraging. The monograph greatly benefited from exchanges at the Max Planck

Institute for International, European and Regulatory Procedural Law in Luxembourg in 2015, the University of Heidelberg in 2015 and 2016 and the Max Planck Institute for Comparative and International Private Law Hamburg in 2016.

I would like to thank all those who discussed the ideas presented in this monograph: Sir Andrew Longmore, Andrew Shutter, Andrew Yianni, Christoph Trebesch, Daniel Peat, Eva Lein, Gabriel Moss QC, Jonathan Blackman, Louise Merrett, Matthew Windsor, Mitu Gulati, Natasha Harrison, Neil Andrews, Pippa Rogerson, Rosa Lastra, Rodrigo Olivares-Caminal, Stavros Brekoulakis, Steven Friel, Yannis Manuelides and many others. Special thanks are due to Sir William Blair for writing such a benevolent foreword. Thanks are also due to the four anonymous reviewers of my monograph.

The Financial Markets Law Committee provided a platform for fruitful discussion, especially for Chapter 7. I wish to thanks the partners in the London office of Cleary, Gottlieb, Steen & Hamilton for affording practical insights in the area of sovereign debt.

Oxford University Press effortlessly transformed disparate texts into a single, uniform and readable document. My friends from Cambridge, London and Yerevan helped, each in their own way. Anna was always there for me. She always provided a more sophisticated view, unencumbered by legal clichés. Finally, I am very grateful to my family.

The views expressed here, including any errors or omissions, are mine alone and do not reflect the views of any other institution or person. The law is as of 30 September 2017.

Dr Hayk Kupelyants
Cambridge
20 November 2017

Foreword

For the time being, in fact for the foreseeable future, much of the legal outcome of sovereign defaults will be dealt with by domestic courts, and the preponderance of these (reflecting governing law and jurisdiction clauses), will be dealt with by the courts of London and New York—as the author puts it, 'bastions of the protection of the pecuniary interests of bondholders'.

In theory, these cases should be relatively straightforward for the courts, in the sense that money due and owing has not been repaid, and standard contractual documentation waives to a greater or lesser degree the immunity that would otherwise be accorded to the sovereign. And in fact, as the author points out, in those cases in which liability is in issue, the summary procedure is often apposite.

In practice, however, these cases are far from straightforward. There is tension between the rights of investors and the duties of a State to care for its people—highlighted in the epic legal battle between NML and Argentina (which is dealt with in these pages in a fair and balanced way). The court may be faced with lending which is alleged to be tainted by corruption, or a debt which is said to be an 'odious debt' (though this is a doctrine which, as the author says, at least for the present is more a creation of academic literature than positive law). Enforcement raises its own raft of sensitivities, as does restructuring and minority rights.

Judges are not insensitive to these often deep-seated and controversial issues. But they have to decide the case according to the law, many of the principles of which are the subject of precedential authority. As the author puts it, domestic courts are not necessarily best suited to weigh the various conflicting and ultimately irreconcilable public policy considerations at play. This is a process that needs to be done and cannot be put off indefinitely. But so far, there is no consensus in the international community, and specifically legal initiatives such as the UK's Debt Relief (Developing Countries) Act 2010 have not been widely taken up.

In this groundbreaking study, Dr Hayk Kupelyants has brought together the law on sovereign defaults to present it as a coherent whole. This coherence gives the book its structure and strength. Focused mainly on the English case law, and that of New York, the subject is covered in its entirety, from contractual framework and documentation, jurisdiction and governing law, to the question of unilateral modification (the author's underlying idea being that necessity on the part of a sovereign debtor does not give an unrestricted right to act above the law), to defences and challenges—the ones which have succeeded and the ones which have not —through to restructurings and enforcement.

Dr Kupelyants argues persuasively that private law mechanisms, and the ordinary deployment of the debt restructuring process, are well tuned to protecting the sovereign debtor, and that judicial case-by-case innovation is the most realistic path for filling the legal vacuum. An understanding of this process is greatly advanced by the publication of Sovereign Defaults before Domestic Courts.

This fine study follows other distinguished contributions from the University of Cambridge in the field. It will bring valuable insights and analysis to practitioners (and of course judges), and all those who seek to make sense of this challenging but ultimately important and absorbing subject.

Sir William Blair
Centre for Commercial Law Studies
Queen Mary University of London
January 2018

Contents

Table of Cases

ENGLISH CASES

US CASES

OTHER DOMESTIC CASES

(I) Argentina

(II) Australia

(III) Austria

(IV) Belgium

(V) France

(VI) Germany

(VII) Hong Kong

(VIII) Italy

(IX) Russia

(X) Spain

(XI) Sweden

(XII) The Netherlands

EUROPEAN COURT OF HUMAN RIGHTS

INTERNATIONAL COURT OF JUSTICE (PERMANENT COURT OF INTERNATIONAL JUSTICE)

INTERNATIONAL ARBITRATION CASES

COURT OF JUSTICE OF THE EUROPEAN UNION

Table of Sovereign Bonds

Table of Legislation, Treaties, and Official Documents

UK STATUTES AND INSTRUMENTS

US STATUTES AND INSTRUMENTS

EU TREATIES, REGULATIONS, AND INSTRUMENTS

INTERNATIONAL CONVENTIONS AND INSTRUMENTS

MISCELLANEOUS

Introduction

I. A PROBLEM STATED

'The progress of the enormous debts which at present oppress, and will in the long-run probably ruin, all the great nations of Europe, has been pretty uniform.'[1] These words of Adam Smith written as early as 1776 in the seminal *Wealth of Nations* could easily have been written today, illustrating the bleak realities of the modern global financial predicament. **I.01**

Sovereign debt obligations account for more than 25% of the world's global debt (as of 2014), approximately US$58 tn.[2] Sovereign debt takes a wide variety of forms and sources. The forms of sovereign debt are multiple: domestic debt and external debt, bonds and syndicated loans, cheques, and trade credits, 'garden-variety' instruments and more sophisticated, 'tailor-made' instruments. The counterparts of the sovereign debtor also vary—funds may be extended by bilateral, multilateral, or private creditors. **I.02**

Notwithstanding this variety of forms and sources, ever since the 1990s there has been a clear shift in international markets in favour of financing sovereigns predominantly through bond markets, rather than syndicated loans. For this reason, sovereign bonds will be the core focus of this book. Official lending and syndicated loans will only be discussed in passing as and when required. **I.03**

Sovereign bonds, whether external or domestic, are at first issued in so-called primary markets, a term of art used to denote the initial issuance of sovereign bonds to subscribers. A typical characteristic of sovereign bonds is that they may later be traded in so-called secondary markets, where sovereign bonds will change hands following the primary issuance of bonds. The secondary markets are the medium through which primary subscribers may assign their rights under the bonds to other actors in financial markets. Such assignees assume risks in the hope of securing a windfall. **I.04**

[1] Adam Smith, *An Enquiry into the Nature and Causes of the Wealth of Nations* (2007) 595.

[2] McKinsey & Company, 'McKinsey Global Institute: Debt and (Not Much) Deleveraging' (2015) 15.

I.05 Notwithstanding the apparent risks of investing into sovereign bonds, private markets have little, if any, hesitation to lend to the State, subject of course to a commensurate interest rate. And the States are rarely prudent in the magnitude of their borrowings: examples of States that overborrow much beyond their repayment capacity abound in history. Reasons for overborrowing are manifold and are beyond the scope of this study. Suffice to say that the direct consequence of overborrowing is that States (developing and developed alike) sooner or later face the harsh reality of lacking the wherewithal to stay current on their debt obligations and the economic growth is no longer sufficient to service the increasing debt and interest payments.

I.06 States have various options at their disposal to deal with the excessive level of public debt, such as the spiking of inflation, imposition of capital controls, and other forms of financial repression.[3] They may also have recourse to bailouts offered by international financial institutions (typically, the International Monetary Fund (IMF)). But in times of extreme indebtedness these measures often prove inadequate and States resort to defaulting and/or restructuring to reduce their mountainous debt.[4] While the prospects of a default or debt restructuring are so daunting as to send shivers through the world of global finance, at times the only optimal solution is the outright default on or restructuring of the sovereign debt despite the significant costs they entail.[5]

I.07 In light of this, it stands to reason that sovereign debt defaults and restructurings are a pervasive feature of the international financial system as it currently stands. Nevertheless, the law has failed to address them systematically through a set of coherent rules. Instead, sovereign debt bankruptcies are addressed on an ad hoc basis through the medium of a contractual renegotiation of sovereign bonds ('sovereign debt restructuring'). Sovereign debt restructurings are in essence a vehicle for the reduction of the State's debt level through the contractual renegotiation with creditors. What will commonly happen is that the State will approach creditors to restructure/reduce its debt composition by exchanging old bonds for new bonds that are more favourable to the debtor ('exchange offer'). Upon obtaining the consent of its creditors to the exchange, the restructuring of sovereign bonds will result in the reduction of the nominal value of bonds, extension of maturities, decrease of interest rate, and combinations

[3] Carmen Reinhart and Kenneth Rogoff, 'Financial and Sovereign Debt Crises: Some Lessons Learned and Those Forgotten' (2013) IMF Working Paper WP/13/266, 4, 9.

[4] Thomas Piketty, *Capital in the Twenty-First Century* (2014) 542, 544–47.

[5] Klaus Adam and Michael Grill, 'Optimal Sovereign Default' (2013) Deutsche Bundesbank No 09/2013.

thereof. The sovereign debt restructuring thus secures some level of debt relief to the insolvent sovereign debtor so as to ensure the sustainability of its debt. Under this practice, bondholders are in fact shouldering the costs of sovereign debt crises (the idea of 'private sector involvement').

As this summary account suggests, the rules on sovereign debt restructurings are rather rudimentary in their scope and nature; they are in essence a technique of purely contractual renegotiation devoid of the intricacies of bankruptcy law proper. The efforts to establish a sovereign bankruptcy regime (akin to the insolvency regimes in domestic laws)—which to some was a panacea for sovereign debt crises and for others a quixotic enterprise[6]—have failed.[7] Most prominently, in the early 2000s, the IMF proposed the creation of the Sovereign Debt Restructuring Mechanism (SDRM), which did not see the light of the day due to the absence of political support. Instead of the statutory mechanism of sovereign debt restructurings, the system that has been put in place relies on adoption of contractual clauses that will ease the operation of sovereign debt restructurings (discussed in Chapter 2). A permanent bone of contention among experts in sovereign debt is which of the following is the most efficacious solution: the establishment of a proper bankruptcy mechanism for sovereigns ('statutory approach') or the mirroring of bankruptcy procedures through the inclusion of contractual clauses ('contractual approach'). I.08

Aggressive holdout litigation may serve to highlight the apparent conflict between the two approaches. In the absence of compulsory bankruptcy protections for sovereigns, a category of holdout creditors—often specialised hedge funds (sometimes pejoratively dubbed 'vulture' funds)—have established the practice of buying distressed sovereign debt or judgments issued against a sovereign on the secondary market at a deeply reduced price to their par. And by consistently refusing to join the renegotiation process and aggressively litigating, they attempt to recover the full value of the debt thus purchased. What happens in practice is that a supermajority of bondholders are cajoled into accepting the 'haircut' (reduction) to their bondholding in view of the precarious nature of the sovereign debtor's economy and finances. By contrast, the remaining 10% of bondholders, often the litigious hedge funds, refuse to exchange their bonds for new, reduced-in-value bonds, attempting to enforce their bonds at face value. I.09

[6] For an overview of sovereign bankruptcy regime proposals, see Udaibir Das, Michael Papaioannou, and Christoph Trebesch, 'Sovereign Debt Restructurings 1950–2010: Literature Survey, Data, and Stylized Facts' (2012) IMF Working Paper WP/12/203, 88.

[7] But see UN General Assembly, 'Towards the Establishment of a Multilateral Legal Framework for Sovereign Debt Restructuring Processes' (2014) UN Doc A/Res/68/304.

I.10 The average recovery rates for this sort of tactics have been estimated to range from three to twenty times the investment in the bonds.[8] Were the sovereign debtors subject to bankruptcy protections, the legal actions by litigious hedge funds would have been stayed and the holdout creditor would have undergone a compulsory reduction of its claims.

I.11 One group of policymakers, organisations, and scholars have consistently underlined the adverse effects of holdout litigation and subjected them to moral obloquy. They have argued that the sort of arbitrage strategies that 'vulture' funds employ have the effect of harassing the sovereign debtor and potentially jeopardising the restructuring process.[9] Opportunistic holdout litigation is said to delay settlement, negatively affect the economic situation of the sovereign debtor, block the access to international capital markets, and increase the costs of restructuring.[10] In addition, the holdout strategy may potentially trigger legal actions from other creditors by sending a clear signal that the sovereign debtor's assets are not unlimited.[11] Further, holdout litigation may limit the ability of the State to use its resources abroad by subjecting these assets to the constant risk of attachment. Lastly, holdout creditors seek to attach the funds that are meant to be used for payment to the majority of creditors and push the sovereign debtor to the brink of default. These deleterious effects obviously exert pressure on the sovereign debtor and the holdout creditor is able to demand a large recovery rate.[12] Empirical data suggests that aggressive holdout litigation may have a negative impact on the pricing of sovereign bonds and creditors may charge less for bonds that face lesser risk of holdout litigation.[13]

[8] Manmohan Singh, 'Recovery Rates from Distressed Debt—Empirical Evidence from Chapter 11 Fillings, International Litigation, and Recent Sovereign Debt Restructurings' (2003) IMF Working Paper WP/03/161, 8.

[9] See generally Anne Krueger, 'New Approaches to Sovereign Debt Restructuring: An Update on our Thinking' (2002) IMF Publication. The UN General Assembly recognised the 'concerns about vulture fund litigation' (UN GA Res A/RES/66/189, External Debt Sustainability and Development, 14 February 2012, para 29).

[10] Julian Schumacher, Christoph Trebesch, and Henrik Enderlein, 'What Explains Sovereign Debt Litigation?' (2015) CESIFO Working Paper No 5319, 1; Jill Fisch and Caroline Gentile, 'Vultures or Vanguards?: The Role of Litigation in Sovereign Debt Restructuring' (2004) 53 Emory LJ 1043, 1092.

[11] Eric Robert, 'Rééchelonnement de la dette ou règlement judiciaire?' in Dominique Carreau and Malcolm Shaw (eds), *La Dette extérieure: The External Debt* (1995) 620; Lee Buchheit and Mitu Gulati, 'Sovereign Bonds and the Collective Will' (2002) 51 Emory LJ 1317, 1320.

[12] Singh (n 8) 13.

[13] Michael Bradley, James Cox, and Mitu Gulati, 'The Market Reaction to Legal Shocks and their Antidotes' (2010) 39 J Leg Stud 289, 312–17. On the truthfulness of the claims on pricing see Chapter 1.

The opposite camp claims that the troubles in sovereign debt markets arise from the weakness of the rights of bondholders. The initiatives to weaken them even further might lead to undesired results. The right of creditors to request repayment of debt is said to ensure the survival and long-term health of debt markets, and is conducive to continued borrowing in the future.[14] I.12

The broader idea underpinning the attitude of the second camp is that too inconsiderate restraints on the activity of litigious hedge funds might have long-term damaging side effects.[15] Litigious hedge funds have their own mission to play: by purchasing bonds in the secondary market they provide liquidity,[16] enable banks to sell off the 'bad' bonds to comply with bank regulatory requirements, create an opposition to the almost exclusive power of the State in sovereign debt restructurings, and impose discipline on sovereign debtors.[17] Devoid of this function, primary bondholders would have been all the more exposed to the wide-ranging bargaining power of the sovereign debtor.[18] Recalcitrant funds thus take on the role of defeating 'opportunistic defaults', ie, defaults where the State, albeit having the capacity to pay up, is unwilling to do so.[19] In addition, the presence of a liquid secondary market may arguably drive down the yields and costs of borrowing for sovereign debtors.[20] I.13

The first camp rebuts this by claiming that in practice, the individual rights of creditors play to the powerful funds that possess the necessary I.14

14 Andrei Shleifer, 'Will the Sovereign Debt Market Survive?' (2003) 93(2) Amer Econ Rev 85.

15 The idea received the imprimatur of the Second Circuit (*Elliott Associates v Banco de la Nacion and Republic of Peru*, 194 F3d 363, 380 (2d Cir 1999) (stressing 'the long term effect' of limiting the rights of creditors). See also John Armour, Antonia Menezes, Mahesh Uttamchandani, and Kristin van Zwieten, 'How Do Creditor Rights Matter for Debt Finance? A Review of Empirical Evidence' in Frederique Dahan (ed), *Research Handbook on Secured Financing of Commercial Transactions* (2015) 13–25 (finding that the reduction of the rights of creditors leads in many cases to more onerous access to credit).

16 Jonathan Goren, 'State-to-State Debts: Sovereign Immunity and the "Vulture" Hunt' (2010) 41 Geo Wash Intl L Rev 681, 692–93. The level and significance of this liquidity is unclear—some argue that it is negligible to justify the holdout tactics of hedge funds (Martin Wolf, 'Holdouts Give Vultures a Bad Name' (2 September 2014) Financial Times). In support of hedge fund litigation, see Hal Scott, 'Sovereign Debt Default: Cry for the United States, Not Argentina' (2006) Washington Legal Foundation Working Paper Series No 140.

17 Natasha Harrison and Fiona Huntriss, 'Hedge Funds and Litigation: A Brave New World' (2015) 10(2) CMLJ 135.

18 For an opposite view, see Schumacher et al (n 10) 22 (who do not find that the presence of secondary markets increases the probability of litigation).

19 On other benefits of holdout litigation, see Fisch and Gentile (n 10) 1051, 1102–05.

20 See for an example of the secondary market of mortgages Vicki Waye, *Trading in Legal Claims* (2008) 215–16.

knowledge and funds to ensure that the judgments are enforced in their favour, whereas the remaining bondholders do not fully enjoy the benefit of enforcement rights.[21] Yet, it is an exaggeration to claim that sovereign debt litigation is necessarily initiated by sophisticated hedge funds—retail bondholders may on occasions litigate, too.[22]

I.15 This debate clearly demonstrates that sovereign debt adjudication conflates issues of policy, principle, pragmatism, and moral choice that are often hard, if at all possible, to reconcile. The principle of recoverability of debt may conflict with the practical inability of the State to meet its financial obligations, and, by contrast, an issue of policy might often prevail over moral choice.[23] A decision-maker would often walk a fine line in manoeuvring between these conflicting and perhaps irreconcilable issues.

I.16 The clash of various considerations in legal disputes is further exacerbated by the political repercussions of one or another solution on a sovereign debt crisis or the fate of a political/economic union. In sovereign debt litigation, politics and economics are never off the court's radar and are inexorably entwined. Ostensibly, neutral domestic courts in the exercise of their discretion are leery to jeopardise political agreements and economic considerations underlying the resolution of sovereign debt crises. The arguments constructed in this book are not oblivious to the *realpolitik* present in the adjudication of international financial transactions, but the book seeks to take a purified view of the legal side of sovereign debt disputes.

I.17 With the failure to establish an international bankruptcy court, the default forums for the resolution of external sovereign debt remain English and New York courts—the bastions for the protection of pecuniary interests of bondholders. Typically, States choose English or New York laws as the governing law of external bonds. It is estimated that English law governs a very sizeable portion of sovereign bonds (around 40% of bonds in the 2000s).[24]

[21] Sönke Haseler, 'Individual versus Collective Enforcement Rights in Sovereign Bonds' (2008) German Working Papers in Law and Economics, 9; Lee Buchheit, 'Supermajority Control Wins Out' (2007) 26 IFLR 21.

[22] See, eg, *Jackson v People's Republic of China*, 550 F Supp 869, 873 (ND Ala 1982); *Fontana v Republic of Argentina*, 415 F.3d 238 (2d Cir 2005) (one of many cases brought by individuals against Argentina). In the context of investment arbitration see *Abaclat and others v Argentine Republic*, ICSID Case No ARB/07/5, Decision on Jurisdiction and Admissibility, 4 August 2011.

[23] See, eg, Chapter 1 (contrasting the sanctity of contract with distributive fairness in the context of sovereign debt litigation).

[24] Michael Bradley and Mitu Gulati, 'Collective Action Clauses for the Eurozone' (2014) 18(6) Rev Fin 2045, 2055–56; Das et al (n 6) 41–43 (showing slightly smaller numbers).

II. OBJECTIVES AND SCOPE

In spite of the practical importance of the topic, it has received little sustained legal analysis. Nor has any attempt been made to combine legal and practical analysis in a comprehensive account of the law and practice governing the resolution of sovereign debt disputes before domestic courts. **I.18**

This monograph examines the resolution of sovereign debt disputes before English courts, and, to a lesser degree, New York courts. The purpose of this monograph is to set out a legal framework for the litigation of sovereign debt and provide guidance to the litigants and adjudicators of sovereign debt disputes alike. The practice of sovereign debt litigation is at times obscure, conducted in the shadow of vague financial covenants and complex negotiation patterns. The discussion focuses on those aspects of sovereign debt litigation which are under-analysed in scholarly writings or unsettled in practice, so as to inform future developments. **I.19**

This book concentrates on diverse litigation tactics and arbitrage strategies available to bondholders and sovereign debtors before English (and New York) courts. In most cases, private creditors may obtain summary judgments with relative ease, which indicates that the defences that the sovereign may rely upon would disclose little prospect of success. That said, often serious issues arise during the stages of assumption of jurisdiction, determination of governing law of sovereign bonds, or substantive resolution of the claims in English proceedings. **I.20**

In the first two chapters, the monograph first examines the theoretical underpinnings of sovereign debt litigation and then sets out the contractual background of sovereign debt litigation. Chapter 3 examines the jurisdiction of English courts and cognate matters (standing, pre-emptive strikes and stays of proceedings, interim measures). Chapters 4 and 5 consider the governing law: Chapter 4 analyses the law applicable to sovereign bonds in the absence of a choice of law clause, and Chapter 5 addresses the power of the State to unilaterally modify the bonds governed by its own domestic law. **I.21**

Chapter 6 addresses the defences in sovereign debt disputes and Chapter 7 examines the challenges to sovereign debt restructurings. Lastly, Chapter 8 set outs the enforcement of sovereign debt and the doctrine of sovereign immunity. **I.22**

A particularity of this monograph is that, in stark contrast to many publications on sovereign debt litigation, it examines both the external bonds **I.23** of a sovereign, namely, the bonds issued in foreign markets, and, to a comparable degree, the domestic bonds, that is, the bonds issued in the territory of the sovereign debtor. As will be seen, domestic debt is increasingly coming to the fore of sovereign debt litigation.

I.24 The adjudication of sovereign debt by international courts and tribunals will be treated only incidentally. Drawing analogies from the public international law of sovereign debt might not be a safe path since public international law may be driven by considerations different from those prevalent under English law.[25]

I.25 Some may be pessimistic about the very need to examine the topic of sovereign debt litigation. It is frequently doubted that holdout litigation poses serious risks to the successful deployment of sovereign debt restructurings.[26] Among other arguments undermining the risks of holdout litigation, scholars sceptically point to the limited incidents of holdout litigations, absence of coordination efforts between holdouts, high costs of minority creditor litigation, necessity of specialised knowledge, and so on. A common claim is that despite the alleged problem of holdout litigation, sovereign debt restructurings have operated smoothly due in part to the extensive sovereign immunity from execution which precludes any chances of judgment recovery[27] and the fact that sovereign's assets are predominantly located within the territory of the sovereign thus excluding the prospects of attachment.

I.26 It is an assumption of this monograph that creditors do have realistic prospects to seize sovereign property—although not without major difficulties—or at least to settle with sovereign debtors. This assumption is supported by three factors. First, the relatively small holdouts to date were often paid in full following the successful completion of a sovereign debt restructuring.[28] Second, sovereign creditors have at times been

[25] *Loan Agreement between Italy v Costa Rica*, 27 June 1998, XXV Reports of International Arbitral Awards 21, 72–74 (distinguishing technical, contractual adjudication in national courts as against public international law adjudication which is more flexible).

[26] IMF, 'A Survey of Experiences with Emerging Market Sovereign Debt Restructurings' (2012) 11; Ran Bi, Marcos Chamon, and Jeromin Zettelmeyer, 'The Problem that Wasn't: Coordination Failures in Sovereign Debt Restructurings' (2011) IMF Working Paper WP/11/265; Moody's Special Comment, 'The Role of Holdout Creditors and CACs in Sovereign Debt Restructurings' (2013).

[27] Netanella Zahavi, *Sovereign Default: Analyses and Remedies* (JSD thesis, Yale Law School, 2005) 157–90; Jeremy Bullow and Kenneth Rogoff, 'A Constant Recontracting Model of Sovereign Debt' (1989) 97(1) J Polit Econ 155, 157 (occasional attachments of sovereign property are far from fully repaying the debt).

[28] Federico Sturzenegger and Jeromin Zettelmeyer, *Debt Defaults and Lessons from a Decade of Crises* (2007) 256–61.

successful in directly attaching sovereign property,[29] tracing sovereign debt and obtaining third-party orders,[30] or securing explicit and wide-ranging waivers of State immunity from execution.[31] The issue is examined in more detail in Chapter 8.

Third, most scepticism focuses on the litigation of sovereign debt disputes, but it seems to miss the point that litigation may play a subdued role in sovereign debt restructuring when the creditor threatens to hold out and litigate, thus prompting the State to settle.[32] The risk of litigation might be a sword of Damocles hanging over the sovereign debtor and might eventually force the debtor to settle on terms favourable to the holdout creditor. Also, it is telling that following the default in 2001, Argentina has not issued any debt in New York as the creditors are likely to attach the proceeds from debt issuance. In the view of the long-lasting threat of attachment and disruptions of normal trade, many sovereigns are willing to pay the holdout creditors either in full or partly (as did Greece with around one-third of all foreign-law governed bonds in 2012).[33] **I.27**

As statistics suggests, sovereign debt litigation is clearly on the rise.[34] No doubt, creditors will not always be able to enforce meaningfully their rights in courts. State immunity and practical considerations may prevent an attempt of litigation and judicial recovery of the contractual entitlement under the bonds. That said, the law and contractual covenants are not epiphenomenal in that they are the background against which the sovereign and its creditors negotiate and upon which they act. The law has the potential for steering sovereign debt negotiations, even though at times it might lack in actual enforcement.[35] **I.28**

29 See, eg, *NML Capital Ltd v Republic of Argentina*, 680 F.3d 254 (2d Cir 2012); *EM Ltd v Republic of Argentina*, 389 F Appx 38 (2d Cir 2010); Singh (n 8) 9–10, 22–24.

30 *NML Capital Ltd v Republic of Argentina*, 699 F3d 246 (2d Cir 2012); *National Union Fire Insurance Co v Congo*, 1991 US Dist LEXIS 21581 (ND Ill 1991) (the claimant sought an order directed at a third party which led to a settlement between the parties). See also Patrick Wautelet, 'Les Fonds Vautours—Vulture funds, Creditors and Sovereign Debtors: How to Find a Balance?' in Mathias Audit (ed), *Insolvabilité des États et dettes souveraines* (2011) 112–14.

31 See, eg, Republic of Estonia, Offering Circular for 5% Notes due 2007 (cited in Mark Weidemaier, 'Disputing Boilerplate' (2009–10) 82 Temp LR 1, 36).

32 See, eg, IMF, 'A Survey of Experiences with Emerging Market Sovereign Debt Restructurings' (2012) 15 (a survey of recent restructurings shows that the overwhelming majority of disputes ended up in settlements).

33 Jeromin Zettelmeyer, Christoph Trebesch, and Mitu Gulati, 'The Greek Debt Exchange: An Autopsy' (2013) 28 Econ Pol 513, 527 (out of twenty-four foreign-law bonds, only 71% agreed to the restructuring, and the remaining 29% were paid in full).

34 Schumacher et al (n 10) 4, 34.

35 For a similar argument in public international law, see Surabhi Ranganathan, *Strategically Created Treaty Conflicts and the Politics of International Law* (2014) 38–41, 94.

III. METHODOLOGY

1.29 This book mostly employs black-letter law analysis. In addition to the legal analysis, the monograph rests on extensive empirical research. It relies on empirical data collected through questionnaires distributed to debt management agencies. Furthermore, the research is enriched through the examination of a dataset of approximately 1,800 bonds (mostly consulted at Thomson One Banker or confidentially provided by market participants). A further practical dimension derives from approximately fifteen interviews with practitioners working in the field of sovereign debt.

1

Theoretical Underpinnings of Sovereign Debt

I. INTRODUCTION

The status of sovereign debt has been and is likely to remain the subject of intense debates so long as there are impecunious governments. And that is for a good reason: how one conceptualises the nature of sovereign debt informs the attitude towards sovereign debt restructurings and litigation. While generalisations cannot do justice to the peculiarities of particular sovereign debt disputes, the determination of the character of sovereign debt and sovereign debt restructurings fosters a more consistent and foreseeable resolution of sovereign debt disputes. **1.01**

The legal rules governing specifically sovereign debt restructurings are predominantly non-existent or, at best, in an inchoate form. Many issues are worryingly left to the pragmatic and ad hoc resolution by practitioners and to the interplay of bargaining powers, politics, and concatenation of events. It would not be an over-exaggeration to claim that no coherent framework exists to resolve sovereign debt crises. Against this background, properly conceptualising the nature of sovereign debt is especially important. **1.02**

That said, the determination of the status of sovereign debt is by no means sufficient in and of itself to yield an all-embracing jurisprudential conception of sovereign debt litigation. However, an abstract evaluation of the nature of sovereign borrowing is crucial for the analysis of certain choices of law and substantive issues implicated in sovereign debt litigation that will be the focus of this book. **1.03**

In what follows, this chapter sets out the theoretical underpinnings of sovereign borrowing and litigation. It first examines the dual nature of sovereign bonds and their restructurings that may be characterised as either private or public, and as either bilateral or multilateral. The chapter then analyses to what extent broader public policy arguments may successfully be adduced in sovereign debt litigation. The chapter also considers the extent to which the concept of insolvency can meaningfully be **1.04** extrapolated to sovereign bankruptcies and whether the considerations of international comity may be adduced in sovereign debt litigation. Lastly, the chapter considers the role of financial markets as the regulators of sovereign debt disputes.

II. CHARACTERISATION

1. Commercial Character of Sovereign Debt Issuance

1.05 Long gone are the days when sovereign bonds were mere 'engagements of honour'.[1] The current understanding is that the creditor advancing funds to the State should not be left to the whims of the sovereign.[2] Revealingly, the choice of 'neutral' laws (almost invariably English and New York laws) to govern sovereign bonds and the demise of absolute immunity of States furnish foreign bondholders with direct legal remedies against the sovereign debtor in default.[3]

1.06 Nowadays few would contest the binding nature of (valid) sovereign debt, except for the doctrine of odious debt.[4] To do so would strike at the heart of the whole system of international finance. Yet, vestiges of the concept of sovereign debt as a mere 'engagement of honour' linger in the idea that the sovereign debt contract is somehow a *contrat aléatoire*,[5] in a sense that, by simply lending to a sovereign, the creditor accepts the inherent risk of the debt being either reduced or repudiated.[6] For many, the *aléatoire* character of sovereign debt flows either from the limited capacity that a bondholder has to enforce one's legal rights through legal remedies,[7] or from the legislative powers that a sovereign debtor enjoys to repudiate or

[1] *Twycross v Dreyfus* (1877) 5 Ch D 605, 611, 616.

[2] Edwin Borchard, 'International Loans and International Law' (1932) 26 Proceedings of the American Society of International Law at its Annual Meeting (1921–69) 135, 147.

[3] Holger Schier, *Towards a Reorganisation System for Sovereign Debt: An International Law Perspective* (2007) 6–8.

[4] On which see Chapter 6.

[5] Germain Watrin, *Essai de construction d'un contentieux international des dettes publiques* (1929) 23; *De Dreux-Breze v France* (Appl No 57969/00) ECtHR 15 May 2001, 9.

[6] Note that the idea of *aléa* in sovereign bonds is independent of the question of the pricing-in of the risk of sovereign default (paras 1.75–1.101), as the latter finds acquiescence in the sovereign default only as a result of a soar in interest rates charged at the time of issuance of debt, whereas the former sees something inherently risky/*aléatoire* in sovereign bonds.

[7] Georges van Hècke, *Problèmes juridiques des emprunts internationaux* (1964) 24–25.

at least modify its debt.[8] A rising number of scholars claim that sovereign debt is, or at least should be, a 'contingent claim' or an 'equity-like instrument', essentially justifying the State's default.[9]

After the initial hurdle of treating sovereign debt as binding is overcome,[10] two conflicting strands emerge in the characterisation of sovereign debt. Sovereign debt may be conceptualised as a public instrument issued by the State in the exercise of governmental authority or, at the least, exhibiting features of a governmental act. In the alternative, sovereign debt may be considered a substantively commercial transaction designed to raise funds, irrespective of the identity of the issuer. Each of the two has its own undeniable merits, given the inherent conflict generated by a public entity's recourse to private sources of funding. **1.07**

The antinomy of the public/private character of sovereign debt has amply been debated in scholarly literature. In the nineteenth and most of the twentieth centuries, sovereign debt was predominantly treated as a sacred instrument through the medium of which the State undertook to raise public funds in addition to the taxation of its residents.[11] Watrin claimed that sovereign debt is a 'regulatory contract' and sovereign debt litigation should be grounded in the principles derived from constitutional or administrative litigation.[12] More recently, others have claimed that sovereign debt restructurings are an exercise of international public authority, the implication being that they should be treated with high deference by international tribunals and national courts.[13] **1.08**

Others wholeheartedly support the private character of sovereign debt.[14] For them, sovereign debt is no different from private debt and should be subject to essentially the same commercial law regime as governs the debt of private debtors. **1.09**

[8] Albert Wuarin, *Essai sur les emprunts d'Etats et la protéction des droits des porteurs de fonds d'Etats étrangers* (1907) 34.

[9] Ashoka Mody, 'Sovereign Debt and its Restructuring Framework in the Euro Area' (2013) Bruegel Working Paper 2013/05, 23–27, 32–33.

[10] The point on the *aléa* will be treated later in this chapter, 1.18.

[11] See, eg, Gaston Jèze, 'Les défaillances d'Etat' (1935) 53 Recueil des Cours 377, 392–93.

[12] Watrin (n 5) 13, 19, 33.

[13] Armin von Bogdandy and Mathias Goldmann, 'Sovereign Debt Restructurings as Exercises of International Public Authority: Towards a Decentralized Sovereign Insolvency Law' in Carlos Espósito, Yuefen Li, and Juan Pablo Bohoslavsky (eds), *Sovereign Financing and International Law: The UNCTAD Principles on Responsible Sovereign Lending and Borrowing* (2013) 39–70.

[14] See, eg, Karl Strupp, 'L'intervention en matière financière' (1925) 8 Recueil des Cours 1, 67.

1.10 In pursuit of the middle ground, Borchard maintained that sovereign bonds are *sui generis* instruments which share private and public features.[15] Despite its apparent appeal, such a qualification would arguably prove unsatisfactory in practice, for it blows both cold and hot. If the *sui generis* character of bonds is affirmed, then the question is in what circumstances should the private or public side prevail over the other side and whether such a determination would not be arbitrary in most, if not all, cases. For *normative* (not merely *descriptive*) purposes, a court would need to determine the dominant character of sovereign bonds.

1.11 Treating sovereign debt as an amalgamation of conflicting elements of public and private may give rise to a cognitive dissonance for the adjudicators. Conversely, establishing the nature of sovereign debt—as either private or public—enables the judges to solve 'hard' cases arising in sovereign debt litigation. Certainly, this might come at the expense of ignoring the other side of sovereign debt issuance, but this seems unavoidable. Sovereign debt does not possess the miraculous wave-particle duality of light, which can manifest as a wave and a particle at the same time.

1.12 Over time, the status of sovereign debt has undergone a paradigm shift. Wrought by the liberalisation of financial markets and the acknowledgement of an equal standing for private bondholders, the debt that a sovereign may incur is now treated as an essentially private transaction in all of its manifestations. Judge Guillaume has neatly summarised the historical development:

> Les dettes souveraines créaient au 19 ème siècle des obligations d'un caractère très particulier du fait qu'elles émanaient d'Etats souverains. Elles étaient d'abord des dettes «souveraines». Au 21 ème siècle, il s'agit avant tout de «dettes», que l'on a fréquemment tendance à traiter en droit comme n'importe quelles autres dettes. Mais de nombreuses incertitudes demeurent et il est difficile de prévoir jusqu'où ira cette évolution de la jurisprudence.[16]
>
> In the nineteenth century, the sovereign debts created very specific obligations since they emanated from sovereign States. They were 'sovereign' debts in the first place. In the twenty-first century, what matters is that they are 'debts', which are treated in law as any other type of debt. But several uncertainties persist, and it is difficult to predict where this evolution will stop. [Author's translation]

1.13 *The law applicable to the characterisation of sovereign debt.* Although the character of sovereign debt is a jurisprudentially intriguing dilemma, properly understood, the issue falls to be determined by the legal system applicable

[15] Borchard (n 2) 15–17.

[16] Guilbert Guillaume, 'La défaillance financière des Etats devant les juges et les arbitres internationaux' (2013), Public Lecture, para 14 (on file with author).

to the sovereign debt. As the discussion below demonstrates, in the cases where English or New York laws govern the reciprocal rights and obligations of parties arising under a sovereign bond, these jurisdictions qualify sovereign bonds as a private, commercial transaction.

Pursuant to this logic, the characterisation that the law of the sovereign debtor might foist on the debt subject to a foreign law is largely irrelevant. Conversely, should the competent court conclude that the domestic law of the sovereign debtor governs sovereign bonds, the characterisation of the sovereign debt under the sovereign's domestic law would be conclusive for the determination of substantive matters. That is, as is customarily the case in the conflict of laws, subject to the exception of public policy of the courts of the forum.[17] **1.14**

So, too, is the issue of characterisation of sovereign debt for the purposes of application of the rules of private international law. The issue of characterisation is for the law of the forum and not for the law of the sovereign debtor. To cite one example, the domestic law of the sovereign debtor is irrelevant at the stage of characterising the sovereign debt in order to determine the law applicable to sovereign bonds in those cases when the law applicable to the bonds is yet to be resolved through the application of conflict of laws principles.[18] The characterisation of sovereign bonds would be exercised in accordance with the law of the forum, ie English law if the matter were brought to the English court. The same would be true in respect of the assumption of jurisdiction under residual rules on jurisdiction.[19] However, in cases when the EU Regulations apply, the characterisation becomes a matter of autonomous meaning of EU law.[20] **1.15**

Characterisation under the applicable English (and New York) law. Under the law of these two jurisdictions, bonds issued by the State are in essence commercial instruments via which the State borrows money from private creditors. In this sense, sovereign bonds are private contracts subject to the common regime of contract and private law. Competent courts are bound to apply ordinary private law tools to the interpretation and performance of sovereign debt instruments. **1.16**

At its strongest point, English and US courts alike have confirmed that sovereign borrowing is a commercial transaction in cases on the sovereign immunity of the borrower States.[21] Can these holdings on the commercial **1.17**

[17] See Chapter 5 applying the public policy exception to domestic-law governed bonds.

[18] See Chapter 4 applying English rules of conflict of laws to the determination of the law governing domestic bonds.

[19] See Chapter 3. [20] Ibid.

[21] *NML Capital Ltd v Republic of Argentina* [2011] UKSC 31, para 111; *Cardinal Financial Investment Corporation v Central Bank of Yemen*, 2000 WL 699384, 13–14 (Longmore J holding

nature of sovereign borrowing serve as a ground for a general affirmation of the commercial nature of sovereign bonds within English and New York laws, in particular in respect of the conflict of laws and substantive law? A consistent approach to sovereign borrowing requires an answer in the positive—the commercial nature of sovereign debt problems must be affirmed across the spectrum of areas where the issue may arise.[22]

1.18 Sovereign bond issuance is no longer perceived as a sovereign prerogative. It is rather a widespread tool for States and private companies alike to raise money on the capital markets. The sovereign usually subjects its debt to some municipal law,[23] and submits to the jurisdiction of foreign courts with an accompanying waiver of State immunity. Sovereign bond disputes are undoubtedly justiciable[24] and sovereign bond restructurings are conducted in compliance with the contractual clauses and provisions of the applicable municipal law. The Act of State doctrine does not apply to the sovereign default as the doctrine does not in principle extend to commercial transactions.[25] Within this framework, the idea of a *contrat aléatoire* and contingent debt, described above, is out of step with fundamental contractual principles which propagate the binding nature of commercial contracts.

1.19 If the commercial premise of sovereign bonds is accepted, then in principle it should not matter to what purpose the State allocates the money raised through the issuance of sovereign bonds. The arbitral tribunal in *Poštová*

that the issuance of promissory notes by the State's central bank, with the purpose of backing up State-to-State borrowing, was not an act done in the exercise of sovereign authority); *Trendtex Trading Corporation v Central Bank of Nigeria* [1977] QB 529 (in respect of letters of credit); *Weltover v Argentina*, 504 US 607 (1992). See also FA Mann, 'The Law Governing State Contracts' (1944) 21 BYBIL 11, 13.

22 See, for instance on the issue of apparent authority, *Themis Capital, LLC v Democratic Republic of Congo and Central Bank of the Democratic Republic of the Congo*, 881 F Supp 2d 508, 526 (SDNY, 2012). Certain forms of sovereign debt evidence stronger public traits as a result of the higher degree of official involvement (State-to-State debt, IMF loans) and it would be wrong to treat them as commercial transactions in most cases, but those are outside the scope of coverage of this book.

23 But see Chapter 4 on the absence of choice of law clauses in domestic sovereign debt.

24 *Crédit Français International SA v Sociedad Financiera de Comercio*, 490 NYS 2d 670, 677 (Sup Ct NY 1985); *NML Capital Ltd v Republic of Argentina* [2009] EWHC 110 (Comm), para 58; Peter Cresswell, William Blair, and Philip Wood (eds), *Butterworths Encyclopaedia of Banking Law* (2013) F-456–58.

25 For details, see Chapter 6. Campbell McLachlan, *Foreign Relations Law* (2014) 530; *Alfred Dunhill of London, Inc v The Republic of Cuba*, 425 US 682 (1976); *Yukos Capital SARL v OJSC Rosneft Oil Co* [2012] EWCA Civ 855, paras 92–94. The District Court in *Allied Bank*, discussed in Chapter 3, applied the Act of State given that the Costa Rican government intervened to cater for the illiquidity of a State-owned bank—the dispute was not thus concerned with the sovereign debt *sensu stricto*; Costa Rica was acting in the capacity of public regulator.

Banka v The Hellenic Republic was anxious to stress that sovereign debt is different in many respects from purely corporate debt.[26] It then went on to highlight that the final use to which the money lent to the State is put did matter for the purposes of ascertaining jurisdiction under Art 25 of the ICSID Convention. Should the debt be used to repay the existing debt of the sovereign, the tribunal would not assume jurisdiction.[27] On merits, the arbitral tribunal in *Italy v Costa Rica* took into account the amount of money that reached the Costa Rican government within the development assistance received from Italy and accordingly awarded lower damages.[28]

Similar enquiries into the final usage of the money lent are highly inappo- **1.20** site in the litigation before national (English and New York) courts. The arbitral tribunal in *Italy v Costa Rica* made it abundantly clear that its enquiry was not a technical, contractual analysis but analysis under international law guided by the considerations of equity.[29] The correct approach under domestic law would be to ignore the purpose behind the debt issuance—only the form of the debt should matter.[30]

The characterisation of internal (domestic) debt is less certain. Much of **1.21** domestic debt is issued under statutes (regulations)[31] or through offering documents.[32] While the characterisation of the domestic debt issued under statutes (regulations) is somewhat uncertain, hesitancy over the contractual nature of such bonds is in principle misplaced. Under US law, the terms inscribed in regulations or statutes that set the basis for the issuance of domestic bonds do not insulate those bonds from the application of contractual principles.[33] Such statutory framework merely acts to incorporate terms and conditions into the contractual arrangement entered into between the government and private creditors.[34]

[26] *Poštová Banka, a.s. and Istrokapital SE v Hellenic Republic*, ICSID Case No ARB/13/8, Award, 9 April 2015, paras 318–24. The award was upheld by the ad hoc committee (*Poštová Banka, a.s. and Istrokapital SE v Hellenic Republic*, ICSID Case No ARB/13/8, Decision for Partial Annulment, 29 September 2016).

[27] Ibid paras 361–65.

[28] *Loan Agreement between Italy v Costa Rica*, Decision of 27 June 1998, Reports of International Arbitral Awards, Vol XXV, 75.

[29] Ibid 72–74.

[30] See, eg, *George W. Cook (U.S.A.) v United Mexican States*, Reports of International Arbitral Awards, 30 April 1929, Vol IV, 510; s 3(3) of the State Immunity Act (1978).

[31] See, eg, in the United States—the Uniform Offering Circular; in China—Regulations on Treasury Bonds of the People's Republic of China.

[32] See, eg, Mexican Tesobonos, Argentine Bonods.

[33] *Von Hoffmann v City of Quincy*, 71 US 535 (1866) (treating the loans issued under statutes as contracts).

[34] In *Perry v United States*, 294 US 330, 348 (1935), the bonds issued by the United States, commercial in nature, referred to US circulars simply 'for a statement of the further rights of the holders of bonds of said series'. That said, the distinction between bonds issued pursuant

1.22 *Comparison with other jurisdictions.* Few jurisdictions would disagree with the basic premise that the issuance of sovereign debt is unequivocally a commercial transaction.[35] In *Dame Hébert c Trésor Public* (1938), the Cour d'Appel of Paris considered a dispute concerning the bonds issued by France in the United States. The court decided that the issuance of bonds was within the jurisdiction of administrative courts because the issuance of sovereign debt 'interests the functioning of the public policy and demonstrates an intention to submit to a special legal regime of public law'.[36] In the court's view, French sovereign bonds were a matter of public policy as they had been issued for the protection of the national currency and constituted an operation of the French treasury. Another weighty reason cited by the court was that the bonds enjoyed special fiscal prerogatives. Seemingly, the only material repercussion of qualifying sovereign debt as administrative, apart from the attribution of competence to administrative tribunals, was the submission of such debt to the law of the sovereign debtor.[37]

1.23 The falsity of the reasoning is exposed the moment one remembers that, as the *note* to the case suggests,[38] all public debt in principle interests the functioning of the treasury and fiscal prerogatives that bondholders may benefit from are not an indication of a special legal regime of public law but merely a waiver of a sovereign's right to tax. Moreover, the purpose pursued in issuing sovereign debt is not conclusive in the determination of its character.

1.24 In 2015, the Tribunal de Grande Instance of Paris confirmed that the bonds issued and guaranteed by the Russian Empire in 1906 and 1908 were immune from the jurisdiction of French courts since they were acts taken in the exercise of governmental authority. The court's only reason was that the Russian Empire accorded fiscal privileges to the bondholders in the

to a statute and those contracted in absence of a statutory framework might be of relevance in international investment arbitration (see *Continental Casualty v Argentina*, ICSID Case No ARB/03/9, Award, 5 September 2008, para 302).

35 Hersch Lauterpacht, 'The Problem of Jurisdictional Immunities of Foreign States' (1951) 28 BYBIL 220, 253, 257–58; van Hècke (n 7) 27–28.

36 Paris, 20 juin 1938, Dame Hébert c Trésor Public, Clunet 1939, 104 (translation is mine). For other French cases, see Lauterpacht (n 35) 262.

37 Van Hècke (n 7) 27. However, the debt owed by the State might not pertain to the public law regime if the debt arises from an assignment of a private debt to the State, whereupon the debt will be treated as a private obligation (Conseil d'Etat, 21 juillet 1972, *Veuve Hermann*, Rev crit DIP, 1974 330, 333).

38 (1939) Clunet 105.

course of issuance of bonds and that was something that a private person could not do.[39]

There is room for arguing that the peculiar judicial system of France, whereby public debt falls squarely within the competence of administrative courts, dictates the qualification of the debt as essentially public activity. Indeed, laws of 26 September 1793 and 17 July 1890 have specifically bestowed the jurisdiction over public debt on French administrative tribunals. **1.25**

2. Sovereign Debt Restructurings

Equally crucial is to correctly characterise sovereign debt restructurings. There is no doubt that the sovereign debt restructuring is a far cry from an 'insolvency regime' in the traditional understanding of the concept, used to denote a formalistic process of debt reduction applicable to individuals and companies. And English and New York courts treat external sovereign debt restructurings as essentially a kind of commercial activity.[40] **1.26**

Italian, German, and Spanish courts have, however, approached sovereign debt restructurings as acts of a public nature. Thus, in a case opposing Italian bondholders and the Republic of Argentina, the Italian Corte di Cassazione agreed with the claimant that the issuance of sovereign bonds was private in nature. However, it (in)famously decided that the acts, which the Argentine government resorted to in the restructuring of its debt (particularly, a moratorium), were sovereign acts taken for the public purpose of protecting the primary need of economic survival of the population in the historical context of a serious national emergency. These acts were therefore shielded by sovereign immunity.[41] This finding was later followed by the Spanish Court of Appeal in the *Pérez Celis* case.[42] A German court has also found that the unilateral modification of bonds was a sovereign measure which attracted sovereign immunity.[43] It was argued that the immunity point in the judgment of the Italian Corte di Cassazione was, however, at odds with established practice given that **1.27**

[39] Tribunal de Grande Instance, *Association Fédérative Internationale des Porteurs d'Emprunts Russes v La Fédération de Russie*, 4 novembre 2015.

[40] See, eg, *Themis Capital, LLC et al v Democratic Republic of Congo and Central Bank of the Democratic Republic of the Congo*, 881 F Supp 2d 508, 526 (SDNY 2012) ('Restructuring debt is a commercial transaction, a paradigmatically private act'); *NML v Argentina*, [2011] UKSC 31, para 108 (per Lord Collins).

[41] Corte di Cassazione, 27 May 2005, decision no 11225 of 27 May 2005, RDIPP, 2005, 1091.

[42] Auto de la Audiencia Provincial de Madrid, Sección 18ª, núm 192/2007, de 19 de septiembre.

[43] Case VI ZR 516/14, Judgment of 8 March 2016.

only the character of the underlying (original) transaction (in this case, issuance of bonds) should determine the commercial nature of a State's activity.[44] This characterisation is considered in Chapters 3 and 8.

1.28 Beyond that, as discussed in Chapter 6 (paras 6.45–6.51), *Allied II*, relying on a US Supreme Court authority on the cross-border insolvency of companies,[45] recognised the effects of the Costa Rican debt restructuring and stayed legal proceedings. The same court then reversed itself in *Allied III*, on the basis that its earlier reasoning had run afoul of the US governmental interests expressed in an amicus curiae brief of the US government.[46] However, the State in *Allied* was acting as a regulator and was not directly involved in the borrowing itself.

3. The Antinomy of Bilateral/Multilateral in Sovereign Lending

1.29 In a typical situation, numerous bondholders subscribe to the sovereign bonds that the State floats on the national or international markets. The entire mass of bondholders is routinely composed of classes of bondholders with each class holding a particular sovereign debt issuance.

1.30 The ties that exist between fellow bondholders vis-à-vis each other, and vis-à-vis the debtor may be treated from two vantage points. First, from a *bilateral* perspective, whereupon the debtor is in a direct, singular contractual relation with each and every one of the bondholders, as are the bondholders vis-à-vis each other. The second perspective is *multilateral* in that the sovereign debtor's contractual counterparty are a group of fellow bondholders, treated as a whole, and with mutual ties within the group of bondholders.

1.31 In the bilateral conception of sovereign debt, the rights of a bondholder are atomistic and are conceptually distinct from the rights of the remainder of fellow bondholders. Under this approach, the solution of the dispute between the debtor and a creditor who initiated litigation should not turn on the stance taken by the other creditors, unless specifically provided in the contractual text. Contractual clauses may establish certain forms of ties between the bondholders (majority action and sharing

[44] Beatrice Bonafé, 'State Immunity and the Protection of Private Investors: The *Argentine Bonds* Case before Italian Courts' (2006) 16 IYBIL 165, 170–76; cf Corte Constitucional, 15 July 1992 (assuming that State guarantees are commercial in nature, cited in Anna de Luca, 'L'immunità degli stati stranieri dalla giurisdizioni civile' in Natalino Ronzitti and Gabriella Venturini (eds), *Le immunità guirisdizionali degli stati e degli altri enti internazionali* (2008) 23).

[45] *Canada Southern Railway Co v Gebhard*, 109 US 527 (1883).

[46] See Chapter 3.

clauses being pertinent examples),[47] provided, of course, that the wording of such clauses is unequivocal.[48] The bondholders may also share stronger or weaker association as a result of the way the bond is issued, eg whether there is a trustee provision, or the bonds are issued as a dematerialised security.

In the multilateral conception of sovereign debt, the group of bondholders, having subscribed to the debt of the same sovereign debtor, is treated as a unitary group, as a community, whereby they share essentially the same financial interests, and for the purposes of vindicating legal rights under bonds, treated as a group of interconnected bondholders.[49] **1.32**

English and New York legal systems, as they currently stand, are firm in asserting that the sovereign debt is a bilateral relation, except for cases expressly stipulated in the sovereign bond contract such that intercreditor relations are established among bondholders. A pertinent example is the majority action clause which vests the majority of bondholders with a wide-ranging power of binding the minority to the debt reduction as it sees fit. But, outside these contractual clauses, the sovereign debt is essentially a bilateral contract. Sovereign bonds do occasionally expressly provide for the independent (detached) character of sovereign bonds,[50] it seems out of caution. **1.33**

In syndicated loans, the interrelation between lenders is based on slightly closer ties. Pursuant to this logic, the Supreme Court of New York in *Credit Français v Sociedad* characterised syndicated lending as a joint venture and prevented a minority creditor from taking an individual action for repayment of contractual debt against the borrower.[51] The characterisation of a **1.34**

[47] On such clauses see Chapter 2; Lee Buchheit and Ralph Reisner, 'The Effect of the Sovereign Debt Restructuring Process on Inter-Creditor Relationships' (1988) 2 U Ill L Rev 493, 495–500, 511–16.

[48] *Nacional Financiera, SNC v Chase Manhattan Bank*, 2003 WL 1878415 (SDNY 2003) (deciding in an action against other creditors alleging breach of the *pari passu* clause that the contract did not create mutual obligations among creditors).

[49] See, eg, Henry Batiffol, *Les Conflits de lois en matière de contrats* (1938) 106–07 (treating sovereign debt holdings as subject to one single law, as the sovereign debt is in principle unitary). See also George Sausser-Hall, 'La clause-or dans les contrats publics et privés' (1937) 60 Recueil des Cours, 651, 753.

[50] *Yucyco Ltd v Republic of Slovenia*, 984 F Supp 209, 220 (SDNY 1997) (citing s 14.3 of the Yugoslavian New Financing Agreement of 1988, namely that 'the amounts payable at any time … to each Creditor shall be a separate and independent debt and each Creditor shall be entitled to protect and enforce his rights arising out of this Agreement, and it shall not be necessary for any other Creditor to be joined as an additional party in any proceedings for such purpose').

[51] *Crédit Français International SA v Sociedad Financiera de Comercio*, 490 NYS 2d 670, 684 (Sup Ct NY 1985).

syndicate as a joint venture is, however, a dubious proposition.[52] Be that as it may, the dispersed group of bondholders does not have the same close association as the lenders in a syndicate. Treating them as some sort of joint venture is plainly erroneous.[53]

1.35 The position under English law is more reassuring. In an interesting twist, US courts, applying English law, came to a different conclusion in respect of the standing of minority creditors in a syndicate. In *Commercial Bank of Kuwait v Rafidain Bank*,[54] decided under English law, the US Court of Appeals for the Second Circuit ('Second Circuit') held that the members of the syndicate had the right to sue the lender. The applicability of English law was later used to distinguish the holding in *The Commercial Bank of Kuwait* from other similar cases on syndicated loans governed by US law.[55]

III. RELEVANCE OF BROADER PUBLIC POLICY ARGUMENTS

1. Broader Public Policy Considerations and their Rejection in Sovereign Debt Litigation

1.36 Allied to the private characterisation of sovereign debt issuance is the question of whether a competent court, seised of a sovereign debt dispute, may (or even ought to) look beyond the terms of the contract or established market practices to the broader interests of the sovereign debtor and its population. Sovereign debtors and academics have shown much imagination in many guises so as to create space for the State's budgetary and social needs, and in that way, affect the judicial determination of a sovereign debt dispute. They claim that lost in a morass of legal argument are a great many adverse consequences of sovereign debt litigation. Adverse consequences commonly cited include the duty of the borrower towards its population,[56] the consideration of human rights in sovereign financing,[57] the responsibility of the international community to fight global poverty

[52] Buchheit (n 47) 503–04; Philip Rawlings, 'The Management of Loan Syndicates and the Rights of Individual Lenders' (2009) 24(4) JIBLR 179, 182; Charles Proctor, *The Law and Practice of International Banking* (2010), para 21.27.

[53] *A.I. Credit Corp v Government of Jamaica*, 666 F Supp 629, 631–32 (SDNY 1987) (holding that the bondholder had individual standing against Jamaica).

[54] 15 F.3d 238, 243 (2d Cir 1994).

[55] *Beal Savings Bank v Sommer*, 8 NY 3d 318, 331 (NY 2007).

[56] Principle I.1, Agency, Principles on Promoting Responsible Sovereign Lending and Borrowing, UNCTAD, 2012.

[57] Juan Pablo Bohoslavsky and Jernej Letnar Cernic (eds), *Making Sovereign Financing and Human Rights Work* (2014); Matthias Goldmann, 'Human Rights and Sovereign

and ensure socio-economic human rights in times of crises,[58] the ethics of and fairness in dealing with an unsustainable debt burden.[59] Comparable attacks against the purely commercial treatment of sovereign bonds may be derived from the positions of such economic and political theories as neo-Marxism, communitarianism, dependency theory, and others.

In this sense, the UN General Assembly—in spite of the opposition from major developed countries—adopted in September 2015 basic principles of sovereign debt restructurings driven by the idea that the existing system is inadequate to resolve the growing incidents of sovereign debt crises.[60] In the 1970s, developing countries (the Group of 77) have expressed their commitment to the establishment of the New International Economic Order in the arena of sovereign debt that will seek to alleviate the pressures of unsustainable stock of debt by sharing the financial burden with creditor countries and the international community.[61] **1.37**

A common theme among many scholars and policymakers is the unfairness of the practice of creditors harassing emerging market debtors into full repayment of the monies due. In an acknowledgement of the State's perspective, sovereignty concerns are often voiced: the unsustainable debt affects the State's autonomy[62] and the State with debt 'overhang' will see its right to development constrained or completely suppressed. The common backdrop of these public policy considerations is to stress the effects of sovereign debt restructurings and the resulting austerity measures on the broader public and, concomitantly, to insist on a lesser role for the rights of creditors in sovereign debt restructurings. **1.38**

Debt Workouts' (2014) (available at http://papers.ssrn.com/sol3/papers.cfm?abstract_id=2330997); Sabine Schlemmer-Schulte, 'Fragmentation of International Law: The Case of International Finance & Investment Law Versus Human Rights Law' (2012) 25 Pac McGeorge Global Bus & Dev LJ 409. We reserve our opinion on the issue of impact of foreign financing on regimes involved in gross human rights violations, on which see, Juan Pablo Bohoslavsky, 'Report on Financial Complicity: Lending to States Engaged in Gross Human Rights Violations' (2015) UN General Assembly A/HRC/28/59, esp para 35.

[58] Margot Salomon, *Global Responsibility for Human Rights: World Poverty and the Development of International Law* (2007); Dimitris Chorafas, *Sovereign Debt Crisis: The New Normal and the Newly Poor* (2011).

[59] Christian Barry, Barry Herman, and Lydia Tomitova (eds), *Dealing Fairly with Developing Country Debt* (2007).

[60] UN General Assembly, 'Basic Principles on Sovereign Debt Restructuring Processes' (2015) UN Doc A/69/L.84.

[61] Milan Bulajic, 'Indebtness of Developing Countries and New International Economic Order' in Detlev Dicke (ed), *Foreign Debts in the Present and a New International Economic Order* (1986) 64–65, 71. See also Programme of Action on the Establishment of a New International Economic Order, UNGA Resolution 3202 (S/VI), 1 May 1974, para II.2.f. and g.

[62] Jubilee Debt Campaign, 'Debt and Public Services' (2007) Briefing.

1.39 The debate is perhaps best captured by two conflicting conceptions of fairness: distributive fairness and procedural fairness.[63] From a distributive viewpoint, it might seem unfair to some that creditors enrich at the expense of seriously indebted countries. Conversely, from the viewpoint of procedural fairness, the compensation of creditors who acquired their debt in a legal and procedurally valid manner is beyond doubt.

1.40 Many commentators query whether the court should be able to sweep under the rug considerations of distributive fairness in the adjudication of sovereign debt disputes. Taking a step back, a legitimate question that the foregoing discussion may prompt is why the commercial side of borrowing and case-specific methodology should not succumb to what may be a severe financial condition of the State. This draws on policy rather than a black-letter argument. The broader public policy repercussions of the sovereign debtor and its populace are undeniably weighty and of great import.

1.41 It is argued here that the courts should virtually never consider broader public policy arguments (justifications for which are not necessarily very convincing) to override contractual language and established legal rules. The reasons are both positive and negative.

1.42 In terms of positive reasons, the pecuniary and non-pecuniary interests of the sovereign debtor are not the sole interests to be considered by foreign courts asked to adjudicate on the dispute. The interests of financial markets, bondholders, creditor States, and other actors should not be discarded with ease. Their interests might and often do clash with the interests of the debtor. A predisposition towards the interests of the impecunious debtor may have unpredictable and backfiring consequences, affecting established market perceptions, the interest rate, rights, and expectations of bondholders. Disregarding contractual rights might cause unpredicted harm and reduce already feeble creditor rights. For one, it may prejudice other States willing to have access to financial markets by raising interest rates prevalent on the market. The financial predicament of the State does not justify recourse to a discretionary, equity-based adjudication of sovereign debt disputes.

1.43 There is scope for the argument that the interests of the State are already met by the widespread practice of collective action clauses (CACs). The contractual *ex ante* drafting, especially its enhanced variations,[64] ensures that holdout creditors are left with little space for harassing sovereign

[63] Christian Barry and Lydia Tomitova, 'Fairness in Sovereign Debt' in Barry et al (n 59) 44–45.

[64] See Chapter 2.

debtors, even if the contractual drafting is the second best after the fully fledged bankruptcy regime for sovereign debt.

Faced with conflicting interests and considerations, one is well advised to err on the side of caution and give full force to the contractual agreement to repay the money as due—embodiment of the principle of *pacta sunt servanda*. **1.44**

In terms of negative reasons, the courts are not well suited to weigh various conflicting and irreconcilable public policy considerations that might arise in sovereign debt litigation (subject to the policy considerations embedded in the law (para 1.52). The District Court for the Southern District of New York ('District Court') in *A.I. Creditor* expressed the general sentiment that it was not the task of the judiciary to evaluate the payment difficulties of a sovereign debtor, but that of the executive branch[65] (or perhaps the international community). Even if payment capacity may be assessed through expert opinions, courts do not have the necessary mandate to do so. Reisman correctly points out that arbitral tribunals (and, by analogy, national courts) should confine themselves to their case-specific methodology and refrain from deviating from it to give effect to the 'systemic implications' of their decisions.[66] It is a matter to be left to the collective wisdom of the legislative power of States and international organisations. **1.45**

The courts forthrightly endorse the view advocated here. In the litigation of sovereign debt disputes, the prevailing consideration is the financial side of the case. Public policy arguments raised by the debtor generally receive short shrift from courts.[67] Rendering a decision by reference to vague policy reasons, bordering on judicial legislation, would defy the commercial predictability of English and New York laws. The basic underpinning of English commercial law is 'contract law minimalism', which shuns extralegal considerations in commercial cases and aspirations to redistribute wealth through commercial contract law.[68] Worthington and Mellon present the unsurprisingly constrained role that public policy **1.46**

[65] *A.I. Credit Corp v Government of Jamaica*, 666 F Supp 629, 633 (SDNY 1987).

[66] Michael Reisman, '"Case Specific Mandates" versus "Systemic Implications": How Should Investment Tribunals Decide?—The Freshfields Arbitration Lecture' (2013) 29(2) Arb Intl 131.

[67] See, eg, *NML Capital, Ltd v Republic of Argentina*, 727 F.3d 230, 245–48 (2d Cir 2013) (rejecting Argentina's various 'public interest' arguments); *Lightwater Corp, Ltd v Republic of Argentina*, 2003 US Dist LEXIS 6156, 13 (SDNY 2003) (dismissing the defence of necessity); *Libra Bank Ltd v Banco Nacional de Costa Rica*, 570 F Supp 870, 882 (SDNY 1983).

[68] Jonathan Morgan, *Contract Law Minimalism: A Formalist Restatement of Commercial Contract Law* (2013), esp 87, 148, 158 (stressing the ineptitude and counterproductiveness of redistributing wealth through contract law).

played in the context of the insolvencies of multinational corporations in England.[69]

1.47 In this context, considerations of the sort described above—human rights, the right of the State to development, and the interests of the populace—cannot be determinative in the litigation of sovereign bond disputes, which is by definition commercial, at least in English and New York courts.

1.48 That said, the UK has accorded the interests of some highly indebted countries additional protection. Indeed, the debt of heavily indebted States has been given special treatment with the introduction of the Debt Relief (Developing Countries) Act 2010. The Act curtails any preying on the debt of sovereign borrowers falling under the definition of Heavily Indebted Poor Countries (HIPC). It should, however, be stressed this is an exception confirming the general rule.

1.49 It is worth stressing in this connection that this is not entirely bad news for the State. The proposition adduced here is a double-edged sword. Not only is the sovereign debtor unable to rely on public policy considerations to get a preferential, *contra legem* treatment, but, for the same reasons, the creditors may not adduce extralegal arguments and considerations to flex the legal rules in their favour.[70]

1.50 Some scholars have attempted to hide policy-charged arguments cloaked in black-letter law arguments. Those who espouse this view find no difficulty in devising esoteric arguments to support the duty of courts to consider systemic implications of their decisions. Some argue that the creditors are under a positive obligation to partake in sovereign debt restructurings and under a negative obligation to refrain from initiating legal actions against the sovereign debtor, irrespective of the contractual rights available under sovereign bonds.[71] The position described tends to derive a duty to renegotiate incumbent upon private bondholders from various sources: the requirement of peaceful settlement of disputes,[72] human rights obligations,[73] and even the threat to peace falling within the

[69] Sarah Worthington and Grainne Mellon, 'Statutory Rules, Common Law Rules and Public Policy in the Global Financial Crisis' (2010–11) 29 Penn St Intl LR 613, 613–25 (but it should be noted that on pp 625–33 they take a more expansive view of the role of public policy in judicial lawmaking).

[70] But see the recent *pari passu* litigation in the US, discussed in Chapter 7.

[71] Although not sharing this premise, Chapter 3 concludes that in contracts with majority action clauses the creditors are indeed under an obligation of standstill, pending the decision by the majority bondholders to refuse or to accept the exchange offer.

[72] Michael Bothe and Josef Brink, 'Public Debt Restructuring—The Case for International Economic Co-operation' (1986) 29 GYIL 86.

[73] Jörn Kämmerer, 'Der Staatsbankrott aus völkerrechtlicher Sicht' (2005) 65 ZaöRV 651, 657 cited in Bogdandy and Goldmann (n 13) 56.

province of the UN Security Council.[74] Others refer to the emerging customary law or general principles of law of sovereign debt restructurings that private creditors should abide by.[75] Continuing the line of imaginative arguments, some scholars contend that creditors are under a legal obligation to negotiate with the sovereign debtor in distress in good faith and to avoid untimely legal actions out of considerations of cooperation, solidarity, and equity.[76] More broadly, Muir-Watt argues for global governance through conflict of laws in, among other spheres, sovereign debt.[77]

Strikingly, many of these principles adduced by those supporting the reform of sovereign debt adjudication are too multifaceted and lack the necessary specificity.[78] Whether there is customary law crystallised in the field of sovereign debt needs to be viewed with strong scepticism. As Waibel shows in the context of UNCTAD Principles on Responsible Sovereign Borrowing and Lending, the claims of customary law of sovereign debt restructurings lack *opinio juris*,[79] and are properly characterised as international 'soft' law.[80] **1.51**

2. Embedded Public Policy Considerations in the Private Law Reasoning

Some may rebut the foregoing by saying that over-reliance on commercial law tools for the resolution of fundamental issues in sovereign debt adjudication is an apologist view of the status quo, and hijacks considerations of human rights and sovereignty. At what point the private law reasoning **1.52**

[74] Matthias Goldman, 'Sovereign Debt Crises as Threats to the Peace: Restructuring under Chapter VII of the UN Charter?' (2012) 4 Go JIL 153.

[75] Bogdandy and Goldmann (n 13) 64–30; Juan Pablo Bohoslavsky, Yuefen Li, and Marie Sudreau, 'Emerging Customary International Law in Sovereign Debt Governance?' (2014) 9(1) CMLJ 55.

[76] Dominique Carreau, 'Rapport du directeur d'études de la section française du centre' in Dominique Carreau and Malcolm Shaw (eds), *La Dette extérieure: The External Debt* (1995) 17; Matthias Goldmann, 'Good Faith and Transparency in Sovereign Debt Workouts' (2014) 10–13 (available at http://www.unctad.info/upload/Debt%20Portal/DWM%20Good%20Faith%20and%20Transparency%2020131223.pdf).

[77] Horatia Muir-Watt, 'Private International Law as Global Governance: Beyond the Schize, from Closet to Planet' (2011) 5 (available at http://works.bepress.com/horatia_muir-watt/1).

[78] Odette Lienau, 'Legitimacy and Impartiality in a Sovereign Debt Workout Mechanism' (2006) Cornell Law Faculty Publications, Paper 1110, 31.

[79] Michael Waibel, 'Out of Thin Air? Tracing the Origins of the UNCTAD Principles in State Practice' in Espósito et al (n 13) 100–03; Florentino Feliciano, 'Report of the Director of Studies of the English-Speaking Section of the Centre' in Carreau and Shaw (n 76) 50.

[80] August Reinisch, 'Debt Restructuring and State Responsibility Issues' in Carreau and Shaw (n 76) 555, 602.

leaves the State devoid of any bankruptcy shield is of serious concern to many scholars.

1.53 In reality, the recognition of the private character of sovereign debt does not make the premise of this book necessarily pro-creditor oriented. Private law mechanisms are well tuned to protecting the sovereign debtor and the ordinary deployment of the debt restructuring process.[81] The application of the private law logic prevents the debtor from raising overreaching defences based on the allegedly public character of the sovereign debt.

1.54 To assuage the concerns of many, it bears emphasising that the commercial courts in England and New York will not close their eyes to public policy considerations in all of their manifestations, thereby acknowledging the debtor State's perspective. It is true that courts will often be confined to their legal straitjacket. Nevertheless, it will be shown over the course of this book that public policy considerations do find subtle expression in private law tools. Indeed, public policy cuts in multiple directions. For one, the rules on State immunity from enforcement shield from attachment all State assets that are not in use for commercial purposes, which represent the lion's share of the sovereign debtor's assets. The onerous rules on State immunity make the litigation of sovereign debt disputes the pursuit of an absolute minority of creditors and often of none. Next, as discussed in Chapter 3, the English courts, in the discretionary exercise of their powers, will pay necessary tribute to the broader repercussions of their decisions by refusing to issue interim and post-judgment measures against impecunious sovereigns. So, too, the English courts will stay legal actions in deference to sovereign debt restructurings out of concern lest the employment of majority action clauses, designed to facilitate the process of reducing sovereign indebtedness, is thwarted.[82] The monograph contains other comparable examples which sustain the latitude that a sovereign debtor may enjoy in the adjudication of its default before English and New York courts.

1.55 As public policy considerations in favour of the sovereign debtor tiptoe into the realm of private law mechanisms, so too do the interests of minority bondholders threatened by rogue sovereign debtors. As Chapter 7 shows, the English courts have designed common law mechanisms to protect the interests of minority bondholders in particularly excessive and abusive restructurings.

1.56 As might be recalled, the premise of the statutory approach to sovereign debt is that legal gaps in the regulation of sovereign debt restructurings

[81] As will be seen in Chapters 3 and 7. [82] See Chapter 3.

are to be filled through statutes or international treaties that institute a sovereign debt restructuring mechanism. Alas, such legislative action might not be forthcoming in practice any time soon.

It is the premise of this book that judicial, case-by-case innovation is the path of least resistance for filling the legal vacuum. Although true that judicial innovation will not modify the system fundamentally, this is not to say that the system is broken in the first place. Admittedly, the system might need some 'tinkering', which may be achieved in many ways, including by judicial innovation. **1.57**

IV. INSOLVENCY ANALOGY

Over the course of history, many States have been de facto bankrupt—historical examples abound.[83] Against this factual background, many have proposed the idea of a sovereign debt bankruptcy mechanism that would provide an orderly mechanism for the restructuring of sovereign debt, analogous to the regime applicable to the bankruptcy of individuals and companies.[84] The proposals to establish a sovereign debt bankruptcy mechanism have been unsuccessful so far. **1.58**

Taking a more audacious stance, some scholars have attempted to extrapolate the domestic concept of bankruptcy to State insolvencies. They argue that when the State in distress faces a situation analogous to the insolvency of individuals or companies, the principles of (national) insolvency ought to be extended to sovereigns. In the view of these scholars, the adjudicator—the national court or arbitrator—should recognise the state of bankruptcy of the sovereign debtor and refuse to issue or enforce a judgment (or arbitral award) in deference to the state of insolvency of the debtor. This would be the case in local personal and corporate insolvencies where proceedings are stayed on the making of a winding-up order.[85] **1.59**

[83] Michael Waibel, 'Staateninsolvenzen in historischer Sicht' in Georg Kodek and August Reinisch (eds), *Staateninsolvenz* (2012) 55.

[84] Kenneth Rogoff and Jeromin Zettelmeyer, 'Bankruptcy Procedures for Sovereigns: A History of Ideas, 1976–2001' (2002) IMF Staff Papers 49; Netanella Zahavi, 'Sovereign Default: Analyses and Remedies' (JSD thesis, Yale Law School 2005) 108–51; François Gianviti, Anne Krueger, Jean Pisani-Ferry, André Sapir, and Jürgen von Hagen, 'A European Mechanism for Sovereign Debt Crisis Resolution: A Proposal' (2010) Bruegel Blueprint Series Vol 10.

[85] Bogdandy and Goldmann (n 13) 64–70; John Fischer Williams, 'Le droit international et les obligations financières internationales qui naissent d'un contrat' (1923) 1 Recueil des Cours 289, 344–46; Schier (n 3) 258–61; Dimitrij Euler and Giuseppe Bianco, 'Breaking the Bond: Vulture Funds and Investment Arbitration' (2013) 31(3) ASA Bulletin 558, 568–69.

What these proposals put forward is a judicially established and supervised bankruptcy regime which would operate as a stay on judicial proceedings in deference to the insolvency of the State.

1.60 The reasoning that is based on the analogy between a sovereign insolvency and corporate insolvency has very little, if any, legal foundation.[86] While there might be room to argue there is a general principle that foreign judgments and arbitral awards will not be issued/executed when the debtor is insolvent,[87] there is little doubt that international law, as it stands now, does not recognise the bankruptcy analogy in the context of sovereign debt.[88] Certainly, the analogy is unlikely to make its way into English law,[89] unless, of course, Parliament paves the way for it, as was the case with the Debt Relief (Developing Countries) Act 2010.

1.61 Examples of judicially imposed insolvency regimes are close to nonexistent. In the early twentieth century, in the absence of a statutory regime applicable to railroads, the US courts devised an equitable remedy to protect insolvent railroads.[90] The remedy—equitable receivership—consisted of appointing a receiver for the insolvent railroad that would take all the measures necessary to reorganise the financially insolvent railroad. The appointment of the receiver acted as an automatic stay on legal actions against the insolvent railroad. In this context, equity receiverships have been cited as a convincing model for the national courts to engage with a sovereign's financial distress.[91] However, as Lubben correctly points out, the model of railroad receiverships may not effortlessly apply to the scenario of a sovereign in distress, partly due to the fact that the former model

[86] Eric Robert, 'Rééchelonnement de la dette ou règlement judiciaire' in Carreau and Shaw (n 76) 653–54.

[87] *Frontier Petroleum Services Ltd v The Czech Republic*, UNCITRAL, Final Award, 12 November 2010, paras 527–30.

[88] Georg Schwarzenberger, 'State Bankruptcy and International Law' in Wybo Heere, *International Law and its Sources. Liber Amicorum Maarten Bos* (1988) 139, 144; cf, on the contrary, Michael Waibel, 'La faillite souveraine en droit: Un Etat peut-il faire faillite?' in Audit, (ed), *Insolvabilité des Etats et dettes souveraines* (2011), 56–61; Michael Waibel, *Sovereign Defaults before International Courts and Tribunals* (2011) 92–93, 97–98, but see p 152 for contrary considerations (citing *C. Itoh Middle East E.C. v The People's Republic of the Congo and the Congolese Redemption Fund*, ICC Arbitration No 6219, 31 July 1990).

[89] The analogy was rejected in *F.G. Hemisphere Associates LLC v Republic of Congo* [2005] EWHC 3103 (Comm), paras 7–8, 13.

[90] David Skeel, *Debt's Dominion: A History of Bankruptcy Law in America* (2003) 48–70, 104–06.

[91] Lee Buchheit and Mitu Gulati, 'Sovereign Bonds and the Collective Will' (2004) 51 Emory LJ 1317, 1322.

was conceived as *in rem* proceedings targeted at the railroad as a bundle of immoveable properties.[92]

Notwithstanding the dearth of judicial authority applying national insolvency principles in the absence of a statutory premise (and even the legality of such analogies),[93] a residual sense of unease remains for two main reasons. First, the bankruptcy analogy has little to commend itself. As Lauterpacht argued in his seminal work *Private Law Analogies*, bankruptcy procedures differ in the content of their rules. Consequently, there is no uniform law of insolvency to begin with.[94] Further, it is no secret that sovereign debt insolvencies and insolvencies of individuals and companies vary in many respects.[95] **1.62**

Secondly, bankruptcy laws are themselves subject to limitations that seek to give meaningful protection to the rights of creditors.[96] If one were to extrapolate the bankruptcy regime from domestic laws, one could not cherry-pick the components of the insolvency regime favourable to the sovereign debtor. Put otherwise, to apply the insolvency analogy, the acts of the insolvent State need to comply with some basic standards or safeguards of insolvency law (such as notice to creditors, fair and equitable treatment of all creditors).[97] One such safeguard is the presence of an impartial third party—the bankruptcy court. The lack of an impartial bankruptcy court that will oversee the bankruptcy procedure of the debtor casts a shadow on the analogy of domestic insolvency.[98] Equally, it is beyond doubt that the courts of a foreign State cannot declare another State bankrupt, appoint a trustee over the debtor State, and seize its **1.63**

[92] Stephen Lubben, 'Out of the Past: Railroads and Sovereign Debt Restructuring' (2004) 35 Geo J Intl L 845, 855–57.

[93] See *Singularis Holdings Ltd v PricewaterhouseCoopers* [2014] UKPC 36, esp paras 38, 83.

[94] Hersch Lauterpacht, *Private Law Sources and Analogies of International Law* (1927) 253, citing pleadings from *Venezuelan Preferential Claim* (1904).

[95] For differences, see ILA, 'State Insolvency: Options for the Way Forward: Hague Conference Report' (2010a) 19ff; Marc Lewyn, 'Foreign Debt—Act of State Doctrine—Unilateral Deferral of Obligations by Debtor Nations Is Inconsistent with United States Law and Policy: Allied Bank International v. Banco Credito Agricola de Cartago' (1985) 15 Ga J Intl & Comp L 657, 666.

[96] Andreas Witte, 'The Greek Bond Haircut: Public and Private International Law and European Law Limits to Unilateral Sovereign Debt Restructuring' (2012) 9(2) Manchester J Intl Econ L 307, 332.

[97] Zahavi (n 84) 221–47.

[98] Andrei Shleifer, 'Will the Sovereign Debt Market Survive?' (2003) 93(2) Amer Econ Rev 85, 89; Ricki Tigert, 'Allied Bank International: A United States Government Perspective' (1985) 17 NYU J Intl L & Pol 511, 522.

assets[99] as an insolvency court has the power to do in respect of private companies.

1.64 Dismissive of the efforts to stretch the insolvency analogy, Zahavi reviewed the practice and the case law on the recovery by bondholders of their contractual debt. She concluded that sovereign debt litigation by minority bondholders does not pose a real risk for the debtors. The chances of successful debt recovery on the judgment against the State are very low. This is due, in no small measure, to the stringent rules on State immunity. As a result, the creditors have very little bargaining power vis-à-vis the State which enjoys extensive powers in the design of the restructuring. This led Zahavi to the conclusion that those who need enhanced protection are the creditors and not the State. By the same token, the function of domestic bankruptcy laws, alongside the award of a fresh start to the debtor, is to maximise the expected return of creditors. Imposing a standstill on the remedies available to creditors might take away the little bargaining power that creditors, as a group, possess.[100]

1.65 Third, the invocation of insolvency is no panacea even under the domestic law of insolvency. In *Mazur Media Ltd v Mazur Media GmbH*, Collins J refused to stay English proceedings that were commenced on the ground of an exclusive jurisdiction clause pending the insolvency proceedings in Germany. The apparent rationale was the mandatory character of the exclusive jurisdictional clause under the Brussels I Regulation.[101]

1.66 There is a more general point to be made in this context. A logically consistent analogy requires the comparison of comparable phenomena. In the absence of a bankruptcy regime, contrasting sovereign debt with modern insolvency regimes based on insolvency statutes is like comparing apples and oranges. It seems more appropriate to draw on historical times pre-dating the adoption of insolvency statutes. Historically, before the advent of insolvency statutes provided a fresh start for indebted individuals courts did not even imagine discharging insolvent debtors or designing some collective procedures for debt relief. It was common practice to imprison bankrupt individuals[102]—Dickens's infamous debtor prison springs to mind.

99 *Republic of Zaire v J.C.M. Duclaux*, Court of Appeal of The Hague, 18 February 1988, (1989) 20 NYIL 296, 300; *W.L. Oltmans v The Republic of Surinam*, Netherlands Supreme Court, 28 September 1990, (1992) 23 NYIL 442.

100 Zahavi (n 84) 157–209, 216, 221–32, 236.

101 [2004] EWHC 1566 (Ch), paras 69–70. See also *Jefferies International Limited v Landsbanki Islands HF* [2009] EWHC 894 (Comm), paras 24–29 (refusing to stay proceedings in deference to the failure of an Icelandic bank).

102 See, eg, John Tribe, 'Discharge in Bankruptcy: An Examination of Personal Insolvency's Fresh Start Function in English Law: Part 2' (2012) 25(8) Insolv Int 117, 118.

Lastly, some scholars have argued in favour of internationalising the Chapter 9 insolvency regime which regulates the insolvency of municipalities in the US.[103] The Chapter 9 regime allegedly grants more leeway to the US municipality than Chapter 11 insolvency proceedings. For this reason, the regime is offered as a better fit for the sovereign debt context. The reasoning suffers from the same flaw as the personal bankruptcy analogies: the competent court in Chapter 9 insolvencies exercises the gateway function by approving the restructuring plan and examining its fairness.[104] Such supervision is blatantly absent in the case of sovereign debt restructurings. Additionally, unlike the financial predicament of municipalities, the US legal system does not cater for the bankruptcy of US States. Congressional bills to introduce such a regime have come to naught.[105] **1.67**

V. THE DOCTRINE OF COMITY AND ITS LIMITS IN SOVEREIGN DEBT LITIGATION

Sovereign debtors have relied, with varying rates of success, upon the defence of the comity of nations in the US judicial practice on the enforcement of sovereign debt. The doctrine of comity applies in those cases where pressing on with the final resolution of a dispute might harm the US government's amicable working relationships with other States and hence the courts are called upon to extend the courtesy of staying legal actions to the defendant sovereign in distress. The conventional rationale behind the doctrine of comity is that the US judiciary should be cautious not to trespass on the spheres which are deemed to be the province of the executive branch. **1.68**

[103] Kenneth Rogoff and Jeromin Zettelmeyer, 'Bankruptcy Procedures for Sovereigns: A History of Ideas, 1976–2001' (2002) 49(3) IMF Staff Papers 470, 482–83, 485; Kunibert Raffer, 'What's Good for the United States Must Be Good for the World: Advocating an International Chapter 9 Insolvency' in Bruno Kreisky Forum for International Dialogue (ed), *From Cancún to Vienna: International Development in a New World* (1993) 64. See also Susan Block-Lieb, 'Austerity, Debt Overhang and the Design of International Standards on Sovereign, Corporate and Consumer Debt Restructuring' (2015) 22(2) Ind J Glob L Stud 487 (offering the analogy with household debt).

[104] See Chapter 7.

[105] David Skeel, 'State Bankruptcy from the Ground Up' in Peter Conti-Brown and David Skeel (eds), *When States Go Broke: The Origins, Context, and Solutions for the American States in Fiscal Crisis* (2012) 191. See also in respect of the bankruptcy regime of Puerto Rico, 'Goodlatte and Marino Statement on Recent Developments Regarding Puerto Rico' (2015) (available at http://judiciary.house.gov/index.cfm/press-releases?id=73F4990C-4D3D-4BD8-B360-D642875054AC).

1.69 The application of the doctrine of comity in sovereign debt litigation is certainly evocative of the public character of the sovereign debt and, if applied consistently, would indicate that the sovereign debt may, in specific contexts, be subject to a *sui generis* legal reasoning. Its rejection, on the other hand, would be yet another indication of the application of private law tools.

1.70 The doctrine of comity has been relied upon to recognise decrees taken by the State to regulate the debt of its nationals,[106] to stay proceedings,[107] and to shield the sovereign from interim measures.[108] At its first invocation in the context of sovereign debt, the doctrine of comity received short shrift in *Allied Bank Int'l v Banco Credito Agricola de Cartago*[109] and later in *Pravin Banker Associates, Ltd v Banco Popular Del Peru and the Republic of Peru.*[110] In *Libra Bank Ltd v Banco Nacional de Costa Rica,*[111] the court discarded the application of the comity defence and denied any effect to the Costa Rican decrees which, as it was decided, subjected the debt of private creditors to an expropriation without adequate compensation. Principle suggests that comity is certainly a consideration in the decision-making of the judge but not one which will be decisive.[112]

1. Application of the Doctrine of Comity of Nations in English Litigation

1.71 An element that divides the litigation in the United States from England is that the doctrine of comity of nations, as understood by English courts, would most probably not serve as a free-standing ground for ordering stay of proceedings in deference to a sovereign debt restructuring. The main application of the doctrine of international comity is found in limiting the use of some allegedly intrusive tools of English commercial litigation, such as anti-suit injunctions,[113] freezing

[106] See Chapter 6. [107] See Chapter 3. [108] Ibid.

[109] 757 F.2d 516 (2d Cir 1985) (discussed in detail in Chapter 6).

[110] 109 F.3d 850, 854 (2d Cir 1997) (discussed in detail in Chapter 3).

[111] 570 F Supp 870 (SDNY 1983).

[112] See Chapters 3 and 6. See also *NML Capital Ltd et al. v Republic of Argentina*, 08 Civ. 6978 (SDNY 2015) ('Comity does not suggest abrogating those judgments, or creating exceptions to the Injunction designed to enforce them'); *Export-Import Bank of the Republic of China v Grenada*, 2012 US Dist LEXIS 116531 (SDNY 2012), 5–6 (referred to the doctrine of comity as one of the factors in deciding to award interim relief).

[113] *Airbus Industrie CIE v Patel* [1999] 1 AC 119, 138; *Star Reefers Pool Inc v JFC Group Co Ltd* [2012] EWCA Civ 14.

orders,[114] etc.[115] In any case, the doctrine of comity will rarely hold sway.[116]

In English law, the function of comity lies in refining the existing rules, rather than acting as a 'general and rhetorical appeal to comity'.[117] Comity acts negatively, and not positively. In *Yukos v Rosneft*, the Court of Appeal considered that comity requires something as a matter of 'restraint rather than abstention'.[118] Asking for a stay of proceedings out of considerations of comity would call for abstention rather than restraint and is likely to trespass on the intrinsic limits of the doctrine of comity as perceived under English law. **1.72**

Hamblen J, in a case on the debt which was transferred by the Bank of Portugal in the restructuring of a highly indebted bank, agreed with the claimant in that case that 'at least at the jurisdictional stage, it is doubtful that there is room for the application of a comity doctrine such as that of act of state in circumstances where it has been determined that the court has jurisdiction under the Brussels Regulation as it is a "civil or commercial matter"'.[119] **1.73**

Given the limited applicability of the doctrine of international comity under English law, Chapter 3 will argue for the stay of judicial proceedings on the grounds of the case management powers of English courts. English judges are more accustomed to resorting to their case management powers than a non-binding rule of public international law in the form of the doctrine of international comity. This does not, of course, prevent them from paying lip service to considerations of comity in the litigation against impecunious sovereigns. However, the framework of case management powers is a more neutral and tenable framework for the stay of proceedings in sovereign debt disputes. **1.74**

114 *Babanaft International Co SA v Bassatne* [1990] Ch 13, 32; *Masri v Consolidated Contractors International (UK) Ltd and others (No 2)* [2009] QB 450, 466 (refusing to make a worldwide freezing injunction against third parties in respect of assets located abroad).

115 Lord Collins of Mapesbury et al (eds), *Dicey, Morris & Collins on the Conflict of Laws*, vol 1 (2012) 6–10. In *Masri v Consolidated Contractors International Co SAL* [2011] EWCA Civ 746, paras 49–53, the Court of Appeal partially overruled a decision appointing a receiver over foreign assets on the grounds of comity. In *The Abidin Daver* [1984] AC 398, 412 comity was cited to support the developing doctrine of *forum non conveniens*.

116 See, eg, *Pearl Petroleum Company Limited v The Kurdistan Regional Government of Iraq* [2015] EWHC 3361 (Comm), para 52.

117 Adrian Briggs, 'Principle of Comity in Private International Law' (2012) 354 Recueil des Cours 65, 92.

118 *Yukos Capital SARL v OJSC Rosneft Oil Company* [2012] EWCA Civ 855, para 87.

119 *Goldman Sachs International v Novo Banco* [2015] EWHC 2371 (Comm), para 112. See also Chapter 3.

VI. RELEVANCE OF PRICING-IN

1.75 There is a widespread perception of financial markets as a great price machine that accurately prices financial risks. In modern times, many are convinced that omniscient financial markets are capable of *ex ante* pricing-in the vagaries of the market. It is a belief shared by many sovereign debt professionals that increased interest rates compensate creditors for the higher risk of default, and by that the market is able to regulate the deficiencies of the regime governing sovereign debt markets.

1.76 The assertion is properly conceptualised in the context of the permanent struggle between conflicting views on the efficiency of markets. Although many shades and variations in economic theories exist, the two contrasting views—laissez-faire liberalism and the State-centred view of market regulation—reveal different perceptions of the role that financial markets have in regulating sovereign debt markets through interest rates.

1.77 On the one hand, the laissez-faire liberalism portrays markets as omniscient and infallible orders that regulate commercial transactions and accurately price in the risks that market actors assume in the course of their business. Hayek advocated non-interference into what he framed as 'spontaneous orders', of which financial markets are an archetypical example. Central planning would, in his view, disrupt 'spontaneous orders' because top-down regulation would seek to control 'a system of interdependent actions determined by information and guided by purposes known only to the several acting persons but not to the directing authority'.[120]

1.78 On the other hand, financial markets are fallible and irrational.[121] Indeed, at every single crisis one can attest to the fallacy of the rational market hypothesis on which regulators ground the international financial edifice.[122] Indeed, the field of behavioural economics has come to challenge the assumption of rationality of market players.[123] Incomplete information and political volatility defy the absolute rationality of financial markets and their ability to effectively price in the risks incurred.[124]

120 Friedrich Hayek, *Law, Legislation and History: Rules and Order* (1973) 51.

121 See, eg, Dan Awrey, William Blair, and David Kershaw, 'Between Law and Markets: Is there a Role for Culture and Ethics in Financial Regulation' (2012) LSE Law, Society and Economics Working Papers 14/2012, 5–6.

122 For the evolution of ideas on the rational market hypothesis, see Justin Fox, *The Myth of the Rational Market: A History of Risk, Reward and Delusion on Wall Street* (2009).

123 For the application in bond markets, see Bodo Herzog, 'A Behavioural Model of European Bond Markets' (2014) 3(3) J Stock Forex Trad 2014.

124 Michael Tomz, *Reputation and International Cooperation: Sovereign Debt across Three Centuries* (2007) 11.

No doubt, the struggle between the two views is a permanent struggle and the differences in practice would appear to be one of degree and not kind. Thus, the views in economics differ as to how fallible (or infallible) the market is and how accurate the price adjustment is.[125] The Chicago school of economics, to mention only one school of thought, is based on the concept that economic actors err, but are correct on average. **1.79**

Conceding certain rationality and effectiveness to financial markets leaves the question of the extent to which such rationality and effectiveness exist in sovereign debt markets. Some practitioners and commentators alike perceive that financial markets may police the conduct of and exact discipline from sovereign debtors, or at least mitigate the effects of their wrongdoings, both *ex post* and *ex ante*. So far as the *ex post* control is concerned, between the nineteenth to early twentieth century, bondholders' self-help organisations were noticeably efficient in ensuring that their members were paid by a government in default as a precondition for further access to finance.[126] In a broader sense, many scholars have stressed the ability of financial markets to foreclose capital markets for sovereign debtors in default and in that way force them to comply with their contractual obligations.[127] The reputation of sovereign debtors and the related threat of seeing capital markets foreclosed make States think twice before defaulting. **1.80**

While the reputational concerns might play a certain role in sovereign debt disputes, the threat of foreclosing capital markets is somewhat exaggerated since markets are in principle forward-looking.[128] The prospects of the repayment of sovereign debt—the question that creditors care about the most—mostly turns on factors other than the previous record of repayment of a sovereign, such as the state of economy of the debtor and external financial conditions.[129] **1.81**

125 Brian Snowdon, Howard Vane, and Peter Wynarczyk, *A Modern Guide to Macroeconomics: An Introduction to Competing Schools of Thought* (1994) 414.

126 Marc Flandreau, 'Sovereign States, Bondholders Committees, and the London Stock Exchange in the Nineteenth Century (1827–68): New Facts and Old Fictions' (2013b) 29(4) Oxford Rev Econ Policy 668; Rui Pedro Esteves, 'The Bondholder, the Sovereign, and the Banker: Sovereign Debt and Bondholders' Protection before 1914' (2013) 17 Europ Rev Econ Hist 389.

127 Jonathan Eaton and Mark Gersovitz, 'Debt with Potential Repudiation: Theoretical and Empirical Analysis' (1981) 48(2) Rev Econ Stud 289; Michael Tomz, *Reputation and International Cooperation: Sovereign Debt across Three Centuries* (2007).

128 Joseph Stiglitz, 'Sovereign Debt: Notes on Theoretical Framework and Policy Analyses' (2002) Initiative for Public Dialogue Working Paper Series 12–13.

129 Ibid 13. For empirical evidence, see Ugo Panizza, Federico Sturzenegger, and Jeromin Zettelmeyer, 'The Economics and Law of Sovereign Debt and Default' (2009) 47(3) J Econ Lit 651, 675–77, 687.

1.82 This section focuses instead on the *ex ante* control of financial markets. Why does this matter? By way of example, consider the choice of law clauses commonly inserted in sovereign bonds. The established practice is that sovereigns subject their bonds either to their domestic law or to the foreign law of a financial centre (commonly English or New York laws). When the bonds are governed by the domestic law of the sovereign, creditors holding such bonds are subject to the risk that the sovereign debtor may modify its own domestic law through an act of parliament in order to reduce the magnitude of its financial indebtedness. This risk has provoked many discussions as to the legality and acceptability of such unilateral modifications of domestic-law bonds and is addressed in detail in Chapter 5.

1.83 While it is hard to place a precise monetary value on a choice of law clause, there is a perception that the governing law affects the interest rate of sovereign bonds. A proponent of the 'market-as-regulator' approach, in the face of such circumstances, may argue that the market should have priced in the sovereign risk inherent in the bonds governed by domestic law; that the investors willing to accept such risk received a higher interest rate in exchange for incurring the risk of unilateral modification of the domestic bonds they hold;[130] and that the loss resulting from a unilateral modification ought to be treated as legitimate and irrecoverable; otherwise, the creditors would be unduly enriched. Similar arguments may apply to other types of legal boilerplate.

1.84 The debate sketched here prompts two questions. First, as a factual enquiry, have the markets been able to price in the risks inherent in the issuance and purchase of sovereign bonds? An answer in the negative will at least cast some doubt on the hypothesis that financial markets are able to price in the risk of default and omnisciently police sovereign bonds markets. Second, as a legal enquiry, assuming a court comes to the conclusion that the risk has indeed been priced in, one is still left with a separate question, namely whether the evidence to the pricing-in is admissible or relevant to the determination of the legality of sovereign default or other wrongdoing.

1.85 *Evidence as to the pricing-in of risks.* It is safe to say that investors incur an undeniable risk by investing into sovereign bonds,[131] in spite of the paradoxical

[130] See in this sense Michael Waibel, 'Opening Pandora's Box: Sovereign Bonds in International Arbitration' (2007) 101 AJIL 711, 754–55; Melissa Boudreau, 'Restructuring Sovereign Debt under Local Law: Are Retrofit Collective Action Clauses Expropriatory?' (2012) 2 HBLR Online 164, 181.

[131] *JP Morgan Chase Bank v Springwell Navigation Corporation* [2008] EWHC 1186 (Comm) (an inherent risk was present in investing into Russian government bonds, or instruments linked to the Russian government bonds, that collapsed in 1998).

banking capital requirements that treat them as risk-free investments.[132] However, even though the legal boilerplate might matter each time a dispute arises and is brought before a court, market players may, and often are, ignorant of the risks that boilerplate contractual clauses entail. Such ignorance or 'optimism bias' is an inherent feature of human behaviour, especially in the context of factual contingencies that are not very likely to materialise.[133] Probability insensitivity[134] casts a big shadow of doubt on the likelihood of investors pricing in the risk of default in calm times, unless the chance of default is foreseeable at the moment of the issuance of bonds. The scepticism towards the ability of financial markets to price in sovereign risk is corroborated by the lack of empirical evidence.

At this point, a line has to be drawn between the pricing of general default (political) risk, on the one hand, and the pricing of the manipulation of contractual provisions, on the other. For the first category, empirical research finds that spreads on the sovereign debt depend on two groups of factors combined: *common explanatory variables*, such as international risk factors, liquidity, quantitative easing, and *country-specific macroeconomic variables*, such as the debt-to-GDP ratio, inflation, tax base, level of investments, risk of exiting a currency union such as the eurozone.[135] In good times, global factors predominantly affect the pricing of bonds;[136] in times of crises, country-specific factors tend to intensify.[137] **1.86**

For the second category—the pricing-in of specific contractual provisions—their pricing by financial markets is much more doubtful. While it is safe to say that certain terms and conditions of bonds are invariably priced in, such as maturities, the pervasive question is whether others, for instance, dispute-resolution-related clauses, are priced, too. **1.87**

When one looks at *private* bond issuances, there are indications that financial markets do indeed price in bond covenants of various sorts.[138] The **1.88**

132 Gemma Varriale, 'Basel Plan to Curb Banks' Sovereign Debt Faces Challenges' (3 February 2015) IFLR.

133 Christine Jolls, 'On Law Enforcement with Boundedly Rational Actors' in Francesco Parisi and Vernon Smith (eds), *The Law and Economics of Irrational Behavior* (2005) 273–79.

134 The general unwillingness to anticipate the occurrence of negative events.

135 For an overview, see Luís Oliveira, José Dias Curto, and João Pedro Nunes, 'The Determinants of Sovereign Credit Spread Changes in the Euro-Zone' (2012) 22 Int Fin Markets, Inst and Money 278, 279–80.

136 Francis Longstaff, Jun Pan, Lasse Pedersen, and Kenneth Singleton, 'How Sovereign Is Sovereign Credit Risk?' (2011) 3(2) Am Econ J 75.

137 Oliveira et al (n 135) 279–80.

138 Michael Bradley and Michael Roberts, 'The Structure and Pricing of Corporate Debt Covenants' (2003) 25–28 (available at http://papers.ssrn.com/sol3/papers.cfm?abstract_id=585882). See also Khalil Torabzadeh, John Roufagalas, and Criss Woodruff, 'Self-Selection

rationale behind the pricing of bond covenants is that the premium on bond covenants is positively correlated to the relative ease with which a disgruntled bondholder may enforce the breach of bond covenants should it wish to enforce the promise to abide by the bond covenant.

1.89 By contrast, covenants contained in the bonds issued by a sovereign debtor may be different. For one, the implicit guarantee of bailouts may make contractual boilerplate irrelevant,[139] although a rational actor does not expect a bailout to occur with certainty. The peculiar context of sovereign bond restructurings and litigation is that the remedies available to ordinary sovereign bondholders may often seem unrealistic in the light of benign sovereign immunity regimes and other defences available to the State against legal actions in foreign courts. There is an intuitive perception of impracticality of legal action against sovereigns which casts doubt on whether the investors would actually go the extra mile to examine intricate bond provisions and price them accordingly.

1.90 Over the years, scholars have examined the pricing of various contractual provisions contained in sovereign bonds. Weidemaier analysed the pricing of the bonds that included sovereign immunity waivers (post-1976: the year of the adoption of the US Foreign Sovereign Immunities Act that introduced relative immunity) and those that did not (pre-1976 when the absolute sovereign immunity was the rule). His evidence rejects the hypothesis that private bondholders priced in sovereign immunity waivers.[140]

1.91 In the 1990s to early 2000s, a debate raged on the effect that the introduction of majority action clauses[141] would have on the pricing of bonds. Empirical studies concluded on the whole there is little evidence of a significant impact of CACs on pricing. Even when the introduction of CACs was found to impact the pricing of bonds, the views differed as to what type of States might benefit from the pricing flexibility delivered by the CACs. One perspective was that the CACs decrease the borrowing costs of financially strong debtors. Conversely, others claimed that the effect of the CACs was to decrease the borrowing costs of financially less viable debtors.[142] The third view was that such an effect only occurred

and the Effects of Poison Put/Call Covenants on the Reoffering Yields of Corporate Bonds' (2000) 9 Intl Rev Econ Fin 139.

[139] Marcos Chamon, Julian Schumacher, and Christoph Trebesch, 'Foreign Law Bonds: Can They Reduce Sovereign Borrowing Costs?' (2014) Mimeo, fn 6.

[140] Mark Weidemaier, 'Sovereign Immunity and Sovereign Debt' (2014) 1 U Ill L Rev 67, 100–01

[141] On which see Chapter 2.

[142] Michael Bradley and Mitu Gulati, 'Collective Action Clauses for the Eurozone' (2014) 18(6) Rev Fin 2045, 2051–54, 2097. See also Elena Carletti, Paolo Colla, Mitu Gulati, and

for mid-level-rated States.[143] Evidence also suggests that the pricing will vary depending on the legal system chosen as the governing law and the forum for litigation.[144] The lower yield of bonds with CACs is explained by the fact that bondholders prefer bonds where the majority can modify the payment terms of bonds.

The evidence on the pricing of *pari passu* clauses was equally inconclusive,[145] although the analyses related more to the pricing of judicial decisions that construed *pari passu* clauses in one way or another. Choi and Gulati's research into the pricing of subordination in sovereign bonds concluded that the effect of subordination was priced when the sovereign debtor was in the vicinity of default—in good times, markets did not attach a monetary value to the contractual boilerplate.[146] The odious character of bonds may also be priced in.[147] **1.92**

On the pricing of choice of law clauses, a study by Gulati, Choi, and Posner compared one Greek law governed bond with one English law governed bond, and found that they had different spreads over the course of Greece's financial predicament and restructuring. Because Greece could modify Greek law governed bonds, and, conversely, was unable to modify English law that governed the remaining bonds, Greek law governed bonds were supposedly a riskier investment for bondholders and, as a consequence, offered higher yields to bondholders willing to assume that risk. Interestingly, the authors observed that the choice of governing law was priced in in Greek law bonds pre-crisis and not only at a later stage when the default of a State became more or less imminent. **1.93**

From this data, the authors concluded that a European-wide mechanism for the orderly treatment of sovereign defaults should adjust the size of haircuts **1.94**

Steven Ongena, 'Pricing Contract Terms in a Crisis: Venezuelan Bonds in 2016' (2016) 11(4) CMLJ 540.

143 Alfredo Bardozzetti and Davide Dottori, 'Collective Action Clauses: How Do They Affect Sovereign Bond Yields?' (2014) 92 J Intl Econ 286.

144 Elena Carletti, Paolo Colla, Mitu Gulati, and Steven Ongena, 'The Price of Law: The Case of the Eurozone Collective Action Clauses' (2016) (available at http://scholarship.law.duke.edu/faculty_scholarship/3543).

145 Stephen Choi, Mitu Gulati, and Eric Posner, 'Pricing Terms in Sovereign Debt Contracts: A Greek Case Study with Implications for the European Crisis Resolution Mechanism' (2011) 6(2) CMLJ 163, 171–72; Michael Bradley, James Cox, and Mitu Gulati, 'The Market Reaction to Legal Shocks and their Antidotes' (2010) 39 J Leg Stud 289 (presenting more conclusive evidence).

146 Stephen Choi and Mitu Gulati, 'The Pricing of Non-Price Terms in Sovereign Bonds: The Case of the Greek Guarantees' (2016) JLFA 1.

147 Stéphanie Collet and Kim Oosterlinck, 'Pricing the Odious in Odious Debts' (2016) Discussion Paper DP11653.

on private investors in correlation with the risks undertaken by investors.[148] In a later piece of research, Gulati, Trebesch, and Zettelmeyer admit that the pricing variations between domestic- and foreign-law governed bonds may have been propelled primarily by choice of court agreements, which invariably go hand in hand with choice of law clauses. Under this interpretation of the data, investors, strictly speaking, priced in the forum for the litigation of disputes and not the governing law.[149]

1.95 A later piece of research by Clare and Schmidlin, drawing on a much larger sample than the study by Choi, Gulati, and Posner and covering Europe-wide securities, claimed that the governing law was priced on the secondary market of bonds when the sovereign debtor, following the primary issuance of the bonds, became prone to default. Their research indicates that in 'good times', ie when the sovereign debtor is not expected to default, the market barely prices in the governing law variable (such limited pricing may well be due to the noise in the information)[150] and if the pricing happens, it occurs in 'bad times'.

1.96 As a general proposition, the 'good times' of sovereign debt issuance will most often coincide with the periods of primary issuance of bonds since private lending is mostly procyclical[151] and the costs of issuance of bonds in 'bad times' may be prohibitive.[152] Conversely, the pricing of bonds, which mostly occurs in 'bad times', will often coincide with the trading of bonds on the secondary market.[153]

148 Stephen Choi, Mitu Gulati, and Eric Posner, 'Pricing Terms in Sovereign Debt Contracts: A Greek Case Study with Implications for the European Crisis Resolution Mechanism' (2011) 6(2) CMLJ 163.

149 Mitu Gulati, Christoph Trebesch, and Jeromin Zettelmeyer, 'International Finance and Sovereign Debt' in Francesco Parisi (ed), *Oxford Handbook of Law and Economics: Volume 3* (2017) 493.

150 Andrew Clare and Nicolas Schmidlin, 'The Impact of Foreign Governing Law on European Government Bond Yields' (2014) (available at http://papers.ssrn.com/sol3/papers.cfm?abstract_id=2406477).

151 Yuefen Li and Ugo Panizza, 'The Economic Rationale for the Principles on Promoting Responsible Sovereign Lending and Borrowing' in Carlos Espósito, Yuefen Li, and Juan Pablo Bohoslavsky (eds), *Sovereign Financing and International Law: The UNCTAD Principles on Responsible Sovereign Lending and Borrowing* (2013) 29.

152 Ugo Panizza, Federico Sturzenegger, and Jeromin Zettelmeyer, 'The Economics and Law of Sovereign Debt and Default' (2009) 47(3) J Econ Lit 651, 664–67. Flandreau sees in this the deficiency of financial markets, in that their ability to discriminate comes in only when it is too late—in times of crises (Marc Flandreau, 'Do Good Sovereigns Default? Lessons of History' in *Sovereign Risk: A World without Risk-Free Assets?* (2013a) BIS Papers No 72, 19).

153 See also Chamon et al (n 139) 3–4 (confirming the finding that the States in distress pay a premium for domestic-law bonds).

Legal import of the pricing-in of risks. Assuming financial markets do indeed price in sovereign risk, the threshold question to be addressed first is at what point in time should the courts consider the pricing: the time of issuance or the trading on the secondary market? It seems that English courts would be more open, if at all, to accepting the financial data on the pricing of bonds as of *the time of issuance of bonds.*[154] The price of bonds traded subsequently on the secondary market is by and large irrelevant. Principle suggests that the trading on the secondary market among creditors cannot affect the rights and obligations of the State. The sovereign is not privy to the sale of bonds after to the issuance of bonds and does not derive any (direct) benefits from the trade on the secondary market. The rights and obligations of the State (and bondholders alike) do not float freely in the air and change their content along with the fluctuations of the secondary market of sovereign bonds. This legal conclusion, with markets mostly pricing in bond covenants only in 'bad times'—which is often likely to coincide with the trading on the secondary market—leads to the conclusion that the pricing of bonds is very unlikely to affect legal rights and obligations as cemented during the primary market issuance. **1.97**

This notwithstanding, for those instances when the primary markets do indeed price in the risks inherent in the subscription to sovereign bonds on the primary market, there is ambiguity as to the legal significance of the pricing-in of sovereign risk. The black-letter law reaction would assert that the argument of the supporters of the 'market-as-regulator' sits uncomfortably with the principle that the evidence preceding the conclusion of contract cannot be adduced for the purposes of contract interpretation.[155] **1.98**

There are two more general points to be made. First, is the pricing of boilerplate contractual provisions always commensurate to the risks undertaken? Prospectuses offering bonds to the general public commonly set out the information necessary for calculating the probability of the occurrence of default. That said, sovereign debt markets may be dominated by impervious information asymmetries or the creditors might fail to process all the available information necessary for the accurate pricing of sovereign bonds, or, more precisely, the probability of triggering of boilerplate provisions. Commentary indicates that bond markets do not accurately reflect economic fundamentals.[156] This makes the idea of accurate pricing **1.99**

[154] *Bank of New York Mellon (London Branch) v Truvo N.V. and others* [2013] EWHC 136 (Comm), paras 83–85.

[155] *Chartbrook Ltd v Persimmon Homes Ltd* [2009] UKHL 38, paras 28–42 (but see the caveat in para 33).

[156] Antonello D'Agostino and Michael Ehrmann, 'The Pricing of G7 Sovereign Bond Spreads: The Times, They Are A-Changin' (2013) ECB Working Paper Series No 1520.

of boilerplate provisions, or, more precisely, the risk of their triggering all the more doubtful. Sovereign defaults may at times be caused by exogenous economic shocks that are unforeseeable at the time of issuance of bonds.[157] On occasion, the State may default opportunistically—even though having the capacity to pay—which is hard to predict forensically.

1.100 Second, does the spread of ten to twenty basis points mean that the investor is to be taken to have acquiesced in the default or other wrongful activity of the State? It is argued that the pricing-in of the governing law implies that the bondholders accept the risk and recognise the legality of the modifications of domestic-law governed bonds.[158] Perhaps more plausibly, it may simply indicate that the bondholders acknowledge the risks of sovereign default and the risk (and costs) that they would incur in challenging the measures to which the sovereign debtor resorts to through litigation/arbitration. It is thought that investors typically price in the political risk and the risk of default in the yields of government bonds, yet that by no means implies that they are willing to accept the risk once it materialises and renounce their rights under the bonds.

1.101 Having said all that, the evidence as to the pricing-in of risks may very rarely play a secondary role in the reasoning of judges. Thus, in *Braka v Bancomer*, a US depositor claimed repayment of deposits placed in a Mexican foreign State-owned bank and later subjected to an exchange control regulation. The judge was anxious to stress that the higher interest rate justified the risk of investing in a foreign bank and eventually found that the Act of State doctrine precluded the adjudication of the dispute over the payment of deposits.[159] Judges are not advised to feel compelled by the theoretical argument of higher interest rates. These are often mere speculation, unsupported by any empirical analysis calculating the extent of interest rates.

[157] Contrast with the empirical analysis showing no correlation between exogenous market factors and the default risk of a sovereign, Alexandre Jeanneret, Eric Paget-Blanc, and Slim Souissi, 'Sovereign Defaults by Currency Denomination' (2014) 4–5 (available at http://papers.ssrn.com/sol3/papers.cfm?abstract_id=2365059).

[158] See Waibel (n 130) 754–55; Boudreau (n 130) 181.

[159] 589 F.Supp 1465, 1471 (SDNY 1984). See also *West v Multibanco Comermex*, 807 F.2d 820, 833 (2d Cir 1987).

VII. RETHINKING SOVEREIGN DEBT ADJUDICATION IN LIGHT OF THE THEORETICAL FRAMEWORK OUTLINED

This book is predicated on the idea that sovereign debt is essentially a commercial activity, and that the courts should employ private law tools to determine rights and obligations under sovereign bonds. The chapter, however, acknowledged that in some cases public policy considerations may find expression in private law tools. **1.102**

The remaining chapters in this book will reflect upon the existing problems in sovereign debt adjudication through the prism of private law. What the pursuit of familiar private law mechanisms will typically do in most cases is simply confirm what is already well known and commonsensical. In this monograph, however, private law mechanisms will instead be resorted to with the single purpose of resolving the salient and under-researched issues that arise in sovereign debt litigation. **1.103**

2

Contractual Background of Sovereign Debt Litigation

One cannot properly comprehend sovereign debt litigation without first placing it in the context of the contractual provisions commonly found in sovereign bonds. The documentation of external bonds has gone from strength to strength over the last decade.[1] External sovereign bonds now include a whole array of clauses, such as collective action clauses (CACs) in various manifestations, choice of law, and choice of court provisions, all of which are designed to facilitate the orderly restructuring of sovereign debt and to ensure certainty in the resolution of disputes. **2.01**

Nowadays, the almost ubiquitous market practice is to include CACs in sovereign bonds. CACs are designed to ensure the orderly resolution of sovereign debt crises and overcome the risk of holdout strategies by minority bondholders. Their introduction into sovereign bonds resonates with the 'contractual approach' to sovereign debt restructurings, whereby the intricacies of the sovereign debt workouts are addressed *ex ante*—through the introduction of various contractual clauses. **2.02**

I. MAJORITY ACTION CLAUSES

Among various CACs, one type of clauses—*majority action clauses*—stand out in that they provide for the 'democratic' governance by the majority of bondholders over and against the will of the minority. Pursuant to this clause, a majority of bondholders (most commonly 75%) has the power to amend the financial terms of bonds and consent to a restructuring of the debt, with binding effect for all bondholders. It is generally assumed that these clauses weaken the chances of holdout litigation in that a bondholder who does not have a blocking position of 25% of bonds is restrained from rebelling against the will of the majority and holding out. **2.03**

[1] Although arguably, sovereign debt documentation provides still far fewer protections than corporate bonds (Philip Wood, 'Bondholders and Banks—Why the Difference in Protections?' (2011) 6(2) CMLJ 188).

2.04 Commonly, in English law governed bonds, the majority of bondholders may modify the bonds if it has amassed the consent of 75% of bondholders, although some bonds may call for the consent of fewer bondholders.[2] Pre-2003, English law governed bonds contained a diminishing quorum requirement: if less than 75% of bondholders were present at the first physical meeting of bondholders, the second meeting required a mere 25% quorum and as low as 18.75% of bondholders could have amended the bonds.[3] This stands in sharp contrast with those bonds that require a unanimous consent of all the bondholders to amend the financial terms of the sovereign debt issuance (pre-2003 New York law governed bonds, German law governed bonds, etc).[4]

2.05 Since 1 January 2013, all eurozone bonds should contain majority action clauses,[5] both in foreign-law and domestic-law governed bonds. The eurozone model clause provides that sovereign bonds might be amended by the consent of the supermajority of 66⅔% of the holders of all outstanding bonds, or 75% of bondholders present at a bondholder meeting.[6] Again, such a decision would have binding effect on the non-consenting minority of creditors (Art 4.12).

2.06 Majority action clauses generally contain two lists of matters each of which requires a different majority. First, there are 'reserve matters' that can only be amended by a vote of a higher percentage of bondholders (often 75% of bondholders). The list of reserve matters commonly includes financial terms of bonds, that is to say, payment-related clauses (amount, maturity, currency, etc), but has increasingly become inclusive of certain protective covenants, such as choice of law and jurisdiction agreements, immunity waivers, definition of events of defaults, and so on,[7] which were considered too important. Then, there are matters that require a lower threshold for amendment (commonly 50% or 66⅔%), discussed below.

2.07 A typical majority action clause will stipulate that:

> [A]ny modification of any provision of these Conditions may be made if approved by an Extraordinary Resolution or a Written Resolution. In these Conditions,

[2] Michael Bradley and Mitu Gulati, 'Collective Action Clauses for the Eurozone' (2014) 18(6) Rev Fin 2045, 2064.

[3] Ibid 2064.

[4] On the historical development of CACs, see Mark Weidemaier and Mitu Gulati, 'A People's History of Collective Action Clauses' (2013) 54(1) Va JIL 51.

[5] Art 12.3 of the Treaty Establishing the European Stability Mechanism.

[6] Art 2.1 of the Common Terms of Reference.

[7] For an extensive definition of reserve matters, see Kingdom of Bahrain, US$1,500,000,000 6.125 per cent Bonds due 5 July 2022, Clause 11(c).

'Extraordinary Resolution' means a resolution passed at a meeting of Noteholders duly convened and held in accordance with the Fiscal Agency Agreement by a majority of at least:

(i) in the case of a Reserved Matter, 75 per cent. of the aggregate principal amount of the outstanding Notes; or
(ii) in the case of a matter other than a Reserved Matter, 66⅔ per cent. of the aggregate principal amount of the outstanding Notes which are represented at that meeting.

Any Extraordinary Resolution duly passed at any such meeting shall be binding on all the Noteholders, whether present or not and whether they voted in favour or not, and all Couponholders.[8]

In the application of a majority action clause, the bondholders will vote within the four corners of the series to which they subscribed. However, the bonds will often stipulate that the 'Series' comprises further issues of bonds which are later consolidated with the original issue.[9] Issuing further bonds in this manner will dilute the voting power in the original bond issuance. The power to issue bonds and consolidate them with earlier issuances may be subject to the prohibition of collusion.[10] **2.08**

Due to the efforts of the EU and international institutions, majority action clauses have been reinforced and may come in the form of *aggregation clauses*. Conventional, non-reinforced majority action clauses are inherently constrained to the four corners of individual series of bonds and do not cater for the need to restructure the whole spectrum of sovereign bond issuances in one strike. Aggregation clauses are thus designed to allow the overall majority of bondholders across a number of sovereign bond issuances to restructure all of the bonds series. Aggregation clauses require both the consent of the aggregate community of bondholders and the consent of bondholders in an individual series of bonds for the restructuring to bind the minority bondholders. To illustrate, the eurozone aggregate clause requires the overall consent of 75% of bondholders combined with the approval of 66⅔% of bondholders in any single series of bonds. EU Model CACs also provide for partial cross-series **2.09**

[8] Republic of Lithuania, Euro 400,000,000 4.85 per cent Notes due 2018, Clause 11(e).

[9] See, eg, Art 1(d) of the Common Terms of Reference; Kingdom of Sweden, General Terms and Conditions for Government Bonds Series No 1057 (2012), p 3; Republic of Philippines, Issue of US$600,000,000 6.00% Notes due 2023 ('[T]he Republic may issue additional notes fungible with outstanding Notes, which would dilute the voting powers of existing Holders of Notes'); Republic of Guatemala, Offering Circular, US$700,000,000 5.750% Notes due 2022, p 18.

[10] On which see Chapter 7.

modification if the proposed modification was not adopted by all the bond series.[11]

2.10 The Model EU aggregation clause provides as follows:

> 2.2 Cross-Series Modification. In the case of a cross-series modification, the terms and conditions of the Bonds and debt securities of any other series, and any agreement governing the issuance or administration of the Bonds or debt securities of such other series, may be modified in relation to a reserved matter with the consent of the Issuer and:
>
> (a)(i) the affirmative vote of not less than 75% of the aggregate principal amount of the outstanding debt securities represented at separate duly called meetings of the holders of the debt securities of all the series (taken in the aggregate) that would be affected by the proposed modification; or
>
> (a)(ii) a written resolution signed by or on behalf of the holders of not less than 66⅔% of the aggregate principal amount of the outstanding debt securities of all the series (taken in the aggregate) that would be affected by the proposed modification;
>
> and
>
> (b)(i) the affirmative vote of more than 66⅔% of the aggregate principal amount of the outstanding debt securities represented at separate duly called meetings of the holders of each series of debt securities (taken individually) that would be affected by the proposed modification; or
>
> (b)(ii) a written resolution signed by or on behalf of the holders of more than 50% of the aggregate principal amount of the then outstanding debt securities of each series (taken individually) that would be affected by the proposed modification.[12]

2.11 It may become apparent that aggregation clauses suffer from a drawback—a single bondholder may still acquire a necessary blocking minority (33⅓%+1) in a single series of bonds and thus obstruct the aggregate restructuring despite the consent of overall bondholders.[13] With this in mind, the IMF[14] and the International Capital Market Association (ICMA),[15] but not the EU,[16] proposed a single series aggregation clause,

[11] Art 2.4 of the Common Terms of Reference.

[12] Art 2.2 of the Common Terms of Reference.

[13] Anna Gelpern, 'How Collective Action Is Changing Sovereign Debt' (2003) 22(5) IFLR 19, 20.

[14] IMF, 'Sovereign Debt Restructuring—Recent Developments and Implications for the Fund's Legal and Policy Framework' (2013) 14; IMF, 'Strengthening the Contractual Framework to Address Collective Action Problems in Sovereign Debt Restructuring' (2014) 15–31.

[15] ICMA, 'Sovereign Bond Consultation Paper Supplement' (2014) 12–14.

[16] Deborah Zandstra, 'New Aggregated Collective Action Clauses and Evolution in the Restructuring of Sovereign Debt Securities' (2017) 12(2) CMLJ 180, 187.

otherwise known as the *enhanced aggregation clause*, whereby the overall majority of bondholders across the board can amend the sovereign bonds, obviating the need to obtain the consent of individual series of bonds.[17] Such aggregation clauses would put an end to the practice of holdout creditors purchasing blocking minorities (either 25%+1 or 33⅓%+1) in a single series of bonds in a move to prevent the State from successfully completing the restructuring.

Exit consents are another technique of 'financial democracy', pursuant to which, when the sovereign debtor restructures its debt by exchanging old bonds for new bonds, it also seeks the consent of the majority of bondholders (most commonly 50%) to amend the terms of the old bonds so as to make them less valuable or practically worthless for the holdout minority. Essentially at their exit, the majority of bondholders modifies essential protective bond covenants of the old bonds, as per the exchange offer, to the detriment of minority creditors. If the minority decides to hold out, it is bound through the operation of exit consents to lose the advantage of certain bond covenants that were removed by the majority from the old bonds. Such terms may be the listing of bonds on stock exchanges,[18] waivers of immunity, cross-default clauses,[19] choice of law clauses, exit covenants (seeking to prevent future restructurings),[20] and, in admittedly rare cases, the redemption of the bonds.[21] It is apparent that this technique is somewhat coercive and aims at fostering 'herding' behaviour.[22] **2.12**

This mechanism is triggered in pursuance of a majority action clause that allows the majority of bondholders (often 50%) to amend the non-financial terms of bonds. Generally, exit consents are put to use in one of two cases: (i) when the bonds do not contain a majority action clause that would provide for the modification of payment-related terms, or (ii) when the sovereign debtor lacks confidence that its offer would be met by **2.13**

[17] Kazakhstan was the first sovereign to follow the ICMA recommendations in respect of single-limb aggregation clauses (Elaine Moore, 'Kazakhstan First to Introduce Post-Argentina Bond Contracts' *Financial Times* (5 October 2014). Vietnam, Mexico, and others followed. It is yet to be seen whether these clauses become the market standard.

[18] Nicolas Piaggio, 'Lessons for Europe: The Pre-Emptive Restructuring of Uruguay' in Eugenio Bruno (ed), *Sovereign Debt and Debt Restructuring: Legal, Financial and Regulatory Aspects* (2013) 205.

[19] Lee Buchheit and Jeremiah Pam, 'Uruguay's Innovations' (2004) 19(1) JIBLR 28, 29–30.

[20] Lee Buchheit, 'How Ecuador Escaped the Brady Bond Trap' (2000) 19(12) IFLR 17, 20.

[21] *Assénagon Asset Management SA v Irish Bank Resolution Corporation Limited* [2012] EWHC 2090 (Ch), paras 50–54.

[22] Christian Engelen and Johann Graf Lambsdorff, 'Fairness in Sovereign Debt Restructuring' (2007) Diskussionsbeitrag Nr V-50-07, 17.

consent of the percentage of bondholders necessary for the modification of financial terms of the bonds (75% of bondholders) (especially so when an aggressive holdout holds 25%+1 of bonds). In such cases, exit consents incentivise potential holdout creditors to accept the new, financially less attractive bonds, almost as if the financial terms were modified through a majority action clause.

2.14 Exit consents work hand in hand with another technique that seeks to give better terms to consenting bondholders. The idea is that if the consenting bondholders are offered bonds with better protections (eg application of English law, negative pledge, cross defaults), this will leave the dissenting bondholders in a worse-off situation which will bite if the State is once again in a situation of financial distress.[23]

2.15 Majority action clauses are a more preferable option for the debtors, for the exit consent technique leaves some, albeit reduced, options for a minority creditor to hold out. But, concomitantly, the threshold required for the operation of a majority action clause is generally set higher than for the exit consents.

2.16 While a significant percentage of sovereign debt (mostly domestic-law governed bonds and debt expressed in a form other than bonds) lack CACs, international sovereign bonds have seen a rapid inclusion of various CACs ever since Mexico's debut issuance in 2003. The introduction of CACs is presumed to assuage the risk of holdout litigation by subjecting the holdouts to the will of the majority of bondholders. Quite how effective CACs are in fending off aggressive holdout litigation is a question of major concern. First, the minority creditor may block the restructuring by buying 25%+1 of bonds unless enhanced aggregation clauses have been introduced into the bonds. This was recently exemplified in the Greek 2012 restructuring where only seventeen out of thirty-six debt issuances, subject to English law, were successfully modified through the use of a majority action clause. As for the remaining debt issuances, the State was unable to persuade 75% of bondholders to restructure the debt.[24]

2.17 The official sector rests its hopes upon the introduction of enhanced aggregation clauses as proposed by the ICMA and IMF. Yet, it will take a considerable amount of time for these clauses to extend to all sovereign

[23] Mitu Gulati and Jeromin Zettelmeyer, 'Making a Voluntary Greek Debt Exchange Work' (2012) 7(2) CMLJ 169, 177–78.

[24] Sean Hagan, 'Debt Restructuring and Economic Recovery' in Lee Buchheit and Rosa Lastra (eds), *Sovereign Debt Management* (2014) 383.

bond issuances.[25] To make matters worse, the introduction of enhanced aggregation clauses is likely to drive litigious distressed debt buyers to the types of sovereign debt that lack CACs in general and aggregation clauses, in particular, including trade credits, domestic debt,[26] official debt, to name a few.

Second, CACs, including aggregation clauses, are not a panacea in any sense: they coordinate the restructuring of bonds issued to private creditors and do not appear in other types of sovereign debt, such as official debt and trade credits. **2.18**

In spite of these limitations, majority action clauses and other CACs are the toolkit of any sovereign debt restructuring and are able to impose discipline on litigious creditors. CACs represent a major shift in the dynamics of sovereign debt renegotiations. With the inclusion of majority action clauses, the sovereign debtor is able to sway a minority of creditors once the majority of creditors, often eager to collaborate with the sovereign debtor, takes the decision to restructure the sovereign debt. **2.19**

One thing that merits particular emphasis is that ever since 2003, majority action clauses became almost ubiquitous in New York and English law governed bonds[27] and other CACs also gained in prominence to varying degrees. With the quasi-ubiquitous introduction of majority action clauses, litigation tactics are bound to undergo significant changes that will inform the discussion in this monograph. Minority creditors are now at the constant risk of being swayed by the majority decision should the sovereign debtor, by sticks and carrots, convince the majority bondholders of the unsustainability of its debt. Following this evolution, holdout creditors are left with the following two main options of litigation: **2.20**

(i) bring pre-emptive litigation before the majority gets the chance to consent to the restructuring and bind the minority (addressed in Chapter 3), or
(ii) challenge the outcome of sovereign debt restructuring *ex post*, after the majority has consented to the terms of the exchange offer (addressed in Chapter 7).

[25] See, however, the impressive uptake of enhanced aggregation clauses as reported by IMF ('Second Progress Report in Inclusion of Enhanced Contractual Provisions in International Sovereign Bond Contracts' (2016)).

[26] Discussed further in Chapter 4.

[27] For an overview of how this change came about, see Stephen Choi, Mitu Gulati, and Eric Posner, 'The Dynamics of Contract Evolution' (2013) 88(1) NYU L Rev 1.

2.21 The third option, of course, would be to acquire a blocking minority (often 25%+1 of bonds). Another option open to distressed debt holders is to invest in financial instruments of a State which are much less legally protective of the interests of sovereign debtors. One such category of debt instruments is the domestic debt of a sovereign. Domestic bonds are less legally fortified as they lack most of the clauses ubiquitously found in external sovereign bonds. They are often silent on the applicable law[28] and competent court, not to mention CACs. Furthermore, and something that may hold additional allure for initial debt investors, domestic bonds may sometimes be perceived to be safer and less prone to the risk of restructuring than external bonds. That said, restructuring of domestic bonds has been done regularly, and not just in the distant past (Russia in 1998 restructured its domestic debt but not its Eurobonds).

II. OTHER CLAUSES

2.22 In addition to majority action clauses, sovereign bonds often contain so-called *disenfranchisement* clauses which are designed to, as the name suggests, disenfranchise (remove from calculations under majority action clauses) the votes cast by certain categories of bondholders controlled by the debtor. In other words, the votes cast by State-controlled bondholders will be ignored when deciding whether a majority action clause has been triggered.

2.23 The EU Model CACs provide:

Outstanding Bonds. In determining whether holders of the requisite principal amount of outstanding Bonds have voted in favour of a proposed modification or whether a quorum is present at any meeting of Bondholders called to vote on a proposed modification, a Bond will be deemed to be not outstanding, and may not be voted for or against a proposed modification or counted in determining whether a quorum is present, if on the record date for the proposed modification:

(c) the Bond is held by the Issuer, by a department, ministry or agency of the Issuer, or by a corporation, trust or other legal entity that is controlled by the Issuer or a department, ministry or agency of the Issuer and, in the case of a Bond held by any such above-mentioned corporation, trust or other legal entity, the holder of the Bond does not have autonomy of decision, where:

(i) the holder of a Bond for these purposes is the entity legally entitled to vote the Bond for or against a proposed modification or, if different, the entity whose consent or instruction is by contract required, directly or indirectly, for the legally entitled holder to vote the Bond for or against a proposed modification;

[28] On the law governing domestic debt, see Chapter 4.

(ii) a corporation, trust or other legal entity is controlled by the Issuer or by a department, ministry or agency of the Issuer if the Issuer or any department, ministry or agency of the Issuer has the power, directly or indirectly, through the ownership of voting securities or other ownership interests, by contract or otherwise, to direct the management of or elect or appoint a majority of the board of directors or other persons performing similar functions in lieu of, or in addition to, the board of directors of that legal entity; and

(iii) the holder of a Bond has autonomy of decision if, under applicable law, rules or regulations and independent of any direct or indirect obligation the holder may have in relation to the Issuer:

(x) the holder may not, directly or indirectly, take instruction from the Issuer on how to vote on a proposed modification; or

(y) the holder, in determining how to vote on a proposed modification, is required to act in accordance with an objective prudential standard, in the interest of all of its stakeholders or in the holder's own interest; or

(z) the holder owes a fiduciary or similar duty to vote on a proposed modification in the interest of one or more persons other than a person whose holdings of Bonds (if that person then held any Bonds) would be deemed to be not outstanding under this Section 2.7.[29]

Many sovereign bonds adopted the disenfranchisement provision as set out in the ICMA Model CACs. Thus, the bonds issued by the Republic of Philippines state: **2.24**

For purposes of determining whether the required percentage of holders of the debt securities of a series has approved any amendment, modification or change to, or waiver of, the debt securities or the Fiscal Agency Agreement, or whether the required percentage of holders has delivered a notice of acceleration of the debt securities of that series, debt securities owned, directly or indirectly, by the Republic or any public sector instrumentality of the Republic will be disregarded and deemed not to be outstanding (except that in determining whether the fiscal agent shall be protected in relying upon any amendment, modification, change or waiver, or any notice from holders, only debt securities that the fiscal agent knows to be so owned shall be so disregarded).

As used in this paragraph, 'public sector instrumentality' means Bangko Sentral, any department, ministry or agency of the Republic or any corporation, trust, financial institution or other entity owned or controlled by the Republic or any of the foregoing, and 'control' means the power, directly or indirectly, through the ownership of voting securities or other ownership interests or otherwise, to direct the management of or elect or appoint a majority of the board of directors or other persons performing similar functions in lieu of, or in addition to, the board of directors of a corporation, trust, financial institution or other entity.[30]

[29] Art 2.7 of the Common Terms of Reference.

[30] Republic of Philippines, Prospectus Supplement to Prospectus dated December 12, 2013, 4.20% Global Bonds due 2024, US$1,500,000,000, p 130.

2.25 The disenfranchisement clauses thus defined do not capture certain market players. First, they do not seem to apply to those entities which are indirectly influenced or will be affected by the lighter debt burden of the State.[31] Second, at least on their face, they do not capture subnational entities. The mechanism of disenfranchisement is addressed in detail in Chapter 7.

2.26 A third group of CACs—*majority enforcement provisions*—unite the enforcement powers in the hands of a group of creditors or a trustee, and thus constrain the enforcement capacity of individual creditors. Among such clauses, prominent are *collective acceleration clauses* that require the approval of a certain threshold of bondholders (usually 25%) to accelerate (make the debt payable and due immediately) the principal. A typical collective acceleration clause provides that:

> If any of the following events (each an 'Event of Default') occurs and is continuing: … then the holders of not less than 25% in the aggregate principal amount of the Notes may, by written notice to the Issuer (with a copy to the Fiscal Agent at its Specified Office), declare the Notes due and payable immediately. Notice of any such declaration shall promptly be given to all other Noteholders by the Issuer. Upon any declaration of acceleration, the principal, interest and all additional amounts payable on the Notes will become immediately due and payable on the date the Issuer receives written notice of the declaration. No delay or omission of any Noteholder shall impair any such right or remedy or constitute a waiver of any such Event of Default.[32]

2.27 Failing such acceleration, the disgruntled creditor is by necessity constrained to an action for the payments missed by the sovereign debtor (up to the point, perhaps, when the cumulative defaults (failure to make interest payments when due) give rise to termination for breach). By contrast, individual acceleration clauses—rarely agreed to by the sovereign debtors—vest a single bondholder with the right to accelerate the payment of the debt.[33]

2.28 The impact of an acceleration clause is often mitigated by a *reverse acceleration clause* which allows the majority (usually 50%) of bondholders to reverse the acceleration achieved by 25% of creditors. A typical clause provides:

> If the Republic receives notice in writing from holders of at least 50 per cent. in aggregate principal amount of the outstanding Notes to the effect that the Event

[31] Stephen Moverley Smith and Heather Murphy, 'Sovereign Bond Collective Action Clauses: Issues Arising' [2015] 2 JIBFL 128A.

[32] Republic of Serbia, Prospectus, 26 September 2011, US$1,000,000,000 7.25 per cent Notes due 2021, Clause 12.

[33] See, eg, Republic of South Africa, Prospectus Supplement, US$2,000,000,000, 5.875% Notes, due 2025, September 12, 2013, p 8.

of Default or Events of Default giving rise to the above mentioned declaration of acceleration is or are cured following any such declaration, the Republic shall give notice thereof in writing to the Noteholders (with a copy to the Fiscal Agent), the Notes shall cease to be due and payable. No such rescission shall affect any other or any subsequent Event of Default or any right of any Noteholder in relation thereto.[34]

Another contractual provision which limits the right of individual creditors to bring proceedings is the *trustee mechanism*. With a certain degree of oversimplification, the latter mechanism confers on the trustee the exclusive right to initiate any legal action and accelerate the sovereign debt. A common criticism of the trustee mechanism is that the trustee almost never takes action of its own initiative. However, a minimum of 25% of bondholders can typically request the trustee to bring claims against the sovereign debtor. *No-action clauses*—precluding individual bondholders from starting legal actions against the debtor—often go hand in hand with the trustee mechanism. Additionally, other clauses also may limit the prospects of holdout litigation: sharing clauses,[35] mandatory prepayment clauses, and so on. **2.29**

Of course, enforcement by the trustee or individual bondholders, provided they have individual standing,[36] is possible only if there is an event of default. Bonds often define events of default as broadly as possible and include the following: **2.30**

1. *Non-Payment:* Uruguay's failure for a period of 30 consecutive days to make a payment of principal or interest when due on any debt security of that series; or
2. *Breach of Other Obligations:* The failure for a period of 60 days following written notice to Uruguay by the trustee or holders representing 25% of the outstanding debt securities of that series to remedy the failure by Uruguay or, where applicable, Banco Central acting on Uruguay's behalf, to observe or perform any of the covenants or agreements provided in the debt securities of that series or the indenture (other than a non-payment default); or

[34] Republic of Latvia, Offering Circular, 20 February 2012, US$1,000,000,000 5.250 per cent Notes due 2017, Clause 9.

[35] Sharing clauses contained in sovereign bonds generally relate to the sharing of the proceeds that the trustee receives and do not as such require sharing of the proceeds from a successful litigation (Allen & Overy Global Law Intelligence Unit, 'Uses and Abuses of Collective Action Clauses in Sovereign Bonds' (2013) 14(3) Bus L Int'l 269, 288).

[36] See Chapter 3.

3. *Cross Default:*
   - Uruguay fails to make a payment when due or within the applicable grace period on public foreign debt issued, or amended as to payment terms, on or after April 10, 2003 having an aggregate principal amount greater than or equal to US$60,000,000 (or its equivalent in other currencies);
   - Any public foreign debt of Uruguay issued, or amended as to payment terms, on or after April 10, 2003 having an aggregate principal amount greater than or equal to US$60,000,000 (or its equivalent in other currencies) is accelerated due to an event of default, unless the acceleration is rescinded or annulled; or
4. *Moratorium:* Uruguay or certain courts declare a general suspension of payments or a moratorium on Uruguay's public foreign debt issued, or amended as to payment terms, on or after April 10, 2003; or
5. *Validity:*
   - The validity of the debt securities of that series is contested in certain formal proceedings by Uruguay or by any governmental entity of Uruguay that has the legal power to contest the validity of the securities;
   - Uruguay denies any of its obligations to the holders of that series under the debt securities or the indenture; or
   - A legislative or constitutional measure or a final decision by a court in Uruguay purports to render any material provision of the debt securities of that series invalid or to prevent or delay the performance of any of Uruguay's material obligations under the securities; or
6. *Failure of Authorisations:* Any law, regulation or governmental authorisation necessary for Uruguay to perform its material obligations under the debt securities of that series ceases to be in full force and effect or is modified in a manner that adversely affects the rights or claims of any of the holders; or
7. *Judgments:* Any of several special types of judgments is levied against all or any substantial part of the assets of Uruguay in connection with a monetary judgment exceeding US$60,000,000 (or its equivalent in other currencies) and Uruguay does not adequately satisfy, bond, contest in good faith, or receive a stay of execution in respect of, such judgment within 45 days; or
8. *Illegality:* Any applicable law, rule or regulation is adopted which would make it unlawful for Uruguay to comply with its obligations described in 'Additional Amounts' above; or
9. *IMF Membership:* Uruguay ceases to be a member of the IMF.[37]

[37] República Oriental del Uruguay, Prospectus Supplement to Prospectus dated July 30, 2013, US$ 2,000,000,000, 4.500% Bonds due 2024, 6 August 2013, pp 5–6.

As an alternative to the trustee mechanism, some bonds provide for the mechanism of fiscal agent. The fiscal agent is an agent of the issuer and carries out mostly administrative tasks. Unlike a trustee, the fiscal agent certainly does not have enforcement powers.[38] **2.31**

Other miscellaneous provisions regulate the enforcement of bonds. Commonly, the *pari passu* clause requires equal treatment with all other unsecured and unsubordinated obligations of the sovereign debtor which is likely to extend the coverage of the clause across all the debt owed by the sovereign debtor. The meaning of the clause is addressed in Chapter 7. **2.32**

Unusually, in a bond issuance of 23 December 2013 that was eventually subscribed by the Russian Federation, Ukraine covenanted to comply with a debt/GDP ratio of 60% along the following lines: **2.33**

> So long as the Notes remain outstanding the Issuer shall ensure that the volume of the total state debt and state guaranteed debt should not at any time exceed an amount equal to 60 per cent. of the annual nominal gross domestic product of Ukraine.[39]

The breach of this covenant was to trigger the Events of Default clause (Art 8 of Terms and Conditions of the prospectus) and allow the 25% of bondholders to accelerate the payment of the principal under the bond and seek legal redress.[40] **2.34**

Lastly, *collective representation* clauses/*creditor engagement* clauses provide for the creation of a creditor committee which will represent bondholders in the negotiations with the sovereign debtor.[41] There is some support for these clauses in international organisations but the clauses are looked at unfavourably by market actors. **2.35**

The extent of proliferation of various CACs in sovereign bonds is hard to calculate. The frequency with which majority action clauses are included in English law governed bonds is hard to measure in view of the enormous size of the universe of sovereign bonds. Extensive research conducted by Bradley and Gulati suggests that majority action clauses, in one form or another, are almost ubiquitous in English law governed bonds, plus around half of all English law governed bonds contain collective **2.36**

[38] See, eg, Republic of Finland, Offering Circular, 10,000,000,000 Euro, Medium Term Note Programme, 29 February 2008, Clause 15 (specifying that the Paying Agent will not act as a trustee).

[39] Republic of Ukraine, US$1,984,838,000 5.00 per cent Notes due 2015, p 28.

[40] Ibid 31.

[41] See, eg, Supplementary Provisions, Standard Aggregated Collective Action Clauses (CACs) for the Terms and Conditions of Sovereign Notes (2014).

acceleration clauses. By contrast, majority enforcement clauses are far from being ubiquitous in sovereign bonds and are thus incapable of assuaging all of the concerns as to aggressive creditor litigation. By 2010, less than 50% of English bonds contained reverse acceleration clauses. The trustee mechanism is also found in less than half of English bonds. As of 2010, only around 50% of sovereign bonds contained disenfranchisement provisions.[42]

2.37 Häseler, using different methodology and covering a different period of time, provides contrasting statistics about the prevalence of CACs and trustee provisions in English law governed bonds. More than half of all English governed bonds, according to his research, do not contain majority action clauses and trustee deeds in a single series of bonds, and merely 2% of English law governed bonds include both.[43] Only 28% of English law governed bonds contain majority action clauses.[44] Häseler locates trustee provisions in only 24% of English law governed bonds.[45]

2.38 Because of the breadth of the database of Bradley and Gulati, covering seventy-five countries and the period 1990–2010, the remainder of this monograph will rely on their empirical data.

2.39 *Dispute resolution clauses* take two forms—jurisdiction or arbitration agreements. For a very long time, the almost exclusive forum for resolving sovereign debt disputes was litigation in court. Jurisdiction agreements almost ubiquitously select either English or New York courts.

2.40 As of recently, arbitration agreements have started making appearance in sovereign bonds. They come in a variety of forms. They can be the exclusive forum for the resolution of disputes arising out of or in connection with the bonds[46] or, alternatively, the bonds will provide that any dispute arising out of or in connection with the bonds shall be referred to and finally resolved by arbitration but the bondholder reserves the right to initiate proceedings in the courts (either of England or New York).[47]

[42] Bradley and Gulati (n 2) 2065–67, 2070–71, 2074.

[43] Sönke Häseler, 'Individual versus Collective Enforcement Rights in Sovereign Bonds' (2008) German Working Papers in Law and Economics, 4–5.

[44] Sönke Häseler, 'Trustees versus Fiscal Agents and Default Risk in International Sovereign Bonds' (2012) 34 Eur J L & Econ 425, 436. Similarly, IMF research finds that as of 2003 only 20% of English law governed bonds contained CACs ('Collective Action Clauses: Recent Developments and Issues' (2003) 15).

[45] Häseler (n 44) 434.

[46] Republic of Azerbaijan, US$1,250,000,000 4.75 per cent Notes due 2024, Clause 17.

[47] Kingdom of Bahrain US$1,250,000,000 5.500 per cent Bonds due 31 March 2020, Clause 16.

3

Jurisdiction and Cognate Matters

I. JURISDICTION

1. Introduction

The traditional understanding, expressed by Borchard, was that 'Courts other than those of the debtor state are likely to consider themselves incompetent; and suits in the courts of the debtor are not likely to be fruitful.'[1] **3.01**

Nowadays, the two most common forums for litigation of sovereign debt disputes, at least external, are London and New York. English and New York courts might well be seised of the dispute over the domestic debt of the sovereign, defined as either the debt that the State floats in its own territory or the debt governed by the law of the sovereign debtor. There are various reasons which explain why the creditors may wish to litigate disputes arising out of domestic bonds of a sovereign before foreign (English) courts. For one, local courts of the sovereign debtor, asked to adjudicate on a sovereign debt dispute, might give unreserved recognition to the legislation of their own parliament which seeks to repudiate or modify the sovereign's bonds. Such cases require local courts to exercise an exceptionally high level of objectivity and impartiality in reviewing the acts of its own legislature when the sovereign debt is (presumably) governed by local law—even more so when the domestic litigation arises in times of economic emergencies, in which case the statutes adopted would be cloaked with public policy.[2] With this domestic bias in mind, it would be rational for foreign bondholders to seek a more favourable foreign forum. **3.02**

2. Service

In sovereign debt disputes, the actions are commonly brought before the Commercial Court in London by serving a claim form. In the US, the **3.03**

[1] Edwin Borchard, *State Insolvency and Foreign Bondholders* (1951) 37.

[2] See the discussion of Argentine and Greek cases in Chapter 5.

proceedings are initiated by a complaint lodged with the US District Court for the Southern District of New York.[3]

3.04 The first step in the process is to properly serve the sovereign debtor. In the UK, the claim form has to be served in compliance with s 12 of the State Immunity Act 1978 (SIA 1978) which requires service through the Foreign and Commonwealth Office to the Ministry of Foreign Affairs of the State concerned (s 12(1)). The State then has two months for acknowledgment of service (s 12(2)).[4] These requirements are applied strictly[5] and no judgment in default of appearance can be entered against the State without proof of compliance with the stipulated requirements (s 12(4)).

3.05 The parties, however, are at liberty to provide for a different mechanism for service (s 12(6)). Often, sovereign bonds will specify that the State has nominated an authorised agent (usually the ambassador in the UK) upon whom process may be served in an action before the English courts.[6] The nomination of the ambassador as the agent for service complicates the service given diplomatic privileges, and the waiver provision may not be an effective waiver of diplomatic privileges. The appointment of a private person (eg, a law firm or the Law Debenture Corporation) avoids the problem of diplomatic privileges.

3.06 In the US, under §1608 of the Foreign Sovereign Immunities Act 1976 (FSIA 1976), the private creditor has various options to serve a complaint upon a foreign State. First, the creditor may serve in accordance with any special arrangement with a State (§1608(a)(1)). Such arrangement will usually take the form of a nomination of an agent within the jurisdiction (often an ambassador). If no special arrangement exists, service may be effectuated in accordance with any applicable international convention (§1608(a)(2)), in particular the Hague Service Convention.[7] Failing this, service may be effected upon the Ministry of Foreign Affairs of the foreign State or to the

[3] In the US, a foreign State may request that a case against it, both on the merits and for the enforcement of a foreign judgment and measures in aid of execution, be removed to federal jurisdiction under 28 US Code §1441. For application, see, eg, *National Union Fire Insurance Company of Pittsburgh v Republic of Congo*, 2005 US Dist LEXIS 6206 (ND Tex 2005).

[4] Compare this with twenty-eight days in the Commercial Court.

[5] *Kuwait Airways Corp v Iraqi Airways Co* [1995] 1 WLR 1147, 1155–56 (finding that the delivery of the writ to the Embassy of Iraq was bad service); *PCL v Regional Government of X* [2015] EWHC 68 (Comm) (service of claim set aside for want of compliance with these requirements).

[6] See, eg, New Zealand, Base Prospectus, Euro Medium Term Note Programme, 5 February 2009, p 51.

[7] The Convention of 15 November 1965 on the Service Abroad of Judicial and Extrajudicial Documents in Civil or Commercial Matters.

US Secretary of State (§1608(a)(3)–(4)). US courts will ensure strict compliance with service requirements.[8] The sovereign will have sixty days after service has been made to serve an answer or other responsive pleading to the complaint (§1608(d)).

3. Applicability of the Brussels Regulation

After effective service, the court needs to establish its jurisdiction over the given dispute and parties. In the UK, there are two coexisting jurisdictional regimes: (i) the Brussels I Recast Regulation on jurisdiction and the recognition and enforcement of judgments in civil and commercial matters (2012) ('Brussels Regulation'); and (ii) national rules of jurisdiction. The first step of any jurisdictional decision is to decide which of the two regimes applies. The Brussels regime would apply if the defendant is domiciled in an EU Member State (Art 5). If the defendant is not domiciled in an EU Member State, the national rules of jurisdiction would apply, subject to Arts 18(1) (consumer contracts), 21(2) (employment contracts), 24 (exclusive jurisdiction), and 25 (jurisdiction agreements) (Art 6 of Brussels Regulation). **3.07**

The Brussels Regulation is thus principally engaged through the domicile of the defendant. The Brussels Regulation expressly covers the domicile of natural persons and companies. The domicile of natural persons is determined by the application of the court's internal law (Art 62). For companies or other legal persons or associations of natural or legal persons, Art 63 provides an EU-wide definition. While it is hard to accommodate the States into this structure, it seems that the modus operandi is to engage the Brussels Regulation if the defendant is an EU Member State,[9] or an EU subnational authority or central bank.[10] If the defendant State is not an EU Member State, the jurisdiction will need to be ascertained on the basis of national law. However, in the latter case, the Regulation will be engaged if **3.08**

[8] *CCM Pension-A, LLC v Republic of Argentina*, 16-cv-1650 (TPG) (SDNY 2016) (holding that the service on the New York branch of Banco de la Nación Argentina was defective since the latter was not an authorised agent of Argentina); *Hardy Exploration & Production (India), Inc v Government of India*, Civil Action No 16-0140 (DDC 2016) (holding that a contractual clause providing for the sending of notices, statements, and other communications by post did not extend to legal notices for the purpose of instituting proceedings).

[9] *Lechouritou v Federal Republic of Germany*, Case C-292/05, [2007] ECR I-1519 (an action against the Federal Republic of Germany where the Court of Justice assumed that the Brussels Regulation applied).

[10] *Grovit v De Nederlandsche Bank NV* [2006] EWCA Civ 953 (an action against the Dutch Central Bank).

the sovereign bonds contain a choice of court agreement in favour of EU courts (Art 6).

3.09 While the Brussels Regulation may in principle apply to actions against EU Member States, it clearly does not apply 'to the liability of the State for acts and omissions in the exercise of State authority (*acta iure imperii*)' and only applies to 'civil and commercial matters' (Art 1(1)). For the purposes of applying the Brussels Regulation, the civil and commercial character of sovereign debt is an autonomous concept determined by reference 'first, to the objectives and scheme of the Convention and, secondly, to the general principles which stem from the corpus of the national legal systems'.[11] The position in English law is not in itself determinative of the autonomous concept under the Regulation.

3.10 Under the established case law of the Court of Justice of the European Union (CJEU, or Court of Justice), contracts entered into by the public authorities other than in the exercise of their public powers, fall within the ambit of the Rome I Regulation.[12] By contrast, claims which arise from an act in the exercise of public powers will be *acta iure imperii* and will not be governed by the Regulation.[13]

3.11 The issuance of bonds, either domestic or external, may hardly be described as an exercise of public powers. Chapter 1 has already established that actions to recover the payments under sovereign bonds are properly characterised as *acta iure gestionis*. The issuance of sovereign bonds is scarcely an exercise of sovereign authority. Rather, it is a mundane exercise of raising funds on private capital markets, akin to what commercial companies do on an everyday basis.

3.12 Recently, the CJEU endorsed this view in holding that actions arising from the Greek debt restructuring of 2012, in particular the unilateral and retroactive introduction of majority action clauses into sovereign bonds (discussed in Chapter 5), were properly treated as 'civil and commercial matters'. The CJEU held that actions against the Greek State couched in terms of breach of property rights and disturbance of ownership, together with a claim for contractual performance, were also 'civil and commercial'.[14] A caveat is due here: the CJEU's preliminary ruling was issued in

[11] *LTU v Eurocontrol*, Case 29/76, [1976] ECR 1541, para 3. [12] Ibid.

[13] *Lechouritou v Greece*, Case C-292/05 [2007] ECR I-1519, para 41.

[14] *Stefan Fahnenbrock et al v Hellenische Republik*, CJEU, Joined Cases C-226/13, C-245/13, C-247/13, and C-578/13, 11 June 2015. Note that Advocate General Bot came to a diametrically opposite conclusion (Conclusions de l'Avocat Général M Yves Bot, le 9 décembre 2014, *Fahnenbrock v Hellenische Republik*, Affaires jointes C-226/13, C-245/13, C-247/13, et C-578/13). For commentary, see Hayk Kupelyants, 'The German Taxpayer and the Greek Sovereign Debt' (2015) Lexis PSL.

respect of the Regulation (EC) No 1393/2007 of the European Parliament and of the Council of 13 November 2007 on the service in the Member States of judicial and extrajudicial documents in civil or commercial matters ('Service of Documents Regulation'). The ruling was corroborated by rather specific objectives and the scheme of the Service of Documents Regulation (mainly acting as a preliminary step to summoning a defendant before an EU Member State court). Furthermore, the request for a preliminary ruling came from German courts where it is not uncommon for defendants to contest the service of documents before proceedings go any further. To be clear, the decision as to the 'civil and commercial' character of a dispute at the stage of service of documents is in principle without prejudice to the jurisdictional and substantive determinations.

That said, it can be argued that for the purposes of the autonomous meaning of the Brussels Regulation, the actions against sovereign acts taken in the course of sovereign debt restructurings ought to be treated as civil and commercial. Much will depend on the way the claims are advanced. In most cases, if the parties have selected foreign law to govern their contract, the choice of foreign applicable law will insulate the contract from foreign statutes. The claimant need not challenge them directly: he could obviate them by pleading their inapplicability. In this instance, the claim will fall to be treated as a contractual claim, with inapplicable public acts constituting mere factual background to the dispute.[15] However, inasmuch as the bonds are governed by foreign law, the sovereign debtor may seek to change the bonds unilaterally in which case the necessary course of action will be to challenge the laws, which modify the substantive obligations in the bonds. In such an instance, the claimant may wish to challenge the public acts on the ground of, for instance, infringement of property rights (as was the case in *Fahnenbrock*). The matter then transforms into a dispute *acta iure imperii* and falls outside the ambit of the Regulation. In this case, jurisdiction will need to be ascertained under national law. **3.13**

4. Grounds of Jurisdiction

Once the applicability of the Brussels Regulation is established, the parties may invoke several grounds of jurisdiction set out in the Brussels Regulation. **3.14**

[15] On which see Chapters 4 and 5. In *Goldman Sachs International v Novo Banco* [2015] EWHC 2371 (Comm), para 71, where Hamblen J held that the statutory transfer of a claim in debt by the Bank of Portugal did not modify the civil and commercial character of a claim, and metamorphose it into an administrative matter. As a result, the dispute was still caught by the Brussels I Regulation.

Jurisdiction Agreements

3.15 First and foremost, English courts may assume jurisdiction pursuant to a choice of forum agreement, which invariably goes hand in hand with a choice of English law. Article 25 will govern all jurisdiction agreements in favour of EU Member States, irrespective of the domicile of parties. Article 25(1) provides that the substantive validity of a jurisdiction agreement is governed by the law of the court designated in the jurisdiction agreement.

3.16 Challenging jurisdiction agreements is often an uphill struggle. In sovereign debt disputes, the State may seek to argue that it did not have the capacity or authority to enter into jurisdiction agreements. The constitutional provisions of many jurisdictions provide, with varying degrees of clarity, for the exclusive jurisdiction of local courts.[16] The arguments on capacity may receive short shrift following the decision in *Law Debenture Trust Corporation plc v Ukraine*.[17]

3.17 In so far as authority is concerned, jurisdiction agreements benefit from the doctrine of severability whereby the jurisdiction agreement will bestow jurisdiction on English courts even if the contract containing the jurisdiction agreement is arguably invalid for want of authority.[18]

3.18 The enforcement of jurisdiction agreements may be complicated in so far as the claimant is not the original subscriber to the bonds. Often, the bonds will be subscribed by financial intermediaries, who will then sell the bonds on the secondary market of sovereign bonds. The immediate subscribers are undoubtedly in a direct contractual relationship with the issuer and are therefore bound by the jurisdiction agreement (which often features in the subscription agreements, too). The issue is whether the beneficial investor is bound by the jurisdiction agreement contained in the prospectus.

3.19 The Court of Justice in *Profit Investment Sim SpA v Ossi* held that if the jurisdiction agreement is included in the prospectus, the court has to verify whether the parties have agreed to the clause. Such agreement will be present if: (i) the contract between the financial intermediary and the issuer expressly mentions the acceptance of the jurisdiction clause or contains

[16] See, eg, George Kahale III, 'State Loan Transactions: Foreign Law Restrictions on Waivers of Immunity and Submissions to Jurisdiction' (1981–82) 37 Bus L 1549.

[17] *Law Debenture Trust Corporation plc v Ukraine* [2017] EWHC 655 (Comm). See Chapter 7 for criticism.

[18] *Deutsche Bank AG v Asia Pacific Broadband Wireless Communications Inc* [2008] EWCA Civ 1091, para 26.

an express reference to that prospectus; (ii) the same enquiry is undertaken in respect of the contract between the financial intermediary and the beneficial investor. If both conditions are satisfied, the jurisdiction clause is regarded as enforceable.

The court then provided an exception to the situation where the first condition is satisfied but the second condition is not. That is to say, the beneficial investor has not consented to the jurisdiction clause by express mention or reference. In that situation, the beneficial investor will be bound by the jurisdiction clause if: (i) the clause is valid as between the issuer and the financial intermediary; (ii) the beneficial investor, by acquiring those bonds on the secondary market from the financial intermediary, succeeded to the latter's rights and obligations attached to those bonds under the applicable national law; and (iii) the beneficial investor had the opportunity to acquaint itself with the prospectus containing that clause, which implies that the prospectus is readily accessible.[19] If this fails too, the court indicated that a usage in international trade or commerce may come to the rescue of the jurisdiction clause, but, as usual, left the identification of such usage to the national court (albeit providing some specific guidance).[20] **3.20**

The decision certainly introduces an element of uncertainty: the sovereign debtor may be exposed to proceedings in a forum different from that specified in a jurisdiction clause if the conditions set out in *Profit Investment* are not satisfied. That said, the risk is less than minimal, since most beneficial investors will fall under one of the grounds enunciated by the Court of Justice. **3.21**

Exclusive Jurisdiction

Under the hierarchical structure of the Brussels Regulation, Art 24 (exclusive jurisdiction) takes precedence over Art 25 (exclusive jurisdiction agreement). In cases where the issue of lack of capacity arises,[21] the State may seek to rely on Art 24(2) as establishing the exclusive jurisdiction of the local courts of the sovereign debtor. However, the argument is likely to fail. First, it is unclear whether Art 24(2) applies to States. The counsel for the claimant in *BVG v JP Morgan* accepted that the said provision may apply to public law institutions,[22] but no such concession was made in **3.22**

[19] *Profit Investment Sim SpA v Ossi*, Case C-366/13, ECLI:EU:C:2016:282, para 36.

[20] Ibid paras 41, 49.

[21] See Chapter 6.

[22] *Berliner Verkehrsbetriebe (BVG) Anstalt Des ŐFfentlichen Rechts v JP Morgan Chase Bank NA* [2010] EWCA Civ 390, para 15.

other cases.[23] Arguably, the reference to 'legal persons' in Art 24(2) may embrace public law institutions and potentially States.

3.23 Second, and more importantly, the Court of Justice held that what is now Art 24(2) covers only proceedings whose principal subject matter is the validity of the constitution, the nullity or the dissolution of the company, legal person or association or the validity of the decisions of its organs. As a result, this provision does not apply to proceedings in which a company pleads incapacity as a defence to an action to enforce a contract.[24]

Special Jurisdiction

3.24 In the absence of choice of forum agreements,[25] the claimant will need to establish special jurisdiction under one of the heads of subject-matter jurisdiction. Article 7(1)(a) provides that in contractual matters, courts of the place of performance of the obligation will have jurisdiction. Article 7(1)(b) provides for special rules for contracts of sale and services. A long-standing debate is whether loans should properly be characterised as services within the meaning of Art 7(1)(b) or whether they fall within the residual category in Art 7(1)(a). The Court of Justice in the recent case *Kareda v Benkö* clarified that a credit agreement is to be characterised as a service within the meaning of Art 7(1)(b).[26] Although the court clarified that its holding applies to credit agreements 'such as that at issue in the main proceedings', it did not seek to clarify what other types of credit agreements may not qualify as services.

3.25 If bonds and loans are 'services', one has to determine where the place of provision of the loan is. The first thing to note is that the place of provision of services within the second indent of Art 7(1)(b) is to be given autonomous meaning under the Brussels Regulation. Identifying the autonomous meaning is easier said than done. Does the autonomous meaning refer to the destination or alternatively, the point of departure of the money transfer? First, Art 7(1)(b) reads 'the services were provided', which may indicate that the court has to consider the final destination.[27] Second, in cases

[23] *Depfa Bank plc v Provincia di Pisa* [2010] EWHC 1148 (Comm), para 71.

[24] *Berliner Verkehrsbetriebe (BVG), Anstalt des Offentlichen Rechts* v *JP Morgan Chase Bank NA*, Case C-144/10, [2011] ECR I-3961. See also *Depfa Bank plc v Provincia di Pisa* [2010] EWHC 1148 (Comm) (denying that the allegations of lack of capacity triggered Art 24(2)).

[25] As will be seen in Chapter 4, domestic law bonds of a significant number of States lack choice of court and law clauses.

[26] *Kareda v Benkö*, Case C-249/16, ECLI:EU:C:2017:472.

[27] Peter Mankowski, 'Article 7' in Ulrich Magnus and Peter Mankowski, *Brussels I Regulation: European Commentaries on Private International Law* (2016) 224; Adrian Briggs, *Civil Jurisdiction and Judgments* (2015) 231.

involving sale of goods, the Court of Justice concluded that the place of delivery under what is now Art 7(1)(a) was the place of final destination.[28]

The Court of Justice in *Kareda v Benkö* went down a different path. It ruled that it is the credit institution which performs the characteristic obligation in a credit agreement since the credit institution grants the sum loaned, *while* the borrower's obligation to repay that sum is derivative from the performance of the service by the lender. The court went on to affirm that the place where the services were rendered is the contractually agreed place of performance, failing which the place of performance is where the lending institution has its registered office.[29] **3.26**

A conundrum which arises is whether the registered office of the lending institution refers to the original credit institution (the financial intermediary upstream the chain of contracts) or the beneficial bondholder who stepped into the shoes of the financial intermediary. The decision of the Court of Justice in *Haeger & Schmidt* would point towards the registered office of the original contracting party.[30] **3.27**

Under the current regime, the parties are free to stipulate the place of performance which will have effect under Art 7(1). To be effective under Art 7(1)(b), the terms and conditions of the bonds have to stipulate the place of payment, since that is the characteristic performance in a credit agreement. The place of repayment, often set out in the bonds, is irrelevant for the jurisdictional purposes. Offering circulars/prospectuses are generally silent as to the place of payment under the bonds: they only provide for the place of repayment. The place of payment is often found in subscription agreements. Some subscription agreements provide that the Joint Lead Managers shall procure the payment of the proceeds of the issue of the Notes to the sovereign debtor (issuer) 'to such account as the Issuer has designated to the Joint Lead Managers'.[31] By leaving the location of the account to be later designated by the debtor, these clauses fail to provide for a jurisdictionally relevant place of payment. Other subscription agreements do stipulate the precise bank account to which money will be transferred,[32] while some bonds merely stipulate that 'the place **3.28**

[28] *Car Trim GmbH v KeySafety Systems Srl*, Case C-381/08, [2010] ECR I-1255.

[29] See also the decision in *Wood Floor Solutions Andreas Domberger GmbH v Silva Trade SA*, C-19/09, [2010] ECR I-2121, paras 42–43.

[30] *Haeger & Schmidt GmbH v Mutuelles du Mans Assurances IARD (MMA IARD)*, Case C-305/13, ECLI:EU:C:2014:2320, paras 43–51. Note, however, that the decision was taken under the Rome I Regulation. For the Brussels Regulation, see, eg, ln, 8 U 44/15.

[31] Confidential Subscription Agreement with a European sovereign debtor.

[32] Confidential Subscription Agreement with an African sovereign debtor.

of performance' is in a certain financial centre.[33] Such stipulations should suffice to establish the jurisdiction of the courts of the place of the bank account.

3.29 If the bonds, by contrast, fall within the ambit of Art 7(1)(a), the place of performance of the obligation relied upon will be determined in accordance with the law governing that obligation as determined by the conflict rules of the court before which the proceedings have been brought.[34] However, if the parties to the contract are permitted by the applicable law to specify the place of performance of an obligation, that agreement is sufficient to establish jurisdiction.[35] The English common law position is that the place of payment is the place where the money is received.[36]

3.30 The discussion so far assumes that the relationship between the claimant bondholder and the issuer is contractual. Nevertheless, in *Kolassa*, the Court of Justice held that in a situation where the bonds are issued through an intermediary, the claim brought by a beneficial investor, Mr Kolassa, against the issuer, Barclays Bank, was non-contractual. This was so since the issuer had not freely consented to a legal obligation with respect to Mr Kolassa in the sense of the Brussels Regulation. And that was so even if, under the national law applicable, Barclays Bank held certain obligations towards Mr Kolassa. The contractual relationship was only between the issuer and the financial intermediary who entered into the contract with the issuer. Therefore, jurisdiction fell to be established under Art 7(2), 'the place where the harmful event occurred or may occur'.

3.31 Applying Art 7(2), the court held that in prospectus liability cases, the court of the place where the investor is domiciled and has its damaged bank account is competent to decide on the claim under Art 7(2).[37] The Court of Justice in *Universal Music v Schilling* sought to circumscribe the pro-claimant holding in *Kolassa*, confining it to its 'specific context'.[38] However, prospectus liability is likely to remain subject to the claimant-friendly ground of jurisdiction established in *Kolassa*. The Austrian Supreme Court made a reference for a preliminary ruling in respect of

[33] See, eg, Hellenic Republic, Deutsche Mark Floating Rate Notes of 1994/2001, DM 1,000,000,000, 18 May 1994, p 9 (the place of performance is Frankfurt am Main).

[34] *Industrie Tessili Italiano Como v Dunlop AG*, Case C-12/76, [1976] ECR 1473.

[35] See, eg, *Česká Spořitelna, a.s. v Gerald Feichter*, Case C-419/11, [2013] EUECJ, paras 54–55.

[36] *Definitely Maybe Ltd v Lieberberg GmbH* [2001] 1 WLR 1745, para 4.

[37] *Kolassa v Barclays Bank plc*, Case C-375/13, EU:C:2015:37. For a more nuanced position, see Matthias Lehmann, 'Prospectus Liability and Private International Law—Assessing the Landscape after the CJEU's Kolassa Ruling (Case C-375/13)' (2016) 12 JPIL 318.

[38] *Universal Music v Schilling*, Case C-12/15, ECLI:EU:C:2016:449, para 37.

the Greek bonds restructured in 2012. The reference proceeds on the assumption that in international bond cases, Art 7(1)(a) is applicable.[39] This assumption does not fit squarely with the decision in *Kareda* which treated 'credit agreements' as services within the meaning of Art 7(1)(b). But, more importantly, the decision does not sit well with the decision in *Kolassa* which treated cases by ultimate investors/bondholders as non-contractual and falling thus within Art 7(2). The Austrian Supreme Court sought to distinguish *Kolassa* on the ground that Art 7 may apply to bearer bonds which represent a direct right against the issuer.

Chapter 7 discusses actions brought by minority bondholders against majority bondholders, who in some way abused their discretion in triggering a majority action clause. The question which arises at this stage is whether the minority bondholder may bring an action against majority bondholders under Art 7(1) ('matters relating to contract'). The action seems predominantly contractual since both minority and majority bondholders are party to the same issuance of bonds, and the rights of majority stem from the terms of the contract. Further, minority creditors are likely to rely on the text of the contract 'to establish the lawful or, on the contrary, unlawful nature of the conduct complained of'.[40] In a somewhat similar context, the Court of Justice held that claims between jointly and severally liable debtors are matters relating to contract.[41] **3.32**

However, under the jurisprudence of the Court of Justice, what matters is whether the party has freely assumed a legal obligation to another.[42] What seems to be clear is that the obligation to act in good faith is imposed on majority bondholders and it is hardly arguable that the majority bondholders have freely assumed an obligation to the minority. If this is correct, the jurisdiction will need to be established under Art 7(2). However, identifying the place of the harmful event in a case involving financial loss is subject to great uncertainties. It is evident that the place where indirect financial damage is felt (eg, the location of the victim's bank account) is not a place where damage is suffered.[43] If the restructuring was agreed at a physical meeting of bondholders, the place of such meeting may constitute the place of the harmful event.[44] If, however, the restructuring was **3.33**

[39] Austrian Oberste Gerichtshof, 10 Ob 34/16x, 24.05.2017. See also Austrian Oberste Gerichtshof, 8Ob125/15p, 29.12.2015.

[40] *Brogsitter v Fabrication de Montres Normandes EURL*, C-548/12, EU:C:2014:148, para 25.

[41] *Kareda v Benkö*, Case C-249/16, ECLI:EU:C:2017:472, paras 26–33.

[42] *Jakob Handte & Co GmbH v Traitements Mécano-chimiques des Surfaces SA*, Case C-26/91, [1992] ECR I-03967.

[43] See, eg, *Marinari v Lloyds Bank*, Case C-364/93 [1995] ECR I-2719.

[44] See, by analogy, *Universal Music v Schilling*, Case C-12/15, ECLI:EU:C:2016:449

conducted by an exchange of communications, as is usually the case in sovereign debt practice, the place of the harmful event may be the place where the communications of the majority of bondholders were forwarded.

Joinder of the Sovereign Debtor

3.34 Failing all the grounds of jurisdiction above, jurisdiction over the State may be established on the basis of Art 8 of the Brussels Regulation. Article 8 permits the joinder of an EU-domiciled party (in our case, an EU Member State) to English proceedings, as a third party in an action on a warranty or guarantee or in any other third-party proceedings, in the court seised of the original proceedings, unless these were instituted solely with the objective of removing him from the jurisdiction of the court which would be competent in his case. This ground of jurisdiction may be used in disputes involving a State's contingent liabilities or when the State is implicated in some other manner in the dispute.

Consumer Contracts

3.35 Special rules for jurisdiction apply in respect of contracts involving consumers. Under Art 18 of the Brussels Regulation, the consumer may bring proceedings not only in the domicile of the defendant, but also at the place of its own domicile. The Court of Justice in *Kolassa* held that the investor could not rely on the favourable regime of what is now Arts 17–19 since there was no contract between the beneficial investor, who bought the bonds from a professional intermediary, and the issuer of bonds.[45]

5. National Rules of Jurisdiction

3.36 The Brussels Regulation will apply in most cases, especially since under Art 25 of the Regulation, all jurisdiction agreements, irrespective of the domicile of the parties, trigger the application of the Brussels Regulation. However, in cases when the Brussels Regulation does not engage, the English courts will assume jurisdiction under national rules of jurisdiction.[46] In so far as the issues of jurisdiction or *forum non conveniens* arise in sovereign debt disputes, the issues are principally no different from ordinary contracts. The principles are well settled to an extent that they

[45] *Kolassa v Barclays Bank plc*, Case C-375/13, EU:C:2015:37, paras 20–35.

[46] However, the Annex to the European Convention on State Immunity of 1972 lists unacceptable grounds of jurisdiction.

do not necessitate extensive treatment in this monograph. Yet, a cursory overview seems appropriate.

The Civil Procedure Rules (CPR) set out the various grounds of residual jurisdiction of English courts.[47] Those that might be relevant in the context of sovereign debt litigation are: 3.37

- a claim is made in respect of a breach of contract committed within the jurisdiction (CPR PD6B 3.1(7));
- the contract is connected with England in any of the following ways (CPR PD6B 3.1(6)):
  - the contract was made within the jurisdiction;
  - the contract was made by or through an agent trading or residing within the jurisdiction, and
  - the contract is governed by English law.

It is conceivable that an English court may assume jurisdiction over the dispute relating to the bonds of a foreign State on one of the grounds listed above. Indeed, it is probable that in practice, the place of missed payments under (domestic) bonds could have been England, or sovereign bonds could have been made and issued in England.[48] Rarely, some bonds may contain a choice of English law but be silent on the choice of forum.[49] In such a situation, the choice of English law in the contract will be a ground of jurisdiction (more precisely, for service out of the jurisdiction). 3.38

That said, having established a ground of jurisdiction, English courts may still refuse to hear the case (give permission to serve out) on the grounds of *forum non conveniens*, ie that England is not the most appropriate forum for the litigation of such disputes. The English court may consider a whole panoply of reasons and factors in deciding which court is the most natural forum for the resolution of sovereign debt disputes. The analysis would largely be a discretionary and fact-specific exercise. 3.39

A particularly relevant and perhaps powerful factor in the *forum non conveniens* equation is the (putative) governing law of sovereign bonds. As discussed in Chapter 4, in the absence of a choice of law provision, English courts may be driven to the conclusion that the law of the lender—for the 3.40

[47] For an example of sovereign debt dispute based on residual jurisdiction, see *Jackson v People's Republic of China*, 550 F Supp 869, 873 (ND Ala 1982) (the sale of bonds in the US territory by the Chinese Imperial Government).

[48] *Trendtex Trading Corpo v Central Bank of Nigeria* [1977] 1 QB 529, 558 (holding that in so far as the letter of credit was issued in London through a London bank, it was 'completely within the territorial jurisdiction of our courts').

[49] See, eg, R Olivares-Caminal, *Legal Aspects of Sovereign Debt Restructuring* (2009) 219.

sake of argument, English law—applies, which will buttress the case for the jurisdiction of English courts.

3.41 If the English court eventually comes to the conclusion that it is not the most appropriate forum under the *forum non conveniens* analysis, there may still be circumstances in which an English court would assert jurisdiction over a foreign sovereign despite such a finding. These factors relate broadly to reasons of justice and legal advantages that the claimant may obtain in English courts, and any injustices in a foreign court which he would avoid by litigating in England.[50]

3.42 Of course, the claimant bears the onus of establishing special and unusual circumstances to demonstrate such (in)justice or legal (dis)advantages. By way of example, the claimant might, successfully or unsuccessfully, claim that domestic courts are barred by domestic legislation from effectively deciding the sovereign debt dispute on the merits; are compelled to engage in discriminatory treatment of foreign bondholder,[51] or perhaps that the State has unilaterally—through an Act of Parliament—modified the extent of its obligations.[52] Yet, merely suspecting that the foreign courts might side with the State is too weak a basis for substantiating injustice in the courts of the sovereign debtor. The claimant should be able to provide positive and cogent evidence as to the existence of substantial injustice within the legal system or judiciary of the sovereign debtor.[53]

3.43 As an argument of last resort, the respondent sovereign may argue that (English) public policy favours leaving the determination of sovereign debt disputes in the hands of the courts of the sovereign, and a sovereign default necessitates the application of public policy rules by the courts of the sovereign debtor. It is true that under English law, public policy may be a powerful argument in the *forum non conveniens* analysis: when the dispute relates to contracts governed by foreign law and the dispute requires application of foreign public policy, English courts would be reluctant to assume jurisdiction over a foreign sovereign.[54] However, nothing suggests such a rule of public policy exists in English law. Further, in cases where English law applies to the contract, the impact of foreign public policy will be harder to substantiate.

[50] *Spiliada Maritime v Cansulex* [1987] AC 460.

[51] On which see Chapter 7 (arguing that discrimination against bondholders is not always objectionable).

[52] On the latter, see Chapter 5.

[53] See, eg, *Ferrexpo AG v Gilson Investments Ltd* [2012] EWHC 721 (Comm), para 96.

[54] *Dupont v Agnew* [1987] 2 Lloyd's Rep 585. Issues of governing law will be treated in detail in Chapter 4.

Finally, failing any grounds of jurisdiction against the State, the bondholder may attempt to join the State as a 'proper and necessary party' if there are pending proceedings against the 'anchor' defendant in England.[55] Thus, a bondholder may bring a claim against a quasi-official or State-owned entity (such as the national railway or oil company), and then seek to join the State as a proper and necessary party to litigate sovereign bonds. In a different situation, the foreign bondholder may bring an action on English law governed sovereign bonds and then seek to join the bonds governed by the domestic law of the debtor, assuming that the court is convinced that this further claim 'arises out of the same or closely connected facts'.[56] The claimant will seek to establish that the defaults under both series of bonds arise from closely connected facts so that the claim on the bonds governed by the domestic law will be joined to the claim on foreign bonds. **3.44**

6. United States

In the US, issues of jurisdiction are entangled with issues of sovereign immunity. Under the FSIA 1976, the court may assume jurisdiction if and in so far as one of the exceptions to sovereign immunity is engaged. With some degree of oversimplification, the exceptions to sovereign immunity are also grounds of jurisdiction. Exceptions to sovereign immunities are treated in detail in Chapter 8. **3.45**

First, the US courts will have jurisdiction if the foreign State has agreed to a choice of forum agreement in favour of US courts, and has thereby waived immunity from jurisdiction (§1605(a)(1) FSIA). Choice of court agreements in favour of US courts are commonplace in sovereign bond documents. The US courts would routinely enforce the agreement of parties, unless the enforcement of the jurisdiction clause would contravene a strong public policy of the forum in which the suit is brought.[57] To our knowledge, no jurisdiction agreement has been declared unenforceable on this ground in a sovereign debt dispute. **3.46**

In the absence of a waiver, private creditors often rely on the commercial activity exception under §1605(a)(2) FSIA: if the sovereign's activity is commercial in nature and has a direct effect in the US, then the US courts may assume jurisdiction and no immunity attaches to such conduct of the State. **3.47**

[55] CPR Practice Direction 6B 3(b). [56] Ibid 4(a).
[57] *Bremen v Zapata Off-Shore Co*, 407 US 1 (1972).

3.48 The direct effect can exist in three variations, each of which is capable of establishing the exception and thus the jurisdiction of US courts:

(1) upon a commercial activity carried out in the United States by the foreign State. The Supreme Court established in *Weltover* that the 'direct effect' under this heading will arise if the designated place of payment is in the US. The residence of bondholders is irrelevant for these purposes;[58]
(2) upon an act performed in the United States in connection with a commercial activity of the foreign State elsewhere; and[59]
(3) upon an act outside the territory of the United States in connection with a commercial activity of the foreign State elsewhere, when that act causes a direct effect in the US.

3.49 Thus, misrepresentations regarding securities issued in a foreign jurisdiction but held by US parties may give rise to 'direct effect' in the US under this heading and deprive the State of immunity.[60]

3.50 Another pertinent exception is the expropriation exception (§1605(a)(3) FSIA). It applies when: (i) the allegedly expropriated property or any property exchanged for such property is located in the US; or (ii) when such property is 'owned or operated by an agency or instrumentality of the foreign state and that agency or instrumentality is engaged in a commercial activity in the United States'. In principle, the aggrieved creditor may need to exhaust local remedies in the courts of the defendant State before it commences proceedings in the US courts under this heading of subject-matter jurisdiction.[61] The Supreme Court has recently raised the threshold for using the expropriation exception: 'Where, as here, the facts are not in dispute, those facts bring the case within the scope of the expropriation exception only if they do show (and not just arguably show) a taking of property in violation of international law.'[62]

[58] *Weltover v Republic of Argentina*, 504 US 607, 619 (1992). See also *Shapiro v Republic of Bolivia*, 930 F.2d 1013, 1019 (2d Cir 1991) (introducing negotiable instruments into the US); *West v Multibanco Comermex, S.A.*, 807 F.2d 820 (9th Cir 1987) (the debtors solicited, marketed, and generally encouraged US investors to deposit monies in their banks).

[59] *Schmidt v Polish People's Republic*, 579 F Supp 23, 27 (SDNY 1984) (treasury notes received as part of payment for a construction contract in Poland, but sold and payable to a finance company in the US).

[60] *Atlantica Holdings, Inc v Sovereign Wealth Fund Samruk-Kazyna JSC*, No 14-917-cv (2d Cir 2016). See also *Callejo v Bancomer*, 764 F.2d 1101, 1112 (5th Cir 1985) (finding that the non-payment to US residents satisfied the test of 'sufficient connection' even when the place of payment was not in the US).

[61] *Republic of Austria v Altmann*, 541 US 677, 715 (2004) (Breyer J concurring).

[62] *Bolivarian Republic of Venezuela v Helmerich & Payne International Drilling Co*, 581 US _, 16 (2017).

In *SI Group Consort Ltd v Ukraine*,[63] the District Court held that the failure to pay does not amount to expropriation. What is necessary is that the State 'nullified or otherwise prevented collection of a valid judgment, effectively confiscating the right to payment'. This is broadly consistent with the principles of public international law.[64] Lastly, the expropriation exception may not apply to the State's own nationals.[65] **3.51**

Along with the exceptions to immunity, the US courts need to comply with the due process requirement in exercising cross-border jurisdiction. However, due process may not apply to foreign sovereigns since they are not treated as a 'person' for the purpose of the Fourteenth Amendment.[66] The Court of Appeal for the Eleventh Circuit considered pragmatically that in any event, the "direct effects" language of §1605(a)(2) closely resembles the 'minimum contacts' language of constitutional due process and these two analyses overlap,[67] although that might have been an exaggeration to some extent. **3.52**

Yet, the due process requirement may apply to the assumption of jurisdiction over State-owned entities. Due process requires the claimant to demonstrate that the defendant has minimum contacts with the jurisdiction, which is alleged to have jurisdiction. The minimum contacts will exist when the defendant purposefully avails itself of the privilege of conducting activities in the forum State, thus invoking the benefits and protections of its law. The Supreme Court in *Daimler AG v Bauman*[68] severely curtailed the general jurisdiction of the US courts by requiring that a corporation's affiliations with a forum be 'so continuous and systematic as to render it essentially *at home*'. It also considered that the reasonableness analysis is superfluous in general jurisdiction cases.[69] **3.53**

For specific jurisdiction cases, the Supreme Court in *Goodyear* confirmed that due process is satisfied, and jurisdiction can be asserted where the corporation's in-State activity was 'continuous and systematic' and gave rise to the episode in suit. Further, it confirmed that the commission of **3.54**

[63] *SI Group Consort Ltd v Ukraine*, 2017 US Dist LEXIS 12515 (SDNY 2017).

[64] For an example see the annulment of State loans by USSR in *Carl Marks & Co v Union of Soviet Socialist Republics*, 665 F Supp 323 (SDNY 1987).

[65] *Josefina Najarro De Sanchez v Banco Central de Nicaragua*, 770 F.2d 1385, 1395 (5th Cir 1985).

[66] *GSS Group v National Port Authority of Liberia*, No 14-7041 (DC Cir 2016). Karen Cross, 'Is a Foreign State a "Person"? Does It Matter?: Personal Jurisdiction, Due Process, and the Foreign Sovereign Immunities Act' (2001) 34 NYU J Intl L & Pol 115. But see *L'Europeenne de Banque v La Republica de Venezuela*, 700 F Supp 114, 122–25 (SDNY 1988).

[67] *S & Davis Intl, Inc v Republic of Yemen*, 218 F.3d 1292, 1303–05 (11th Cir 2000).

[68] 134 S Ct 746 (2014).

[69] For a detailed analysis, see Linda Silberman, 'Daimler AG v. Bauman: A New Era for Judicial Jurisdiction in the United States' (2014/2015) 16 YPIL 217.

certain 'single or occasional acts' in a State may be sufficient to render a corporation answerable in that State with respect to those acts, although not with regard to matters unrelated to the forum connections.[70]

3.55 The District Court found in *Parex* that Sberbank's (an instrumentality of the Russian Federation) use of accounts at the Bank of New York for the transaction in dispute and its practice of conducting other similar transactions using New York banks established Sberbank's 'minimum contacts' with this jurisdiction.[71] However, an agreement to make payments in the US, in the absence of any other jurisdictional contacts, is not sufficient to confer personal jurisdiction over the debtor.[72]

3.56 The reasonableness test, which applies only in specific jurisdiction cases, requires the balancing of a range of factors: the burden on the defendant; the interests of the forum State; the plaintiff's interest in obtaining relief; the interstate judicial system's interest in obtaining the most efficient resolution; the shared interest of the several States in furthering fundamental substantive social policies, and, in the international context, the procedural and substantive policies of other nations whose interests are affected by the assertion of jurisdiction.[73]

3.57 Moreover, the District Court found in *Parex*, in addition to addressing the exceptions in the FSIA and Due Process, that the claimant needs to overcome the *forum non conveniens* burden. Crucially, it ruled that if the contract giving rise to the dispute was not enforceable in the foreign forum, the US courts would not stay their proceedings in favour of a foreign court.[74]

7. Standing

3.58 Two issues of standing arise. The first is whether the individual bondholder may institute proceedings under the bonds which contain a trustee mechanism. In other words, does the trustee have an exclusive right to sue? This issue of standing is addressed in Chapter 7, which explains that the exclusive right to bring proceedings is usually vested in the hands of

[70] *Goodyear Dunlop Tires Operations, SA v Brown*, 564 US 915, 923 (2011).

[71] *Parex Bank v Russian Savings Bank*, 116 F Supp 2d 415, 422 (SDNY 2000).

[72] *L'Europeenne de Banque v La Republica de Venezuela*, 700 F Supp 114, 125 (SDNY 1988).

[73] *Asahi Metal Industry Co v Superior Court of California*, 480 US 102 (1987). For a commentary, see Linda Silberman, '*Goodyear* and *Nicastro*: Observations from a Transnational and Comparative Perspective' (2012) 63 SCLR 591.

[74] *Parex Bank v Russian Savings Bank*, 116 F Supp 2d 415, 426–27 (SDNY 2000) (holding that Russia was not the appropriate forum since the contract at hand will not be enforceable in Russia). See also *Banco Metropolitano v Desarrollo de Autopistas*, 616 F Supp 301 (SDNY 1985) (dismissing the claim against Banco de Guatemala on the ground of *forum non conveniens*).

a trustee. Yet in practice, because of the low compensation levels and risks inherent in litigation, trustees are hardly incentivised to initiate proceedings. And that makes court litigation illusory in many cases. The possibility of implied limitation of individual action is examined in Chapter 1.

The second issue of standing is whether the beneficial holder of bonds may sue the sovereign debtor in a situation where it did not purchase the bonds directly from the State but from financial intermediaries/depositories. The established practice is, with some degree of simplification, that the State will issue bonds to banks (financial intermediaries) and they will in turn sell the bonds to their customers, the beneficial holders. In this chain of contracting, the financial intermediaries will be registered as owners of the bonds in central depositories. Only a few systems are based on a direct holding where the investor will be the legal holder of bonds/shares.[75] **3.59**

The bonds often record the status quo and stipulate, with certain variations in the language, that the title in the bonds rests with the registered bondholder and no one who is not a registered bondholder has any right under the Contracts (Rights of Third Parties) Act 1999 to enforce any of the Terms and Conditions of the Notes.[76] The exclusion of the Contracts (Rights of Third Parties) Act 1999 is of course without prejudice to any rights the bondholder may enjoy apart from the Act (s 7(1) of the Act). Other bonds clearly stipulate that only the bearer of the bonds may claim payment of the principal and interest.[77] **3.60**

In *Secure Capital SA v Credit Suisse AG*, Hamblen J rejected the action brought by the ultimate beneficiary under bearer notes. The financial structure involved investors/participants at various levels. The bearer notes were deposited with a common depository (Bank of New York Mellon) who was agreed to be the bearer of the bonds. The notes were registered in a central depository (Clearstream in Luxembourg) where another financial entity held the registered account, which contained an entry for the claimant. Hamblen J found that under English law, the obligations of the issuer were owed to, and only to the bearer. Accordingly, the beneficial investor had no direct claim against the issuer of the bonds.[78] **3.61**

[75] Philip Wood, *Set-off and Netting, Derivatives, Clearing Systems* (2007) para 18-073.

[76] See, eg, Romania, Information Memorandum, EUR 7,000,000,000 Global Medium Term Note Programme, p 39; Republic of Azerbaijan, US$1,250,000,000 4.75 per cent Notes due 2024, 13 March 2014, Art 18.

[77] See, eg, Hellenic Republic, Offering Circular, Euro 150,000,000, Fixed to CMS Spread Linked Notes due 2021, 8 June 2006, pp 5–6.

[78] [2015] EWHC 388 (Comm), para 55.

3.62 Whether this decision is the last word is unclear (the appeal is pending against the decision of Hamblen J). Wood countenances the 'no look-through' (cell structure) system where a beneficial investor's claim lies against his top tier holder (financial intermediary) and not against the issuer. However, he notes that in English law, each financial intermediary holds the securities on trust for the beneficiary. As a result:

> the beneficiary's remedy is not, as in the [US] UCC, solely limited to action against the intermediary-trustee. If the trustee fails to act, the beneficiary can act but must join the trustee in court proceedings. This preserves the ability of a beneficiary to act if the intermediary fails to do so.[79]

3.63 The trustee can thus be joined in the court proceedings through the *Vandepitte* procedure.[80]

3.64 In many sovereign debt cases heard and decided before the US courts, sovereign debtors have not sought to contest the standing of beneficial owners. Yet, in two cases where the issue has arisen, the language of the bond documentation specified that the registered owner of the bonds was the sole holder of bonds and to institute proceedings, the beneficial owners had to obtain the authorisation of the registered owner. In *Fontana v Republic of Argentina*, and in light of this language, the Second Circuit required proof that the action had been authorised by the registered owner, which was the Depository Trust Company.[81] In *Allan Applestein v Province of Buenos Aires*, it was established on the record that the registered owner authorised the legal actions, albeit *ex post*, and this, the District Court held, satisfied the requirement of standing.[82] Judge Griesa in the District Court was particularly unwelcoming of such challenges to the standing of beneficial owners and the requirement of authorisation, which to him was a mere formality.[83]

3.65 All this is of course subject to the assumption that English and New York laws apply to the issue of standing. In *Secure Capital SA v Credit Suisse AG*, the issue was whether the beneficial investor under bearer bonds registered in Clearstream (Luxembourg) could have a right of action against the issuer of the bonds. The beneficial investor sought to characterise the issue as one of property (and later 'deemed possessory right'), and argued that this issue was to be decided by *lex situs*, namely the law of Luxembourg.

[79] Wood (n 75) paras 18-025, 18-035-18-038.

[80] *Vandepitte v Preferred Accident Insurance Corporation of New York* [1933] AC 70.

[81] 415 F.3d 238 (2d Cir 2005).

[82] 415 F.3d 242 (2d Cir 2005). In *Million Air Corp v Republic of Argentina*, No 04 Civ 1048, 2005 US Dist LEXIS 23904 (SDNY 2005), Argentina waived the requirement of authorisation.

[83] See Judge Griesa's reaction, recorded in *Fontana v Republic of Argentina*, 415 F.3d 238, 240 (2d Cir 2005).

The law of Luxembourg seemed to provide that the beneficial investor may exercise the rights of the registered owner, including by bringing actions against the issuer of the bonds.

Hamblen J disagreed and ruled that the matter was contractual since it is 'artificial to seek to divorce that question [whether the beneficial investor has rights against the issuer] from the rights which Secure Capital is seeking to enforce which are clearly (and admittedly) contractual rights'. He also placed reliance on an excerpt from *Dicey, Morris & Collins*, which specified that 'a person's (proprietary) entitlement to be treated as a "holder" as against other claimants, will normally be determined in accordance with the lex situs, but the question whether the instrument carries with it rights against the issuer (and questions concerning the exercise of those rights) will, ultimately, be matters for the law governing the instrument'.[84] To support his contractual characterisation, the judge also referred to *Raiffeisen Zentralbank Osterreich v Five Star Trading*, where Mance LJ characterised the claim under an assignment as a contractual issue.[85] **3.66**

There is, however, a second way of analysing the issue. In the preceding paragraph, the editors of *Dicey, Morris & Collins* state that 'the question whether a "bearer bond" is capable of carrying with it the right to claim … from the issuer should ultimately be determined, not by the law of place where the bearer instrument was situated at the time of its negotiation, but by reference to the law governing those rights and the issuer's corresponding obligations'.[86] It may reasonably be questioned whether this solution, designed for bearer bonds with a physical place of transfer which will vary from one case to another, should perforce apply to modern global notes. What characterises global notes is the stability and predictability of their *lex situs* both for the issuer and all the participants in the chain of contracting. Furthermore, if the matter is within the Rome I Regulation, whether the issue of standing against the issuer is contractual will be a matter of autonomous characterisation. And there are strong indications that the autonomous characterisation would subject the relationship between the issuer and the beneficial holder to the law of registration of securities.[87] Lastly, the decision in *Raiffeisen* was based on what **3.67**

[84] [2015] EWHC 388 (Comm), para 51. [85] [2001] QB 825.

[86] Lord Collins of Mapesbury et al (eds), *Dicey, Morris & Collins on the Conflict of Laws*, vol 2 (2012) paras 33–388.

[87] Recital 56, Regulation (EU) No 909/2014 of the European Parliament and of the Council of 23 July 2014 on Improving Securities Settlement in the European Union and on Central Securities Depositories and Amending Directives 98/26/EC and 2014/65/EU and Regulation (EU) No 236/2012 Text with EEA relevance ('Such national corporate and similar law under which the securities are constituted govern the relationship between their issuer and holders or any third parties').

is now Art 14(2), which expressly subjects 'the relationship between the assignee and the debtor' to the law governing the debt.

3.68 In any case, the ultimate bondholder is likely to enjoy standing, past the financial intermediaries, in international investment arbitration.[88]

8. Class Actions

3.69 Outside competition law proceedings, English law does not recognise full-blown collective actions à la US class actions. While the CPR provides for multiparty actions in the form of representative parties (Part 19.II) and Group Litigation Orders (Part 19.III), the characteristic of these actions is that they operate on an opt-in basis, unlike class actions in the US, and the court enjoys discretion in granting the Group Litigation Order.

3.70 In the US, class action litigation is much more prominent. However, to bring a class action, the class has to be 'ascertainable', that is to say, 'sufficiently definite so that it is administratively feasible for the court to determine whether a particular individual is a member'.[89] To ensure ascertainability, the Second Circuit imposed the requirement of continuous holding, ie, the class members had to possess beneficial interests in a particular bond series from the date of the complaint through to the date of final judgment. Otherwise, the bonds could trade hands after a class had been certified and it would then become impossible to determine which bonds were part of a class action.[90]

3.71 Concerned with an orderly and uniform deployment of sovereign debt restructurings, Buchheit and Gulati argue for the mechanism of class actions as a way of introducing court-supervised restructurings of sovereign debt. They contend that in a certified mandatory class action, the judgment or the settlement will bind the whole class of bondholders, eliminating any concerns about holdout litigation.[91] However, the attempts to initiate class actions against sovereign debtors have so far mostly failed in the US courts: US judges have refused to certify too large classes of sovereign bondholders because the sheer size of the classes made them unmanageable.[92] That said, ICSID arbitration seems to be more accommodating of

[88] *Abaclat and others v The Argentine Republic*, ICSID Case No ARB/07/5, 4 August 2011, Decision on Jurisdiction and Admissibility, paras 359–60; *Ambiente Ufficio SPA and others v The Argentine Republic*, ICSID Case No ARB/08/9, 8 February 2013, Decision on Jurisdiction and Admissibility, para 327.

[89] *Brecher v Republic of Argentina*, No 14-4385 (2d Cir 2015).

[90] Ibid.

[91] Lee Buchheit and Mitu Gulati, 'Sovereign Bonds and the Collective Will' (2004) 51 Emory LJ 1352–57.

[92] *H.W. Urban GmbH v Republic of Argentina*, 2003 US Dist LEXIS 7868 (SDNY 2003); *Seijas v Republic of Argentina*, 606 F.3d 53 (2d Cir 2010); Olivares-Caminal (n 49) 140–52, esp 148;

mass claims in respect of sovereign debt disputes, as illustrated in *Abaclat v Argentina*.[93] As always, there is a caveat: the requirement of substantive unity of the 'dispute', recognised in the jurisdictional decision in *Alemanni v Argentina*,[94] might act to prevent excessively wide-ranging mass claims.

II. STAY OF PROCEEDINGS

1. Introduction

Buchheit has asserted that the tactics that litigious hedge funds have usually employed is to wait for the restructuring to be completed and only then bring legal actions. The apparent rationale for avoiding pre-emptive strikes is that it might spread the contagious desire for litigation among other creditors, and, by precipitating further litigation, would eventually deplete the foreign assets of the sovereign available for attachment, already limited in scope and number.[95] It has been speculated that the reluctance to bring pre-emptive strikes might also account for the fear that legal actions intended to frustrate a forthcoming restructuring would not be accommodated due to concerns of comity[96] or for the desire to hold back until the sovereign has received a debt relief that would increase the likelihood of a sovereign being willing to agree to a private deal with the recalcitrant creditor.[97] **3.72**

With the almost ubiquitous introduction of majority action clauses into sovereign bonds, minority creditors might find it extremely risky to wait for the restructuring to be completed. They might easily be swayed by the decision of the majority with little or no possibility to review the outcome of the restructuring, unless exceptional circumstances are manifest.[98] **3.73**

David Skeel, 'Can Majority Voting Provisions Do It All?' (2002) 52 Emory LJ 417, 423. But see *Jackson v People's Republic of China*, 550 F Supp 869, 873–74 (ND Ala 1982) (class certified).

[93] *Abaclat and others v Argentine Republic*, ICSID Case No ARB/07/5, Decision on Jurisdiction and Admissibility, 4 August 2011.

[94] *Giovanni Alemanni and others v The Argentine Republic*, ICSID Case No ARB/07/8, Decision on Jurisdiction and Admissibility, 17 November 2014, paras 287–94.

[95] Lee Buchheit, 'Sovereign Debt Litigation' (1999) Memorandum for the International Monetary Fund 8, 10; Lee Buchheit, 'Act of State and Comity: Recent Developments' in David Sassoon and Daniel Bradlow (eds), *Judicial Enforcement of International Debt Obligations* (1987) 106.

[96] EMTA, 'Preliminary Analysis of Creditor Litigation in the Non-HIPC Sovereign Debt Restructuring Context' (2009) 3–4.

[97] John Coffee and William Klein, 'Bondholder Coercion: The Problem of Constrained Choice in Debt Tender Offers and Recapitalizations' (1991) 58(4) U Chi L Rev 1207, 1223.

[98] On which see Chapter 7.

3.74 Against this background, often the only viable strategy that dissatisfied creditors are left with in the face of majority action clauses—putting aside the purchase of a blocking minority—is to bring immediate, pre-emptive legal actions to obtain a (summary) judgment, before the majority of bondholders is given the chance to amend the terms of sovereign bonds.[99] By bringing pre-emptive strikes at the eleventh hour the holdout creditor seeks to avoid being tied down by the decision of the majority. The effort is to initiate proceedings and obtain a (summary) judgment before the majority has taken the decision to bind the minority to a debt restructuring.

3.75 In practice, the decision by the majority might, and often does, take time which will offer recalcitrant creditors a window to bring legal actions in the meantime. Before the restructuring has hit its stride and the majority has been given the chance to alter the terms of the bonds, the State usually defaults on its payments, thus offering a cause of action for pre-emptive strikes.[100] It is documented that this happens in more than 50% of sovereign debt restructurings[101] and that at least nine sovereign debt restructurings were affected by pre-restructuring litigation (based on publicly available information).[102] Challenging a pre-emptive debt restructuring, that is to say, a debt restructuring prudently initiated before an event of default, may lack a cause of action.[103]

3.76 In a short course of time, before the restructuring is completed, a holdout creditor is able to obtain a summary judgment in a streamlined manner. It is true that in most cases the creditor, even equipped with a summary judgment, might not be able to attach sovereign property at the time of declaration of default by the State. This is due to the substantial hurdles that the sovereign immunity against enforcement establishes,[104] however,

[99] In this sense see IMF, 'Proposed Features of a Sovereign Debt Restructuring Mechanism' (2003), para 27.

[100] Michael Bradley and Mitu Gulati, 'Collective Action Clauses for the Eurozone' (2014) 18(6) Rev Fin 2045, 2095–96.

[101] Udaibir Das, Michael Papaioannou, and Christoph Trebesch, 'Sovereign Debt Restructurings 1950–2010: Literature Survey, Data, and Stylized Facts' (2012) 6, 35–36; IMF, 'A Survey of Experiences with Emerging Market Sovereign Debt Restructurings' (2012) IMF Working Paper WP/12/203, 7–9.

[102] Christoph Trebesch, 'Debt Restructuring Delays: Measurement and Stylized Facts' in Robert Kolb (ed), *Sovereign Debt: From Safety to Default* (2011) 174. For the breakdown by sovereign debt restructurings, see Christoph Trebesch, 'Debt Restructuring Delays' (2010) Table A2, p 31 (available at https://sites.google.com/site/christophtrebesch/research).

[103] However, an investor who wants to challenge a pre-emptive debt restructuring may face fewer hurdles before international investment tribunals (see *Continental Casualty Company v Republic of Argentina*, ICSID Case No ARB/03/9, Award, 5 September 2008, para 229).

[104] Allen & Overy Global Law Intelligence Unit, 'Uses and Abuses of Collective Action Clauses in Sovereign Bonds' (2013) 14(3) Bus L Intl 269, 277.

it would not preclude obtaining a summary judgment in the hope of enforcing it later.[105]

The question is whether such pre-emptive actions should be stayed in one way or another. There have been attempts to eliminate or at least constrain the risks of pre-emptive litigation both at the level of a statutory sovereign debt restructuring mechanism and contractual clauses. At the statutory level, scholars and policymakers have stressed that the stay of actions ought to be a necessary component of the sovereign debt restructuring mechanism,[106] whereas others have opposed the idea of a stay as an intrusion into the rights of private creditors.[107] When the IMF came up with its far-reaching and ambitious proposal of establishing the sovereign debt restructuring mechanism in 2002 and 2003, its proposal did not go as far as to propose an automatic stay of legal action but only a stay approved by the majority of creditors.[108] **3.77**

A statutory or contractual provision prescribing stay of proceedings has, however, never seen the light of the day. In a move to eliminate the risk of pre-restructuring litigation through contractual clauses, proposals have been put forward to introduce 'initiation clauses' that would provide a cooling-off period between the event of default and the restructuring of the debt in the pendency of which holdout creditors would not be able to sue the sovereign debtor. Such clauses could provide a breathing space for the debtor and time to trigger the operation of majority action clauses. In spite of the clauses being well intentioned, the market felt negatively about the inclusion of such clauses,[109] which explains why the proposal remained a dead letter.[110] **3.78**

105 It is for this reason that the proposals to impose a standstill rule limited to the enforcement of a judgment will not suffice (Matthias Goldmann, 'Necessity and Feasibility of a Standstill Rule for Sovereign Debt Workouts' (2014) 5).

106 David Skeel, 'Can Majority Provisions Do It All?' (2003) 52 Emory LJ 417, 423–24 (at least a stay on asset seizures); Philip Power, 'Sovereign Debt: The Rise of the Secondary Market and its Implications for Future Restructurings' (1995–96) 64 Fordham L Rev 2701, 2767–68; Patrick Bolton and David Skeel, 'Inside the Black Box: How Should a Sovereign Bankruptcy Framework Be Structured?' (2004) 53 Emory LJ 763, 782–83 (arguing for a creditor referendum on a stay).

107 Steven Schwarcz, 'Sovereign Debt Restructuring: A Bankruptcy Reorganization Approach' (2000) 85 Cornell L Rev 956, 985 (the costs of a stay would outweigh the perceived benefits of minimising the collective action problem).

108 IMF (n 99) paras 24, 35–40; IMF, 'The Design of the Sovereign Debt Restructuring Mechanism—Further Considerations' (2002), paras 132, 136.

109 IMF, 'The Design and Effectiveness of Collective Action Clauses' (2002) 17.

110 'Initiation clauses' are different from contractual clauses that require the amicable settlement before initiating judicial proceedings. While the sole arbitrator Fouchard in an arbitral award against the Congo relating to the repayment of the debt considered that this provision imposed a duty to negotiate in good faith (and found a general principle of commercial law

3.79 This section would instead proffer a judicially imposed stay of proceedings. Introducing a clause into sovereign bonds to impose judicial stays is Sisyphus labour fraught with uncertainties and requires the concerted reaction of major governments and international financial institutions, as was the case with the introduction of majority action clauses in 2003. The proposals to introduce standstills on payments and creditor litigation through the medium of the IMF[111] may never be implemented. For that reason, a judicially imposed stay on legal actions is perhaps the path of least resistance.

3.80 The discussion in paras 3.82–3.90 will present arguments for and against a term that courts may imply into sovereign bonds, to the effect that actions brought pre-emptively—in breach of majority action clauses—should be stayed. The discussion in paras 3.91–3.112 will then argue, in the alternative, for the judicious application of case management powers so as to ensure that pre-emptive strikes brought before English proceedings are stayed in favour of sovereign debt restructurings. The examination in paras 3.113–3.118 will consider the circumstances where the stay of proceedings will not be opportune. Finally, the analysis in paras 3.119–3.127 will consider the interrelation between the principle of finality of judgments and the exercise of majority powers.

3.81 One thing that needs to be made clear at the outset is that the reasoning in favour of the stay of pre-emptive strikes is not based on policy grounds. As the discussion below will demonstrate, the criticism towards pre-emptive strikes is purely legalistic based on the idea that pre-emptive strikes are properly treated as actions brought in breach of and sidestepping majority action clauses to which the litigious creditor has consented by subscribing to the bonds containing such clauses.

2. The Implied Term to Stall Pre-emptive Strikes

The Modification of the Financial Terms of Sovereign Bonds

3.82 When the defendant argues that the dispute is in the course of renegotiation, but the claimant disagrees, the court is unlikely to stay proceedings on the ground of renegotiation.[112] Things may change if there is a majority action clause. On their face, majority action clauses do not inhibit

to that effect) (ICC award n 6219 (1990) 117(4) JDI 1047, 1050–51), English courts are likely to have reservations about the enforceability of such clauses.

[111] Barry Eichengreen, 'Can the Moral Hazard Caused by the IMF Bailouts Be Reduced' (2000) Geneva Reports on the World Economy Special Report I, 19–31.

[112] *Sempra Energy International v Republic of Argentina*, ICSID Case No ARB/02/16, Decision on Objections to Jurisdiction, 11 May 2005, para 108.

pre-emptive legal actions by holdout creditors. That said, one cannot fail to notice the inherent conflict between two types of clauses—majority action clauses and choice of forum agreements. Choice of forum clauses vest jurisdiction into English (or other) courts to hear claims to recover payments under the bonds, while majority action clauses vest the majority of bondholders with the power to amend the very contractual entitlements which the minority creditor may recover through court adjudication. In both cases, one cannot fail to notice the consent of the parties to submit to/abide by an extrinsic decision—either to the decision of a court in the case of a choice of forum agreement, or to the decision of a majority of bondholders in the case of a majority action clause.

This perhaps non-accidental overlap may provide an impetus to race to **3.83** the court. The holdout creditor will be motivated to seise the court having jurisdiction under the choice of court agreement. Conversely, the sovereign debtor will have the incentive of triggering the majority action clause as early as possible.

Would English courts assume jurisdiction over a dispute when there are **3.84** parallel efforts to restructure the debt through a majority action clause? In the absence of a clear provision for preponderance of the restructuring efforts over the jurisdiction of English courts, the initial reaction of English courts would be to assume jurisdiction on the basis of a jurisdictional clause. In a parallel context, English courts are of the view that in case the contract contains two conflicting jurisdiction agreements, bringing an action in accordance with one of them does not amount to oppressive or vexatious conduct.[113]

Yet, one cannot deny that the entire sovereign debt workout, as a result of **3.85** the interplay of choice of forum agreements and majority action clauses, may be fragmented between these two 'forums' in so far as the sovereign debt restructuring process is in a sense a *sui generis* 'forum'.[114] Although nothing is inherently wrong with pre-emptive strikes brought before national courts, the litigation and judgment risks would undoubtedly undermine the very purpose behind majority action clauses which are designed with the smooth and uniform sovereign debt restructurings in mind. By initiating premature litigation and obtaining a judgment for the full face value of its contractual entitlement, the holdout creditor comes close to frustrating the objective and purpose of majority action clauses.

[113] *Catlin Syndicate Ltd v Adams Land & Cattle Co* [2006] EWHC 2065 (Comm).

[114] Richards J treated Swiss mandatory conciliation proceedings as a 'court' for the purposes of the *lis pendens* rule under the Lugano Convention on Jurisdiction and the Recognition and Enforcement of Judgments in Civil and Commercial Matters of 2007 (*Lehman Brothers Finance AG v Klaus Tschira Stiftung GmbH et al* [2014] EWHC 2782 (Ch)).

3.86 One, and seemingly the most natural legal ground for ordering coordination between majority action clauses and choice of forum agreements, is for a court to decide that, on a true construction of majority action clauses, they contain an implied term that would prohibit untimely legal actions in breach and contravention of such clauses. For that, one would need to overcome the hurdle of establishing the necessity of implication. Under English law, the reasonableness of a to-be-implied term is not sufficient—the term has to be necessary.[115] While the establishment of the necessity of a term in fact might prove an uphill struggle, the court will have greater leeway when implying contractual terms in law. In doing so, the judge will look for a term which the nature of the contract might call for, or the law will imply this term as a necessary incident of a group of contracts.[116] In the quest for the implication of terms applicable to a group of contracts, the court will take into account the 'wider considerations', such as questions of reasonableness, fairness, and the balancing of competing policy considerations,[117] as well as reasonable expectations of parties.[118]

3.87 The implication of terms into majority action clauses appears never to have arisen in a reported judicial decision. Drawing on analogous situations, one can notice numerous contractual clauses which are given effect via a stay of English proceedings. The list of such clauses includes mediation clauses, arbitration clauses, adjudication clauses, and expert panel determinations.[119] It is true that these clauses generally require resort to the alternative dispute resolution as a preliminary step which cannot be bypassed by recourse to the court. Nevertheless, the creativity of the English courts to read through the lines and imply terms into the contract may be strong enough to stay premature litigation initiated by a minority bondholder, who consented to be bound by a decision of the majority of bondholders, and then sought to renege on its consent by initiating pre-emptive litigation. The English courts have consistently entertained actions where one party has breached clauses stipulating all sorts of *'agreed-to-be-prohibited behaviour'* (such as, settlement agreements).[120] Majority action clauses,

[115] *Marks and Spencer plc v BNP Paribas Securities Services Trust Company (Jersey) Limited* [2015] UKSC 72; *Scally v Southern Health & Social Services Board* [1992] 1 AC 294, 307.

[116] *Liverpool City Council v Irwin* [1977] AC 239, 255; *Scally v Southern Health & Social Services Board* [1992] 1 AC 294, 307.

[117] *Crossley v Faithful & Gould Holdings* [2004] 4 All ER 447, para 36.

[118] Ewan McKendrick, *Contract Law: Text, Cases and Materials* (2014) 362–65.

[119] See, eg, *Channel Tunnel Group v Balfour Beatty Ltd* [1993] AC 334, 353 (exercising its inherent jurisdiction to stay proceedings in favour of a clause which provided for an expert panel reference and, if necessary, subsequent arbitration proceedings); *Sunrock Aircraft Corp Ltd v Scandinavian Airline Systems Denmark–Norway–Sweden* [2007] EWCA Civ 882.

[120] Adrian Briggs, *Agreements on Jurisdiction and Choice of Law* (2008) 306–07.

by contrast, provide for *agreed-to-be-bound behaviour*—to be bound by the decision of a majority of bondholders.

That said, some justifiable scepticism might still subsist as to how well founded the argument of implied terms is. As described above, financial markets were reluctant to introduce 'initiation' clauses into sovereign bonds.[121] This suggests that the silence as to the prohibition of pre-emptive strikes in sovereign bonds might not be accidental. Another problem with implied terms is that in accordance with English law, a term will not be implied if it contradicts the express terms of the contract. In this case, arguably an express choice of forum clause. Should the argument on implied terms fail in court for these or other reasons, the parties may rely in the alternative on the case management powers of English courts, discussed below. **3.88**

Modification of Non-Financial Terms of the Bonds

As described in Chapter 2, the majority power may also be wielded through the technique of exit consents. Exit consents are employed if the bonds in question allow modification of non-financial terms of the bonds by some majority to render the bonds less attractive, and thereby encourage participation in an exchange. As explained in subsection 4 below, it is arguable that in contrast to the modification of financial terms of sovereign bonds, the issuance of a judgment by a competent court does not necessarily prevent the majority from modifying the non-financial covenants of sovereign bonds that do not necessarily pertain to the core of the judgment. The object of a summary judgment is the repayment of the principal and interest, rather than the confirmation of and merger with the non-financial covenants, whatever they might be. As an example, if the majority of bondholders is asked by the sovereign debtor to modify the waiver of immunities clause, it may very well do so but that should not serve to stay the proceedings brought by the creditor for recouping its investment in judicial proceedings. **3.89**

The stay of proceedings would also be rejected in a situation where the creditor that owns 25% and more of outstanding bonds is able to accelerate **3.90**

[121] IMF (n 109) 17; Lex Rieffel, *Restructuring Sovereign Debt: The Case for Ad Hoc Machinery* (2003) 223–24 (in respect of 'standstills'). See also *Société Commerciale de Belgique (Belgium v Greece)*, 1939 PCIJ Series A/B, 177 ('the Court is not entitled to oblige the Belgian Government … to enter into negotiations with the Greek Government with a view to a friendly arrangement regarding the execution of the arbitral awards which that Government recognizes to be binding: negotiations of this kind depend entirely upon the will of the parties concerned').

the debt and bring action in English courts, but the sovereign debtor feels confident to amass the necessary amount of bonds (often 50%) to reverse the acceleration of the bonds and requests stay of proceedings. The creditor should be able to proceed once it has satisfied the requirements of the acceleration clause. If the majority of bondholders—instigated by the debtor—wish to reverse the acceleration, they would be wise to hasten.

3. Case Management Powers of English Courts to Stall Pre-emptive Strikes

3.91 English courts will be reluctant to stay their proceedings out of considerations of comity or in order to prevent the squandering of debtor's assets.[122] If there is a choice of forum clause in favour of English courts, the English courts will feel compelled, and rightly so, to assume jurisdiction over the disputed sovereign debt. However, as will be shown below, the absence of a clear ground for staying proceedings would not prevent the English courts from staying the proceedings on case management grounds.[123] Under English law, strong and compelling reasons might justify stay of proceedings pursuant to the wide-ranging case management powers of English courts.[124]

3.92 English courts retain broad case management powers permitting the court to regulate the content and progress of civil litigation so as to achieve the overriding objective of dealing with the case justly (CPR 1.1).[125] To achieve this aim, the court holds a general case management power to stay proceedings (CPR 3.1(2)(f)) which it may exercise when either the parties agree, or the court, of its own initiative, considers that a stay would be appropriate.

3.93 The following discussion argues that case management powers, as well as the inherent jurisdiction of English courts,[126] is the tool that will permit the Commercial Court—the jurisdiction to be seised with the actions over

[122] *Jefferies International Limited v Landsbanki Islands HF* [2009] EWHC 894 (Comm), paras 33–36 (in the context of the Icelandic financial crisis).

[123] *Halifax Financial Services Ltd v Intuitive Systems Ltd* [2000] 2 TCLR 35, 46.

[124] *Jefferies International Limited* (n 122), paras 33–34; Richard Fentiman, *International Commercial Litigation* (2015) 461.

[125] Neil Andrews, *English Civil Procedure: Fundamentals of the New Civil Justice System* (2003) 337.

[126] The Privy Council stated that the stay of proceedings can be sought both under case management powers or the inherent jurisdiction of the English courts (*Texan Management Ltd v Pacific Electric Wire & Cable Company Ltd* [2009] UKPC 46, para 76). On inherent jurisdiction, see Martin Dockray, 'The Inherent Jurisdiction to Regulate Civil Proceedings' (1997) 113 LQR 120.

sovereign bonds—to stay its proceedings before the restructuring process under a majority action clause is finalised. Staying the proceedings brought by holdout creditors permits the sovereign debtor to put to use, or at least attempt to put to use, the majority action clauses contained in sovereign bonds held by litigious creditors.

The inherent jurisdiction and case management powers of English courts provide a solid ground for the stay of English proceedings so as to disallow concurrent proceedings. In *Reichhold Norway ASA v Goldman Sachs International*,[127] the claimant, Reichhold, started arbitration proceedings, with their seat in Norway, against Jotun under a sale agreement. However, prior to that, Reichhold initiated proceedings in the English courts against Goldman Sachs—the adviser to Jotun in connection with the sale transaction—on the ground of negligent misstatements about the transaction. **3.94**

On a true construction of the sale agreement, there was a coherent arrangement between the parties under which Reichhold had a remedy for any misleading or inaccurate information solely against Jotun that could be brought in arbitration. Pending the decision in arbitration, Goldman Sachs requested stay of English 'satellite'[128] proceedings. The Commercial Court took the view that bringing two concurrent proceedings was nothing but a tactical move on the part of Reichhold. The court ordered a stay of proceedings on the ground of the inherent jurisdiction under s 49(3) of the Supreme Court Act 1981 and active case management powers. **3.95**

Reichhold appealed on the ground, among others, that it was not a proper exercise of case management powers to prevent a claimant from proceeding with a claim properly brought before the English court unless he, the claimant, had exhausted the remedies against another party in foreign arbitration. Sir Thomas Bingham MR held that the order of stay of proceedings was appropriate in the event given the presence of *rare and compelling circumstances*.[129] **3.96**

Under the case law that developed in furtherance of the principles laid down in *Reichhold*, the power to stay proceedings on the ground of case management powers was held to apply with equal force even when, unlike the scenario in *Reichhold*, the defendant in English proceedings **3.97**

[127] [1999] CLC 486, 492. See also *Donohue v Armco Inc* [2001] UKHL 64 para 24 (holding that the claimant may 'show strong reasons, sufficient to displace the other party's prima facie entitlement to enforce the contractual bargain').

[128] As per *Ledra Fisheries Ltd v Turner* [2003] EWHC 1049 (Ch), para 17.

[129] *Reichhold Norway ASA & Anor v Goldman Sachs International* [2000] 1WLR 174.

who asked for a stay was a claimant in foreign proceedings.[130] Precisely this type of situation arises in sovereign debt litigation in the presence of majority action clauses where the sovereign debtor, a defendant in English proceedings, is the one triggering the restructuring of the sovereign debt. While English courts would never bind a party to foreign proceedings to which it is not a party,[131] this consideration would be irrelevant in the context of sovereign debt litigation since the holdout creditor consented to be bound by the decision of the majority of fellow bondholders.

3.98 So, too, the presence of a choice of forum clause in favour of English courts does not act as an absolute impediment to the stay of English proceedings on the ground of case management powers. Some courts have held that more rare and compelling circumstances must be shown in the particular event,[132] whereas others were sceptical about differentiating between degrees of rarity and compellability.[133] What would qualify as rare and compelling circumstances is hard to define and would indeed be a fact-intensive enquiry. However, it is submitted that an untimely legal action that frustrates the purpose of a majority action clause and the orderly restructuring of sovereign debt would meet the high threshold required for a stay of proceedings on case management grounds.

3.99 What might sway a judge is the idea that a holdout creditor, who has consented to a majority action clause, should not be allowed to make a preventive strike in the English courts for the purposes of dodging a decision by the majority of creditors. Having agreed to abide by the decision of the majority of bondholders, holdout creditors are unable to appear with clean hands before English courts. Of course, if the sovereign debtor fails to secure the consent of the bondholders to amend the terms of bonds, the minority creditor who has had its claim stayed on the grounds of case management powers, may resume its claim and request interest for the period during which the proceedings are adjourned.[134]

3.100 The solution proposed here would be inapposite to the sovereign debt that lacks majority action clauses—in such a case nothing in principle stands in the way of holdout litigation, subject of course to considerations of comity described in Chapter 1 (para 1.68). Likewise, it is senseless to

[130] *Ssangyong Motor Distributors Ltd v Daewoo Cars Ltd, Daewoo Corporation* [1999] WL 33453544, paras 10, 11.

[131] *Equitas Ltd v Allstate Insurance Co* [2008] EWHC 1671 (Comm), para 72.

[132] Ibid para 66.

[133] *The Princess of the Stars* [2012] EWCA Civ 1341, para 22; *Messier Dowty Ltd v Sabena SA* [2000] 1 All ER (Comm) 101.

[134] *Prifti v Musini Sociedad Anonima de Seguros y Reaseguros* [2005] EWHC 832 (Comm), paras 30, 32.

stay proceedings when the litigant creditor has a blocking position in a particular issuance of bonds that would permit him to impede any collective decision by the majority of bondholders.

A recent case clarifies the status and level of the recognition afforded to majority action clauses before English courts. In *The Princess of the Stars*,[135] a passenger cargo vessel sank in a typhoon. The owners of cargoes made numerous claims against the insurer of the vessel's cargo liability in the courts of the Philippines. In parallel, the English reinsurer initiated proceedings in the English courts against the Philippine insurer under an exclusive jurisdiction clause contained in the reinsurance contract. **3.101**

The reinsurance contract provided that to compensate the insurer, the reinsurer was under an obligation to follow all the terms, conditions, and *settlements* of the original insurance policy ('a follow settlements clause'). Arguing that the reinsurers should wait for the insurer to settle the claims (whether by agreement or by paying any judgment sum), the insurer asked for the stay of English proceedings, as a matter of case management, pending the decision in Philippine proceedings, so as to give meaningful effect to the follow settlements clause. The court rejected the argument, albeit 'with little enthusiasm' on the part of two judges, on the technical ground that under the follow settlements clause, the reinsurer was not required to compensate the insurer for the loss settled which did not fall within the risks covered by the terms of the reinsurance policy. The reinsurance policy contained a typhoon warranty that exempted the reinsurer from any liability, notwithstanding any clause contained in the reinsurance policy, if the vessel sailed into a typhoon. The purely technical ground upon which the court predicated the rejection may be read to suggest that the court was ready to accept that a follow settlements clause might be a good reason for the stay of proceedings had the insurance policy not contained a typhoon warranty clause. In the unusual situation of such occurring, the follow settlements clause would have bound the reinsurer and the appellant's case for giving effect to the follow settlement clause would have tipped the scales in favour of a stay of English proceedings. **3.102**

The analogy with majority action clauses is apparent. In a typical situation, a minority creditor would be bound by the decision of the majority of bondholders taken during the sovereign debt restructuring. By the same token, the reinsurers would be bound by the settlement achieved by the insurer in another forum. What distinguishes *The Princess of the Stars* from sovereign debt restructurings is that minority holders of sovereign debt are squarely bound by the settlement reached in sovereign debt **3.103**

135 [2012] EWCA Civ 1341.

restructuring, whereas the reinsurers in *The Princess of Stars* were able to profit from the loopholes left in the follow settlements clause.

3.104 A cognate question is whether the stay of English proceedings on case management grounds would breach the right to fair trial of a minority creditor under Art 6 of the ECHR. Put otherwise, the question is whether the stay of proceedings would place considerable strain on the right of access to justice, even more so when the parties have opted for the exclusive jurisdiction of English courts.

3.105 In *Reichhold Norway ASA v Goldman Sachs International*, the Court of Appeal decided that the presence of rare and compelling circumstances would assuage the concerns that were likely to arise as to the breach of Art 6 of the ECHR.[136] In the same vein, *Racy v Hawila* rejected an allegation of breach of Art 6 resulting from a case management stay.[137]

3.106 This replicates the patterns seen in other contexts: the stay of proceedings on *forum non conveniens* grounds and the issuance of anti-suit injunctions. The rationale underpinning the exercise of jurisdiction for both these legal tools is the availability of an effective legal remedy. English courts will order stay of proceedings on the *forum non conveniens* grounds only if they are satisfied that no one party would be denied an effective remedy in the alternative forum.[138] It has been consistently held that substantial injustice would not be inflicted upon one of the parties in the alternative forum if the party were merely exposed to a lower quantum of damages.[139] By the same logic, any claims by the minority of creditors that they would face substantial injustice in the sovereign debt restructurings are bound to fail, given that the possible haircut of the sovereign debt does not amount to the deprivation of an effective remedy. On the contrary, it gives effect to the agreement of creditors to abide by the operation of the majority action clause. In *Bramelid and Malmström v Sweden*, the European Commission of Human Rights drew a distinction between voluntary and compulsory arbitrations, holding that normally Art 6 would be irrelevant in the case of voluntary arbitrations where the party has consented to submit to arbitration.[140]

3.107 Even if one were to assume that the stay of proceedings brought in breach of a majority action clause might potentially breach the right to fair trial, the holdout creditor would still need to establish that the limitation of the

[136] *Reichhold Norway* (n 129) 186. [137] [2003] EWHC 1611 (Ch), para 67.

[138] See, eg, *Cornelly v RTZ Corporation* [1998] AC 854.

[139] *Lubbe v Cape* [2000] 1 WLR 1545, 1554; *Herceg Novi (Owners) v Ming Galaxy (Owners)* [1998] C.L.C. 1487.

[140] (EComHR Application 8588/79 and 8589/79) 12 October 1982.

right of access to justice was not proportionate under the human rights standards. The essentials would appear to be: (1) the public interest of referring a holdout creditor to sovereign debt restructurings by staying judicial proceedings; and (2) the timing of a potential sovereign debt restructuring. So far as the first point is concerned, constraints over the right of access to courts should be proportionate to the public interest pursued and the right circumscribed.[141] Thus the enquiry is whether the United Kingdom has any public interest in protecting a foreign State from holdout litigation by ensuring the integrity of sovereign debt restructurings, and whether such a concern would qualify as public interest under the case law of the European Court of Human Rights (ECtHR). Evidently, a foreign State is not part of the 'public' of the United Kingdom. That said, on the issue of whether the UK Debt Relief Act (restraining the amount recoverable under the bonds) breaches the right of property under the European Convention on Human Rights (ECHR), Wautelet argues that there is a strong public interest in shielding States in distress from holdout creditors who prey on sovereign debtors. And, even more so, the premise of the Act is to give effect to English public policy in not enforcing such debt in full—this is reflected both in the terms of the Act (ss 5 and 7 refer to 'public policy'), and also reflected in the Explanatory Notes (s 32). The concept of 'public interest', extensively construed by the ECtHR, may extend to the goal of assisting distressed States—a concern shared by the whole international community.[142]

As for the second factor, the ECtHR has found that in properly determining the reasonable time of a public hearing, the court is obliged to take into account the individual circumstances of the particular case.[143] In the ECtHR case law, delays over three years at a single jurisdictional stage have been held not to be unreasonable on the grounds of a sensitive political climate and the need for the court to consider many sources of information, including witnesses.[144] Long delays in foreign forums are also a **3.108**

[141] *Shirayama Shokusan Co Ltd v Danovo Ltd* [2004] 1 WLR 2985, para 39; *Steel and Morris v United Kingdom* (2005), para 62; *Acimovic v Croatia* (2005), para 29; *Ernst v Belgium* (2004), para 48; Steven Greer, *The European Convention on Human Rights: Achievements, Problems and Prospects* (2006) 252; *Gambazzi v Daimler Chrysler Canada*, C-394/07, [2009] ECR I-02563, para 29.

[142] Patrick Wautelet, 'Les Fonds Vautours—Vulture Funds, Creditors and Sovereign Debtors: How to Find a Balance?' in Mathias Audit (ed), *Insolvabilité des États et dettes souveraines* (2011) 159, 160, 162.

[143] *Zimmerman and Steiner v Switzerland*, 13 July 1983, para 24.

[144] *Tričković v Slovenia* (Appl no 39914/98) ECtHR 12 June 2001, para 67; *Angelucci v Italy* (Appl no 12666/87) ECtHR 19 February 1991, para 15; Mark Janis, Richard Kay, Anthony Bradley, *European Human Rights Law: Text and Materials* (2008) 818.

material factor militating against a stay of English proceedings under case management powers.[145]

3.109 Obtaining the consent of a considerable number of bondholders might indeed require time. However, recent sovereign debt restructurings have been conducted at a surprisingly high speed.[146] The average duration of 'post-Brady era' (since 1998) sovereign bonds restructurings is thirteen months.[147] One could argue that the use of or threat to use majority action clauses could accelerate, though not always substantially, the overall speed of a sovereign debt restructuring. Debt restructurings of Pakistan (1999), Ukraine (2000), and Moldova (2002) took only four months. The restructuring of the debt of Uruguay was completed in a record time of two months. Nearly all the restructurings mentioned were governed by English law and included majority action clauses. The entire Greek debt reorganisation was completed in nine months.[148] Exceptions include the case of Dominica (2004) where the restructuring took fifteen months, and Seychelles (2009), which took nineteen months (both of them, though, contained majority action clauses), and of course Argentina (2002) with forty-two months.[149] Of course, there is a risk that pre-default restructurings may be said to be shorter than they are in reality, because considerable groundwork for the restructuring may be done beforehand, whereas in post-default restructurings there is a starting point from which one may calculate the duration of the restructuring. Be that as it may, modern sovereign debt restructurings are generally conducted in a prompt manner.

3.110 Once the initial hurdles for a case management stay are overcome, the case management order should not become an order of substance since its function is to regulate the procedure before the English courts. Generally speaking, imposing conditions over the process of the sovereign debt workout would amount to an exorbitant exercise of the court's jurisdiction.[150] However, the Commercial Court is in no way precluded from staying its proceedings on condition that the sovereign debtor is accorded a limited period of time to obtain the consent of the majority of bondholders; in case the sovereign debtor fails to successfully trigger the operation

[145] *The Princess of the Stars* [2012] EWCA Civ 1341, para 27.

[146] Christoph Trebesch, 'Delays in Sovereign Debt Restructurings', unpublished paper 22.

[147] Ibid 7–8, 10; Das et al (n 101) 28.

[148] Allen & Overy Global Law Intelligence Unit, 'How the Greek Debt Reorganisation of 2012 Changed the Rules of Sovereign Insolvency' (2012) 16.

[149] IMF, 'A Survey of Experiences with Emerging Market Sovereign Debt Restructurings' 8, 14–15.

[150] *Shirayama Shokusan Co Ltd v Danovo Ltd* [2004] 1 WLR 2985, para 23; *Halsey v Milton Keynes General NHS Trust* [2004] EWCA Civ 576, para 14; G1.9(b) of the Admiralty and Commercial Court Guide.

of the majority action clause, English proceedings will resume. Another, more stringent, condition that the court might stipulate is for the debtor to transfer the (portion of) its debt into an escrow account, pending the activation of the majority action clause and the money would be paid if the restructuring fails.[151]

A distinct issue of legal litigation arbitrage arose in *Black Diamond Offshore v FCC*.[152] The creditors held two different debt instruments of a single Spanish company: (1) notes governed by English law and subject to the jurisdiction of English courts; and (2) the syndicated debt subject to Spanish law and courts. In their capacity as holders of the English debt, the creditors requested a declaration from a Chancery Division judge that the initiation or completion of Spanish restructuring proceedings was an Event of Default which would entitle them to accelerate the English law debt. The Spanish debtor company requested stay of English proceedings, among other things, arguing that the only interest pursued in requesting a declaratory judgment was to confer a collateral benefit upon the holders of the Spanish debt, to later use it in Spanish restructuring proceedings. The judge declined the request of the case management stay as she was convinced that the creditors did indeed have interest in English proceedings, including the certainty as to the right to accelerate the debt and sell it on the secondary market. **3.111**

Would the judge have reached the same conclusion if the Spanish debt instrument contained a provision obliging the holders of Spanish debt to be bound by the restructuring? It is possible. Addressing the argument that English proceedings were trying to subvert the choice of jurisdiction agreement in favour of Spanish proceedings, the judge found that jurisdiction agreements did not govern restructuring proceedings in any event.[153] This might suggest that in the context of sovereign debt restructurings, the court might have stayed proceedings started by creditors who, backing two horses, requested a declaratory judgment from English proceedings to subvert a majority action clause. **3.112**

3. Exceptions to the Stay of Proceedings

Actionable Restructurings

Confusion might arise as to whether the stay of proceedings is a principled policy or a pragmatic presumption which may be overcome in **3.113**

[151] For a proposal to introduce escrow account payments in case of standstills, see Jonathan Eaton, 'Standstills and an International Bankruptcy Court' (2002) 14.

[152] [2015] EWHC 1035 (Ch).

[153] Ibid para 51.

particularly compelling circumstances. In other words, can the disgruntled minority bondholder, by adducing certain exceptional circumstances, make a case against the mandatory stay of proceedings to obtain a judgment from English courts, notwithstanding a majority action clause incorporated in the bonds?

3.114 It bears emphasising that the stay of proceedings on case management grounds is a discretionary exercise. English courts retain the power to refuse the request to stay proceedings if they are convinced that that is the appropriate course of conduct. As a matter of principle, the stay of proceedings may be overcome if the manner and the outcome of the handling of the sovereign debt restructuring are actionable in court. Other chapters of this book address restructurings that are actionable:

(1) the passing of legislation to retroactively introduce majority action clauses into sovereign bonds (Chapter 5); and
(2) the repudiation or expropriation of the debt or the presence of some other factors that would justify a review of sovereign debt restructuring in truly exceptional circumstances (Chapter 7).

3.115 In the unreported legislation arising from the introduction of the Irish Subordinated Liabilities Order, both parties agreed that in usual circumstances the English courts would not allow a legal action before the decision by the person who has the power to modify the rights of creditors was taken. However, the claimant argued that the tender was coercive in nature and proceedings should not be stayed. The matter did not receive judicial resolution as a result of the settlement of the dispute.

Waiver of the Right to Request Stay of Proceedings

3.116 Subsection 2 argued for the stay of proceedings brought in breach of a majority action clause. However, hardly anyone is able to predict what the reaction of financial markets would be if the English courts were to adopt the stance outlined above. The effect on the secondary market of bonds is hard to foresee, as the stay of proceedings might undermine the value of trading on the secondary market.

3.117 In the (unlikely) situation that markets are disturbed by such an approach, the parties are at full liberty to negotiate a full waiver of objections to the exercise of jurisdiction by English courts along the following lines: 'Each party waives objection to the English courts on grounds of inconvenient forum or *otherwise* as regards proceedings in connection with ...'. This would leave case management stay out of the question[154] or at least make it much harder to obtain.[155]

Under many sovereign bonds, the waiver to the exercise of jurisdiction by English courts extends only to stays on the ground of *forum non conveniens tout court,* without the all-encompassing 'otherwise'.[156] English law governed Greek bonds provide that: 'The Republic hereby irrevocably waives any objection which it may have now or hereafter to the laying of the venue of any such Proceedings in any such court and any claim that any such Proceedings have been brought in an inconvenient forum.'[157] Whether this formulation waives the right of the Greek government to request stays on case management grounds is ambiguous. **3.118**

4. Interference of the Majority Power of Bondholders with the Finality of English Judgments

Modification of Financial Terms

If the argument for the stay of proceedings pending the restructuring eventually fails before English courts, the court will most certainly issue a summary judgment against the State. The question that may arise is whether the majority of bondholders may wield its majority powers once a favourable judgment has been issued. **3.119**

The dominant narrative is that once the holdout creditor obtains a favourable judgment from the court, the decision of the majority of bondholders is incapable of overruling the judicial ruling.[158] Certainly, this position seems to hold true in respect of the financial terms of the bonds (the amount of debt, payment date, and currency): the sovereign debtor, after losing a case to the holdout creditor in court, cannot mount a collateral **3.120**

[154] *National Westminster v Bank plc v Utrecht-America Finance Co* [2001] CLC 442, para 19.

[155] *Standard Chartered Bank (Hong Kong) Limited v Independent Power Tanzania Limited* [2015] EWHC 1640 (Comm), 109, 131 (holding that in spite of said waiver, the court enjoys residual discretion to stay its proceedings where there are particularly strong or exceptional grounds that such a stay will be granted).

[156] See, eg, The Republic of Austria, Euro 30,000,000,000, Medium-Term Note Programme, 16 September 2003, Clause 18(b).

[157] See, eg, The Hellenic Republic, Euro 250,000,000 Fixed to Floating Rate Capped Government Bonds due 2024, 5 July 2005, Clause 14(b).

[158] International Law Association, 'International Monetary Law Committee: Berlin Conference' (2004) 7; Edwin Borchard, *State Insolvency and Foreign Bondholders* (1951) 354–56; Southan Harati, 'Loan Rescheduling and Third Parties' (1987) 6 IFLR 44. A mere notice of litigation would not be sufficient to prevent the use of majority action clauses.

attack against the judgment by triggering the majority action clause so as to reduce the amount due and already fixed in the judgment. It can be argued with confidence that the judgment perpetuates the contents of the bond as of the date of judgment, subject of course to the right of appeal. What the certainty of law requires is that the final judgment of a court withstands subsequent attempts of revision, whether through another set of judicial proceedings or a contractual modification clause.

3.121 In addition to the *res judicata* effect of judgments, the doctrine of merger of judgment—according to which the cause of action is merged and thus assimilated with the judgment—may be held to prevent the exercise of majority powers once a binding judgment settles the dispute between the parties. The main thrust of the doctrine is that the cause of action is assimilated with the judgment, however it may be read to suggest that the clauses of the contract may also be merged with the judgment. Thus, in *Director General of Fair Trading v First National Bank plc*, the covenant to pay interest was said to merge into the judgment unless parties 'agree that a covenant to pay interest will not merge in any judgment'.[159] Of course, the issue of interest is somewhat specific given that following the issuance of the judgment the statutory interest rate would apply which requires delineating the statutory interest rate from the contractual.

3.122 Putting the issue of interest aside, controversy surrounds the second strand of the doctrine of merger—the assimilation of the clauses of the contract with the judgment (and not the cause of action *sensu stricto*)—to the extent that it is not clear whether it is good law. On the other side of the Atlantic, the District Court in a sovereign debt claim was sceptical of the contemporary relevance of the doctrine of merger as it was barely distinguishable from *res judicata*. The court was more willing to reason in terms of *res judicata* rather than extinguishment of an instrument upon the issuance of a judgment.[160]

3.123 If the finality of a judgment were to 'trump' the power of the majority to modify the financial terms of the bonds, the holdout creditor could simply take the necessary steps to obtain a judgment from the English courts and await the prospects of a successful enforcement of the judgment. The enforcement of the judgment would simply be a matter of time.

[159] [2002] 1 AC 481, 487–88. See also *Standard Chartered Bank v Ceylon Petroleum Corp* [2011] EWHC 2094 (Comm) (the contract expressly extending the obligation to pay interest to the period after the judgment and therefore not merging with the judgment). See in the same vein *Westinghouse Credit Corp v D'Urso*, 371 F.3d 96 (2d Cir 2004).

[160] *Export–Import Bank of the Republic of China v Grenada*, 13 Civ 1450, 4–5 (SDNY 2013). See more in detail Restatement (Second) of Judgments, §18 (1982).

3.124 Sovereign debt markets are cognisant of the inherent limitations of the collective power of bondholders vis-à-vis final judgments. Some bonds provide that a majority of bondholders may rescind a notice of acceleration of bonds or 'such decision to institute litigation',[161] but stop short of providing power to rescind an entitlement under a final judgment. Other bonds expressly provide that the reverse acceleration clause cannot be operated after 'a judgment or decree for payment of the money due has been obtained'.[162]

3.125 An ancillary question is whether the majority of bondholders may modify the bonds in respect of which the holdout has started proceedings before the English courts and the determination of which is pending before the judge. Should the majority swiftly agree to the restructuring before a summary judgment is issued, there does not seem to be much that a bondholder may do other than be bound by the terms of the binding restructuring. The majority power may also waive default, but it is unclear whether such power extends to pending proceedings brought by a creditor.[163] If grounds for waiving the sovereign debtor's default are present (eg, the curing of the State's default), the waiver of default renders the issuance of the judgment moot.

Modification of Non-Financial Covenants

3.126 A related issue is whether, assuming the holdout creditor obtains a (summary) judgment, majority action clauses or exit consents may still operate to the detriment of the creditor holding a judgment by modifying the non-financial covenants of the bonds. Put otherwise, assume that a creditor obtained a summary judgment in respect of the bonds that contained a waiver of sovereign immunity; could the majority, through a majority action clause or an exit consent, wield its power to restrict or completely eliminate the waiver of sovereign immunity after the issuance of the judgment?

3.127 The initial reasoning would be that the same kind of considerations that apply to the modification of financial terms of sovereign bonds should perforce be extended to non-financial covenants. The doctrine of merger of judgment could be argued to insulate the bonds from the operation of the exit consent technique that would seek to modify non-financial covenants. Nevertheless, the judgment is rendered in respect of the financial

[161] See, eg, The Hellenic Republic, Offering Circular, €600,000,000 2.085% Inflation Linked Notes, due 25 July 2057, p 13.

[162] See, eg, The Democratic Socialist Republic of Sri Lanka, Offering Circular, US$1,000,000,000, 6.25% Bonds due 2021, 20 July 2011, p 122.

[163] *McClelland v Norfolk Southern Railroad Co*, 110 NY 468, 479 (NY 1888) (highlighting the uncertainty).

matters of the sovereign debt, such as the principal and interest. The doctrine of merger goes so far as to merge the cause of action only,[164] and not the entire contract. By implication, the non-financial covenants of the bond are not set in stone by the judgment, and, in principle, can be modified through the exit consent.

5. The Stay of Proceedings in the US

3.128 It is clear that debt restructuring measures do not bind non-consenting creditors.[165] However, the extent to which judicial proceedings may be stayed in deference to a pending sovereign debt restructuring is more unclear. The issue arose in *Pravin Banker Associates, Ltd v Banco Popular Del Peru and the Republic of Peru.* Following a severe economic crisis, Banco Popular Del Peru, a Peruvian State-owned bank, failed to pay the interests due to Pravin Bankers Association, a US bank association. Soon after this default, Banco was put into liquidation, administered by the Peruvian Central Bank.

3.129 Pravin persistently refused to join the liquidation process and Brady Plan negotiations.[166] Instead, it initiated litigation in US courts. In *Pravin I*, the district court stayed its proceedings for six months, so as not to interfere with the liquidation of the impecunious Banco. There are two views of the judgement's *ratio:* first, the stay was ordered within the narrow confines of the principle of recognition of foreign bankruptcy proceedings;[167] second, the stay was based on broader considerations of comity that may equally be applied in the context of a sovereign–creditor relationship.[168] The stay was further extended for two months to enable the negotiations with the Bank Advisory Committee (a committee of Peru's major creditors) to proceed, and the parties to provide additional information on the Peruvian debt (*Pravin II*).[169] In the judicial proceedings that resumed after the two-month pause, Peru argued that Pravin threatened the renegotiation process of the Peruvian debt on the basis that legal action by the holdout creditor Pravin posed a substantial risk of reopening the floodgates of

[164] See s 34 of the Civil Jurisdiction and Judgments Act 1982 ('No proceedings may be brought by a person in England and Wales or Northern Ireland on a cause of action in respect of which a judgment has been given').

[165] *Lloyds Bank plc v The Republic of Ecuador*, 1998 US Dist LEXIS 3065, 33–34 (SDNY 1998).

[166] Brady Plan was a framework for the negotiation of the debt owed by the Latin American countries, supervised by the IMF.

[167] *Petition of Tam*, 170 BR 838, 844 (Bankr SDNY 1994).

[168] *Pravin Banker Assocs Ltd v Banco Popular del Peru*, 165 Bankr 379, 387 (SDNY 1994) (distinguishing *Allied* on the grounds that the restructuring *in casu* was still pending and conformed to the mandates of US policy in that it was an IMF-directed restructuring).

[169] *Pravin Banker Assocs Ltd v Banco Popular del Peru*, 11 WL 102840 (SDNY 1995).

the lawsuits stayed by the committee of Peru's creditors. This slippery slope argument notwithstanding, the District Court denied the claimant's motion to dismiss or stay proceedings, and granted summary judgment to Pravin.[170]

On appeal, Peru argued that the District Court had wrongly declined to apply the principle of comity on the facts of the case. The Second Circuit, citing *Hilton v Guyot*,[171] confirmed that, as a matter of principle, US courts would give deference to proceedings that take place in foreign countries and would usually refuse to review the acts of foreign governments. In spite of this, the Second Circuit noted that the principle of comity is not an imperative rule of law and should not be applied to Peru's Brady negotiations if it would contravene US governmental policies.[172] In its judgment, the court contrasted two conflicting governmental policies: (1) the need to enhance participation in the foreign debt restructuring under the Brady Plan;[173] and (2) the need to ensure the enforceability of foreign debts, particularly the enforcement of debts owed to US lenders. The court held that the latter policy—that of the enforceability of contractual debt—was held to prevail over the former, relying on the amicus brief of the US government submitted in *Allied III* and on the overriding principle that participation in the restructuring process should strictly be on a voluntary basis.[174] The Second Circuit refused to stay proceedings indefinitely since that would have transformed the voluntary negotiations into a de facto judicially enforced bankruptcy procedure. Emphasis on comity was not sufficient to allay fears of intrusion with private contractual rights. **3.130**

However, the court expressly left open the question whether the circumstances of that case justified a stay of the proceedings to allow the completion of Peru's negotiations with its creditors without unduly threatening the ultimate enforceability of the debt.[175] The judge in the *Allan Applestein* case was perplexed by how to reconcile this latter pronouncement with the main finding of the *Pravin* case, ie, the refusal to stay proceedings.[176] **3.131**

[170] *Pravin Banker Assocs Ltd v Banco Popular del Peru*, 895 F Supp 660 (SDNY 1995).

[171] 159 US 113, 164 (1895) (international comity is 'the recognition which one nation allows within its territory to the legislative, executive or judicial acts of another nation').

[172] *Pravin Banker Associates, Ltd v Banco Popular Del Peru and the Republic of Peru*, 109 F.3d 850, 854 (2d Cir 1997).

[173] The question is whether the court would have given the status of a governmental policy to a restructuring not under the Brady Plan which was, it will be recalled, a programme supported by the US government.

[174] Another question left open is whether the governmental policy would be as strong in a case when the lender is not American.

[175] *Pravin Banker Associates* (n 172) 856.

[176] *Allan Applestein Ttee Fbo D.C.A Grantor Trust v The Province of Buenos Aires*, 2003 US Dist LEXIS 7128, 9 (SDNY 2003).

On a close reading of the case, it appears that the Second Circuit was implying that a *definite* stay of proceedings, as contrasted to an *indefinite* adjournment of proceedings, might have been appropriate where the court could expect with more certainty that the definite, temporary stay of proceedings would permit the successful closure of the restructuring. Nevertheless, the Second Circuit found that the District Court had not abused its discretion in refusing to stay the proceedings or the execution of the judgment temporarily, which was the sole permissible ground for reviewing the decision of the District Court.

3.132 A series of US cases followed the approach enunciated in *Pravin III*.[177] In *EM Ltd v The Republic of Argentina*,[178] the District Court held that the creditor had an unconditional right to collect the sums due under the bonds agreement, in spite of a pending sovereign debt restructuring (in that case, the Argentine bonds explicitly provided that the bonds are 'unconditional ... obligations of the Republic').[179] In *A.I. Credit Corp v Government of Jamaica*,[180] Jamaica halted the payments under its foreign debt obligations and started a series of restructuring processes. In an action brought by a bondholder for the repayment of debt, the court discarded any considerations of the severe economic situation of Jamaica on the grounds that it was not the function of a court to evaluate the consequences to the debtor of its financial default, nor the foreign policy or other repercussions of Jamaica's default.

3.133 In a similar vein, two other US cases refused to stay proceedings pending the completion of restructuring—*Lightwater Corporation Limited v The Republic of Argentina*[181] and *Allan Applestein Ttee Fbo D.C.A Grantor Trust v The Province of Buenos Aires*[182] (although in both cases, the courts granted a limited short-term stay of proceedings, awaiting decision on the admissibility of two class actions of Argentine bondholders then pending before US courts). In both cases, the wording, nonetheless, seems to be more nuanced in comparison with *Pravin III*. Both judgments held that '[t]he debt restructuring situation was uncertain as to possible success and timing' and declined the motions for stay of proceedings. In light of this linguistic difference, it is arguable that the courts introduced two other considerations into the equation of comity—timing of the restructuring and the chances of its success.

[177] Among others, see *Banco Cafetero (Panama) Ltd v The Republic of Peru*, 1995 US Dist LEXIS 11840 (SDNY 1995).

[178] 2003 US Dist LEXIS 15975 (SDNY 2003).

[179] Ibid 3–6.

[180] *A.I. Credit Corp v Government of Jamaica*, 666 F Supp 629, 633 (SDNY 1987).

[181] 2003 US Dist LEXIS 6156 (SDNY 2003).

[182] 2003 US Dist LEXIS 7128 (SDNY 2003).

All these cases concerned bonds that did not feature majority action clauses. For bonds with majority action clauses, the defendant may raise arguments based on the implication of terms and case management powers, as described above. **3.134**

III. INTERIM MEASURES IN SOVEREIGN DEBT LITIGATION

1. Interim measures before US courts

In a line of cases, US courts denied orders of attachment when that would have had adverse consequences on the ability of States to restructure their debt, and, to a lesser degree, the economy of the sovereign debtor. In the District Court judgment *NML Capital Ltd v Republic of Argentina*[183] and in the appeal judgment *EM v Republic of Argentina*,[184] holders of Argentine bonds asked for a prejudgment order to attach the contractual right of Argentina in respect of old bonds that were to be transferred back to Argentina after the restructuring process had been finalised. Under the restructuring plan, Argentina was to cancel those old debts, once received, and issue new bonds. The attachment, as requested, would have had the effect of averting the cancellation of the bonds and stripping Argentina of any interest in pursuing the restructuring. As a consequence, the sovereign debt restructuring would have been derailed had the old bonds been attached by a court order. The District Court, invoking the discretionary nature of attachments and restraining notices, vacated the prejudgment and post-judgment remedies alike, as they substantially threatened the Argentine sovereign debt restructuring.[185] **3.135**

In *Capital Ventures International v Republic of Argentina*,[186] the holdout creditor of Argentine Brady bonds, Capital Ventures International (CVI), sued Argentina and sought attachment of the collateral over Brady Plan bonds. CVI did not intend to attach the part of the collateral that was supposed to be paid at the ongoing restructuring, but rather the remaining part which was to revert back to Argentina. Thus, the order of attachment did not pose an immediate risk to the restructuring at hand. Nonetheless, the District Court rejected the application for an order of attachment, partly **3.136**

[183] 2005 WL 743086 (SDNY 2005). [184] 131 Fed App 745 (2d Cir 2005).

[185] See also *Greylock Global Opportunity Master Fund v Province of Mendoza*, 2004 US Dist LEXIS 20356, 12–14 (SDNY 2004) (in deciding to grant an interim injunction, the public interest of a public province going through an economic crisis is a factor to consider).

[186] 443 F.3d 214 (2d Cir 2005).

because the order of attachment could have created 'confusion' during the restructuring process.

3.137 On appeal, the Second Circuit, in a move to fortify the right of creditors to assert their rights in court, held that the District Court did not have unfettered discretion to refuse interim measures.[187] It conceded, though, that the prevailing public interest may trump an order of attachment. That said, the Second Circuit found that the restructuring was already over at the crucial time of the appeal proceedings and therefore no confusion could have arisen at that time. It is readily apparent that this case is distinguishable from *NML Capital Ltd* and *EM*, as here the order of attachment did not pose any substantial risk to the restructuring of the Argentine debt.

3.138 In *Export–Import Bank of the Republic of China v Grenada*,[188] Grenada asked the court to set aside restraining notices over its immune assets. In its reply, Grenada outlined the (potential) harm that would result from restraining notices, in particular pushing the State-owned company to the brink of financial insolvency. The court embraced Grenada's demand for a number of reasons, including the public interest against keeping the restraining notices over the assets of a sovereign. The judge noted that the commitment to the principles of comity and respect for the relationship between the US and Grenada disfavoured the imposition of a restraining notice.

3.139 *Elliott Associates v The Republic of Peru and Banco de la Nacion* is a case that went even further in its effort to shield the debtor and its economy from attachment orders.[189] Elliott Associates asked for a prejudgment attachment of the assets of the defendants, alleging default by Banco de la Nacion and failure to perform under a guarantee by the Republic of Peru. The defendants Banco de la Nacion and the Republic of Peru asserted that the attachment order should be refused on the discretionary grounds as it might unravel the Brady Plan renegotiations.

3.140 The court held that Elliott bore the burden of establishing the need for attachment. It could not simply rely on concerns that Peru might fail to enforce the ensuing judgment. This was especially so since Elliott had intentionally declined to partake in the restructuring process, and thus had knowingly taken the risk of unenforceability. The court also alluded to the support by international institutions and the US to the voluntary restructuring of the Peruvian debt, which fortified the desire not to derail the restructuring by prejudgment attachments.

[187] Ibid 222.
[188] 2012 US Dist LEXIS 116531 (SDNY 2012).
[189] 948 F Supp 1203 (SDNY 1996).

Elliott relied on *Allied III* and *Pravin III* arguing that policy arguments would not be sufficient justification to defeat the entitlement of a private creditor to a judgment. The court retorted by drawing a line between the cases relied upon by Elliott in that they related to the final resolution of the dispute on the merits, and the order of attachment sought by the claimant. It was clear that ordering such an attachment was at the court's discretion, and, as a corollary of broad discretion, the court could recognise the significant repercussions that an attachment might have on the pending Brady Plan and the Peruvian economy. As a result, the court rejected the order of attachment.[190] **3.141**

On the other side of the spectrum, the US courts were willing to stress that they would not apply the doctrine of comity if the State was unwilling to pay to discourage other creditors from litigating in the hope of securing a windfall,[191] or if the State refused to honour previous judgments emanating from the US.[192] By contrast, when the State expressed a good-faith willingness to negotiate, the public interest and the concern for the 'health of the nation' reappeared in the reasoning of the court.[193] **3.142**

In *NML v Argentina*, the Second Circuit took the unprecedented move of making concessions to the sovereign debtor in the form of an 'alternative payment formula'. In this case, the creditors obtained a third-party injunction against the banks 'aiding and abetting' the Republic of Argentina in breaching its obligations under the *pari passu* clause.[194] The upshot of the breach of the injunction could have been serious—default on other debt obligations of Argentina. **3.143**

Conscious of the draconian nature of the injunction granted, the court's order read as follows: **3.144**

> [I]t is hereby ordered that, on or before March 29, 2013, Argentina submit in writing to the court the precise terms of any alternative payment formula and schedule to which it is prepared to commit.
>
> The court directs that, among the terms specified, Argentina indicate: (1) how and when it proposes to make current those debt obligations on the original bonds that have gone unpaid over the last 11 years; (2) the rate at which it proposes to repay debt obligations on the original bonds going forward; and (3) what assurances, if

[190] On the merits stage, Elliott, however, managed to get an order of attachment (*Elliott Associates v Banco de la Nacion*, 194 FRD 116, 117 (SDNY 2000)).

[191] *Kensington International Ltd v Republic of Congo*, Docket No 05-1988-cv, 14–15 (2d Cir 2006).

[192] *NML Capital Ltd v Republic of Argentina*, 2015 US Dist LEXIS 30625, 47–48 (SDNY 2015), affd 644 Fed Appx 98 (2d Cir 2016).

[193] *NML Capital Ltd v Republic of Argentina*, 2016 US Dist LEXIS 20633 (SDNY 2016).

[194] For details, see Chapter 7.

any, it can provide that the official government action necessary to implement its proposal will be taken, and the timetable for such action.[195]

3.145 The Second Circuit there still seemed to require full payment ('to make current those debt obligations on the original bonds') but might have been open for proposals to pay the debt in an alternative manner ('how and when'). In theory, the alternative payment formula could have meant payment in alternative methods of payment, such as debt-equity swaps, bonds in the amount of full face value and so forth. The order did not produce any results as Argentina eventually elected to defy the injunction.

3.146 It is unlikely that the courts would be as merciful were the issue at stake to be a request to issue a judgment. Such a lenient stance towards the sovereign debtor would only be taken in respect of interim relief, when, practically speaking, the consequence of the relief sought might be destructive or, at least, seriously harmful to the interests of the sovereign debtor or, indeed, third parties.

3.147 This line of cases on interim and post-judgment measures is often completely misunderstood. It is cited for the general proposition that US courts will provide broad deference to sovereign debt restructurings.[196] In reality, the reasoning in the cases is strictly limited to the stage of interim injunctions or post-judgment freezing injunctions. The reluctance to award interim and post-judgment measures against impecunious States is a somewhat trivial exercise of discretionary powers which may be influenced to some extent by the considerations of comity.

2. Interim measures before English courts

3.148 English courts may be rather cautious, too, when asked to issue interim or post-judgment measures against impecunious States. This cautiousness was explicit in the judgment in *Camdex International Ltd v Bank of Zambia (No 2)*,[197] where the Court of Appeal took a deferential approach in granting interim injunctions. Camdex, an assignee of the rights of the Central Bank of Kuwait, entered summary judgment against the Central Bank of Zambia. On failing to satisfy any part of the judgment debt, Camdex

[195] *NML Capital Ltd v Republic of Argentina*, Order, Docket No 12-105 (L) (2d Cir 2013).

[196] Armin von Bogdandy and Mathias Goldmann, 'Sovereign Debt Restructurings as Exercises of International Public Authority: Towards a Decentralized Sovereign Insolvency Law' in Carlos Espósito, Yuefen Li, and Juan Pablo Bohoslavsky (eds), *Sovereign Financing and International Law: The UNCTAD Principles on Responsible Sovereign Lending and Borrowing* (2013) 66–67; dissenting opinion of Justice Lübbe-Wolff, para 93 in Argentina Necessity Case (Judgment), 2 BvM 1/03, Bundesverfassungsgericht, 8 May 2007, (2007) 101(4) AJIL 857, 860.

[197] [1997] 1 WLR 632.

obtained a freezing injunction restraining removal of the assets of the Bank of Zambia from England and Wales.

The Bank of Zambia had previously arranged for the printing in England of bank notes for later issuance in Zambia, which Camdex targeted by a freezing injunction. The Bank of Zambia applied to the court for release of the unissued bank notes on the grounds that their export was of considerable importance to the Zambian economy. As a result of inflation in Zambia, more high denomination currency was needed for the operation of the Zambian economy and the Bank of Zambia was charged with the task of issuing high value local currency in Zambia and exchanging it with the low value currency. The Bank of Zambia, appealing to the general equitable discretion of the English courts to grant or withhold injunctions, argued that the issue of these notes in Zambia was of great importance to the Zambian economy and accordingly the notes should be released. Camdex's response was that it was entitled to repayment whatever the circumstances were. **3.149**

The Court of Appeal, in a speech delivered by Sir Thomas Bingham MR and with whom Phillips and Aldous LJJ concurred, recognised that it was a novel situation, where the enforcement of a claim was said to threaten, or certainly jeopardise, the economic survival of a State. He recognised that Zambia was highly indebted to international financial institutions and the economic predicament of the country would intensify were it to default on its obligations. It was established on the record that the debt of Zambia amounted to US$7bn, and it had assets of some US$115m of which more than half were encumbered. The situation was one in which severe national hardship to the people of Zambia would have followed if the State defaulted on its international obligations. **3.150**

Sir Thomas Bingham MR concluded that the Bank of Zambia, grievously short of funds, could not be blamed if it sought to pay its creditors on a pro rata basis even if that meant that each of them recovered less than what they were owed. It was a legitimate concern to ensure that Zambia did not default on the sums due to international financial institutions, namely the World Bank and the IMF. Accordingly, the court decided to vary the freezing injunction to exempt the bank notes from its ambit. **3.151**

Certainly, the factual situation in *Camdex (No 2)* is in some respects different from that of a sovereign debt restructuring. In *Camdex (No 2)*, the hardship to the Zambian economy that could have resulted from an inadequate money supply might have been higher than the damage resulting from a legal action thwarting a sovereign bonds restructuring. However, on another view, the risks of derailing a debt restructuring and leaving a national economy without national currency share many similarities. **3.152**

In both, there are serious countervailing reasons for denying a request of interim or post-judgment measures—the hardship to the national economy and the jeopardising of a restructuring, respectively.

3.153 In circumstances other than those prevailing in *Camdex (No 2)*, English courts were more accommodative of requests for interim or post-judgment measures. Thus, the Court of Appeal in an earlier judgment concerning the same dispute between the same parties was in principle open to making a third-party debt order. The Court of Appeal correctly considered that a private litigant is entitled to vigorously enforce its rights against an impecunious sovereign debtor and no public ground can be asserted against it.[198]

[198] *Camdex International Ltd v Bank of Zambia and others (No 2)* (1997) Times Law Reports, 28 January 1997 ('His Lordship was similarly unimpressed by the invocation of considerations of comity. Of course Zambia was a foreign friendly state and of course one recognised that state's acute need for hard currency. The rules of law, however, dictated that judgment debtors should pay their debts and that if they failed to do so all the usual methods of execution should be open to their creditors.').

4

Governing Law of Sovereign Bonds

I. INTRODUCTION

In the UK, the governing law of bonds is to be determined pursuant to the Rome I Regulation. The Regulation provides that the parties are free to agree to the governing law of bonds (Art 3) and in the absence of such choice, the governing law is determined under Art 4 of the Regulation. Although it was historically considered that sovereign debt could not be governed by a municipal law other than that of the sovereign debtor,[1] there is now no disagreement that States are at liberty to submit sovereign bonds to a foreign law of their choice.[2] External sovereign bonds issued by emerging market economies ubiquitously contain choice of law clauses in favour of the law of an established financial centre, often London or New York. A small percentage of sovereign bonds contain choices of Japanese, German, Italian, or Luxembourg laws. A principle permeating these legal systems is that choice of law clauses are binding and enforceable. **4.01**

Choice of law clauses need not be formulated in express terms. Buchheit, Gulati, and Tirado examined a clause commonly found in sovereign bonds, which stipulates that all payments are to be subject to the laws, regulations, and directives in the place of payment. Rather unusually, the clause in Cypriot bonds subjects all payments 'to any applicable fiscal or other laws, regulations and directives' *tout court*, without the qualifying caveat of 'in the place of payment'. The authors argued that this linguistic formulation entitled Cyprus to subject payments under the bonds to the Cypriot law even if the place of payment is outside Cyprus,[3] and, as the case may be, to use the clause as a legal basis for restructuring the bonds through legislative amendments. Similarly worded clauses found in Ukrainian (and other) bonds have invited comparable reasoning.[4] **4.02**

[1] Mauro Megliani, *Sovereign Debt: Genesis, Restructuring, Litigation* (2015) 188.

[2] Wolfgang Friedmann, *Law in a Changing Society* (1972) 472–73.

[3] Lee Buchheit, Mitu Gulati, and Ignacio Tirado, 'The Problem of Holdout Creditors in Eurozone Sovereign Debt Restructurings' (2013) 4 JIBFL 191, 193.

[4] Joseph Cotterill, 'Ukraine's Bonds: A Little Local Leverage' (26 March 2015) FT Alphaville.

4.03 This interpretation is by no means the only reasonable construction of the clause. Understanding the clause as subjecting the bonds to the law of the sovereign debtor eviscerates the enquiry as to why the law of that debtor should apply in the first place. In other words, why is it the '*applicable*' fiscal or other law? To apply the law of the sovereign debtor requires it to be applicable under the choice of law rules of the prorogated forum or under the contract in question.

4.04 In most cases, the omission of the qualifying 'at the place of payment' would not result in a different result. In any case, English choice of law rules associate the applicability of a fiscal or other rule with the place of payment. First, English courts would only apply the mandatory provisions of the place of performance of the contract (Art 9(3) of the Rome I Regulation), discussed below. (Note that US law may adopt a broader view of the applicability of mandatory provisions.[5]) Second, formalities of the contractual performance are also for the law of the place of performance (Art 12(2) of the Rome I Regulation).

4.05 Moreover, the bonds in question come with a distinct choice of law provision. One should not presume that the parties to the bonds had two governing laws or perhaps the option of *depéçage* in mind at the time of drafting the bonds. Properly understood, clauses on 'applicable fiscal and other laws' do not necessarily conflict in any meaningful way with the choice of law provision.

4.06 Leaving aside the cases where the bonds contain choice of law clauses, either express or tacit, considerable controversy surrounds the determination of the law applicable to sovereign debt in circumstances where the parties have remained silent as to the governing law of the transaction in question. Empirical research shows that choice of law clauses are in no way ubiquitous in internal (domestic) bonds, which constitute the main focus of this chapter (external bonds, as explained, invariably contain a choice of law provision). The chapter thus addresses the question what law applies to domestic bonds in absence of a choice of law provision.

4.07 First a few words of introduction about domestic debt. Alongside international bonds issued in international financial centres, States commonly float domestic debt in their own territory.[6] Domestic debt has seen steady growth since the recent financial crisis,[7] although the rise of domestic bond

[5] Restatement (Second) on Conflict of Laws (1969) §§187–88.

[6] Federico Sturzenegger and Jeromin Zettelmeyer, *Debt Defaults and Lessons from a Decade of Crises* (2006) 58.

[7] Ken Miyajima, Madhusudan Mohanty, and Tracy Chan, 'Emerging Market Local Currency Bonds: Diversification and Stability' (2012) BIS Working Papers No 391,

markets in developing countries pre-dates the crisis. The domestic sovereign debt, including its governing law, remains one of the least researched topics in the sovereign debt literature.

4.08 To determine how often, if ever, governing law provisions appear in domestic bonds, questionnaires were sent to debt management agencies of EU Member States and major national economies (Brazil, China, India, the Russian Federation, the US, etc).[8] Among other questions, the survey asked whether domestic bonds of the particular State contained a choice of law provision. The responses received show that most domestic debt issuance lacks express choice of law clauses. While the bonds issued by many developed countries, such as Italian, Portuguese, Irish, and pre-restructuring Greek bonds,[9] are often expressly subjected to their local law, the number of bonds with no choice of law clauses is large. Out of eighteen responses received, domestic bonds of eight States did not have a choice of law clause, namely Albania, Brazil, Bulgaria, Costa Rica, Cyprus, Czech Republic, Lithuania, and Uruguay. Even when choice of law clauses appear in sovereign bonds, they may be lacking in retail bonds (Belgium). In the UK, a governing law provision expressly specifying English law was first introduced in 2007, and only applies to gilts first issued after 20 August 2007.[10] The gilts floated before 20 August 2007 were silent on choice of law matters.[11]

4.09 When the domestic debt issued by the State is subscribed to by its own residents, the law of the sovereign debtor will govern its own domestic debt under any system of the conflict of laws.[12] In such a situation, the debt

1–2; Paloma Acevedo, Enrique Alberola, and Carmen Broto, 'Local Debt Expansion and Vulnerability Reduction: An Assessment for Six Crisis-Prone Countries' (2008) BIS Papers No 36; UNCTAD, 'Domestic and External Public Debt in Developing Countries' (2008) UNCTAD Discussion Papers, 7–9.

8 From forty-two questionnaires sent, eighteen responses were received: Albania, Argentina, Australia, Belgium, Brazil, Bulgaria, Costa Rica, Cyprus, Czech Republic, Denmark, Estonia, Finland, Hungary, Latvia, Lithuania, Switzerland, the United Kingdom, and Uruguay.

9 IMF, 'A Survey of Experiences with Emerging Market Sovereign Debt Restructurings' (2012) 14.

10 The Information Memorandum relating to the Issue, Stripping and Reconstitution of British Government Stock (published on 20 August 2007 and subsequently updated on 15 August 2011) s 103.

11 See, eg, 2% Index-Linked Treasury Stock 2035, Issue of £675,000,000, United Kingdom, 2 December 2003 (no choice of law clause).

12 See, eg, *Kahler v Midland Bank* [1950] AC 24, 28; *Zivnostenska Banka v Frankman* [1950] AC 57, 69–70. See also *Re United Railways of Havana and Regla Warehouses Ltd* [1961] AC 1007, 1067–68 (per Lord Denning); Clive Schmitthoff, 'The International Government Loan' (1937) 19(4) J Comp L & Intl L 179, 193.

will in all respects be domestic. Nevertheless, with the advent of financial globalisation and the interconnectedness of capital markets, domestic debt may no longer qualify as domestic at all times. The reality is that the domestic debt might and often does contain foreign elements. One of the followings grounds might be relied upon to distinguish domestic from foreign indebtedness:

- the residence of bondholders;
- currency;[13]
- the place of marketing of bonds; or
- the law governing the debt (jurisdiction of local courts).[14]

4.10 So far as the first two elements are concerned, the domestic debt may be, and in practice is often held by foreign residents, and to a lesser degree, denominated in foreign currency.[15] Thus, in the restructurings of Russian (1998) and Ukrainian (1998) domestic debt, external creditors held a considerable number of bonds restructured (40% in the case of Russia).[16] Involvement of foreign residents introduces a foreign (international) element into the legal characterisation of the domestic debt, which, as will be seen, will be decisive in the conflict of laws analysis. With that in mind, the distinction between domestic and external debt needs to be found somewhere else.

4.11 The conventional theory draws the line between domestic and external bonds on the basis of the place of the marketing of bonds.[17] According to Borchard, external debt is the debt marketed abroad, whereas domestic

[13] Art 6, Law of the Russian Federation on the Particularities of the Issuance and Trading of State and Municipal Securities (1998).

[14] IMF, 'Sovereign Debt Restructuring Mechanism—Further Considerations' (2002) 12. Similarly, no single criterion is used in defining 'External Indebtedness', a definition used by many sovereign bonds. 'External Indebtedness' is either defined through the place of issuance (see, eg, Commonwealth of Bahamas, US$100,000,000, 7.125% Notes due 2038, p 32), currency (see, eg, Arab Republic of Egypt, US$1,000,000,000, 5.75% Notes due 2020, p 82), or governing law (see, eg, Republic of Slovenia, €1,500,000,000, 4.700%, Notes due 2016, p 18).

[15] Henrik Enderlein, Christoph Trebesch, and Laura von Daniels, 'Sovereign Debt Disputes: A Database on Government Coerciveness during Debt Crises' (2011) 30 J Intl Mon & Fin 1, 12 (in six domestic debt restructurings large shares of domestic debt were held by foreign residents); Carmen Reinhart and Kenneth Rogoff, 'The Forgotten History of Domestic Debt' (2008) NBER Working Paper 13946, 45–48; Kevin Cowan, Eduardo Levy-Yeyati, Ugo Panizza, and Federico Sturzenegger, 'Sovereign Debt in the Americas: New Data and Stylized Facts' (2006) Working Paper of Inter-American Development Bank No 577, 21.

[16] Udaibir Das, Michael Papaioannou, and Christoph Trebesch, 'Sovereign Debt Restructurings 1950–2010: Literature Survey, Data, and Stylized Facts' (2012) IMF Working Paper WP/12/203, 8, 24–25; Anna Gelpern and Brad Setser, 'Domestic and External Debt: The Doomed Quest for Equal Treatment' (2004) 35 Geo J Intl L 795, 800.

[17] League of Nations Study Committee Report, II Econ and Finan (1939b) II.A 10, 6–7.

debt is the debt floated within the territory of the sovereign debtor.[18] In the *Canevaro Brothers* case, the sovereign debt was characterised as domestic for the simple reason that it was 'created and payable' in the territory of the sovereign, and accordingly, the nationality of the current holders of bonds and the currency did not meaningfully affect the characterisation of the debt.[19]

Yet, nowadays this position is problematic for two main reasons: (1) the difficulties associated with defining the market; (2) the blurring of the place of issuance in today's globalised financial world. First, the concept of a market is cloaked with uncertainty, and to be effective, requires additional characterisation. Several additional features can define a market: the place of advertisement of bonds, the place of physical trading, the place of entering into the contract, the location of contracting parties or the place of payment—either by the bondholders to the debtor or vice versa. The adoption of any of these factors as the defining characteristic of the market ultimately would depend upon the policy that the person qualifying the market follows.[20] **4.12**

Second, the current patterns of domestic debt issuance blur the distinction between domestic and external bonds based on the criterion of the place of issuance or marketing—a phenomenon that the issuing State presumably is aware of. Broadly speaking, capital markets are not segmented as they used to be, and the issuance of bonds usually transcends borders. The delocalisation of financial markets challenges the usefulness of markets as a connecting factor.[21] **4.13**

Tellingly, although domestic bonds are often sold through auctions organised within the territory of the sovereign or listed on domestic stock exchanges, domestic bonds are often marketed abroad and targeted to foreign residents. Developed countries (eg, Belgium) market their domestic debt abroad as a general practice. Sovereign bond auctions are usually advertised on the website of the competent State authority (either the **4.14**

[18] Edwin Borchard, *State Insolvency and Foreign Bondholders*, vol 1 (1951) 75.

[19] *Canevaro Brothers (Italy v Peru)*, 3 May 1912 (1912) 6 AJIL 746, 750 (but refraining from inquiring what the decision would have been had the debt been owed to foreign residents at the time of the restructuring of bonds).

[20] Herbert Kronke, 'Capital Markets and Conflict of Laws' (2000) 286 Recueil des Cours 245, 300–01; Francisco Garcimartín Alférez, 'Cross-Border Listed Companies' (2007) 328 Recueil des Cours 9, 78–79.

[21] Kronke (n 20) 368; Robert Ahdieh, 'Making Markets: Network Effects and the Role of Law in the Creation of Strong Securities Markets' (2003) S Cal L Rev 277, 284, fn 20. See also the finding of the District Court that the admittedly domestic bonds of Argentina, governed by its domestic law, were offered outside Argentina (*NML Capital Ltd v The Republic of Argentina*, 2015 US Dist LEXIS 30625, 40–41 (SDNY 2015)).

ministry of finance or the debt management agency) for direct purchase, and the information is potentially targeting a wider audience than local residents.[22] In practice, domestic retail bonds (to be purchased directly by the investor, without the 'middle man') are traded through the online platforms of the sovereign debtor (most prominently, in Italy).[23]

4.15 It is true that certain countries have a system of primary dealers who have the right to participate in sovereign bond auctions to the exclusion of other (foreign) participants.[24] Yet, in other jurisdictions, primary dealers may be foreign banks or financial institutions.[25] Bypassing the auction format, and instigated by the worsening of the issuing environment brought on by the financial crisis of 2008, some States also use syndication and private placement as a selling technique.[26] Certain States permit the direct purchase of their bonds on such international trading systems as Euroclear.[27] All of this opens the holdings of domestic debt to foreigners.

4.16 The *Norwegian Loans Case*, brought before the International Court of Justice (ICJ), highlights the confusion that may arise in defining the market of sovereign bonds.[28] Espousing the claims of French nationals, France argued that the bonds issued by Norway were clearly international and thus evaded the application of the domestic legislation of Norway which purported to nullify the gold clauses contained in the bonds. In its pleadings, France relied upon several characteristics of Norwegian bonds to establish their international character: the bonds

[22] Order no 60 of the Ministry of Finance of the Russian Federation on the Emission of Internal Bonds of the Russian Federation on International Capital Markets of Bonds, 25 February 2011.

[23] The purchase of retail bonds, although limited in practice, can nevertheless be an attractive option for foreign creditors, for two reasons: (1) retail bonds, generally purchased by domestic retail bondholders, are unlikely to be restructured for the reasons of domestic politics; (2) foreign creditors can easily construct a blocking position in the relatively small-scale issue of retail bonds.

[24] Hans Blommestein, 'Responding to the Crisis: Changes in OECD Primary Market Procedures and Portfolio Risk Management' (2009) 2 OECD Journal: Financial Market Trends, 12. In the EU, only thirteen Member States use the system of primary dealer (Economic and Financial Committee, 'Progress Report on Primary Dealership in EU Public Debt Management' (2000), EFC/ECFIN/665/00-En-fin, 1).

[25] Jakob de Haan, Sander Oosterloo, and Dirk Schoenmaker, *Financial Markets and Institutions: A European Perspective* (2012) 143.

[26] Hans Blommestein, 'Responding to the Crisis: Changes in OECD Primary Market Procedures and Portfolio Risk Management' (2009) 2 OECD Journal: Financial Market Trends, 3–8; Mark De Broeck and Anastasia Guscina, 'Government Debt Issuance in the Euro Area: The Impact of the Financial Crisis' (2010) IMF Working Paper WP/11/21, 9–10.

[27] Scott Rose, 'Russia Sees Risks as Foreigners Amass Government Ruble Bonds' (26 July 2013) Bloomberg News.

[28] *Norwegian Loans Case (France v Norway)*, 1957 ICJ Rep 9.

were placed with beneficiary bondholders in several jurisdictions and were drafted in different languages, the repayment of the debt was stipulated in various optional currencies and jurisdictions, the bonds were listed on stock exchanges located in several jurisdictions, and the holders of the bonds were almost exclusively foreign.[29] In its counter-memorial, Norway pursued the argument that the bonds held by the French residents were in reality traded within the territory of Norway as evidenced by various criteria: the loan contracts with intermediary banks were concluded in Norway, drafted in Norwegian, denominated in Norwegian currency, and Norway always figured as one of the alternative jurisdictions of payment. Additionally, the identity of holders of bearer bonds was irrelevant.[30] The ICJ did not resolve this complex issue. Instead, it relied on the self-judging Declaration accepting the compulsory jurisdiction of the ICJ that left the determination of whether the dispute fell within the national jurisdiction to the Norwegian government.[31] This excluded the competence of the ICJ to hear the matter since Norway had maintained throughout the proceedings its reliance on the domestic character of the dispute.

The foregoing discussion shows that the dividing line between domestic and international bonds on the grounds of residence, currency, and place of marketing is extremely porous. In light of this, the fulcrum of the dichotomy remains the law governing the debt and the submission to local courts.[32] Or so it is argued. As for the jurisdiction of local courts, it is a misleading criterion in and of itself, given that choice of forum clauses are merely procedural.[33] Further, the multiplicity of jurisdictional grounds renders this factor somewhat dubious. **4.17**

Even the former factor—the application of the law of the sovereign debtor—is at least equivocal in international finance since sovereign bonds may lack a choice of law clause. Further discussion will demonstrate that **4.18**

[29] Mémoire Soumis par le Gouvernement de la République Française, 20 décembre 1955, 29–30; Réplique du Gouvernement Français, 20 février 1957, 386–89 (available at www.icj-cij.org).

[30] Contre-Mémoire du Gouvernement du Royaume de Norvège, 20 décembre 1956, 263 (available at www.icj-cij.org).

[31] *Norwegian Loans Case* (n 28) 23.

[32] UNCTAD, 'Domestic and External Public Debt in Developing Countries' (2008) UNCTAD Discussion Papers, 4–5; Cowan et al (n 15) 8; Carmen Reinhart and Kenneth Rogoff, *This Time Is Different: Eight Centuries of Financial Folly* (2011) 8 (subjection to national jurisdiction).

[33] *Abaclat and others v The Argentine Republic*, Decision on Jurisdiction and Admissibility of 4 August 2011, ICSID Case No ARB/07/5, para 379 (affirming the procedural character of choice of forum agreements).

the quasi-automatic application of the law of the sovereign debtor to its domestic debt is at best doubtful.

II. APPLICABILITY OF ROME I REGULATION

4.19 It is a common belief that sovereign issuers proceed on the assumption that local law implicitly governs all domestic debt.[34] However, it is suggested here that this general assumption often rests on an insecure foundation and ignores the conflict of laws rules applicable in the English (and other) courts. Assuming that sovereign debt litigation is brought before English courts, the common regime of the commercial conflict of laws, as embedded in the Rome I Regulation, would control the determination of the law governing domestic bonds.

4.20 Two threshold matters first need to be overcome to apply the Rome I Regulation. First, the Regulation applies exclusively to 'civil and commercial matters' (Art 1(1)). This has been discussed in Chapter 3 in respect of the Brussels Regulation and the same analysis is likely to apply to the Rome I Regulation (Recital 7).

4.21 Second, Art 1(1)(d) of the Rome I Regulation excludes 'negotiable instruments' from the scope of its application 'to the extent that the obligations under such other negotiable instruments arise out of their negotiable character'. Weber comments that bonds are not covered by the then Rome Convention (currently, the Rome I Regulation) as the issuance of bonds is excluded from the coverage of the Rome I Regulation, and instead regulated by the choice of law rules contained in the Bills of Exchange Act of 1882.[35] An entire line of English cases, discussed below, which applied common rules of private international law to the determination of the governing law of bonds defies this view. Arguably, Weber's view might hold true for bonds which serve as means of payment under a related contract and thus are subject to a special conflict of laws regime,[36] but the exclusion would not apply to those bonds which are autonomous agreements for the borrowing of money, such as sovereign bonds. Further, the Giuliano–Lagarde Report clarified that '[n]either the contracts pursuant to which such [negotiable] instruments are issued nor contracts for the

[34] Georges Delaume, *Legal Aspects of International Lending and Economic Development Agreements* (1967) 92; ILA, 'The Hague Conference Report: Sovereign Insolvency Study Group' (2010b) 9.

[35] Stefan Weber, 'The Law Applicable to Bonds' in Hans van Houtte (ed), *The Law of Cross-Border Securities Transactions* (1999) 31.

[36] On which see Peter Cresswell, William Blair, and Philip Wood (eds), *Butterworths Encyclopaedia of Banking Law* (2013) F-228, 251.

purchase and sale of such instruments are excluded' from the coverage of the Rome I Regulation.[37] Additionally, Plender and Wilderspin argue that 'negotiable' in the sense of the Rome I Regulation implies the ability to transfer a title to property, for instance, bills of lading in respect of goods shipped.[38] Be that as it may, this book will not address this controversy since obligations specific to the negotiable character of negotiable instruments, for instance, the bearer's right to bring an action against the drawer irrespective of contractual obligation,[39] or the acquisition of title to a bond free from set-offs and defects in title,[40] are outside the ambit of this book.

1. The Law Applicable under Art 4(1)(b)

Having established the applicability of the Rome I Regulation, the general rule contained therein is that contracts shall be governed by the law of the country where the party required to effect the characteristic performance of the contract has his habitual residence at the time of the conclusion of the contract (Arts 4(2) and 19(3) of the Rome I Regulation).[41] The Court of Justice in *Kareda v Benkö* established that a credit agreement is a type of service, albeit under the Brussels Regulation. Under Art 4(1)(b), in contracts for the provision of services, the law that applies is the law of the service provider. Similarly, the Court of Justice in *Kareda v Benkö* established that the credit institution provides the characteristic performance, since the borrower's obligation to repay that sum is derivative from the performance of the service by the lender.[42] Unless and until the lender releases the funds, the borrower would not be under an obligation to reimburse the debt.[43] **4.22**

Even if the bonds are not services within the meaning of Art 4(1)(b), it seems that in any case the lender/bondholder provides the characteristic **4.23**

[37] Giuliano–Lagarde Explanatory Report to the Rome Convention on the Law Applicable on Contractual Obligations [1980] OJ C 282/1, 11.

[38] Richard Plender and Michael Wilderspin, *The European Private International Law of Obligations* (2009) 110. For a contrary view arguing that bonds are indeed negotiable instruments, see Ravi Tennekoon, *The Law and Regulation of International Finance* (1991) 19, 164–65.

[39] Plender and Wilderspin (n 38) 110.

[40] Philip Wood, *Conflict of Laws and International Finance* (2007) para 2-020.

[41] Compare the more flexible conflict of laws methodology employed by the US courts in the context of sovereign bonds (*Salah Turkmani v The Republic of Bolivia*, 193 F Supp 2d 165, 177 (DDC 2002)).

[42] *Kareda v Benkö*, Case C-249/16, ECLI:EU:C:2017:472. See also Kronke (n 20) 349. For a contrary view, see Pietro Franzina, 'Sovereign Bonds and the Conflict of Laws: A European Perspective' in Pasquale Nappi et al (eds), *Studi in onore di Luigi Costato* (2013) 11.

[43] For a similar reasoning in the context of supply and promotion of products, see *Print Concept v GEW* [2002] CLC 352.

performance. The editors of *Dicey, Morris & Collins*, when examining the law applicable to a loan contract between a bank and a customer, suggest that the bank provides the characteristic performance and the law of the lender bank should thus govern the loan contract.[44]

4.24 In *Molton Street Capital LLP v Shooters Hill Capital Partners LLP*, a US broker dealer sold bonds issued in the US by a third party to a dealer located in the UK. It was conceded that in a contract for the sale of bonds, the seller of the bonds was the characteristic performer.[45] Here, one needs to draw a distinction between two situations. One is where the debtor issues bonds to investors. In this case, the subscribing investors provide a 'service' by lending the funds. In the second scenario, which was the case in *Molton*, a trader sells the bonds to the wider public. The trader is not the person raising funds, but he is merely an intermediary selling a chose in action to the investors. In this case, the seller of the bonds is the person providing the characteristic performance under Art 4(1)(a). In light of this distinction, the concession made in *Molton* should only be taken to apply to the second scenario. This dichotomy allows us to reconcile *Molton* with the earlier authorities that the lender is the characteristic performer.

4.25 The resulting conclusion is that the law of the habitual residence of the (initial) bondholder (usually, the financial intermediary who purchases the bonds) governs the contractual aspects as between the sovereign and the bondholder.[46] This challenges the conventional assumption that the law of the sovereign debtor applies to domestic bonds in all cases. By that, it might awaken the sleeping giant in the sense that sovereign bonds might be governed by a law other than that of the sovereign debtor notwithstanding the latter's assumptions.

4.26 Although principle suggests that the law of the creditor governs the rights and obligations under sovereign bonds, in practical terms, there are a number of complications to consider. As mentioned above, it is commonplace for domestic bonds to be subscribed to by lenders resident in various jurisdictions. To apply the law of the habitual residence of the lender would result in the undesirable consequence of submitting the domestic debt to a mosaic of governing laws of each and every lender.[47] This would

[44] Lord Collins of Mapesbury et al (eds), *Dicey, Morris & Collins on the Conflict of Laws*, vol 2 (2012) 2057; Peter Kaye, *The New Private International Law of the European Community* (1993) 182.

[45] [2015] EWHC 3419 (Comm), para 92.

[46] See, eg, *Haeger & Schmidt GmbH v Mutuelles du Mans Assurances IARD (MMA IARD)*, Case C-305/13, ECLI:EU:C:2014:2320, paras 43–51 (finding that when the first forwarding agent has been replaced by the second forwarding agent, the court has to apply the law of habitual residence of the first forwarding agent).

[47] Megliani (n 1) 198–99.

give rise to a situation where, as a function of the habitual residence of the creditor, the sovereign debtor might be subject to different legal systems and consequently, varying levels of obligations.

This drawback becomes all the more acute in collective actions (class actions, representative actions), where a group of bondholders, conceivably from various jurisdictions, are grouped in one single action. In such a scenario, the court seised of the dispute would face a diversity of laws as a function of the variety of habitual residences of the creditors in a collective action. To apply the law of the defendant sovereign, as the law manifestly more closely connected to the dispute, is unlikely to occur in collective actions.[48] Nonetheless, the multiplicity of laws is not necessarily an impediment to a collective action—one case management solution available to the court would be to form subgroups of claimants subject to a single law,[49] or to locate common issues that although subject to different law may be treated functionally alike.[50] **4.27**

To deal with this ominous legal conundrum on a more principled basis, commentators put forward alternative connecting factors. It has been contended that the most appropriate connecting factor for private loans is the law of the lead (manager) bank. If loans are advanced by more than one leading manager, then the law of one or more of the lead managers which happens to coincide with the law of the fiscal agent or trustee would apply.[51] The inadequacy of this solution for domestic bonds lies in the fact that the agent of the sovereign debtor will often be somewhat linked to or indissociable from the sovereign debtor (such as the central bank of the debtor), rather than to the bondholders who provide the characteristic performance. Of course, the aforesaid suggestions are merely *de lege ferenda* solutions to a situation that is unsatisfactory from a practical point of view. **4.28**

Nevertheless, there is no denying that subjecting the sovereign debt to one single law may be a legitimate pursuit since it increases predictability and precludes the subjection of the State to mutually conflicting obligations. The line of reasoning of some old judgments, although few and far **4.29**

[48] Eva Lein, 'Jurisdiction and Applicable Law in Cross-Border Mass Litigation' in Fausto Pocar, Ilaria Viarengo, and Francesca Clara Villata (eds), *Recasting Brussels I* (2012) 169–70; Linda Silberman, 'The Role of Choice of Law in National Class Actions' (2007–08) 156 U Pa L Rev 2001, 2022–24, 2031; Astrid Stadler, 'Conflicts of Laws in Multinational Collective Actions—A Judicial Nightmare?' in Duncan Fairgrieve and Eva Lein (eds), *Extraterritoriality and Collective Redress* (2012) 207–08.

[49] Stadler (n 48) 208, 212–13; Lein (n 48) 171.

[50] Stadler (n 48) 208, 211.

[51] André Jacquemont, *L'Emission des emprunts euro-obligataires* (1976) 176; Megliani (n 1) 196–97.

between, favours the submission of domestic bonds to one single law.[52] This can be achieved by applying the escape clause in Art 4(3).

2. Escape Clause (Art 4(3))

4.30 Under Art 4(3), the governing law of the contract may be displaced, provided that some other law 'is manifestly more closely connected' to the bonds. The threshold is avowedly set very high. The court in *Molton Street Capital LLP v Shooters Hill Capital Partners LLP* stressed that the Rome I Regulation has raised the threshold under Art 4(3):

> The text and architecture of Article 4 of the Rome I Regulation is very different from that of the Rome Convention. In particular, the test is no longer expressed as one of closest connection; the test is that contained in the rules set out in Articles 4.1 and 4.2, which are no longer expressed as presumptions or as being subject to the closest connection test; and the closest connection test has become an 'escape clause' to be applied only where it is clear that the connection is manifestly closer to a country other than that dictated by the tests in Articles 4.1 and 4.2 so that they are to be disregarded. The word 'clear' reflects what the ECJ had already said was the effect of Article 4.5 of the Rome Convention in the Interfrigo case, but the word 'manifestly' suggests a more stringent standard than before, as does the elevation of the criteria in Articles 4.1 and 4.2 to tests from mere presumptions of closest connection. The new language and structure suggests a higher threshold, which requires that the cumulative weight of the factors connecting the contract to another country must clearly and decisively outweigh the desideratum of certainty in applying the relevant test in Article 4.1 or 4.2.[53]

4.31 There are potentially three legal systems that may satisfy the requirement of manifestly more close connection: the law of the sovereign debtor, the law of the market of issuance, and the law of the majority of bondholders. These are addressed in turn.

Law of the Sovereign Debtor

4.32 Historically, the law of the sovereign debtor applied as a matter of a presumption. An excursus into the history of this presumption is necessary

[52] *Smith v Weguelin* (1869) LR 8 Eq 198, 213 (holding that 'the same law should regulate the whole' of loan obligations contracted by the sovereign); *Goodwin v Robarts* (1876) 1 App Cas 476, 495; PCIJ, *Serbian Loans Case*, Ser A, No 21 (1929), 42 (attempting to determine a single law to govern the network of relations between various bondholders and the sovereign debtor, implicitly rejecting the possibility of subjecting the bonds to diverse laws). See also the decision of the Swedish Supreme Court in *Skandia Insurance Company Ltd v Swedish National Debt Office* (1937) 18 BYBIL 215, 216.

[53] [2015] EWHC 3419 (Comm), para 94.

before deciding whether and when the law of the sovereign debtor may be manifestly more closely connected with the bonds.

Historical Presumption of Application of the Law of the Sovereign Debtor

It was often contended in the past that private contracts with the sovereign, both with the central government and local authorities,[54] are subject to the rebuttable presumption that the law of the State governs the contract between a State and a private person.[55] Under this paradigm, financial instruments issued by the State in its territory are commonly believed to be 'creatures' of the law of that State.[56] **4.33**

The Permanent Court of International Justice (PCIJ) in *Serbian and Brazilian Loans* applied the presumption to the bonds issued by the Serbian and Brazilian governments and held that the debt contracted by Serbia and Brazil was subject to Serbian and Brazilian laws, respectively (although, French law applied to the determination of the currency of payment). The PCIJ reasoned that the sovereign debtor could not be presumed to subject its obligations to any law other than its own.[57] **4.34**

The presumption, in principle rebuttable, was not rebutted on the facts of the case. The following array of factors strongly pointed towards the law of sovereign debtor: **4.35**

- the debt was issued under special laws that laid down conditions relating to the bonds;
- these laws were cited in the bonds;

[54] *Mount Albert Borough Council v Australasian Temperance and General Mutual Life Assurance Society* [1938] AC 224, 239.

[55] Borchard (n 18) 67; FA Mann, 'The Proper Law of Contracts Concluded by International Persons' in FA Mann, *Studies in International Law* (1973), 220; Jean-Flavien Lalive, 'Recent Version: Abrogation or Alteration of an Economic Development Agreement between a State and a Private Foreign Party' (1961–62) 17 Bus Law 434, 436, fn 7; *Smith v Weguelin* (1869) LR 8 Eq 198, 213; *Skandia Insurance Company Ltd* (n 52) 215, 216; Conseil d'Etat 28 novembre 1958, 'Dame Langlois' (1960) Clunet 444; *Gouvernement Ottoman c. Comptoir d'escompte et consorts*, Trib civ de la Seine, 3 mars 1875 (1877) Sirey 25.

[56] US–Mexican General Claims Commission, *George Cook v United Mexican States* (1927) RSA IV 213, 215.

[57] Ser A, No 21 (1929), 42, No 22 (1929), 121. See also Separate Opinion of Judge Sir Hersch Lauterpacht in the *Case of Certain Norwegians Loans (France v Norway)* (1957) ICJ Rep 37; Separate Opinion of Abdel Badawi in the *Case of Certain Norwegians Loans (France v Norway)* (1957) ICJ Rep 30; *Saudi Arabia v Aramco* (1963) 27 ILR 117, 167.

- the bonds were bearer bonds which presupposed that the identity of their holders was irrelevant and the individuality of the issuer only was fixed and unchangeable;
- all creditors were not located in one single State and the bonds were consequently not issued in one single State; and
- even if the entire sovereign debt were to be entirely issued in a single State, that would not suffice to refute the conclusion that the law of the sovereign governed the debt given that the payments of principal and interest were made in diverse States.

4.36 Judge de Bustamante in his Dissenting Opinion explained the presumption of applying the law of the sovereign debtor on the ground that sovereign loans were in essence contracts of adhesion.[58] This rationale is somewhat ill-considered. Arguably, the fact that sovereign bonds were contracts of adhesion should lead to the opposite conclusion.[59] At the stage of negotiations and drafting, private subscribers of sovereign bonds may often be bereft of the opportunity to negotiate the terms of the contract. Due to the operation of the principle of contract interpretation *contra proferentem*, expressly referred to in the decision of the PCIJ in *Brazilian Loans*,[60] the adhesive nature of sovereign bonds should have been construed as a factor militating against the law of the sovereign debtor.

4.37 The rationale of *Serbian and Brazilian Loans* was echoed in a 1950 judgment of the Privy Council in *Bonython v Commonwealth Australia*.[61] First, the Board determined that if the loan agreement concluded with the sovereign debtor was denominated in the currency of the sovereign debtor, the implication would be—other factors being considered—that the proper law of the contract is the law of the sovereign debtor.

4.38 It is suggested here that the conclusion of the Privy Council is counter-intuitive to the economic underpinnings of the issuance of sovereign bonds in local currency. In the late 1990s, the economists Eichengreen, Hausmann, and Panizza advanced the concept of 'original sin'—the general inability of most States to borrow abroad in their own currency irrespective of their

[58] Dissenting Opinion in the *Brazilian Loans Case*, Ser A, No 21 (1929) 130.

[59] Henry Batiffol, *Les Conflits de lois en matière de contrats* (1938) 200–02 (albeit for private contracts).

[60] Ser A, No 21 (1929), 114. Provided, of course, that the doctrine has any role to play in debt contracts (William Bratton, 'The Interpretation of Contracts Governing Corporate Debt Relationships' (1983–84) 5 Cardozo L Rev 371, 380–81). Sovereign bonds are not strictly speaking contracts of adhesion, given that the underwriters would generally negotiate the terms and conditions of sovereign bonds.

[61] [1951] AC 201.

'credit history'.[62] The implication is that developing States are inclined to develop domestic (internal) markets for bonds denominated in local currency,[63] to deal with insufficient demand for bonds denominated in their own currency and issued abroad and also to address currency mismatches arising out of borrowings in foreign currency.[64] The issuance of bonds in local currency is thus merely a reflection of economic realities and practicality and it ought not to be counted as a major connecting factor.

Albeit in a commercial context not involving a sovereign, Lord Radcliffe correctly noted that there is not necessarily a correlation between the currency of the obligation and the proper law of the contract.[65] No apparent reason exists to reach a different conclusion for the bonds of a sovereign debtor. The choice of currency of sovereign bonds may simply be tied to considerations of currency mismatches, balance of payments, desire to de-dollarise the economy, and more broadly, with other political and economic factors.[66] **4.39**

The Privy Council in *Bonython v Commonwealth of Australia* then stated more broadly that if the sovereign debtor was a party to a contract that would be of great, if not decisive, weight in determining the proper law of the contract[67]—a classical expression of the presumption of the application **4.40**

[62] Barry Eichengreen and Ricardo Hausmann, 'Exchange Rates and Financial Fragility' (1999) NBER Working Paper 7418; Barry Eichengreen, Ricardo Hausmann, and Ugo Panizza, 'Currency Mismatches, Debt Intolerance and Original Sin: Why They Are Not the Same and Why It Matters' (2003) NBER Working Paper 10036; Ricardo Hausmann and Ugo Panizza, 'Redemption or Abstinence? Original Sin, Currency Mismatches and Counter-Cyclical Policies in the New Millennium' (2010) CID Working Paper No 194.

[63] Barry Eichengreen, Ricardo Hausmann, and Ugo Panizza, 'Original Sin: The Pain, the Mystery, and the Road to Redemption' (2002) Paper prepared for the conference Currency and Maturity Matchmaking: Redeeming Debt from Original Sin 15; BIS 'The Development of Bond Markets in Emerging Economies' (2001) BIS Paper No 11; IMF, 'Local Securities and Derivatives Markets in Emerging Markets: Selected Policy Issues' (2003) IMF Financial Markets Quarterly.

[64] Oliver Bush, Katie Farrant, and Michelle Weight, 'Reform of the International Monetary and Financial System' (2011) Bank of England Financial Stability Paper No 13, 17.

[65] *Re United Railways of Havana and Regla Warehouses Ltd* [1961] AC 1007, 1060. For a contrary view, see Julius Weigert, *The Abrogation of Gold-Clauses in International Loans and the Conflict of Laws* (1940) 5–7.

[66] On diverse factors affecting the composition of government debt, see Allan Drazen, 'Towards a Political–Economic Theory of Domestic Debt' (1997) NBER Working Paper 5890; Peter Diamond, 'National Debt in a Neoclassical Growth Model' (1965) 55(5) Am Econ Rev 1126; Eduardo Levy Yeyati, 'Dollars, Debt, and International Financial Institutions: Dedollarizing Multilateral Lending' (2007) 21(1) World Bank Economic Review 21.

[67] For *dicta* that might be read in the same way, see *Smith v Weguelin* (1869) LR 8 Eq 198, 213; *Goodwin v Robarts* (1876) 1 AC 476, 494. *Rex v International Trustee for the Protection of Bondholders* [1937] AC 500, 566 rejected such an extensive reading of these cases.

of the law of the sovereign. Conversely, in the case *Rex v International Trustee for the Protection of Bondholders A.G.*,[68] decided thirteen years earlier, the House of Lords underplayed the status of the sovereign in determining the governing law of sovereign bonds. The dispute arose in relation to the bonds issued by the UK government in New York. Following the issuance of the bonds, the US Congress passed a general piece of legislation repealing gold clauses contained in bonds. The crux of the case was thus the identification of the law governing the contracts: were New York law to be found to govern British bonds, it would substantially alleviate the financial obligations of the UK government through the abrogation of gold clauses. The King's Bench and the Court of Appeal decided that because the UK government was a party to the contract, the bonds were governed by English law despite all the connecting factors to the US (issuance in the US territory, denomination of the bonds in US currency, the principal location of payments in New York based on a value estimated by reference to US coins, and bonds being secured by a pledge agreement with a US bank).

4.41 The House of Lords reversed the judgment of the Court of Appeal holding that New York law governed the bonds. What was crucial in the reasoning of the Law Lords was that common conflict of laws principles governing the determination of the law applicable to contracts were applicable with equal force to the contracts to which the sovereign was a party. The court was persuaded that the fact the sovereign was a party to the contract carried great weight, but it was not decisive and was only one factor in assessing the proper law of the contract. Upon the assessment of all the factors at hand, the House of Lords came to the conclusion that New York law governed the bonds issued by the UK government.

4.42 A certain logical discrepancy is discernible between the two cases. In *Rex*, the House of Lords stated that the fact the State is a party to the contract carries great weight, but is not conclusive. Instead, it is merely a factor in determining the proper law of bonds, whereas in *Bonython*, the Privy Council acknowledged that the very same fact had great weight, 'if not decisive'.

4.43 It has been suggested that the difference between *Rex* and *Bonython* (and *Serbian and Brazilian Loans*) can best be explained by the fact that in the former case, sovereign bonds were issued in a single country which lent itself more easily to the proper law of the contract. Whereas in the latter cases, the bonds were issued in more than one country, giving credence to

[68] [1937] AC 500.

the submission of the bonds to the law of the debtor as a common denominator.[69] Additionally, most connecting factors in *Rex* pointed towards the law of the US. By contrast, in the *Serbian and Brazilian Loans* cases, the presumption of the application of the law of the sovereign debtor was strongly supported by other important indices.[70]

Yet, the reasons for distinguishing between the two decisions are more profound than these factors. The House of Lords in its decision in *Rex* was clearly guided by the progressive argument that sovereign bonds should be governed by the common rules for determining the applicable law (although a cynic would claim that the House of Lords rendered a political decision in favour of the UK government and the Treasury). The ruling of the House of Lords in *Rex* is commercially sound since submitting sovereign bonds to the law of the sovereign debtor and leaving the bondholders to the mercy of the sovereign debtor might often be disquieting.[71] Delaume, criticising the outdated decision of the PCIJ in *Serbian and Brazilian Loans*, argued that the sovereign character of the borrower does not warrant subjecting sovereign bonds to the law of the sovereign debtor.[72] **4.44**

Subjecting sovereign debt contracts to the law of the sovereign debtor, as a matter of presumption albeit rebuttable, appears anachronistic. Properly understood, sovereign bonds are to be subjected to the same common conflict of laws rules as any other commercial contracts. Both English[73] and foreign[74] progressive case law follows this direction by applying the common choice of law rules to sovereign borrowing. **4.45**

Formerly, the presumption in favour of the application of the law of the sovereign debtor was heavily buttressed by the fact that the debt of the **4.46**

[69] Note, 'Decisions of National Tribunals involving Points of Public or Private International Law' (1937) 18 BYBIL 210, 218; Wilfred Jenks, 'The Authority in English Courts of Decisions of the Permanent Court of International Justice' (1939) 20 BYBIL 1, 6.

[70] Jenks (n 69) 6.

[71] Note, 'Conflict of Laws and the Gold Clause in Foreign Government Bonds' (1937) 46(5) Yale LJ 891, 895; Bruno Zanghirati, 'Sovereign Indebtedness: The Complex Relations between Banks and States' (1896–97) 7 IYBIL 133, 145.

[72] Delaume (n 34) 101–02. See also Jean-Flavien Lalive, 'Unilateral Alteration or Abrogation by either Party to a Contract between a State and a Foreign National' in Symposium on the Rights and Duties of Foreigners in the Conduct of Industrial and Commercial Operations Abroad, *Rights and Duties of Private Investors Abroad* (1965) 271; Cresswell et al (n 36) F-305. Contra see Georges Sausser-Hall, 'La clause-or dans les contrats publics et privés' (1937) 60 Recueil des Cours 651, 754.

[73] *The Metamorphosis* [1953] 1 WLR 543, 547.

[74] George van Hecke, *Problèmes juridiques des emprunts internationaux* (1964) 75–76 (citing Swedish, Austrian, and Norwegian cases).

sovereign debtor could only be adjudicated in the courts of the sovereign debtor due to the operation of the rules of State immunity. This point strongly implied the application of the law of the sovereign debtor to its debt.[75] However, as the dilution of the absolute sovereign immunity has evidenced, the realities of the globalised world and the current climate of opinion are opposed to such a facile presumption of subjecting domestic debt to the volatility of the whims of the law of the sovereign debtor.

The Law of the Sovereign Debtor under Art 4(3)

4.47 Although the presumption of applying the law of the sovereign debtor is a relic of the past, it remains to be seen whether, on a thorough analysis of all relevant connecting factors, the old presumption may return through the back door of the 'manifestly more closely' connection.

4.48 The application of the law of the sovereign debtor has the undeniable advantage of assembling the entire sovereign debt under the umbrella of one single legal system.

4.49 In evaluating the law manifestly more closely connected to the domestic debt, the following factors, in addition to the ones referred to in the *Serbian and Brazilian Loans* cases above, might give cause to favour the law of the sovereign debtor:

- the need to observe the sovereign's regulatory requirements;
- the habitual residence of beneficial bondholders;[76]
- the language of the bonds which will almost invariably be the language of the sovereign debtor, though this latter does not carry much weight,[77]
- the currency; and
- the place of agents and other indicia depending on the circumstances of the particular case.[78]

4.50 On the other hand, in cases when a foreign party subscribes to the domestic debt of the sovereign debtor, several elements of the transaction tend to be foreign. If the residence of bondholders is outside the territory of the sovereign debtor, the funds are likely to flow from the local banks of bondholders. Furthermore, the fiscal or paying agent of the sovereign debtor

[75] Schmitthoff (n 12) 192–93.

[76] *Haeger & Schmidt GmbH v Mutuelles du Mans Assurances IARD (MMA IARD)*, Case C-305/13, ECLI:EU:C:2014:2320, paras 43–51 (finding that the habitual residence of the second forwarding agent should be taken into account in locating the manifestly more closely connected law).

[77] Delaume (n 34) 91. But the language of the contract might not carry great weight.

[78] Davidson Sommers, Aaron Broches, and Georges Delaume, 'Conflict Avoidance in International Loans and Monetary Agreements' (1956) 21 L & Contemp Prob 463, 472.

may make the payments of interests over the bonds to the foreign bondholder's foreign bank account, or else to a clearing system which might be either Clearstream Banking (Luxembourg) or Euroclear Bank (Belgium) even for domestic bonds.

An argument, which clearly resonated with the PCIJ judges in *Serbian and Brazilian Loans*, concerned the bearer character of the bonds issued by the sovereign. The PCIJ held that the identity of holders of bearer bonds was volatile in that the bonds were easily tradable in the secondary market of sovereign bonds. The only identity that was established and definite was that of the sovereign debtor. In the modern settings of private international law, the argument of the volatility of the identity of bondholders can be easily dispensed with. Under Art 19 of the Rome I Regulation, the relevant point in time for the determination of the governing law is that of the time of the conclusion of the contract (and, accordingly, the trading on the secondary market carries no import). **4.51**

If one views all the connecting factors from a distance, commercial reason or commercial significance is the benchmark against which any connecting factor should be measured for the purposes of applying the escape clause under Art 4(3) of the Rome I Regulation.[79] The benchmark, however, cannot easily be applied in the sovereign debt context: how can a State's acts be measured as against their commercial significance if they are, to varying degrees, dictated by the political–economic considerations of a sovereign? Similarly, it might be too far-fetched to say that some connecting factor should be taken into account as commercially significant—for instance, the issuance of bonds under a statute, when it is mandated by the national rules of the sovereign debtor. Such factors denote considerations alien to the commercial nature of bonds and are largely incomparable to such commercially significant connections as the domicile of foreign creditors and the place of repayment of the debt. **4.52**

This shows that objective connecting factors in a sovereign context, in their pure and unbent form, do not carry the same commercial significance. Given the specificity of the sector, fact- and context-specific interpretation of objective factors might be called for. It is true that certain objective connecting factors, which translate into reality the political–economic considerations of the sovereign debtor, may link the contract with the local law of the sovereign debtor. **4.53**

For example, the issuance of bonds under a statute, and having express references to the statute in the bonds as was the case in the *Serbian and* **4.54**

[79] Richard Fentiman, *International Commercial Litigation* (2015) 210–14.

Brazilian Loans cases, may seem a factor pointing in favour of the law of the sovereign debtor.[80] Arguably, it could evidence an implied intention to submit the bonds to the law of the sovereign debtor (Art 3(1) of the Rome I Regulation). While not absolute,[81] this connecting factor at hand can be subject to other, equally reasonable interpretations. First, the citation of a statute in the text of the bonds may merely act as incorporating terms and conditions into the contractual arrangement entered into between the government and private creditors. Thus, in *Perry v United States*, the bonds issued by the US referred to US circulars 'for a statement of the further rights of the holders of bonds of said series'.[82] Second, the reference to a statute in the text of bond documents often indicates the legitimacy and legality of the issuance of bonds under the constitutional regime of the sovereign,[83] and does not necessarily imply that the parties implicitly have chosen the law of the sovereign debtor. Domestically, many governments have a limitation over the amount of the debt that they may borrow.[84] This is all the more evident in the practice of those States that guarantee the debt of foreign States: by the operation of their constitutional provisions, States wishing to guarantee loans issued by a foreign State in the territory of the former are compelled to pass statutes authorising the assumption of liability over foreign States' bonds.[85]

4.55 The argument sketched here does not deal with the scenario where the sovereign debtor, in accordance with its law, is compelled to contract under its own law. If a sovereign debtor's local law precludes it from choosing a foreign law to govern its contracts, this should be a strong, though not decisive, factor for the submission of State contracts to its local law.[86] In such circumstances, the presumption of application of the law of the sovereign would be difficult to rebut.[87]

[80] *Mount Albert Borough Council v Australasian Temperance and General Mutual Life Assurance Society* [1938] AC 224, 239 (in respect of local authorities),

[81] *Apple Corps v Apple Computer* [2004] EWHC 768, para 63.

[82] *Perry v United States*, 294 US 330, 348 (1935).

[83] See, eg, Art 115(1) of the Basic Law of the Federal Republic of Germany on which see in detail, Paul Kirchhof, 'The Public Debt, Democratic Principles and the Rules of Law' in Detlev Dicke (ed), *Foreign Debts in the Present and a New International Economic Order* (1986) 339.

[84] See, eg, Treaty on Stability, Coordination and Governance in the Economic and Monetary Union, 2 March 2012.

[85] Borchard (n 18) 108.

[86] Cresswell et al (n 36) F-306.

[87] Derek Bowett, 'State Contracts with Aliens: Contemporary Developments on Compensation for Termination or Breach' (1988) 59 BYBIL 49, 53.

Law of the Market

The intuitive inclination, as expressed in the mainstream approach, would be to subject domestic bonds to the place of their marketing. Delaume suggests that the law applicable to bonds ought to be the law of the market where the funds were raised and repaid and where the contract was signed.[88] Likewise, Kronke argues for the submission of bonds to the law of the market of issuance as that would ensure uniform calculation and administration procedures, as well as equal treatment of private creditors.[89] **4.56**

After all, it may be reasonable to expect a foreigner purchasing bonds targeted to local residents in the territory of a sovereign to submit to the law of the latter sovereign. Indeed, it might come as a surprise to a sovereign that its bonds issued in its own territory purchased by foreigners would for some reason be subjected to a law other than its own municipal law. But one might wonder whether the place of issuance of domestic bonds is as easily discernible nowadays as it was in the early or mid-twentieth century. As shown above, the place of marketing of bonds is no longer so clear-cut as it used to be. **4.57**

On a more principled basis, as argued in Chapter 1, in commercial debt placements, the debtor is tied to bondholders through bilateral relations. With the bilateral nature of the sovereign bond issuance affirmed, the market of the issuance of bonds does not have the same unifying character and it could be discarded as a mere *lex loci contractus*, which is a discredited connecting factor and unlikely to sway the decision under Art 4(3). **4.58**

Against this, Batiffol has suggested that the issuance of bonds is a transaction that has a single purpose of raising economic resources and it should be treated as a unitary complex.[90] In his view, piecemeal solutions to the law governing various relations of the sovereign debtor with private creditors are incongruent with the anatomy of sovereign bonds. In spite of this, it remains true that the contract for purchase of bonds remains bilateral and autonomous for the purposes of ascertaining the applicable law. The unitary (or multilateral) character of sovereign bonds is only a shorthand for painting the process of the day-to-day raising of the funds by sovereigns. **4.59**

[88] Delaume (n 34) 86–88, 91, 100. [89] Kronke (n 20) 349–50.

[90] Henry Batiffol, *Les Conflits de lois en matière de contrats* (1938) 106–07 (arguing that the unity of the State's debt calls for the application of its own law).

4.60 It is not a coincidence that the only instance where the Rome I Regulation submits financial instruments to the law of the market relates to the trading in multilateral systems (including exchanges). Under Art 4(1)(h) of the Rome I Regulation, contracts traded in multilateral systems which bring together or facilitate the bringing together of multiple third-party buying and selling interests in financial instruments will be subject to the law of that multilateral system. Multilateral systems are highly organised and centralised markets that hinge on the application of a single governing law.[91] This explains the submission of such trading to the law of the place of exchange. Tellingly, the Rome I Regulation is silent in relation to other markets of financial instruments, including the markets for the placement of bonds.

Law of the Majority of Bondholders

4.61 Recitals 20 and 21 of the Rome I Regulation indicate that to locate the law manifestly more closely connected to the transaction, account should be taken, among other things, of other contracts that have a very close relationship with the contract at hand. The enquiry under Art 4(3) might thus consist in locating the law of the principal chunk of all bondholders (by the percentage of the bonds held), and then linking all other closely connected contracts to it.

4.62 Yet, the argument is misconceived. Sovereign bond contracts are not genuinely connected contracts since they can operate separately and individual bondholders can often bring claims separately from other bondholders, unless the contract provides otherwise.[92] More principally, the general principles of conflict of laws suggest that each particular relation of a sovereign debtor with a creditor should be governed by a separate law. The Privy Council in *Bonython v Commonwealth of Australia* disfavoured the search for one common law to govern the entirety of contractual relations between the sovereign and various bondholders.[93]

4.63 Returning to the concept of domestic bonds, one might wonder whether the distinction between domestic and external bonds remains feasible in light of the foregoing analysis in this chapter.[94] None of the criteria mentioned above which seemingly demarcate domestic bonds from external

[91] Michael McParland, *The Rome I Regulation on the Law Applicable to Contractual Obligations* (2015) 415.

[92] See Chapter 1. [93] [1951] AC 201, 222.

[94] Writers have since long noted the artificiality of the distinction (Anna Gelpern, 'Domestic Bonds, Credit Derivatives, and the Next Transformation of Sovereign Debt' (2008) 83 Chi-Kent L Rev 101, 133; UNCTAD (n 32) 5).

bonds appear to be stark enough to support the distinction. From a legal perspective, a more precise distinction lies simply between the bonds that contain a choice of law clause and those bonds that have omitted such a clause.

3. Mandatory Provisions

It is common practice for parties to a sovereign bond to select a foreign legal system (mostly English or New York law) to regulate their rights and obligations arising under the bonds. Yet, a variety of laws of the sovereign debtor may purport to apply both to the issuance of sovereign bonds and to the process and the content of sovereign debt restructurings. Examples abound: contract formalities, taxation, exchange regulations, currency controls, laws on moratorium, etc. **4.64**

This section will consider whether these laws could qualify as mandatory and trump the otherwise applicable governing law. It is clear that if the law, which applies to the contract is the law of the foreign sovereign, all the provisions mentioned will apply as part and parcel of the governing law. However, based on the evidence before it, the court may reach the conclusion that a law other than the law of the sovereign debtor applies to the bonds. In this case, certain provisions of the sovereign's legal system may still purport to apply. **4.65**

The preliminary issue to address is that bonds often provide that a declaration of moratorium constitutes an event of default. If the declaration of moratorium is found to be a mandatory provision, it is beyond doubt that the event of default clause may not in itself preclude the application of the declaration of moratorium, which qualifies as an overriding mandatory rule.[95] **4.66**

There are several ways to give effect to what may be loosely defined as foreign mandatory provisions. **4.67**

Article 3(3) of the Rome I Regulation

Article 3(3) of the Rome I Regulation provides for the application of non-derogable provisions: **4.68**

> Where all other elements relevant to the situation at the time of the choice are located in a country other than the country whose law has been chosen, the choice of the parties shall not prejudice the application of provisions of the law of that other country which cannot be derogated from by agreement.

[95] See Chapter 6, section II.

4.69 Article 3(3) allows the application of any provision, which cannot be derogated from by agreement and thus casts the net very widely. However, the non-derogable provisions apply only if all the elements are located in the jurisdiction whose non-derogable provision purports to apply.

4.70 The Court of Appeal in *Santander* examined the application of non-derogable provisions to interest rate swap agreements entered into between Portuguese public sector transport companies and a Portuguese bank, under ISDA Master Agreements subject to English law and jurisdiction. Portuguese transport companies sought to rely on various provisions of Portuguese law by claiming that they were non-derogable provisions within the meaning of Art 3(3). The court had to identify first whether all the elements relevant to the situation pointed towards Portugal. As a delineating exercise, Sir Terence Etherton MR drew a distinction between 'elements relevant to the situation' in Art 3(3) and 'close connection' in Art 4 of the Rome Convention and held that 'elements relevant to the situation' was a wider concept. It was not constrained exclusively to factors of a kind which connect the contract to a particular country for the purpose of identifying the proper law in the absence of an express choice.

4.71 The Master of the Rolls then approved the evaluation of the 'elements relevant to the situation', as conducted by the judge of first instance, Blair J. The judge referred to the following factors to find that Art 3(3) did not engage: the right to assign to a bank outside Portugal; the use of standard international documentation; the practical necessity for the relationship with a bank outside Portugal; the international nature of the swaps market in which the contracts were concluded; and the fact that back-to-back contracts were concluded with a bank outside Portugal in circumstances in which such hedging arrangements are routine.[96]

4.72 *Dexia* involved somewhat comparable swap agreements, albeit with a stronger link to Italy. There, only two of the elements from *Santander* were present, namely the use of standard international documentation, in the form of the ISDA Master Agreement, and the routine back-to-back contracts concluded with banks outside Italy. The Court of Appeal considered that notwithstanding this difference, each of these two factors was enough on its own to demonstrate an international and relevant element in the situation such that it was impossible to say that 'all elements (other than the choice of law) relevant to the situation' were located in Italy.[97]

[96] *Banco Santander Totta Sa v Companhia Carris De Ferro De Lisboa Sa* [2016] EWCA Civ 1267, paras 65–67.

[97] *Dexia Crediop SPA v Comune di Prato* [2017] EWCA Civ 428, paras 130–34.

4.73 In the context of sovereign bonds, one could imagine situations where the State, having agreed to the choice of English law, would seek to engage its domestic non-derogable provisions through the backdoor of Art 3(3). If the creditor is local to the sovereign debtor, the latter may argue that all the elements of the transaction are within its jurisdiction and therefore non-derogable provisions of its law apply notwithstanding a choice of English or New York law. However, it is likely that plentiful extraneous elements will exist to evade the application of Art 3(3). First, the claimant bondholder has subscribed to the bonds together with other bondholders, some of whom might be foreign. Second, the element of back-to-back contracts that was cited with approval in *Santander* and *Dexia* has a corollary in sovereign debt issuance, where the financial intermediary would often purchase the bonds only to resell them to beneficial investors in other jurisdictions. Third, while the Eurobonds documentation is not as uniform as the Master ISDA Agreement, it is at least arguable that by subscribing to Eurobonds, parties intended to insert an element of international finance into their transaction.

Overriding Mandatory Provisions

4.74 Overriding mandatory provisions under Art 9 of the Rome I Regulation is a narrower concept than non-derogable provisions and only comprises those provisions 'the respect for which is regarded as crucial by a country for safeguarding its public interests, such as its political, social or economic organisation, to such an extent that they are applicable to any situation falling within their scope, irrespective of the law otherwise applicable to the contract under this Regulation' (Art 9(1)).

4.75 Art 9(2) provides for the application of the overriding mandatory provisions of the forum. The application of those provisions is unlikely to be a common occurrence in sovereign debt litigation.

4.76 Sovereign debtors could avail themselves of Art 9(3) which allows for the application of the overriding mandatory provisions of a foreign State:

> Effect may be given to the overriding mandatory provisions of the law of the country where the obligations arising out of the contract have to be or have been performed, in so far as those overriding mandatory provisions render the performance of the contract unlawful. In considering whether to give effect to those provisions, regard shall be had to their nature and purpose and to the consequences of their application or non-application.

4.77 Assuming that the sovereign debtor's legislation qualifies as an overriding mandatory provision within the sense of Art 9(1), several conditions need to be satisfied to apply the overriding mandatory provisions of the sovereign debtor. First, a condition *sine qua non* for the application of overriding mandatory provisions is that the place of performance of obligations arising out of the contract has to be in the country whose overriding provisions purport to apply.

4.78 How is the place of performance determined? Harris reasons that the place of performance should be determined in two steps: (1) the place of performance provided in the contract and failing that; (2) it will be a matter for the autonomous meaning of the Regulation.[98] The editors of *Dicey, Morris & Collins* contend that the place of performance is to be determined by the governing law of the contract.[99] Bonomi considers that the place of performance is to be determined by the contractual agreement of parties, failing which the place of performance is to be determined by the governing law of the contract.[100] Another alternative is to apply the law of the forum to determine the place of performance of the obligation.

4.79 The agreement of parties to a contractually stipulated place of payment will be decisive. However, the ambiguity is whether it denotes the place of payment of funds to the State or the place of repayment by the State. Chapter 3 established that for the jurisdictional purposes, the place of provision of services is the place of payment only. However, for the purposes of applying overriding mandatory provisions, the court will need to identify the exact obligation affected by the mandatory provision and locate its place of performance. If the overriding mandatory provision seeks to affect the obligation to repay, then the court will need to identify the contractually stipulated place of repayment. That place in the sovereign bond documentation is often in the jurisdiction of creditors and therefore outside the territorial scope of the overriding mandatory provisions of the sovereign debtor.

4.80 If, however, the sovereign bond documentation is silent as to the place of payment/repayment, the place of performance can be determined in two ways: applying the autonomous meaning of the place of performance or leaving the matter to the governing law of the contract. In the first scenario, while there is no autonomous meaning under the Rome I Regulation, under Art 7(1) of the Brussels Regulation the place of provision of a credit agreement is the place where the lending institution has its registered office.[101] In light of the synergy between the two Regulations (Recital 7),

[98] Jonathan Harris, 'Mandatory Rules and Public Policy under the Rome I Regulation' in Franco Ferrari and Stefan Leible (eds), *The Rome I Regulation* (2009) 315.

[99] Lord Collins of Mapesbury et al (n 44), vol 2, para 32-096.

[100] Andrea Bonomi, 'Article 9' in Ulrich Magnus and Peter Mankowski, *Rome I Regulation: European Commentaries on Private International Law* (2017) 647.

[101] *Kareda v Benkö*, Case C-249/16, ECLI:EU:C:2017:472.

the position under the Brussels Regulation may be extrapolated to apply under the Rome I Regulation.

Yet, it is at least arguable that the autonomous definition in Art 7(1) developed for jurisdictional purposes may fail to reflect the nuances and purposes of Art 9(3) of the Rome I Regulation.[102] Unlike Art 7(1) of the Brussels Regulation, Art 9(3) does not refer to the place of performance of a single obligation (place of provision of services) but to the place of performance of 'the obligations arising out of the contract'. **4.81**

If, however, to determine the place of performance, the English court needs to apply the law governing the contract and that law happens to be English law, then the common law position is that the place of the obligation to pay is the place where the money is to be received.[103] In practice, the place where the money will be received will be outside the territory of the sovereign debtor and thus outside the reach of its overriding mandatory provisions. If, by contrast, the place of (re)payment is within the territory of the State, its mandatory provisions may apply.[104] This is consistent with the practice of several foreign jurisdictions, which in deciding on the enforcement of foreign exchange regulations, refused to apply any foreign exchange regulations when the payments were to be made outside the territory of the sovereign who adopted such rules.[105] **4.82**

The solution, both under the Brussels Regulation and English common law, has the advantage of predictability for credit institutions who may legitimately predict what overriding mandatory rules will apply over the course of performance of the contract. An additional benefit is that the State will not be tempted to frustrate or modify the contract by adopting mandatory rules in the vicinity of default. **4.83**

In a case decided under English common law, *Ispahani v Bank Melli Iran*,[106] the funds were withdrawn from Bangladesh in breach of Bangladeshi exchange controls and paid into a London bank account. At the interlocutory stage of proceedings, the Court of Appeal found that it was reasonably arguable that the acts were conducted in Bangladesh whose exchange regulations were breached. The case is unusual in that it may give effect to the mandatory provisions of the country of origin of payments and not **4.84**

[102] Bonomi, 'Article 9' in Magnus and Mankowski (n 100) 645–46.

[103] *Definitely Maybe Ltd v Lieberberg GmbH* [2001] 1 WLR 1745, para 4.

[104] *De Beéche v South American Stores (Gath & Chaves) Ltd* [1935] AC 148 (bills of exchange handed over in Chile where the controls were adopted).

[105] *Central Hanover Bank and Trust Company v Siemens& Halske A.G.*, 15 F Supp 927 (SDNY 1937); Martin Domke, *International Loans and the Conflict of Laws: A Comparative Survey of Recent Cases* (1937) 11–20.

[106] [1997] All ER (D) 124.

the place of final destination of payments. However, the case can be supported since the parties intended to commit or procure the commission of illegal acts in the territory of Bangladesh[107] within the meaning of *Foster v Driscoll*.[108]

4.85 Second, a foreign mandatory provision will only be given effect if it renders the performance of the contract unlawful. 'Unlawful' is wide enough to capture most overriding mandatory provisions in sovereign debt disputes, however the mere unenforceability of the contract may not qualify as 'unlawful'.[109]

4.86 Third, the exercise under Art 9(3) is discretionary. The court has to consider the nature and purpose of the foreign mandatory provisions, and the consequences of their application or non-application. The discretion of the court is multi-factored, but one thing that will not pass unnoticed is the attempt to avoid the obligations by relying on (retrospective) mandatory provisions. In *Eurobank Ergasias SA v Kalliroi Navigation Company Ltd*, the judge was particularly taken by the fact that the party relying on illegality 'was very keen to have the finance in place' arguably in breach of mandatory provisions.[110]

4.87 In parallel to Art 9(3) of the Rome I Regulation, issues of foreign illegality are also governed by English common law. The Court of Justice has confirmed that Art 9(3) does not preclude overriding mandatory provisions 'from being taken into account as a matter of fact, in so far as this is provided for by a substantive rule of the law that is applicable to the contract pursuant to the regulation'. Article 9(2) and (3) thus does not seek to supersede rules of substantive law which take into account foreign overriding mandatory provisions.[111] An example of such a national substantive law in English law is the line of cases following *Foster v Driscoll*[112] and *Regazzoni v KC Sethia*.[113]

4.88 Article 9(3) and English common law share certain traits. Principally, to trigger both regimes, the place of performance of obligations has to be in the country whose mandatory provisions purport to apply. Mandatory provisions of any other country cannot be applied or taken into account. Of course, the English courts are not bound to apply the autonomous

[107] Charles Proctor, *Mann on the Legal Aspect of Money* (2012) 451–52.

[108] [1929] 1 KB 470.

[109] Trevor Hartley, *International Commercial Litigation: Text, Cases and Materials on Private International Law* (2015) 672.

[110] [2015] EWHC 2377 (Comm), paras 38–40.

[111] *Republik Griechenland v Grigorios Nikiforidis*, Case C-135/15 [2016] ECR EU:C:2016:774.

[112] [1929] 1 KB 470.

[113] [1958] AC 301.

meaning of the place of performance when applying English substantive law and the place of performance will be determined by English law.

Unlike the discretionary test in Art 9(3), the common law provides for an almost automatic application of the foreign illegality laws. The English court need not engage in the analysis of the nature, purpose, and consequences of the application of foreign laws. This ostensibly mechanical application of foreign illegality laws explains why defendants would often resort to the common law provisions: the claimant may not defeat the operation of foreign illegality laws by seeking to affect the discretionary decision-making of the judge. **4.89**

Article VIII(2)(b) of the IMF Agreement

Article VIII(2)(b) of the Bretton Woods Agreement in effect gives effect to foreign exchange regulations of IMF Member States. It reads: **4.90**

> Exchange contracts which involve the currency of any member [of the International Monetary Fund] and which are contrary to the exchange control regulations of any member maintained or imposed consistently with this agreement shall be unenforceable in the territories of any member.

The first thing to note is that Art VIII(2)(b) does not supersede the English common law on illegality but merely supplements it.[114] However, it is open to debate whether Art VIII(2)(b) is a conflict of laws rule or a procedural mechanism which applies irrespective of the governing law of the contract or alternatively, if it is a rule of the governing law of the contract. It would be hard to imagine that Art VIII(2)(b) would be treated as part of the substantive provisions of a legal system.[115] Instead, each court is likely to apply it as a matter of its *lex fori*, irrespective of the governing law of the contract. In any case, Art 25 of the Rome I Regulation preserves the application of international conventions which lay down conflict of laws rules relating to contractual obligations. **4.91**

English courts have given a narrow construction to Art VIII of the IMF: 'exchange contracts' are nothing but contracts for exchange of currency.[116] US courts have also adopted a narrow interpretation of 'exchange **4.92**

[114] *Ispahani v Bank Melli Iran* [1997] All ER (D) 124. See also *Republic Griechenland v Grigorios Nikiforidis*, Case C-135/15, ECLI:EU:C:2016:774.

[115] Weber, 'The Law Applicable to Bonds' in van Houtte (n 35) 39.

[116] *Ispahani v Bank Melli Iran* [1997] All ER (D) 124; *Wilson, Smithett & Cope Ltd v Terruzzi* [1976] QB 683. In support of this position, see, eg, Lester Nurick, 'The IMF Articles of Agreement' in David Sassoon and Daniel Bradlow (eds), *Judicial Enforcement of International Debt Obligations* (1987) 107.

contracts'.[117] Thus, sovereign bonds, loans, deposits, and letters of creditors will not qualify as 'exchange contracts' within the meaning of Art VIII(2)(b). Further, Art VIII(2)(b) may not apply when the foreign exchange regulation regulates the currency of repayment in case of a restructuring and the creditor has the discretion to resort to a restructuring.[118]

4.93 By contrast, European jurisdictions have taken a more expansive approach to 'exchange contracts' to include all contracts that 'in any way affect a country's exchange resources', thereby potentially including international loan agreements in the definition of exchange contracts.[119]

117 *Libra Bank Ltd v Banco Nacional de Costa Rica*, 570 F Supp 870, 897 (SDNY 1983); *J. Zeevi & Sons, Ltd v Grindlays Bank (Uganda) Ltd*, 37 NY 2d 220 (NY 1975).

118 *Weston Banking v Turkiye Garanti Bankasi*, 57 NY 2d 315, 326 (1982).

119 George Weisz, Nancy Schwarzkopf, and Mimi Panitch, 'Selected Issues in Sovereign Debt Litigation' 12(1) U Pa J Intl Bus L 1 (1991), 1–2. In support of this position, see Dominique Carreau, 'Rapport du directeur d'études de la section française du centre' in Dominique Carreau and Malcolm Shaw (eds), *The External Debt* (1995) 22. But see Armin von Bogdandy and Mathias Goldmann, 'Sovereign Debt Restructurings as Exercises of International Public Authority: Towards a Decentralized Sovereign Insolvency Law' in Espósito Carlos, Li Yuefen, and Bohoslavsky Juan Pablo (eds), *Sovereign Financing and International Law: The UNCTAD Principles on Responsible Sovereign Lending and Borrowing* (2013) 63 (German courts do not accept the expansive interpretation of Art VIII).

5

Unilateral Modification of Sovereign Domestic-Law Bonds

I. INTRODUCTION

The unilateral modification of sovereign bonds has recently loomed large following the Greek sovereign debt restructuring of 2012. In the wake of a severe financial crisis, Greece sought to restructure its Greek law governed bonds, only to face the requirement of unanimous consent for the amendment of the terms of bonds and the lack of majority action clauses in the sovereign bond documentation. To ensure higher participation of bondholders in the restructuring, the Greek parliament passed the Greek Bondholders Act on 23 February 2012, which retroactively incorporated majority action clauses into the Greek law governed bonds. Under the majority action clause, two-thirds of the bondholders were given the power to amend the entire mass of Greek law governed bonds, provided there was a quorum of 50% of the face value of all the bonds.[1] The specificity of this majority action clause was that it applied across the entire mass of Greek sovereign bonds, and not bond by bond—a proviso which precluded individual bondholders from tactically blocking the restructuring in a single bond issue.[2] **5.01**

This manoeuvre was achievable because the absolute majority of Greek bonds (more than 85%) were governed by Greek law, and hence were within the reach of the Greek parliament. Although the retrospective inclusion of collective action clauses (CACs) caused considerable consternation in financial markets,[3] the restructuring was successfully completed. Old Greek law bonds were exchanged for new bonds which this time contained a choice of English law. As a matter of English law, the **5.02**

[1] Art 1(4) of the Rules of Amendment of Titles Issued or Guaranteed by the Hellenic Republic with Bondholders' Agreement, 23 February 2012.

[2] Jeromin Zettelmeyer, Christoph Trebesch, and Mitu Gulati, 'The Greek Debt Exchange: An Autopsy' (2013) 28 Econ Pol 513, 525.

[3] See, eg, Report of the IIF Joint Committee on Strengthening the Framework for Sovereign Debt Crisis Prevention and Resolution (2012) 14; Josiane Kremer and Lukanyo Mnyanda, 'Norway Oil Fund Rejected Greek Debt Swap, CEO Slyngstad Says' Bloomberg (16 March 2012).

inclusion of an English choice of law clause would in future insulate the bonds from unilateral changes of law by the Greek parliament.[4] Thus, in *National Bank of Greece and Athens v Metliss*, the House of Lords was adamant that a Greek moratorium act should not affect contractual relations governed by English law.[5] Conversely, in cases where the loans were subject to a foreign law, the English courts took the view that the rights and obligations under a loan agreement were the province of its governing law and would give effect to, among other things, foreign moratorium acts and foreign exchange regulations.[6]

5.03 The lesson to be learned from the Greek debt restructuring of 2012 is that in cases when the law of the borrowing State governs sovereign bonds, the State may seek to amend its law in a unilateral and retrospective fashion.[7] And the State may seek to do so even when the bonds contain a majority action clause which contemplates the very modification sought by the State (eg, the State seeks to redenominate its bonds but there is a majority action clause which vests in the majority the power to redenominate the bonds).[8]

5.04 However, controversy surrounds the exercise of such power. The general assumption was and still is that the State has the power to amend the terms of the bonds governed by its local law as it sees it fit and these changes need to be accepted as part and parcel of the applicable law.[9] The proponents of this view argue that the investors consciously accept the

[4] *NML Capital Limited v Republic of Argentina* [2011] UKSC 31, para 108; *Wight v Eckhardt Marine GmbH* [2003] UKPC 37, para 15.

[5] *National Bank of Greece and Athens v Metliss* [1958] AC 509, 529–30; *Global Distressed Alpha Fund I Limited Partnership v PT Bakrie Investindo* [2011] EWHC 256 (Comm) (holding that a foreign restructuring does not affect the debt governed by English law).

[6] *Re Helbert Wagg & Co Ltd* [1956] Ch 323; *Zivnostenska Banka v Frankman* [1950] AC 57, 69–72; *Kahler v Midland Bank* [1950] AC 24.

[7] For further examples of unilateral modifications of sovereign bonds, see Matthias Audit, 'La dette souveraine appelle-t-elle un statut juridique particulier?' in Matthias Audit (ed), *Insolvabilité des Etats et dettes souveraines* (2011) 72. In 2010, Ireland introduced subordinate liabilities orders (SLO) whereby the Ministry of Finance could unilaterally amend the terms of the bonds between a nationalised bank and the creditor. Creditors argued that given that the banks were nationalised the State was wearing two hats when passing this legislation. Creditors brought actions before Irish and English courts. The bonds contained a choice of English law clause. The cases settled.

[8] John Dizard, 'Delusional Lawyering Won't Save European Bonds' *Financial Times* (24 February 2017).

[9] Rodrigo Olivares-Caminal, *Legal Aspects of Sovereign Debt Restructuring* (2009) 29; Pierre Mayer, 'La neutralisation du pouvoir normatif de l'Etat en matière de contrats d'Etat' (1986) 113 JDI 5, 48; Michael Gruson, 'Controlling Choice of Law' in Michael Gruson and Ralph Reisner, *Sovereign Lending: Managing Legal Risk* (1984) 51, 65–66; Philip Wood, 'Selected Aspects of International Loan Documentation and Rescheduling' in Lars Kalderén and

risk of unilateral legislative changes[10] à la Greece by subscribing to the bonds governed by the local law of the sovereign debtor. Therefore, they ought to assume that the law might change over time.[11]

The competing line of thought suggests that it would be inconsistent with the principle of *pacta sunt servanda* and legitimate expectations of creditors to recognise the changes to local law adopted by the sovereign who is simultaneously a party to the contract it seeks to amend unilaterally.[12] How can a party to a contract, whatever its status, change the terms of the contract in a unilateral fashion and eviscerate any vested rights that a party contracting with the sovereign debtor by mutual agreement enjoys?[13] A State should not be its own judge.[14] If it were possible to change the legislation unilaterally of the State's own volition, this school of thought contends that the scope for abusive legislating and debt repudiation would be far-reaching. Such action is also macro-economically suboptimal as it is liable to lead to a political risk premium for the bonds issued by sovereigns under their local law.[15] **5.05**

An intermediate position is advocated by Mann who sets forth a distinction between legislative amendments of general reach—adopted within the ambit of the State's power to regulate—and those directly aimed at **5.06**

Qamar Siddiqi (eds), *Sovereign Borrowers: Guidelines on Legal Negotiations with Commercial Lenders* (1984) 125; Georges Delaume, *Legal Aspects of International Lending and Economic Development Agreements* (1967) 118; Edwin Borchard, *State Insolvency and Foreign Bondholders*, vol 1 (1951) 14–15; Karl Strupp, 'L'intervention en matière financière' (1925) 8 Recueil des cours 1, 65, 93 (with the exception of arbitrary amendments to State bonds).

10 Garcia Amador, 'Second Report on State Responsibility' (1957) 2 ILC Yearbook 104, 119.

11 On the issue of pricing and accepting the risk of unilateral changes, see Chapter 1.

12 Jean-Flavien Lalive, 'Recent Version: Abrogation or Alteration of an Economic Development Agreement between a State and a Private Foreign Party' (1961–62) 17 Bus Law 434, 440–56; George Ray, 'Some Reasons for the Binding Force of Development Contracts between States and Foreign Nationals' (1960–61) 16 Bus Law 942; Leo Kissam and Edmond Leach, 'Sovereign Expropriation of Property and Abrogation of Concession Contracts' (1959) 28 Fordham L Rev 177, 204–12.

13 The idea of protecting vested rights in the determination of the time element in conflict of laws was highlighted in the 1981 Resolution of the Institut du Droit International (Institut du Droit International, 'The Problem of Choice of Time in Private International Law' (1981) para 6), though the usefulness of the doctrine is very limited (Etienne de Szaszy, 'Les conflits de lois dans le temps' (1934) 47 Recueil des cours 145, 196–98; John McNulty, 'Corporations and the Intertemporal Conflict of Laws' (1967) 55 Cal L Rev 12, 19, 38). On the application of the doctrine of vested rights in the US, see the Dissenting Opinion of Justice Strong in *Sinking-Fund Cases*, 99 US 700, 742 (US Ct Cl 1878).

14 John Fischer Williams, 'Le droit international et les obligations financières qui naissent d'un contrat' (1923) 1 Recueil des Cours 289, 315.

15 Hal Scott and Anna Gelpern, *International Finance: Law and Regulation* (2012) 403–04.

contracts to which the State is a party.[16] Under this approach, a private creditor may not complain of unilateral changes to the legislation governing the contract which are not directly addressed to the contractual relations which the State has undertaken. Another intermediate position is to draw a distinction between the abrogation of fundamental terms of the bonds and the abrogation of ancillary clauses/obligations.[17]

5.07 And lastly, Buchheit and Gulati, supporting the retrospective introduction of majority action clauses into Greek bonds, drew on the argument, among others, that majority action clauses are a technique in spirit of the established practice of sovereign debt restructurings.[18] This begs the obvious question of what the established practice is and why it should matter.[19]

5.08 The legality of unilateral amendments to sovereign domestic bonds has not yet been tested in any judicial or arbitral proceedings[20] and the speculations have mainly been limited to analyses concerning the human right to property[21] and the international law of expropriation.[22] The lingering

16 FA Mann, 'State Contracts and State Responsibility' (1960) 54 AJIL 572, 576–77, 581–85, 588. The distinction is criticised by Mayer (n 9) 48, 65.

17 McNulty (n 13) 36.

18 Lee Buchheit and Mitu Gulati, 'Restructuring a Nation's Debt' (2010) 29 IFLR 46, 49. See also, Report of the Joint Committee on Strengthening the Framework for Sovereign Debt Crisis Prevention and Resolution (2012) 15 (chastising unilateral modifications of bonds, but making an exception for the introduction of CACs consistent with the market practice).

19 Note that the threshold of two-thirds, used in the unilateral majority action clauses in Greek bonds, in conjunction with an aggregation clause, is at odds with the then prevalent market practice of using the threshold of three-quarters of bondholders (Mitu Gulati and Jeromin Zettelmeyer, 'Engineering an Orderly Greek Debt Restructuring' in Christoph Paulus, *A Debt Restructuring Mechanism for Sovereigns: Do We Need a Legal Procedure?* (2014) 122).

20 *Abaclat and others v The Argentine Republic,* ICSID Case No ARB/07/5, Decision on Jurisdiction and Admissibility, 4 August 2011; *Ambiente Ufficio SPA and others v The Argentine Republic,* ICSID Case No ARB/08/9, Decision on Jurisdiction and Admissibility, 8 February 2013; *Giovanni Alemanni and others v Argentine Republic,* ICSID Case No ARB/07/8. The tribunal in *Poštová banka, a.s. and Istrokapital SE v Hellenic Republic,* ICSID Case No ARB/13/8, Award, 9 April 2015, in a challenge of the 2012 Greek debt restructuring, declined jurisdiction over the case. See, however, *Mamatas c. Grèce* (Requêtes nos 63066/14, 64297/14 et 66106/14) CEDH 21 juillet 2016 (holding that the unilateral introduction of CACs into Greek law governed bonds did not contravene the ECHR).

21 Patrick Wautelet, 'The Greek Debt Restructuring and Property Rights: A Greek Tragedy for Investors?' in André Alen, *Liberae Cogitationes: Mélanges Marc Bossuyt* (2013) 903; Stephen Choi, Mitu Gulati, and Eric Posner, 'Pricing Terms in Sovereign Debt Contracts: A Greek Case Study with Implications for the European Crisis Resolution Mechanism' (2011) John M Olin Law & Economics Working Paper No 541, 17–18; Alexander Metallinos, 'The Greek Sovereign Debt' in Eugenio Bruno (ed), *Sovereign Debt and Debt Restructuring: Legal, Financial and Regulatory Aspects* (2013) 26–29.

22 Delaume (n 9) 118–124; Andreas Witte, 'The Greek Bond Haircut: Public and Private International Law and European Law Limits to Unilateral Sovereign Debt Restructuring'

uncertainty over the issue requires revisiting the issue from the viewpoint of English conflict of laws.

Before doing so, a preliminary question arises. It has been suggested that a distinction has to be drawn between unilateral modifications of the local law by the sovereign and defaults under sovereign bonds. In the first case, it is argued, the sovereign debtor does not breach any express contractual provisions and therefore no cause of action should arise against the sovereign.[23] The falsity of the logic is exposed the moment one remembers that the State is bound by the original, intact version of the contract and the introduction of new contractual provisions inconsistent with the original contract amounts to a breach of contract.[24] Sovereign bondholders consent to release the necessary funds under the original, unamended sovereign bond documentation. In their eyes, the unilateral modification is as much a breach of contract as a non-payment under bonds. **5.09**

II. CONSTITUTIONALITY OF THE UNILATERAL REPUDIATION OR MODIFICATION OF SOVEREIGN BONDS

The initial step for an English court may be to review the foreign statute that purports to modify the bonds in a unilateral manner as to its constitutionality. It is arguable that the courts of the forum (in this case, England) have the power to review the constitutionality of the statutes of a foreign State (the sovereign debtor).[25] **5.10**

Assuming that the courts of the forum do indeed enjoy such powers, the limitations on the constitutional review of foreign statutes are several. **5.11**

(2012) 9(2) Manchester J Intl Econ L 307 (arguing that retrofit CACs amount to expropriation); Melissa Boudreau, 'Restructuring Sovereign Debt under Local Law: Are Retrofit Collective Action Clauses Expropriatory?' (2012) 2 HBLR Online 164 (no expropriation).

23 Choi et al (n 21) 4–5.

24 Ivar Alvik, *Contracting with Sovereignty: State Contracts and International Arbitration* (2011) 253.

25 FA Mann, 'On the Sacrosanctity of the Foreign Act of State' (1965) 14(3) ICLQ 985 (the constitutionality of a foreign State's statute may be put into question if the validity of the foreign law comes in question incidentally in an action on a contract to be performed abroad, citing *Buck* v *Attorney-General* [1960] 2 WLB 1038, 1042); Kurt Lipstein, 'Proof of Foreign Law: Scrutiny of its Constitutional Validity' (1967) 42 BYBIL 265 (in principle accepting the review of constitutionality of a foreign statute); Pierre Mayer, 'L'arbitre international et la hiérarchie des normes' (2011) 2 Revue de l'arbitrage 361; *A/S Tallinna Laevauhisus v Estonian State Steamship Line ('The Vapper')* (1947) 80 Ll L Rep 99 (CA) (cited by Campbell McLachlan, *Foreign Relations Law* (2014) 528).

English judges could not examine the constitutionality of the foreign statute should the local courts of the sovereign themselves not have the power to do so or if the exclusive power of constitutional review were concentrated in the hands of a local specialised court, by necessity excluding the power of foreign courts.[26] Kahn-Freund suggested that a court is empowered to review whether the foreign law had been properly enacted, however, it could not review the conflict of the foreign statute with the substantial provisions of the constitution.[27]

5.12 Should such power be accepted in principle, and following the reasoning to its logical conclusion, one might argue that it would not be legitimate for the English courts to rule on the legality of a domestic debt restructuring, unless the claimant bondholder has brought a constitutional action in the courts of the sovereign debtor.[28] Nevertheless, forcing such a 'local remedy' may seem unwise if the remedy is ineffective,[29] which might often be the case in times of economic and social turmoil. Equally, it does not seem that if the local courts of the sovereign debtor come to the conclusion that the statute modifying sovereign bonds is constitutional, that would necessarily prevent the English courts from holding that the same statute offends English public policy.

III. CONFLICT OF LAWS ANALYSIS

5.13 If an English judge were to assess the unilateral modification of domestic bonds through the prism of English conflict of laws, the orthodox position is clear. The well-established position is that the governing law is not frozen at the time of entering into a contract and courts will apply the law as it exists from time to time.[30] The transitory rules of the foreign applicable law will, as a result, be given full effect.[31]

[26] Lipstein (n 25) 266–77.

[27] Otto Kahn-Freund, 'Constitutional Review of Foreign Law?' in Werner Flume, Hugo Hahn, Gerhard Kegel, and Kenneth Simmond (eds), *International Law and Economic Order, Festschrift für F. A. Mann* (1977) 210, 217–19.

[28] In this sense, see Patrick Kinsch, *Le Fait du prince étranger* (1994) 218–19.

[29] Ibid. [30] *Re Helbert Wagg & Co Ltd* [1956] Ch 323, 342.

[31] Lord Collins of Mapesbury et al (eds), *Dicey, Morris & Collins on the Conflict of Laws*, vol 1 (2012) 68, 71–72; Philip Wood, *Conflict of Laws and International Finance* (2007), para 2-009; Kurt Lipstein, 'The General Principles of Private International Law' (1972) 135 Recueil des cours 97, 222; Vicente Lucas, 'Conflicts of Laws in International Lending Transactions—Governing Law and Choice of Forum' in Dominique Carreau and Malcolm Shaw, *Dette extérieure: External Debt* (1995) 439. For criticism of the approach, see Celia Wasserstein Fassberg, 'The Intertemporal Problem in Choice of Law Reconsidered: Israeli Matrimonial Property' (1990) 39 ICLQ 856, 876–77.

That said, the readiness of courts to apply the transitory laws of the sovereign is, as is always the case in the conflict of laws, constrained by the public policy exception.[32] This chapter will argue that a claimant in proceedings before English courts may advance the argument that the unilateral modification of bonds is inconsistent with English public policy. **5.14**

The first issue that needs to be addressed is the threshold of public policy in the context of a unilateral modification of sovereign bonds. Under Art 21 of the Rome I Regulation, to eschew the application of the otherwise applicable foreign law, that law has to be 'manifestly incompatible' with the public policy of the forum. The Court of Justice established that a court might resort to the defence of public policy where the enforcement of a foreign judgment (and *mutatis mutandis* the application of foreign law) 'would be at variance to an unacceptable degree with the legal order of the State in which enforcement is sought' (and application of the foreign law is sought).[33] Allied to this is the requirement to demonstrate that the unilateral modification is inconsistent not merely with domestic public policy but with international public policy in England, that is to say the core principles that cannot be derogated from even in situations presenting cross-border elements.[34] The Court of Justice determined that public policy cannot solely be invoked on the ground of a mere discrepancy between the law of the forum and the foreign court.[35] Public policy seeks to 'protect legal interests which are expressed through a rule of law, and not purely economic interests'.[36] This is thus a demanding standard but the pertinent question is, however, how demanding it is in the face of a unilateral and retrospective modification of the rights of creditors. **5.15**

English courts have at times applied a lower threshold of public policy to unilateral and retrospective legislation. In *Lynch v Provisional Government of Paraguay*,[37] a Paraguayan decree retroactively invalidated the will of the ex-dictator of the country, with the intended effect in England and elsewhere. The English court seised of the dispute refused to give effect to the retroactive changes adopted in the legislation as that would be 'both inconvenient and unjust' (the old nomenclature for public policy exception). Some of the glosses on the holding in *Lynch* is that the law governing the succession to moveables is the law of the domicile at the time of **5.16**

[32] Lord Collins of Mapesbury et al (n 31) 75–76; Christian Gavalda, *Les Conflits dans le temps en droit international privé* (1955) 325.

[33] *Krombach v Bamberski*, Case C-7/98 [2000] ECR I-1935, para 37.

[34] Stéphanie Francq, 'Article 45' in Ulrich Magnus and Peter Mankowski, *Brussels I Regulation: European Commentaries on Private International Law* (2012) 874.

[35] *flyLAL-Lithuanian Airlines v Starptautiskā lidosta Rīga VAS*, Case-302/13, ECLI:EU:C:2014:2319, para 48.

[36] Ibid para 56. [37] (1871) LR 2 P & D 268.

the death,[38] or the law retroactively invalidating the will of the ex-dictator of the country was a penal law that would not lend itself to enforcement in English courts.[39] An equally valid interpretation is that the retroactive application of the will of an ex-dictator was shocking to the conscience of the judge and triggered the application of the public policy exception.[40]

5.17 *Adams v National Bank of Greece* concerned mortgage bonds that were issued by a Greek bank in the United Kingdom.[41] The bonds were guaranteed by another Greek bank, which was later amalgamated with a third Greek bank. Initially, a Greek parliament statute declared the third bank to be the universal successor of the obligations previously held by the two amalgamated banks, including the obligations of guarantee under the mortgage bonds. Although, as it was decided in the lower court, the proper law of the bonds was English law,[42] Greek law was the law applicable to the issues of status, including the succession as between two entities through amalgamation.

5.18 Four days after the bondholder obtained a favourable decision from an English court, the Greek parliament passed a law which excluded from the succession of the third bank the obligations arising out of foreign currency bonds and de facto absolved the third bank of any liability under the English law governed bonds. In a new action brought against it in the English courts, the new Greek bank argued that this statute should be accorded full recognition in England because the succession was a question of status properly falling within the reach of Greek law. Rebuffing the argument, three Law Lords held that it would be neither just nor convenient to recognise the effects of retrospective alterations that in effect sought to alter or discharge the obligations accrued pursuant to English law governed obligations.[43] While Greek banks had personality separate from the Greek State, the latter had globally profited or intended to profit from the legislation.[44] The Greek parliament's evasive approach to obligations undertaken by the Greek banks clearly influenced the decision that the House of Lords reached.[45]

[38] John Morris, 'The Time Factor in the Conflict of Laws' (1966) 15(2–3) ICLQ 422, 428; Pippa Rogerson, *Collier's Conflict of Laws* (2013) 289–90.

[39] Michael Pryles, 'The Time Factor in Private International Law' (1980) 6 Monash U L Rev 225, 231.

[40] Jan Grodecki, 'Conflict of Laws in Time' (1959) 35 BYBIL 58, 67–68.

[41] [1961] AC 255.

[42] *Metliss v National Bank of Greece and Athens, The Times* (13 July 1956) 4.

[43] Compare a similar US Supreme Court decision in *Broughton v Pensacola*, 93 US 266 (1876).

[44] Mayer (n 9) 66.

[45] *Adams v National Bank of Greece* [1961] AC 255, 290, followed in *Goldman Sachs International v Novo Banco* [2015] EWHC 2371 (Comm), para 104.

Lord Denning took a more nuanced approach which echoes the intermediary position taken by Buchheit and Gulati enunciated above. He first qualified the Greek parliament's legislation as pertaining to the status of companies and hence governed by the Greek law. This qualification notwithstanding, he held that the exclusion of liability of the third, amalgamated company 'is such an unusual provision in an amalgamation, and is so inconsistent with the essence of the transaction, that there is no comity of nations which requires the English courts to recognise it'.[46] An open question is whether Lord Denning's analysis in terms of usualness and comity is more compliant with the review of the legislative acts of a foreign State, evidencing a heightened level of deference to a foreign legislator.[47] **5.19**

These cases denote a lower threshold of public policy in respect of foreign retroactive legislation. This can tentatively be explained by the idea—affirmed by *Phillips v Eyre*[48]—that the retroactive application of law is a deviation from the common practice of the nations of mankind[49] and may be inconsistent with public policy.[50] Thus, the retrospective *and* unilateral character of these modifications may trigger the defence of public policy. **5.20**

Kahler[51] and *Zhivnstenska*[52] are the cases commonly cited for the proposition that to refuse their application the foreign retrospective laws have to be 'penal or confiscatory'. However, upon closer examination, it transpires that these two cases did not concern the retroactive application of foreign law. At all material times in those cases, including the date of entering into contract, foreign currency regulations were in force in the territory of the foreign State.[53] **5.21**

While defining the correct threshold of public policy is undoubtedly helpful, one is still left with the task of identifying the precise contents of English public policy in relation to the unilateral modification of a sovereign's domestic-law bonds. To elucidate the contents of English public policy, English courts typically refer to the comparable English domestic **5.22**

46 *Adams v National Bank of Greece* (n 45) 290.

47 In support of Lord Denning's approach, see Jan Grodecki, 'The Greek Bond Cases' (1961) 24(6) MLR 701, 711.

48 (1870) 6 QB 1, 23.

49 See for common law countries, Ben Juratowitch, *Retroactivity and the Common Law* (2008) (arguing for a general presumption against the retroactivity of statutes for the sake of certainty and liberty).

50 *Corporación Mexicana De Mantenimiento Integral v Pemex-Exploración Y Producción*, No 13-4022 (2d Cir 2016), 32.

51 *Kahler v Midland Bank* [1950] AC 24, 27.

52 *Zivnostenska Banka v Frankman* [1950] AC 57, 72.

53 *Kahler v Midland Bank* [1950] AC 24, 28; *Zivnostenska Banka v Frankman* [1950] AC 57, 71, 77.

practice on the subject.[54] Equally useful is the practice of foreign States in defining the extent of the public policy exception.[55] Given the paucity of authorities on the matter, this chapter undertakes a similar enquiry: if retrospective legislation of a certain sort is unobjectionably accepted in the domestic practice in England and foreign States, the public policy exception would not inhibit the recognition of comparable foreign legislation. If, by contrast, unilateral modifications of sovereign bonds are generally condemned in international practice, this can (and perhaps should) inform the approach of English courts. With this in mind, the following analysis addresses English and foreign judicial practice, although few and far between, on the unilateral modification of State contracts, in particular, sovereign bonds.

5.23 Drawing on the analysis of judicial practice, the section argues against the fully fledged right to modify unilaterally domestic-law bonds in sovereign debt restructurings. Such comparative research suggests that the State in issuing debt and later embarking on its restructuring is acting in a private capacity and should not be allowed to modify its debt in a unilateral fashion.

1. The Position in England and Overseas as a Basis for the Conflict of Laws Analysis

England and Wales

5.24 The orthodox view in English domestic law is that the UK Parliament has absolute supremacy and any legitimate expectations can be overcome by a properly worded statute.[56] The conventional doctrine was expressed by Bowett as follows:

> Indeed, in English law not only is 'stabilization' impossible against future legislation but, because of the doctrine of Parliamentary supremacy, no English court could challenge the assertion that Parliament was acting in the public good.[57]

5.25 A line of English cases upholds the view that the sovereign, when entering into contracts, is certainly not enjoined from using its sovereign

[54] *Starkowski v Attorney-General* [1954] AC 155, 174; *Phillips v Eyre* (1870) 6 QB 1, 17.

[55] *Starkowski v Attorney-General* [1954] AC 155, 174; *Frontier Petroleum Services v Czech Republic*, UNCITRAL, Award, 12 November 2010, para 528 (referring to the jurisprudence of other courts on matters of public policy in the context of insolvency law).

[56] See, eg, *R v Secretary of State for Education and Employment, ex parte Begbie* [2000] 1 WLR 1115, para 53: 'It is common ground that any expectation must yield to the terms of the statute under which the Secretary of State is required to act.'

[57] Derek Bowett, 'State Contracts with Aliens: Contemporary Developments on Compensation for Termination or Breach' (1988) 59 BYBIL 49, 58.

prerogatives so as to amend the scope of its contractual obligations.[58] Thus, the Court of Appeal in *William Cory and Son Ltd v City of London* held that the City of London, as the port health authority, could not be held liable for passing by-laws which imposed further conditions on the private contracting party, even though the by-laws made the contract commercially impossible to perform. An administrative body charged with statutory powers for public purposes is incapable of divesting itself of such powers or fettering itself in the use of such powers. Thus, any clauses purporting to do so will be held invalid.[59] Yet, there is a caveat: all this is true, unless the public company is entering into 'trading contracts'.[60]

On the other hand, opinions are uttered with increasing frequency that the supremacy of Parliament is no longer as absolute as it was historically.[61] Judge Higgins expressed her voice in favour of that development as early as 1977: **5.26**

> [I]t is widely accepted that no compensation is due for government legislation which adversely affects individual contracts. The answer to this must surely be that there is no reason why that principle should apply to contracts to which the government itself is party.[62]

To date, the courts have never ruled on the question of whether the UK Parliament can retrospectively and unilaterally abrogate mercantile or financial obligations that the government has undertaken to abide by.[63] Irrespective of its status in modern English law,[64] the doctrine of executive necessity, according to which the Crown can renege on its assurances 'as to what its executive action would be in the future', does not extend to commercial contracts which the government should perform 'like anybody else'.[65] **5.27**

[58] FA Mann, 'Sovereign or Fisc?' (1960) 9 ICLQ 691.

[59] *William Cory and Son Ltd v City of London* [1951] 2 KB 476, 485; *Ayr Harbour Trustees v Oswald* (1883) 8 App Cas 623, 638–40.

[60] *William Cory and Son Ltd v City of London* [1951] 2 KB 476, 487; *Birkdale District Electric Supply Company v Corporation of Southport* [1926] AC 355.

[61] *Jackson v Attorney-General* [2006] 1 AC 262, 302–03; Trevor Allan, *Constitutional Justice: A Liberal Theory of the Rule of Law* (2003) 201–42; Jaime Arancibia, *Judicial Review of Commercial Regulation* (2014) 144 (advocating review of commercial regulation on the ground of its proportionality).

[62] Rosalyn Higgins, 'The Availability of Damages for Reliance by Government on Executive Necessity' in Flume et al (n 27) 33.

[63] Carol Harlow and Richard Rawlings, *Law and Administration* (2009) 341–42.

[64] *Robertson v Minister of Pensions* [1949] KB 227; John Mitchell, *The Contracts of Public Authorities* (1954) 53–55.

[65] *The Amphitrite* [1921] 3 KB 500, 501.

5.28 The Court of Appeal in *Page v Commissioners of Crown Lands* affirmed that the contracts entered into by the Crown contain an implied term to the effect that the Crown is not precluded from taking measures for the public good.[66] However, recognising that a court may enquire into the importance of the public interest invoked by the governmental agency,[67] Devlin LJ stressed that:

> That does not mean that the Crown can escape from any contract which it finds disadvantageous by saying that it never promised to act otherwise than for the public good.

5.29 The Court of Appeal then drew a crucial distinction between acts of the Crown entered into for the purposes of public good and those taken 'for the purpose of achieving a particular result under the contract in question'—a distinction which resonates with the one proposed by Mann above. As explained by Lord Denning in *Czarnikow v Rolimpex*,[68] the State would seek to achieve a particular result under a contract when it intends 'to avoid its own liabilities under a particular contract or contracts'. It follows from this that if a particular course of action is taken by the State for the public good, such as health, public morals, or safety, then the action may well be defendable. Note that the actions taken in *Page* were adopted under wartime powers. However, actions taken so as to put into effect a discharge of onerous obligations cross the line.[69] Mayer, intuitively following this stance, cites a compelling example based on the abrogation of gold clauses: the abrogation of gold clauses will generally seek to reduce inflation, however, when applied to State contracts, it will retain another function, ie, reducing the debt of the State.[70] That said, quite how extensive such a review would be, and quite where the line between the two types of measures would lie, is unclear.[71]

5.30 In principle accepting this distinction for domestic purposes, Lord Wilberforce in *Czarnikow v Rolimpex* (with whom Lords Fraser and Keith

[66] [1960] 2 All ER 726, 736.

[67] Peter Cane, *Introduction to Administrative Law* (2011) 235–37.

[68] [1978] QB 176, 194.

[69] See also *Smith Kline & French Laboratories (Australia) Limited v Secretary to the Department of Community Services and Health* [1990] FSR 617, 651 where the distinction is well highlighted.

[70] Mayer (n 9) 49; Pierre Mayer, 'Mandatory Rules of Law in International Arbitration' (1986) 4(2) Arb Intl 274, 291.

[71] The House of Lords in *Czarnikow, Ltd v Rolimpex* [1979] AC 351 held that a ban on export taken by the Polish government was taken for the public good when the performance of the contract would have affected currency (ibid 370), or when the action taken is 'to avoid serious domestic, social and political effects and to avoid loss of foreign exchange' (ibid 364). However, this case has to be read in light of the fact that the contract in *Czarnikow* contained an express *force majeure* clause.

agreed) was reluctant to apply said distinction to the arguably distinct context of dealings with foreign sovereigns,[72] whereas Lord Salmon felt no hesitation in doing so.[73] Reason suggests siding with Lord Salmon. If domestic analogies (combined, perhaps, with a comparative analysis) were not well suited to the scrutiny of foreign retroactive legislation, one would be left with applying only the foreign constitutional law, the inherent limitations of which have been exposed above. The alternative would be to have no standard against which one could ever review the attempts of a foreign sovereign to frustrate its own contracts.

There is some authority for the proposition that the retrospective abrogation of gold clauses may infringe English public policy. In *New Brunswick Ry v British and French Trust Corporation Ltd*,[74] Lord Maugham LC suggested that an abrogation of a gold clause by a statute 'cannot be held to diminish or destroy the rights of an English creditor, and it may be added without compensation, after he has commenced an action in this country. A fortiori is such a statute incompetent to affect the course of justice here after trial and judgment.' The editors of *Dicey, Morris & Collins* treat this as an 'isolated *dictum*'.[75] **5.31**

In light of this discussion, the solution under English law is at best unsettled, necessitating an analysis of the practice of foreign States on this subject.[76] This is all the more necessary given the lack of a specific precedent under English law on the modification of financial obligations of the State, which, as the discussion of the US law will evidence, present a peculiarity which calls for the application of special rules. **5.32**

The United States

The position in US law is less murky. In a landmark judgment *Perry v United States*, the US Supreme Court emphatically confirmed the view that the US government cannot unilaterally renege through legislative amendments on its contractual obligations embedded in governmental bonds.[77] **5.33**

[72] *Czarnikow, Ltd v Rolimpex* [1979] AC 351, 363–64. [73] Ibid 370.

[74] [1939] AC 1, 24. [75] Lord Collins of Mapesbury et al (n 31) para 32-189.

[76] *Starkowski v Attorney-General* [1954] AC 155, 174; *Frontier Petroleum Services v Czech Republic*, UNCITRAL, Award, 12 November 2010, para 528.

[77] 294 US 330 (1935). See also *Woodruff v Trapnall*, 51 US 190 (1850) (holding that the State of Arkansas could not repeal with retrospective effect a section in the charter of a State-owned bank that provided that 'that the bills and notes of said institution shall be received in all payments of debts due to the state of Arkansas'). For insurance contracts, see *Lynch v United States*, 292 US 571 (1934). Conversely, the Supreme Court decided that the government may unilaterally and retrospectively modify the contracts of private parties (*Norman v Baltimore & O.R. Co*, 294 US 240, 304–05 (1935)).

The case arose in the context of the Great Depression of 1929. To deleverage the public and private debt alike, the US Congress passed the Joint Resolution of 1933, which abrogated all gold clauses contained in loan agreements, including those issued by the US government.

5.34 When a disgruntled bondholder challenged the abrogation of the bonds it held, the Supreme Court first distinguished between, on one hand, the powers of Congress to control or interdict the contracts between private parties, and on the other hand, to alter or abrogate the substance of its own engagements under which it borrowed money. For the latter cases, the Supreme Court established the 'fundamental principle' that the validity and integrity of public debt should not be questioned and the abrogation of gold clauses in sovereign bonds was to be without effect. This followed from the confirmation that when Congress enters into binding legal obligations, they are in essence similar to the obligations incurred by private parties and hence Congress does not enjoy police powers (power to regulate) to abrogate its own engagements.

5.35 In a similar vein, the US Supreme Court in *Murray v City of Charleston* stated that:

> States and cities when they borrow money and contract to repay it with interest are not acting as sovereignties, but their contracts have the same meaning as that of similar contracts between private persons, and hence instead of there being in the undertaking of a state or city to pay a reservation of a sovereign right to withhold payment, the contract should be regarded as an assurance that such a right will not be exercised.[78]

5.36 It is worth contrasting the ruling in *Perry* with the decision of the House of Lords in *Rex v International Trustee*, where the same US legislative act, the Joint Resolution of 1933, was recognised as abrogating the gold clauses in the bonds issued by the UK government. The difference is that in *Perry*, the debtor (the US Congress) sought to reduce its own obligations through domestic legislation, whereas in *Rex v International Trustee*, the UK government merely relied on a foreign statute (which benefited the UK government immensely).

5.37 Mann, referring to *Perry v United States*, suggested that '[t]here would seem to be no justification for founding upon this exception [*Perry v United States*] a general principle of law applicable to state loans', given that the decision in *Perry* was expressly based on the provisions of the US Constitution.[79] One has to disagree with the learned author's reading of *Perry*. It is true that the Supreme Court relied on various provisions of the

[78] 96 US 432, 445 (1877).

[79] FA Mann, 'State Contracts and State Responsibility (1960) 54 AJIL 572, 586, 590.

US Constitution in its analysis of the constitutionality of the Joint Resolution of 1933, in particular the 14th Amendment of the US Constitution which provides that '[t]he validity of the public debt of the United States, authorized by law ... shall not be questioned'.[80] However, this provision, as the US Supreme Court expressly stated, merely confirms a fundamental principle applicable both to the bonds issued after and those issued before the adoption of the Amendment. The unacceptability of unilateral changes to government bonds was not a mere peculiarity or idiosyncrasy of the US constitutional regime. The principle was indeed fundamental, for it derived its force from the general framework of contract law which governed contractual undertakings of the US government, as well as from the implied ability of the sovereign to bind itself contractually as a manifestation of its sovereignty.

As a general proposition of US constitutional law, the power of Congress to unilaterally modify contracts strictly correlates with the level of police powers inherent in the contract that is sought to be modified.[81] The crux of the problem would generally lie in distinguishing between (i) purely financial obligations, such as the bonds in *Perry v United States*, where no or little police power is engaged. The Supreme Court has confirmed that 'financial obligation ... may not be said automatically to fall within the reserved powers that cannot be contracted away',[82] and (ii) a modification of sovereign bonds conducted in the context of the exercise of a police power.[83] Although the precise scope of police powers is hard to ascertain,[84] purely financial obligations do not seem to involve police powers strong enough to vest the Congress with the power of unilateral modification or repudiation.[85] **5.38**

Quite surprisingly, the Supreme Court eventually determined that the revocation of the gold clause did not result in any actual damages.[86] It may well be the case that there was no majority in the Court for a finding that the US government could not abrogate gold clause *and* be required to pay **5.39**

[80] As well the 5th Amendment.

[81] Mitchell (n 64) 106; *Lynch v United States*, 292 US 571, 579 (1934).

[82] *United States Trust Co v New Jersey*, 97 S Ct 1505, 1519 (1977) (concerning a repeal of a statutory covenant that provided a guarantee to the creditors).

[83] *Lynch v United States*, 292 US 571, 580 (1934). One such example may be the exercise of police powers in times of war.

[84] Mitchell (n 64) 90–97.

[85] *United States Trust Co v New Jersey*, 97 S Ct 1505, 1518–19 (1977) ('[w]hatever the propriety of a State's binding itself to a future course of conduct in other contexts, the power to enter into effective financial contracts cannot be questioned').

[86] A similar result was reached in *Nortz v United States*, 294 US 317, 328–30 (1935), and in *Smyth v United States*, 302 US 329, 355–56 (1937).

damages. But the reasoning behind what seems to be a U-turn from the preceding reasoning of the Supreme Court may be more complex. Gold coins had already been withdrawn from circulation—an action that the Supreme Court did not judge to be arbitrary or capricious—which barred the repayment of the debt in gold. Neither was the claimant able to establish the amount of currency equivalent to the promised gold coin for the simple reason that the market of gold was at the time subject to strict regulations. The claimant's action would therefore result in damages exceeding the nominal value of the bonds, which the Supreme Court was leery to award. Nor did the claimant establish any loss in respect of buying power as a result of the abrogation of the gold clause, for the value of bonds had soared due to the falling price level and thereby the claimant would have been unjustly enriched upon the payment of damages.[87] Four justices strongly dissented from the holding that no damages were available to the bondholder.

5.40 In so deciding, this part of the judgment effectively defeats the finding of unconstitutionality of the Joint Resolution of 1933 and in fact bolsters Congress in its economic reforms by denying effective relief to the bondholder.[88] Relying upon, what seems to be, the pyrrhic character of this victory, it has been suggested that no damages should arise out of the unilateral modification of the bonds by the Greek parliament in the course of the 2012 bond restructuring since the bonds were already rated as 'junk' bonds.[89] The argument is based on flawed understanding. The situation in *Perry v United States* was not ordinary since the gold clauses, although protected by the fundamental prohibition on modifying unilaterally sovereign bonds, impeached the power of the US Congress to exercise monetary regulation by withdrawing gold from the national economy.[90] In contradistinction, in the Greek debt restructuring episode of 2012, the insertion of CACs into Greek law bonds resulted from no apparent police powers of the Hellenic Republic. Furthermore, influential authorities contend that *Perry v United States* was ostensibly limited to the actions brought exclusively by local bondholders, who and only who were subject to the compulsive gold regulation within US territory, whereas foreign bondholders

[87] Richard Timberlake, *Constitutional Money: A Review of the Supreme Court's Monetary Decisions* (2013) 198, 204.

[88] Henry Hart, 'The Gold Clause in United States Bonds' (1934–35) 48 Harv L Rev 1057, 1080, 1087, 1098–99; John Dawson, 'The Gold Clause Decisions' (1935) 33(5) Mich L Rev 647, 658.

[89] Boudreau (n 22) 179, 183.

[90] *Perry v United States*, 294 US 330, 357 (1935); Hart (n 88) 1074; Dawson (n 88) 656–57.

should see no obstacle to availing themselves of the action in damages against the government.[91]

In light of the Supreme Court's decision not to award damages, one might think that the prohibition on unilateral changes is a rule with no teeth. But there is a cluster of cases which actually prohibited unilateral modification of sovereign bonds and restored the bondholder to its original position: *Lynch v US*[92] at the federal level, and at the municipal level—*Murray v City of Charleston*,[93] *US Trust Co v New Jersey*,[94] and *Flushing Natl Bank v Municipal Assistance Corp for City of N.Y.*[95] These cases show that the holding in *Perry* was not a simple rhetorical attempt at obtaining a majority in a divided court but was a case where the existence of the police power to regulate gold affected the outcome of the case. **5.41**

So far as individual US States are concerned, the Contract Clause of the US Constitution directly prohibits US States from passing laws that retroactively affect contractual obligations, including the obligations under bonds, unless the impairment of contractual rights is both reasonable and necessary to serve an important public purpose.[96] In assessing the later requirement, the court should enquire whether the public purpose pursued could have been attained by less drastic measures, and if the public purpose should have been foreseeable at the time of signature of the contract.[97] The US courts have gone to considerable length to stress that the desire to reduce the level of government expenditure is not in itself sufficient to justify abrogation of financial contracts. The State cannot ground its refusal to meet its legitimate financial obligations in the desire to divert the funds intended for the repayment of creditors to the promotion of the public good.[98] **5.42**

[91] Borchard (n 9) 138, fn 51; Martin Domke, *La Clause 'dollar-or': la non-application de la legislation américaine aux emprunts internationaux* (1935); Charles Fenwick, 'The Gold Clause Decision in Relation to Foreign Bondholders' (1935) 29 AJIL 310; Georges Sausser-Hall, 'La clause-or dans les contrats publics et privés' (1937) 60 Recueil des Cours 651, 762; Gaston Jèze, 'Les défaillances d'Etat' (1935) 53 Recueil des cours 377, 414. See also *Brazilian and Serbian Loans* cases where the French legislation prohibiting gold clauses was held to be limited to domestic contracts (PCIJ, *Serbian Loans Case*, Ser A, No 21 (1929), 44).

[92] *Lynch v United States*, 292 US 571, 580 (1934).

[93] 96 US 432, 445 (1877).

[94] *United States Trust Co v New Jersey* (n 85).

[95] 40 NY2d 731 (1976).

[96] On the application of the Contract Clause to bonds, see James Ely, *The Guardian of Every Other Constitutional Right: A Constitutional History of Property Rights* (1998) 95, 97–98; *Von Hoffmann v City of Quincy*, 71 US 535, 549 (1866); *United States Trust Co v New Jersey* (n 85). Note that the Contract Clause does not apply to the US government.

[97] *United States Trust Co v New Jersey* (n 85) 1521–22.

[98] Ibid 1519, 1521; Mitchell (n 64) 95.

5.43 Quite when an act of legislation taken in times of financial dire straits will be in breach of the Contract Clause is somewhat uncertain. In *Faitoute Iron & Steel Co v City of Asbury Park*, a case decided prior to the enactment of the favourable regime of Chapter 9 of the US Bankruptcy Code on the bankruptcy of municipalities, the US Supreme Court had to rule on the validity of a New Jersey statute that established a regime for restructuring the debt of a highly indebted municipality. The restructuring regime shared similar traits to a majority action clause—the restructuring plan was contingent upon receiving the consent of the supermajority of bondholders which would thereby bind the minority (but only upon obtaining the *ex ante* judicial approval). In a challenge to this regime based on the Contract Clause, the Supreme Court held that the introduction of this restructuring regime did not impair the Contract Clause in light of the fact that the raising of taxes would not have brought the municipality back to solvency.[99]

5.44 Nevertheless, the precedential value of *Faitoute*, ostensibly overturned by Congress,[100] may hardly be extended to other instances of unilateral modifications of municipal (sovereign) bonds. A later decision, *US Trust*, distinguished *Faitoute* on the grounds that the debt restructuring in *Faitoute* was exceptional since it was performed for the benefit of creditors as evidenced by the consent of the supermajority of bondholders, and the fact that the price of bonds soared after the debt restructuring.[101] Two lower US court decisions have equally questioned the holding in *Faitoute*.[102] Thus, the court in *George Hardin v The Village of Mount Prospect* noted the atypical character of the facts in *Faitoute*, where the creditors enjoyed extended protection, ie, the bankruptcy repayment plan required approval of 85% of all creditors, and non-consenting creditors were to be bound by the plan only after a State court determined that the municipality could not otherwise pay its creditors and that the repayment plan was in the best interest of all creditors.[103] In the recent litigation over the insolvency of Puerto Rico, the US District Court for the District of Puerto Rico examined the legality of Puerto Rican restructuring procedures that would have allowed the

99 *Faitoute Iron & Steel Co v City of Asbury Park*, 316 US 502 (1942).

100 11 USC §903(1) (proscribing composition that would bind non-consenting creditors); Clayton Gillette, 'What States Can Learn from Municipal Insolvency' in Peter Conti-Brown and David Skeel (eds), *When States Go Broke: The Origins, Context, and Solutions for the American States in Fiscal Crisis* (2012) 111–12.

101 *United States Trust Co v New Jersey* (n 85) 1520–21; cf to high 'exit yields' following the Greek debt restructuring of 2012 showing that the investors remained sceptical about the sustainability of Greek debt (Zettelmeyer et al (n 2) 527).

102 *In re Jefferson County, Alabama*, 465 BR 243, 293 (ND Ala Bankr 2012); *George D. Hardin, Inc v Village of Mount Prospect*, 99 Ill 2d 96, 104–06 (S Ct Ill 1983). See also the dictum in *United States v Bekins*, 304 US 27, 51 (1938).

103 *George Hardin v The Village of Mount Prospect*, 99 Ill 2d 96, 105 (S Ct Ill 1983).

public corporations to restructure their debt with the authorisation of the Government Development Bank, majority of creditors and a special court. The Court distinguished the authority in *Faitoute* on the ground that the valid restructuring in *Faitoute* merely extended maturities and reduced interest rates, but did not go so far as to allow a haircut to the principal.[104]

In another case reinforcing the doubts over the wide precedential value of *Faitoute*, *Flushing Natl Bank v Municipal Assistance Corp for City of N.Y.*, the New York Court of Appeal decided that a moratorium on the short-term obligations of New York City was illegal.[105] It is striking that so innocuous a tool as the debt moratorium was judged unacceptable in *Flushing Natl Bank*, whereas a full-scale debt restructuring involving interest rate reduction and extension of maturities in *Faitoute* was squarely upheld.[106] The following reasons, not only of degree but of kind, are put forward to explain the difference in treatment: **5.45**

(1) In *Faitoute*, the State did not unilaterally impose the restructuring on the creditors, but introduced a regime whereby 85% of the creditors could consent to the terms of the restructuring (we will return to this point later).
(2) In *Faitoute*, the debt restructuring was *ex ante* reviewed and approved by a court.[107]

Upon a closer look, secondary differences between *Faitoute* and *Flushing Natl Bank* appear: **5.46**

(1) *Conditions relating to the financial capacity of the debtor*. In *Faitoute*, the financial crisis was judged to be unforeseen, whereas in *Flushing Natl Bank* it was deemed to be foreseeable;[108] in *Flushing Natl Bank*, the city of New York had the capacity to increase its taxes to pay the debt, whereas in *Faitoute* the court was persuaded that the further levying of taxes would not rescue the municipality.

[104] *Franklin California Tax-Free Trust et al v Commonwealth of Puerto Rico*, 2015 US Dist LEXIS 14855, 67 (DPR 2015).

[105] 40 NY2d 731 (1976). Conversely, in the context of one and the same financial emergency, a wage freeze was found to be constitutional (*Subway-Surface Supervisors Assoc v New York City Transit Authority*, 44 NY 2d 101 (1978)).

[106] *Flushing Natl Bank* was met with a legislative change in Chapter 9, see An Act to Amend Chapter IX of the Bankruptcy Act to Provide by Voluntary Reorganization Procedures for the Adjustment of the Debts of Municipalities, Pub L No 94-260, 94th Cong, 2d Sess (1976).

[107] Holger Schier, *Towards a Reorganisation System for Sovereign Debt: An International Law Perspective* (2007) 254–55.

[108] On the history of the 1970s bankruptcy of the city of New York, see David Skeel, 'States of Bankruptcy' (2012) 79 U Chic L Rev 677, 727–29.

(2) *Conditions relating to the conduct of the sovereign debt restructuring.* In *Flushing Natl Bank*, the legislature was selective as to the creditors to bear the burden of the moratorium and the creditors affected were denied court access.

5.47 The application of the two main benchmarks of *Faitoute*—the consent of creditors and judicial review—may be rather misguiding if extrapolated to sovereign debt restructurings. First, creditors are often cajoled into giving consent. The States often obtain the consent of creditors through varying degrees of economic coercion and duress. The borderline between cases of voluntary consent or coercion of bondholders is often thin.[109]

5.48 Second, it has strongly been argued that the favourable reasoning of *Faitoute* should not apply to sovereign debt restructurings because the current regime of sovereign debt restructurings lacks an impartial third party capable of reviewing the restructuring of the sovereign debt.[110] There are two potential existing candidates for such a role—local courts of the sovereign and external courts. Local courts of the State in default often lack the impartiality required. In *Faitoute*, the supreme court of the State was the competent jurisdiction to sanction the restructuring programme of a municipality which is likely to indicate sufficient distancing between the impartial third party—the court of a State—and the debtor in distress, namely, a municipality, the political subdivision of the State. By contrast, in sovereign debt restructurings the foreign residence of bondholders justifies the need for an international tribunal which could review and approve the terms of the debt restructuring programme *ex ante*. As for the control by external courts (mostly New York and English courts), the extent of their *ex post* review of the debt restructuring programmes is very lightweight, as seen in Chapter 7.

The Russian Federation

5.49 Coherent with the authority in *Perry v United States*, the Russian courts have come down in favour of the proposition that the State does not enjoy the power to modify its bonds in a unilateral fashion. In the aftermath of the Russian sovereign debt crisis of 1998, the government of the Russian Federation issued a decree which sought to restructure its domestic bonds in a unilateral manner. A local holder of Russian foreign-currency

[109] Christoph Trebesch, Henrik Enderlein, and Laura von Daniels, 'Sovereign Debt Disputes: A Database of Government Coerciveness in Debt Crises' (2012) 31(2) J Intl Mon & Fin 250.

[110] Schier (n 107) 255.

domestic bonds, OOO Rusatommet, sued the Ministry of Finance and the government of the Russian Federation requesting payment under the original terms of the Russian bonds and challenging the unilateral restructuring. The Federal Moscow District Arbitraj (Commercial) Court of the Russian Federation held that the restructuring decree was issued within the constitutional competence of the government to regulate the market of securities and the internal and external debt of the Russian Federation, and consequently, should prevail over the contractual obligations of the State.[111]

The Presidium of the Supreme Arbitraj (Commercial) Court of the Russian Federation chastised the District Arbitraj court for the misplaced reliance on the governmental decree. It held that the government loan was subject to the contractual regime prescribed by Art 817 of the Civil Code of the Russian Federation which expressly provided that State loans could only be modified by the mutual consent of contracting parties.[112] Furthermore, the court held that the application of the governmental decree with the effect of unilaterally modifying the State loans would violate the right to property, enshrined in the Russian Constitution. **5.50**

However, the court added a proviso that the lower courts should enquire into the existence of a State-imposed moratorium, subject to an extensive judicial review, and referred the case to the lower courts (no moratorium was found in the event).[113] It is perplexing why the court was ready to grant legal effect, albeit subject to a judicial review, to the moratorium, while denying effect to a governmental decree purporting to restructure the sovereign debt. Arguably, the moratorium acts only as a temporary stay on legal claims, whereas the decree had irreversible consequences on the rights of bondholders. The deferral of payment maturities (although within the confines of reasonableness) was also supported by the decision of the Russian Constitutional Court, which received the imprimatur of the European Court on Human Rights.[114] **5.51**

[111] Decision No KG-A40/723-00, 16 March 2000.

[112] Decision No 2453/00, 13 February 2002.

[113] Decision No KG-A40/6804-02, 28 October 2002.

[114] *Malysh and others v Russia* (Appl No 30280/03) ECtHR 11 February 2010; cf *Lobanov v Russia* (Appl No 15578/03) ECtHR 2 December 2010 (finding that the failure to convert Soviet bonds into Russian promissory notes made the repayment impossible and thus breached Art 1 of Protocol 1).

Germany

5.52 In a 1962 judgment, the German Federal Constitutional Court recognised the legislative cancellation, without any compensation, of the Third Reich's government debt.[115] It held inter alia that the legislative cancellation of the debt did not fly in the face of the right to property embedded in the German Basic Law (the German Constitution). One is struck by the inconsistency of this judicial pronouncement with a much later pronouncement of the same judicial instance on the Argentine debt restructuring of 2001, where the court found that Argentina could not avail itself of the exception of the state of necessity in restructuring its debt in the time of a severe crisis.[116]

5.53 The rather peculiar facts of the case explain the 1962 judgment by which the Federal Constitutional Court embraced so draconian a measure. The legislative cancellation in question was based on the express provisions of the German Basic Law. Art 134(4) delegated the legislator with the task of regulating the debt of the Third Reich, while Art 135(a) ('Old obligations') stipulated that federal legislation might exempt the German State from complying with the obligations accrued by the Third Reich. In applying these constitutional provisions, the German parliament passed in 1957 the Act on War Reparations that declared the debt owed by the Third Reich cancelled.

5.54 It transpires from this overview that the legislative annulment of the debt, endorsed by the Federal Constitutional Court, did not relate to the debt of the Federal Republic of Germany contracted in the ordinary course of its existence but rather incurred by its predecessor, the Third Reich. The peculiarity of the Third Reich's debt justified its express regulation in the German Basic Law.

Argentina

5.55 In 1998–2002, Argentina was struck by a severe economic crisis which led the State, among other things, to a forceful debt restructuring and alleged repudiation of its debt. The crisis has sparked a welter of cases before ICSID tribunals and foreign courts. Interestingly, local Argentine courts also were seised of the actions of dissatisfied bondholders, who argued

[115] Case 1 BvR 987/58, Judgment of 14 November 1962, BVerfGE 15, 126.

[116] Joined Cases Nos 2 BvM 1-5/03 & 2 BvM 1-2/06, 60 Neue Juristische Wochenschrift 2610 (2007), in (2007) 101(4) AJIL 857. See, in a similar vein, Cases XI ZR 193/14 and XI ZR 47/14, Judgments of 24 February 2015 (rejecting, among others, Argentina's claim that majority action clauses represent general practice binding upon minority creditors, even though the bonds do not contain express provision to that effect).

that the pesification of sovereign bonds expressed in foreign currency and the statutory prohibition on reaching any kind of agreement with hold-out bondholders flew in the face of the rights embedded in the Argentine Constitution.

Underlying the judicial enquiry of the Supreme Court, and of other judicial instances seised of similar requests, was the standard of reasonableness of the measures adopted. In *Brunicardi, Adriano c/ Banco Central*, the Supreme Court held that a mere deferral of the payment did not amount to a substantial degradation or concealed confiscation of the property, and was reasonable considering the financial situation present at the time of its adoption. In *Civit Félix Guillermo v Poder Ejecutivo Nacional*, the Court of Appeal decided that the pesification of the bonds together with the diminution of the guarantee provided to the bondholder crossed the line. It declared the decrees effecting such amendments unconstitutional albeit holding the bondholder to the reduction of interest rate.[117] **5.56**

In respect of the constitutionality of compulsory pesification, the Supreme Court in *Galli*[118] upheld the decision of the Argentine government to pesify bonds, considering that the financial situation in the country was such as to justify such a course of conduct. In deciding that the pesification legislation did not confiscate sovereign bonds, the Supreme Court was clearly guided by certain statutory mechanisms that the Argentine government introduced to minimise the loss suffered by the bondholders from the forcible conversion of currency. Such mechanisms were the inclusion of a consumer-based inflation index so as to profit from the economic growth when the crisis abates, and the option to partake in future public debt exchanges in foreign currency. **5.57**

Another measure that Argentina resorted to over the course of the restructuring and that proved rather controversial was the Law No 20,617 which prohibited negotiating or reaching any type of agreement with the creditors who held out from the initial debt restructuring. The Supreme Court judges in *Galli* were divided in their *obiter* statements as to the constitutionality of such statute. Lower courts did not speak with a single voice—some of the courts decided that the rights of bondholders were left untouched by the Law No 20,617,[119] whereas others applied the law on its face.[120] **5.58**

117 Rodrigo Olivares-Caminal, *Legal Aspects of Sovereign Debt Restructuring* (2009) 342–49.

118 *Galli, Hugo Gabriel y otro c/ Poder Ejecutivo Nacional*, 5 April 2005.

119 See, eg, *Belohlawek v Poder Ejecutivo Nacional*, 28 August 2007. These courts, however, held that the payment under the bonds was deferred.

120 See, eg, *Di Nicolo, Pietro v National Executive Powers*, 15 June 2006.

5.59 At a different level, Argentine courts have confirmed something that was implicit, namely that recognising a foreign judgment against Argentina resulting from the sovereign debt restructuring which seeks to circumvent the debt restructuring process would contravene Argentine public policy and therefore could not be afforded recognition.[121]

Greece (and Imprimatur of the European Court of Human Rights)

5.60 Following the 2012 sovereign debt restructuring, multiple holders of Greek bonds brought legal actions in local Greek courts challenging the constitutionality of the unilateral and retroactive introduction of majority action clauses into Greek law governed bonds. The Greek Council of State dismissed the action by holding that the introduction of majority action clauses did not violate the Greek Constitution and the European Convention on Human Rights (ECHR) on numerous grounds.[122] First, it held that the legislative act introducing CACs did not result in actual damage to bondholders: only the subsequent modification of the bonds by the majority of bondholders inflicted the actual damage. The distinction strikes as too formalistic: but for the majority action clauses, the majority of bondholders would have been incapable of reducing the debt owed to the bondholders with the binding effect on minority bondholders.

5.61 Further elaborating on the argument of 'no harm', the Council of State reasoned that in the absence of a restructuring, Greece would have been unlikely to perform on the bonds through constant economic growth and the bondholders would inexorably have suffered a bigger loss had the restructuring failed.[123] Following the successful restructuring, the bonds enjoyed a higher creditor rating and were valued at least at the same price level as the one preceding the restructuring.

5.62 Second, the Council of State found that the introduction of CACs satisfied the proportionality requirement under the ECHR. It also determined that the prohibition in the Greek Constitution to expropriate without full compensation applied only to rights *in rem* and not to contractual rights.

[121] *Claren Corporation c/ Estado Nacional (Artículos 517/518 CPCC Exequátur) s/ Varios*, 6 March 2014.

[122] The discussion is based on Ioannis Glinavos, 'Casenote: Decision 1116–1117/2014 (21.3.14) of the Greek Council of State (Συμβούλιο της Επικρατείας)' (2014) (available at http://papers.ssrn.com/sol3/papers.cfm?abstract_id=2445568); Dimitris Tsibanoulis and Iakovos Anagnostopoulos, 'The Greek PSI and the Litigation Surrounding It' (2014) 2 Rev Int des serv fin/Intern Rev Fin Serv 18; Yannis Erifillidis, 'Legislative Measures to Prevent Greece's Economic Collapse: A Step Too Far?' (2014) 7 JIBFL 468.

[123] Cf Gloster LJ's argument in Chapter 7, Coda.

Lastly, the Greek Council of State highlighted that national emergency prompted the introduction of CACs and the measures resorted to were necessary and proportionate for the protection of the public interest. The judgment was accompanied by a strong dissent of seven out of twenty judges. **5.63**

Having exhausted local remedies, the disgruntled creditors initiated proceedings before the European Court of Human Rights. The Court largely confirmed the findings of the Council of State and held that the unilateral introduction of CACs into Greek law governed bonds did not amount to a breach of the ECHR, namely the right to property (Art 1 of Protocol 1) and the prohibition of discrimination (Art 14).[124] First, the Court established that the modifications of bonds did not amount to a 'deprivation of property' within the meaning of the first paragraph of Art 1 of Protocol 1 since the bondholders had made an investment the value of which could fluctuate as a function of the uncertainties of the markets and the economic situation of the issuing State. **5.64**

The Court, however, considered that the unilateral modification did amount to an 'interference' with the right to property. That said, that interference was justified on the facts for an array of reasons: (a) the State enjoyed a wide margin of appreciation in times of economic crises; (b) the interference was prescribed by law; (c) was in the public interest; (d) was proportionate given that Greece was in the situation of 'imminent insolvency', the commercial value of the bonds was already affected by the insolvency of the State and the bonds were subject to a risk of default. **5.65**

IV. INTERIM CONCLUSIONS

Subject to the discussion of tolerable unilateral modifications in the next section, there are two conclusions to draw from the perusal of this case law (especially the common law portions): **5.66**

(1) the sovereign debt issuance is subject to the common regime of private contracts; and
(2) the State does not enjoy police powers to alter the obligations it has entered into in a unilateral manner, or at least there are limits to those police powers.

It is true that the capacity to regulate and unilaterally abrogate State contracts is strictly correlated to the degree of the public interest involved.[125] **5.67**

[124] *Mamatas c. Grèce* (Requêtes nos 63066/14, 64297/14 et 66106/14) CEDH 21 juillet 2016.
[125] Lalive (n 12) 453–54; Peter Cane, *Introduction to Administrative Law* (2011) 236–37.

Clearly, the principle of *pacta sunt servanda* is not absolute and might be subject to exceptions in certain spheres such as natural resources.[126] Unlike other spheres where the State might be called to exercise its sovereign prerogatives more often, in the field of financial contracts the public interest is not directly at the forefront.[127] The US Supreme Court has correctly noted that purely financial contracts with the State do not in principle give rise to police powers.[128]

5.68 That said, the prohibition to modify sovereign bonds unilaterally is without prejudice to three distinct matters. First, the argument presented here is restrained exclusively to situations where the State purports to change the express terms of the contract. Changes to the broader legislative framework of the sovereign debtor, adopted within its right to regulate, that might have collateral effect on the financial expectations of investors (eg, currency rate fluctuations or tax measures) are assumed to be objectionable to a much lesser degree.[129] The argument is that the expectations of creditors, not expressly set out in the contract, should more effortlessly yield to the State's right to regulate. Conversely, financial terms expressly agreed upon are believed to give rise to higher and more stable expectations.

5.69 Looking at the matter more pragmatically, the State may use the threat of modifications of the broader legal framework as a measure of coercion on the bondholders in an effort to force them to accept the terms of a debt restructuring. This tactic was used by New Zealand in 1933 when the parliament imposed on domestic bondholders a 33% tax on interest paid under those domestic bonds that were not voluntarily converted into new, restructured bonds.[130]

5.70 In any event, the scope of unilateral amendment of the general legal environment that will affect the extent of the State's obligations has dwindled in relevance with the increasing sophistication of the modern bond

[126] Munir Maniruzzaman, 'State Contracts with Aliens: The Question of Unilateral Change by the State in Contemporary International Law' (1992) 9(4) J Intl Arb 141; Derek Bowett, 'Claims between States and Private Entities: The Twilight Zone of International Law' (1986) 35 (4) Cath U L Rev 929, 935.

[127] Borchard (n 9) 282.

[128] *United States Trust Co v New Jersey* (n 85) 1519.

[129] Borchard (n 9) 261–62; *National & Provincial Building Society, the Leeds Permanent Building Society and the Yorkshire Building Society v The United Kingdom* (Appl No 21319/93) ECtHR 23 October 1997, paras 80–81. One of the possible ways of assessing the legality of such changes is to consider the effects of economic regulation, the degree of interference with the legitimate expectations, and the character of governmental action (*Eastern Entreprises v Apfel*, 524 US 498, 500 (1994); *In re Persky* 134 BR 81, 93–94 (Bankr EDNY 1991)).

[130] Michael Reddell, 'The New Zealand Debt Conversion Act 1933: A Case Study in Coercive Domestic Public Debt Restructuring' (2012) 75 Reserve Bank of New Zealand Bulletin 38.

documentation. The sovereign bond documentation often explicitly elevates various parts of the legal system onto the sovereign bond terms and conditions. A cursory overview of bonds shows that the following matters, among others, are covered by the bond documentation: taxation, currency, interest payments, transfer of bonds, and prescription. For instance, in respect of the currency fluctuations, bonds often stipulate that:

> If the amount received or recovered is less than the amount expressed to be due to the recipient under any Note, Receipt or Coupon, the Republic shall indemnify it against any loss sustained by it as a result. In any event, the Republic shall indemnify the recipient against the cost of making any such purchase.[131]

Second, the modes of payment (not the substance of the debt) is a matter subject to the State's prerogative to regulate. As a matter of example, the Permanent Court of International Justice held in the *Serbian and Brazilian Loans* that although Serbian and Brazilian laws applied as regards the substance of the debt, French law applied to the currency of payment since the place of payment was in France.[132] Similarly, the French Conseil d'Etat judged that for the debt payable in France, French law would govern the conversion rate of the currency of the payment, even though the obligation was subject to some other law.[133] This fits rather neatly into the principle of conflict of laws that the method of payment shall be governed by the place of its performance.[134] **5.71**

Lastly, a separate and complex issue is whether sovereign bonds, irrespective of their governing law, may be treated as property and be affected by the legislation of the country in the clearing system of which they are registered. For example, the legislation of the State of the location of the clearing system may constrain the transferability of the title to the bonds outside the clearing system or may introduce statutory novation by transferring the liability of the debtor to another person. It needs to be stressed that the English courts have historically been adamant in subjecting the release or transfer of securities to the proper law of the contract, and not to the law of the place where the securities were situated.[135] An idea that **5.72**

[131] See, eg, cl 16 of the offering circular of the Medium Term Note Programme of the Republic of Austria, 23 March 2007.

[132] *Case Concerning the Payment in Gold of the Brazilian Federal Loans Issued in France (France v Brazil)*, Judgment No 15 (1929) Ser A, 122; *Case Concerning the Payment in Gold of the Serbian Federal Loans Issued in France (France v Serbia)*, Judgment No 14 (1929) PCIJ Ser A, 44.

[133] Conseil d'Etat 28 nov 1958, Dame Langlois (1960) Clunet 444.

[134] Art 12(2) of the Rome I Regulation on the Law Applicable to Contractual Obligations; *Serbian and Brazilian Loans Cases*, PCIJ, Ser A, No 21 (1929); No 22 (1929).

[135] *Kahler v Midland Bank* [1950] AC 24, 28; *Zivnostenska Banka v Frankman* [1950] AC 57, 81–83. See also *Re Helbert Wagg & Co Ltd* [1956] Ch 323, 339–40.

received the imprimatur of the Privy Council is that measures short of expropriation are subject to the proper law of the contract.[136]

1. Tolerable Types of Unilateral Modification of Sovereign Bonds

5.73 It remains true that, assuming the State is on the verge of bankruptcy, the extreme financial burden can seriously affect the proper function of the State. Financing—in aggregate, not bond by bond—goes to the heart of the State's public interest and its capacity to deliver a wide range of public goods. State infrastructures might not exist or might not be able to be maintained without what might seem to be a necessary sovereign debt restructuring.

5.74 Having said that, an idea permeating this monograph is that the state of necessity of a sovereign debtor does not give an unrestricted carte blanche to act *ultra legum*. With that idea in mind, this chapter has argued that the State does not have the power to modify unilaterally its domestic-law bonds. While that is the starting point of enquiry, the private creditor would still need to convince the English courts that the unilateral modification is *manifestly* in breach of public policy. To do something exceptional—refuse recognition of a law on the ground of public policy—the foreign legislation ought to be manifestly in breach of public policy.[137]

5.75 It is submitted here that certain more or less innocuous unilateral modifications may fail to meet the bar of manifest breach of public policy:

(1) Unilateral modification of bonds when conjoined with a valid exercise of power to regulate. To draw on the examples discussed here, a valid exercise of power would include the regulation of gold (*Perry v United States*) or the exercise of wartime powers (*Page v Commissioners of Crown Lands*; the German repudiation of the debt of the Third Reich). In those instances, the modification of bonds speaks in a fundamental manner to the concurrent exercise of a police power. This explains why in *Perry v United States*, where the police power relating to gold regulation was at stake, the Supreme Court refused to award damages to the aggrieved bondholder, but in a case decided a year earlier, in *Lynch v US*, the Supreme Court upheld the validity of war insurance contracts in spite of a legislative act that purported to annul them.[138]

[136] *Wight v Eckhardt Marine GmbH* [2003] UKPC 37, para 15.

[137] *Kuwait Airways Corp v Iraqi Airways Comp* [2002] UKHL 19, para 29.

[138] *Lynch v United States*, 292 US 571, 580 (1934).

(2) Declaring a moratorium (stopping payments for the duration of the moratorium) or re-profiling bonds (extending maturities of bonds). This was implicit in the Russian litigation, discussed above.[139] Proving the manifest contrariety of these two ventures to the English public policy would undeniably be a burdensome task.[140]
(3) Injection of majority action clauses (or other CACs) into contracts that did not have them in the first place is more uncertain. The retrospective introduction of a regime to restructure debt did, however, receive judicial imprimatur in *Faitoute* (with important constraints) and the judgment of the Greek Council of State.[141]

Furthermore, one could temper the effects of the public policy exception by relying on the so-called *public policy attenué*. In other words, the idea that the public policy exception would only be triggered when the application of the foreign law, allegedly in breach of manifest principles of the legal system of the forum, is also detrimental to the interests of the forum (eg, interests of local claimants).[142] **5.76**

The foregoing analysis demonstrates that public policy is largely an unruly horse and prudent lenders might be better advised to deal with the transaction risk by *ex ante* tools. Risk-averse bondholders would be better insulated from unilateral amendments brought in by the sovereign debtor through the insertion of stabilisation clauses into sovereign bonds.[143] **5.77**

One is left with perhaps not the most beguiling idea that whether the retrospective legislation contravenes public policy is at the end an issue of balancing.[144] That the sovereign can amend its legislation is beyond cavil. It is also beyond cavil that a State may not rely on the very event it has itself **5.78**

[139] See also Marc-Philippe Weller, *Die Grenze der Vertragstreue von (Krisen-)Staaten: Zur Einrede des Staatsnotstands gegenüber privaten Anleihegläubigern* (2013).

[140] See, however, *Allied III*, discussed in Chapter 6, that has equated the moratorium of debt with a taking of contractual rights. For criticism, see Dominic Carreau, 'La nouvelle decision américaine Allied Bank International ou un retour ambigu à la protection juridique des créanciers dans la procédure des rééchelonnements de detters internationales' (1986) 113 JDI 123, 124–25.

[141] See, however, Chapter 7 (the vesting in a third party of the power to modify the rights under the bonds without the consent of bondholders is likely to attract the opprobrium of English courts).

[142] See in this sense *Russian and English Bank v Baring Brothers* [1936] AC 405, 422 (leaving English creditors unpaid is unjust).

[143] Note that the status of stabilisation clauses is controversial (see, eg, Paul Lagarde, 'Le nouveau droit international privé des contrats après l'entrée en viguer de la Convention de Rome du 19 juin 1980' (1991) 80(2) Rev Crit 287).

[144] FA Mann, 'The Time Element in the Conflict of Laws' (1954) 31 BYBIL 217–47, 240; Erwin Spiro, 'The Incidence of Time in the Conflict of Laws' (1960) 9 ICLQ 357, 377–78.

brought into existence to frustrate its own mercantile undertakings.[145] The difficulty is the haze that overlies the boundary between what is acceptable as a legitimate change of contractual terms and what is not. There is no denying that the State has a wide interest in regulating the volume and content of the debt in the national economy. National sovereignty is unimaginable without a significant degree of economic independence and freedom in regulating national economy. However, such power needs to be carefully balanced against the fairness of the action of the State that seeks to interfere with its own obligations.

[145] Kinsch (n 28) 276–85; Christoph Schreuer, *State Immunity: Some Recent Developments* (1988) 110–11.

6

Defences to Repayment

Having examined issues of jurisdiction and governing law, this chapter turns to substantive matters arising in sovereign debt litigation. Section I will examine the obligation to repay and the attacks mounted against it. Section II will consider the defences that a sovereign debtor can raise against the recovery of the payments under the bonds. **6.01**

I. OBLIGATION TO REPAY

In English law (and the New York courts, for that matter), the private creditors will seek repayment by bringing an action in debt for the principal due, plus the interest accrued on the money. It is a fundamental principle that the creditor may thus recover its contractual entitlement in full (ie, the par value of bonds plus the interest). **6.02**

The action in debt is unlike, and not to be confused with, the action in damages where the claimant seeks to recover the damages arising from a breach of contract,[1] and where the issue of evaluation of damages is often acutely posed (eg, mitigation of damages). The distinguishing feature here is that in an action for an agreed sum, the claimant seeks to recover, as of right, a fixed sum of money and no major controversy arises over the quantum of payment. In transactions involving a reciprocal exchange of money, the courts, as a rule, order repayment of the nominal value of the money agreed in the contract. Of course, the calculation of payments under the bonds can be plagued by complications in class actions where the judge may be tempted to issue an aggregated judgment without individualised calculations,[2] however, this is a separate matter. **6.03**

The interest rate in an action in debt will depend on the drafting of the contract and the governing legal system. Some Argentine bonds provided for a floating interest rate under which the contractual rate of interest changed from time to time based on changes in the then-current 'market **6.04**

[1] For a distinction between actions for damages and actions for debt, see Harvey McGregor, *McGregor on Damages* (2016) para 1-005.

[2] *Puricelli v Republic of Argentina*, 2015 US App LEXIS 13944 (2d Cir 2015).

yield' on regular Argentine fixed rate bonds in the secondary trading markets. The floating interest rates proved disastrous for Argentina where the interest rate was 101% at one point.[3] Interest on interest, otherwise known as compound interest, is recognised both in English law[4] and New York law.[5] Once a judgment has been entered into, the judgment interest rate applies instead of the contractual rate. In England, it is 8% post-judgment (s 17 of the Judgments Act 1838). In New York State, it is currently 9% (NY CPLR §5004).

6.05 English law subscribes to the nominalism of monetary obligations, whereby the nominal value of the debt is not subject to adjustment following inflation.[6] If a foreign law applies to the bonds, it may provide for a mechanism for adjusting for inflation. For instance, in a bond-related dispute under the US–Peru Trade Promotion Agreement, the bondholder sought to contest the calculations under Peruvian law that recognised the possibility of increasing the value of bonds because of hyperinflation.[7]

6.06 This is the state of current positive law. The law is clear—the creditor is entitled to full repayment. Section I discusses whether deviations from this rule are possible, that is to say, whether bondholders may receive less than full reimbursement.

6.07 All the alternative proposals below share one common objective: they seek to reduce the amount of the debt owed to the private creditors. They do not rely on the majority action clauses or other contractual provisions specifically designed to ease sovereign debt restructurings. Rather, they seek to devise a substantive law approach in favour of the sovereign debtor. Consequently, the substantive approach, outlined below, may also apply in respect of the sovereign debt that does not contain collective action clauses (CACs) (such as, State-to-State bonds bought on the secondary market).

6.08 This section will contain references to the position in public international law. However, the solutions in public international law are not easily transposable into municipal law. In *Italy v Costa Rica* the arbitral tribunal, chaired by Pierre Lalive, drew a distinction between the technical level (level of contractual provisions) and the equitable decision-making under

[3] Matt Levine, 'Argentina's Bond Fight Comes Down to its Worst Bonds' *Bloomberg View* (8 February 2016).

[4] *Sempra Metals Ltd v Inland Revenue Commissioners* [2007] UKHL 34.

[5] New York General Obligations Law §5–527.

[6] Charles Proctor, *Mann on the Legal Aspect of Money* (2012) Intro III.01.

[7] *Gramercy Funds Management LLC and others v Republic of Peru*, Notice of Intent to Commence Arbitration (2016).

public international law where the award of compensation is guided by other considerations.[8]

There is a growing counter-trend that proffers less than full repayment to the sovereign bondholders and relies on the market value of the bonds as opposed to their nominal value. For the purposes of this section, market value is defined as the price at which the bonds change hands on the secondary market of sovereign bonds. The market value is unavoidably lower than the bond's nominal value in the case of a sovereign debtor in distress, representing the distrust that the financial market has in the State's financial sanity. **6.09**

Various grounds for, and methods of, reducing the contractual entitlement down to the market value have been proposed. Waibel, adducing international legal decisions, suggests the exceptional character of financial crises, the State's limited payment capacity, and the need to avoid unjust entitlement of creditors to awards less than the nominal value of bonds—the fair market value or even less. He calculates the market value by using the net present value of the old bonds, discounted by the yield of the new debt.[9] **6.10**

Glinavos suggests that investors should receive the fair market value of bonds, which for him is the amount invested in the purchase of bonds.[10] This resonates with the position under French law. Under Art 1699 of the French Civil Code (*retrait des droits litigieux*), the assignor receives the money paid for the assignment of credit when the debt is disputed, not the nominal value. **6.11**

Lastly, Bohoslavsky argues that the bondholders should bear responsibility for abusive (excessive) lending to the States. The backbone of the argument, allegedly derived from the legal systems of a number of developed countries, is that speculative bondholders should bear responsibility for lending to the State already buried under excessively high levels of debt. The responsibility should come in the form of a set-off or subordination of abusive loans to those classified as not abusive.[11]

[8] *Loan Agreement between Italy v Costa Rica*, Decision of 27 June 1998, Reports of International Arbitral Awards, Vol XXV, 72–75.

[9] Michael Waibel, *Sovereign Defaults before International Courts and Tribunals* (2011) 301–08, 312–15. For the case law in the opposite direction, see Michael Waibel, 'Opening Pandora's Box: Sovereign Bonds in International Arbitration' (2007) 101 AJIL 711, 756.

[10] Ioannis Glinavos, 'Haircut Undone? The Greek Drama and Prospects for Investment Arbitration' (2014) 5 J Intl Disp Settl 475, 494–96.

[11] Juan Pablo Bohoslavsky, 'Responsibility for Abusive Granting of Sovereign Loans' (2008) 14 Law & Bus Rev Am 495. See also Kunibert Raffer, 'Risks of Lending and Liability of Lending' in Christian Barry, Barry Herman, and Lydia Tomitova (eds), *Dealing Fairly with Developing Country Debt* (2007) 127–32.

6.12 These views are essentially attempts to resolve the problem of holdout litigation. They put forward a view that the problems of holdouts may be more satisfactorily addressed by finding a substantive law solution under English law (or New York law) that would limit the rights of distressed debt investors to request full nominal value.

6.13 The grounds adduced in favour of using the market value as the benchmark for the repayment of sovereign debt are numerous, but the reasons against are overwhelming and more convincing. The following analysis would suggest that awarding the market value of bonds is suboptimal on many levels. Even if in practice the creditors might settle for less than the nominal value of bonds, it is imperative that they should enjoy the right to claim the nominal value as of right should they wish to do so.

6.14 Having outlined the various grounds for the partial compensation of bondholders, some clarification is required regarding whose debt entitlement should be reduced. At its strongest, the proponents of the market value compensation claim that the payments to all private bondholders—both initial and secondary—should be equally decreased. At its weakest, it is proposed that the reduction of the creditor rights should affect the holders of sovereign bonds who acquired the bonds on the secondary markets or, even narrower, 'vulture' funds.

1. Risk of Default

6.15 The proponents of less than full compensation often allege that the risk of default is a risk that a creditor assumes with open eyes when purchasing the bonds of a State in distress or even in the vicinity of default. If the risk of non-payment does not materialise over time, the creditor will see its bonds completely paid. However, should the circumstances decline and the State default, the sovereign bondholder is bound to the payment of the market value of the bonds, rather than the nominal value. Sovereign bonds do not give an absolute right to repayment and bondholders engaging in speculation should not earn a windfall on their initially limited investment. According to the proponents of this view, this should be all the more the case when the investor purchased an interest in the sovereign debt after the event of default.

6.16 The argument strikes one as specious. On the conceptual level, the investor is contractually entitled to recover the par value of bonds. The bondholder, who acquired the bonds on the secondary market at a steep discount, agreed to pay as little as 10–20% of the nominal value and accept the risk of default, only in the hope of recovering the whole amount due under the bonds. The larger the discount on the par value on the secondary market, the larger the risk undertaken by the bondholder. The risk undertaken is mitigated by the more or less certain probability of the recovery of the full value. Otherwise, such risks would not be taken by reasonable commercial parties.[12]

Hobhouse LJ, in a slightly different context of champerty defence and validity of assignment, neatly expresses the point in the context of an assignment of the debt of impecunious State entity at a sheer discount: 'If … assets of the defendant can be found which are amenable to execution, the plaintiff may at the end of the day have made a profit on the transaction.… [W]hy else should a commercial entity purchase a debt?'[13] **6.17**

It may well be argued that the risks inherent in the sovereign debt lie with the sovereign debtor. By issuing bonds, the sovereign debtor accepts the risk of changed economic and financial conditions, as well as of the financial difficulties. It is commonly accepted that the party who has been assigned the performance under the contract is under the obligation to perform it notwithstanding changing economic conditions and costs of such performance (unless, of course, it can raise a valid defence, as discussed in Section II). **6.18**

2. Abusive Lending

Even though the contention might have factual grounding in certain sovereign debt crises (1980s crises in Latin America spring to mind), the counterarguments are not particularly difficult to formulate. First, the legal basis of such argument is shaky and is not tenable in positive law.[14] Examples of abusive lending, derived from national legal systems that are isolated and subject to stringent conditions, do not justify the emergence of a general principle of law that may be extended to the ordinary commercial situation where a State has overborrowed. The State enters into financial markets of its own volition, almost exclusively with the advice of sophisticated legal and financial counsel. In England, the lender is not subject to a general duty to advise a borrower about the prudence or soundness of the borrowing, unless the lender has assumed specific contractual responsibility. In ordinary scenarios, the State would not ask the lenders for advice on its debt burden and whether the debt is sustainable. Nor do the lenders **6.19**

[12] *Pravin Banker Associates Ltd v Banco Popular del Peru*, 912 F Supp 77 (SDNY 1996) (rejecting attempts to reduce the recoverable principal on the ground that the creditor bought it at a steep discount).

[13] *Camdex International Ltd v Bank of Zambia* [1998] QB 22, 35.

[14] Roberto McLean, 'Legal Aspects of the External Debt' (1989) 214 Recueil des Cours 31, 106–07.

owe a duty of care to borrowers when lending money. The rules are, however, not as strict for consumer (individual) credit.[15] Moreover, the circumstances where the lender will owe a fiduciary duty to the customer are narrowly constrained: the courts would look for vulnerability, reliance/dependency, an ascendant position, or capacity to influence so as to place a fiduciary duty on the lender.[16] In light of these principles, in so far as the scholars claim abusive lending acts to shield or reduce the liability of the sovereign debtor, shifting the burden for overborrowing onto the financial markets amounts to avoiding one's own responsibility for imprudent borrowing.[17]

6.20 Second, it is a commonsensical principle that the sovereign debtor may not raise the argument of abusive lending against the claimant who might have purchased the bonds on the secondary market and in no way contributed to the abusive lending. Should, for argument's sake, the claimant be the original bondholder, having lent in excess and without due diligence of the State's financial health, it cannot be held liable for the aggregate overborrowing ensured by the mass of lenders who collectively contributed to the over-indebtedness of the debtor.

6.21 Third, the lending to a debtor with high levels of debt is perhaps better conceptualised not as abusive lending, but as high-risk and high-yield investment which bets on the financial recovery of the State. By providing the funds to an over-indebted State, the creditor expects that the State has a chance of recovery and will be able to fully repay the debt.

6.22 At a policy level, an argument can be made that overzealous lending presents a systematic issue and should be treated as such. Valid as that may be, it is hardly an issue for the judicial development of law.

3. Unjust Enrichment

6.23 This argument will not carry the day in English law since the debtor will struggle to pinpoint any unjust factor, such as lack of consideration, undue influence, and so on. The question of unjust enrichment may only arise when the loan is invalid and the lender claims that the debtor is unjustly enriched by the money provided without a valid loan agreement.[18] Schreuer goes further and suggests that crisis-like situations may in themselves be grounds for a claim of unjust enrichment and cites either

[15] Parker Hood, *Principles of Lender Liability* (2012) 194–95, 204. [16] Ibid 247–49.

[17] See, eg, *JP Morgan Chase Bank v Springwell Navigation Corporation* [2008] EWHC 1186 (Comm) (finding that an inherent risk was present in investing into Russian government bonds, or instruments linked to the Russian government bonds, that collapsed in 1998).

[18] See below para 6.108.

the outbreak of war or change of territorial sovereignty.[19] He then, however, continues:

> [W]ith international law in its present state of development, restitution for unjustified enrichment can be considered hardly more than a decision-technique to be applied once the basic policy decisions have been made, and not a normative principle or general rule from which specific 'correct' decisions can be logically derived.[20]

4. Fairness

Waibel claims that awarding the fair market value would ensure intercreditor equity: it is nothing but fair to award a comparable level of damages to creditors, both holdout and consenting.[21] In *Salah Turkmani v Republic of Bolivia*,[22] the defendant claimed that the damages of a private creditor are necessarily constrained to the level of damages accorded in the Paris Club Agreement. The court correctly confirmed the voluntary character of debt restructurings and derived from it that the agreement of the Paris Club would not bind a private creditor litigating before domestic courts.[23] The case is very much to the point: a creditor may not be forced into accepting the haircut that other creditors have consented to (absent, of course, a triggered majority action clause). Holding all the groups of creditors to the same level of repayment of the debt might wreak havoc on the secondary market of sovereign bonds. Predicting the broader repercussions of such an outcome on the practice and pricing of sovereign debt is difficult, and testing it in real life does not seem to be a well-thought-through step. **6.24**

In *National Fire Insurance v Congo*,[24] the claimant attempted to enforce an English judgment arising out of a loan agreement in the courts of the United States. Among other arguments, Congo claimed that the recognition of the judgment would fly in the face of the principles of equity and international law. Congo argued that recognising and enforcing a judgment would be against the restructuring agreement that Congo had entered into with all but one of its commercial creditors, namely the holdout creditor in those proceedings. The court strongly rebutted the argument on the ground that participation in the restructuring ought to be voluntary. The mere fact that the enforcement of contractual rights might **6.25**

[19] Christoph Schreuer, 'Unjustified Enrichment in International Law' (1974) 22(2) Am J Comp L 281, 289–93.

[20] Ibid 301. [21] Waibel, *Sovereign Defaults* (n 9) 313–14.

[22] 193 F Supp 2d 165, 181 (DDC 2002).

[23] See, to the same effect, ICC award n 6219, (1990) 117(4) JDI 1047, 1052–53.

[24] *National Union Fire Ins Co v People's Republic of the Congo*, 729 F Supp 936 (SDNY 1989).

have adverse effects upon the Congo was not sufficient to render the exercise of contractual rights illegitimate. The court added that it was not the appropriate institution to make a policy judgment, namely to weigh the potential harm to the sovereign debtor against the harm to the claimant if the court refused to enforce the judgment.

6.26 A precedent does exist for less than full compensation. Under the UK Debt Relief (Developing Countries) Act (2010),[25] in actions against heavily indebted poor countries (HIPC), the creditors are able to recover only the debt as reduced in accordance with the HIPC Initiative. The statute is, however, by definition limited to HIPC only—the countries which the international community has agreed to treat in a beneficial manner. In Belgium, under the Loi relative à la lutte contre les activités des fonds vauteurs, adopted on 12 July 2015, if a Belgian judge determines that a fund is acting as a 'vulture', the fund may only recover the discounted price paid for the bonds, and not their full value. Importantly, this provision applies irrespective of the governing law of bonds (Art 1).

6.27 There is a more general point to be made in respect of the Debt Relief (Developing Countries) Act (2010). The Act was expressly constrained to HIPC. Should the legislature have wished to let other sovereign debtors benefit from such reduction, it could have specified such in the Act. The courts might prefer not to embark on an innovative interpretation of English contract law where the legislature has chosen to remain silent on the contracts of all debtors, other than HIPC.

6.28 Two further counterarguments can be invoked. First, from a policy perspective, too blunt a limitation of the rights of 'vulture' funds might come at the expense of damaging the secondary market of the sovereign debt and the free assignability of sovereign debt. Even more so, damaging the secondary market would have direct negative repercussions on the primary sovereign market. The whole *raison d'être* of the secondary market is to counteract the weak enforcement mechanisms in the primary markets.[26] Trading on the secondary market is not necessarily a speculation in that it has a social function, namely, to provide money to bondholders who exchange their non-performing loans for liquidity.

[25] For analysis, see Michael Waibel, 'Debt Relief to Poor Countries: Rules v. Discretion' (2010) 25(5) BB & FLR 295. Jersey and Guernsey have announced plans to pass a similar law. More generally about such statutes, see Elizabeth Broomfield, 'Subduing the Vultures: Assessing Government Caps on Recovery in Sovereign Debt Litigation' (2010) 2 Colum Bus L Rev 473.

[26] Fernando Broner, Alberto Martin, and Jaume Ventura, 'Enforcement Problems and Secondary Markets' (2007) NBER Working Paper 13559.

More generally, the proposed overhaul of the payment system in the sovereign debt litigation might have negative spillovers to the markets of sovereign bonds and thus make the litigation of sovereign debt disputes, already an adventurous exercise, the pursuit of very few. This would undermine the whole business model of hedge funds specialising in the purchase and litigation of sovereign debt on the secondary market. The whole point of providing liquidity to the holders of sovereign bonds and preserving the often coveted secondary market of bonds might disappear for the hedge funds should the only remedy that a secondary market purchaser receive be the market value or less. **6.29**

The arguments that propose to reduce the full compensation arising out of sovereign default are all the more pronounced and have a higher likelihood of being upheld in investment treaty arbitration.[27] There is a trend advanced by a number of international investment tribunals not to afford full compensation to the investors engaged in speculative trading who acquired the debt after the investment declined in value.[28] **6.30**

In international investment law, the fact that the claimant bought the securities in the secondary market at a heavy discount could be a relevant consideration in deciding whether he was treated in a fair and equitable way at the time of default and/or restructuring. In investment arbitration this is captured by the mitigation of damages rule. By contrast, in English contract law, an action for an agreed sum of money is not subject to the requirement of mitigation. **6.31**

Lienau, in her lucid historical analysis of the doctrine of odious debt, contends that the principle of consistent repayment of sovereign (illegitimate) debt in all circumstances is historically charged. It is based on the assumptions of political neutrality, reputational stability, and creditor uniformity, as well as the conception of sovereignty and the model of 'agency' between the government and the people. Drawing on the historical examples of Costa Rica and the USSR, she highlights that 'the degree to which creditor interactions are competitive or consolidated ... may affect the degree to which the rule of continuous debt repayment is stable'.[29] At the expense **6.32**

[27] For a discussion, see Waibel, *Sovereign Defaults* (n 9) ch 13.

[28] *RosInvestCo UK Ltd v The Russian Federation*, SCC Case No V079/2005, Final Award, 12 September 2010, para 664ff; *Renta 4 SVSA et al v The Russian Federation*, SCC No 24/2007, Award, 20 July 2012, paras 195–219; *African Holding Company of America, Inc and Société Africaine de Construction au Congo SARL v La République Démocratique du Congo*, ICSID Case No ARB/05/21, Decision on Jurisdiction and Admissibility, para 80 (expresses serious doubts as to the activity of vulture funds). For other cases, see Waibel, *Sovereign Defaults* (n 9) 297, 301–08, 312–15. See also *Eagle Pencil Co, Inc*, 27 April 1959 (1966) 30 ILR 128, 130 (reduction of bank deposits by 30% given the 'abnormal' situation in pre-revolution Russia).

[29] Odette Lienau, *Rethinking Sovereign Debt: Politics, Reputation and Legitimacy* (2014) 28.

of oversimplification, her argument is that in a system where creditors are competitive, some of them might forgo the requirement of consistent repayment of sovereign debt, thus affecting the stability of such a rule.

6.33 The principle of full and consistent repayment of the debt is not modified just because at some points in history in Costa Rica and the USSR the lenders decided to waive their entitlement to consistent repayment. The principle of debt repayment remains valid, yet whether it will be applied in the current economic or political environment is an altogether different question.

6.34 Although ostensibly limited to the issue of odious debt, one should warn against extending this type of extralegal, historically charged argument to the principle of consistent repayment in general. By entering into sovereign debt obligations, and absent any contentions of odiousness (quaere whether this doctrine is good law), the sovereign debtor is bound to its contractual obligations and the courts should resist calls for undermining the commercial basis of sovereign debt issuance.

II. DEFENCES

6.35 It is usual for a bondholder to move for a summary judgment upon the bonds. In English litigation, the claimant can obtain a summary judgment if the defendant has no real prospect of successfully defending the claim or issue (CPR 24.2). In the US, the court will grant summary judgment if the movant (either claimant or defendant) shows that there is no genuine dispute as to any material fact and the movant is entitled to judgment as a matter of law (Rule 56, Federal Rules of Civil Procedure).

6.36 In most cases, the sovereign debtor, who defaulted on the bonds, will have no real prospect of succeeding on the claim. The fact of default will rarely be contested and most legal defences raised by the State in financial litigation will receive short shrift from the English and New York courts. Nevertheless, some defences have prospects of success in sovereign debt litigation.

6.37 The discussion below examines the defences under English and New York laws and is not concerned with defences available in international law, specifically the defence of necessity.[30]

[30] On which see August Reinisch, 'Necessity in Investment Arbitration' (2010) 41 NYIL 137; Michael Waibel, 'Two Worlds of Necessity in ICSID Arbitration: *CMS* and *LG&E*' (2007) 20 LJIL 637.

1. Relevance of Events of Default Clause

Before proceeding with the discussion of defences, a preliminary point needs to be raised. It is at least arguable that the Events of Default Clause ubiquitously found in sovereign bond documentation may colour the defences that a State can raise. Often, sovereign bonds provide that an Event of Default (which has the effect of accelerating the payment of the principal) will arise if: **6.38**

(5) ***Validity***:
  (a) the Republic, or any governmental body with the legal power and authority to declare such series of debt securities and the related Fiscal Agency Agreement invalid or unenforceable, challenges the validity of such series of debt securities or the related Fiscal Agency Agreement;
  (b) the Republic denies any of its obligations under such series of debt securities or the related Fiscal Agency Agreement; or
  (c) any legislative, executive or constitutional measure or final judicial decision renders any material provision of such series of debt securities or the related Fiscal Agency Agreement invalid or unenforceable or prevents or delays the performance of the Republic's obligations under such series of debt securities or the related Fiscal Agency Agreement;

(6) ***Failure of Authorisations***: any legislative, executive or constitutional authorisation necessary for the Republic to perform its material obligations under the series of debt securities or the related Fiscal Agency Agreement ceases to be in full force and effect or is modified in a manner materially prejudicial to the holders of the debt securities.[31]

Pursuant to this provision, challenges to the validity and even denial of obligations are treated as Events of Default. In a similar vein, some bonds (by El Salvador[32] and Trinidad and Tobago)[33] contain a clause which provides for payment in a certain currency irrespective of any laws or regulations: **6.39**

Judgment Currency. All payments required to be made hereunder by the Republic shall be in U.S. dollars, regardless of any law, rule, regulation or statute, whether

[31] Republic of Philippines, Prospectus Supplement to Prospectus dated December 12, 2013, US$1,500,000,000, 4.20% Global Bonds due 2024, pp 121–22.

[32] Republic of El Salvador, Offering Circular, US$800,000,000 5.875% Notes due 2025, Clause 18.

[33] Republic of Trinidad and Tobago, Offering Circular, US$550,000,000, 4.375% Notes due 2024, Clause 17.

now or hereafter in existence or in effect in any jurisdiction, which affects or purports to affect such obligations.

6.40 The question is whether these provisions can act as a barrier to the raising of legal defences in court proceedings. The issue arose in *Elliott Associates v Banco de la Nacion and Republic of Peru*,[34] where Peru agreed to pay the amounts due 'regardless of any law, regulation or order'. The District Court first established that under New York law, a sovereign may waive a statutory or even a constitutional provision enacted for his benefit or protection, assuming a private right is involved and the public interest is not. On the facts, the Court held that a champerty statute involved public interest and could not be waived.

6.41 It stands to reason that these types of clauses are not treated as capable of genuinely insulating the bonds from genuine defences, mandatory rules, or valid legislative changes adopted by the sovereign debtor. Most of these will in one way or another involve public interest. If the State adopts a legislative act recognised by English courts or relies on a defence under English law to challenge the validity of a bond, the Event of Defaults clause cannot prevent such reliance. Upon an event of default, the bondholder will only be able to accelerate the debt, merely to find the terms and conditions of bonds it possesses already altered by unilateral modifications of the sovereign debtor (if applicable).[35]

6.42 Further, bonds may often contain warranties or be accompanied by legal opinions regarding the validity of the bonds, including their compliance with the constitutional principles of the sovereign debtors. Properly understood, the legal effect of any warranties or legal opinions is a matter to be determined by the governing law. Thus, if, for instance, the State raises an issue of legal capacity, the relevance of warranties is a matter for the law governing capacity.[36]

2. Act of State

6.43 In the recent *Belhaj v Straw*, Lord Neuberger, in the majority, set the boundaries of the Act of State doctrine. For him, the doctrine is composed of three rules. First, English courts will recognise, and will not question, the effect of a foreign State's *legislation* or other laws in relation to any acts which take place or take effect within the territory of that State. Second, English courts will recognise, and will not question, the effect of an *act* of a foreign

[34] 12 F Supp 2d 328 (SDNY 1998).

[35] Peter Cresswell, William Blair, and Philip Wood (eds), *Encyclopaedia of Banking Law* (2013) F-310.

[36] On State capacity, see para 6.89 below.

State's executive in relation to any acts which take place or take effect within the territory of that State. The third rule is the non-justiciability or abstention, or in the terminology of Lord Sumption, international act of a State.[37] To cite an example, in *Law Debenture Trust Corporation plc v Ukraine*, Blair J held that the allegations of duress and threat of force made by Ukraine against Russia were non-justiciable.[38] Importantly, it was earlier confirmed that while sovereign immunity may be waived, the doctrine of Act of State or non-justiciability may not.[39]

The doctrine of Act of State may feature prominently in the litigation of various disputes involving sovereign defendants. However, it shall have no application to sovereign defaults given that the doctrine does not in principle extend to commercial transactions.[40] In commercial cases, if a State adopts laws and regulations to govern or modify its own debt, then their application will be determined by the conflict of laws principles canvassed in this book. If the court reaches the conclusion that the governing law of sovereign bonds is English or New York law, or indeed any legal system other than that of the sovereign debtor, those regulations will have no application.[41] If, by contrast, the bonds are subject to the laws of the foreign State, the claimants may need to challenge the legality of such laws, perhaps by arguing that they are inconsistent with English public policy.[42] The challenge of foreign legislation will have the result of triggering the Act of State doctrine, but so long as the challenge is based on the doctrine of public policy, the English court will not be precluded from reviewing its consistency with public policy.[43] **6.44**

The Act of State doctrine may apply when the State acts in its public capacity by regulating the foreign debt of local entities. In 1981, following a severe economic crisis, the Costa Rican government passed a decree prohibiting all external debt payments without the consent of its Central Bank, to ensure the uniformity of the renegotiation of the Costa Rican external debt. Soon thereafter, the Costa Rican Central Bank deferred the release of foreign currency intended for the repayment of external debt, which caused three Costa Rican State-owned banks to default on their **6.45**

37 [2017] UKSC 3, paras 120–24. On non-justiciability, see *Buttes Gas and Oil Co v Hammer* [1982] AC 888.

38 *Law Debenture Trust Corporation plc v Ukraine* [2017] EWHC 655 (Comm), paras 295–308.

39 *High Commissioner for Pakistan in the United Kingdom v Prince Mukkaram Jah* [2016] EWHC 1465 (Ch), para 89.

40 Campbell McLachlan, *Foreign Relations Law* (2014) 530; *Alfred Dunhill of London, Inc v The Republic of Cuba*, 425 US 682 (1976); *Yukos Capital SARL v OJSC Rosneft Oil Co* [2012] EWCA Civ 855, paras 92–94.

41 Unless these regulations qualify as overriding mandatory provisions (see Chapter 4).

42 See Chapter 5.

43 *Belhaj v Straw* [2017] UKSC 3, paras 37, 83, 106.

external debt obligations. Here, the Costa Rican government intervened to cater for the illiquidity of a State-owned bank—the dispute was not thus concerned with the sovereign debt *sensu stricto*; Costa Rica was acting in the capacity of public regulator.

6.46 A disgruntled creditor, Allied, sued in the US courts to recover on promissory notes issued by the three Costa Rican banks. The District Court held that the Act of State doctrine barred the review of the Costa Rican decrees, which prevented any further consideration of the matter (*Allied I*).[44] Allied appealed before the Second Circuit. The Second Circuit, relying on the doctrine of comity, decided that the US courts should recognise the decrees and resolutions of Costa Rica because they were consistent with US bankruptcy law, as well as US foreign policy in support of the renegotiation of foreign debts (*Allied II*).[45] Applying the authority in *Canada Southern Railway Co v Gebhard*—a case on the recognition of foreign schemes of arrangement[46]—the Second Circuit analogised sovereign debt default with the bankruptcy of a company. It held that Costa Rica's attempts at restructuring/reorganisation should be given effect and, relatedly, pending actions should be stayed to allow for the orderly reorganisation of the Costa Rican external debt. Further, the court considered that 'Costa Rica's prohibition of payment of debt was not a repudiation of the debt but rather was merely a deferral of payments while it attempted in good faith to renegotiate its obligations.'[47]

6.47 Following the decision of the Second Circuit, the US government submitted an amicus brief in which the US government expressed its support for granting priority to the enforceability of loan agreements over the comity to external debt restructurings. The US brief contained two reasons for not extending comity to the Costa Rican restructuring: (1) permitting Costa Rica to deny its private creditors their contractual rights would discourage grants of future loans; (2) allowing Costa Rica to alleviate its debt in that fashion would disincentivise sovereign debtors from undertaking necessary economic reforms.[48] Giving effect to the Costa Rican restructuring would be at odds with pivotal US interests, particularly that of the effective functioning of the international financial infrastructure.[49]

[44] 566 F Supp 1440 (SDNY 1983). [45] 733 F2d 23 (2d Cir 1984).

[46] 109 US 527 (1883). [47] Ibid 11.

[48] Marc Lewyn, 'Foreign Debt—Act of State Doctrine—Unilateral Deferral of Obligations by Debtor Nations Is Inconsistent with United States Law and Policy: Allied Bank International v. Banco Credito Agricola de Cartago' (1985) 15 Ga J Intl & Comp L 657, 667.

[49] Ricki Tigert, 'Allied Bank International: A United States Government Perspective' (1985) 17 NYU J Intl L & Pol 511, 519.

6.48 In the light of the newly emerged expression of the official policy of the US government, the Second Circuit in *Allied III* reheard the case en banc, being advised that it had misconstrued the US government policy, and eventually reversed itself.[50]

6.49 The Second Circuit discarded the application of the Act of State doctrine since the *situs* of the debt was not in Costa Rica, but in New York. This was so for two main reasons: (1) US courts had jurisdiction over the defendants; (2) the payment was to be made in New York in US dollars. As for the acts of foreign governments purporting to have extraterritorial effect, they fall outside the scope of the act of State doctrine and should be recognised by the courts only if they are consistent with US law and policy. The Second Circuit affirmed that the unilateral modification of debts was not so consistent.[51] (In 1982, Congress adopted the so-called Second Hickenlooper Amendment,[52] whereby the court cannot refuse to decide on an expropriation claim on the grounds of the Act of State.[53])

6.50 The court also found that Costa Rica's debt restructuring was inconsistent with the US policy of voluntary negotiations as it purported to unilaterally repudiate the debt owed to Costa Rica's private creditors. Costa Rica's unilateral restructuring also contravened the established IMF procedures of restructuring the debt which were based on the cooperative adjustment of international debt problems. The Second Circuit reinforced its conclusions by relying on the text of the loan contract. The text provided that the default would not be excused if the Central Bank failed to provide the currency necessary for repayment. In the same spirit, the Second Circuit did not reiterate the bankruptcy analogy and reversed the decision on the doctrine of Act of State.

6.51 The Second Circuit in *Allied III* followed the US governmental policy on sovereign debt restructurings, as expressed in the amicus curiae, as if it were bound by the latter.[54] This interrelation between judicial and

50 757 F 2d 516 (2d Cir 1985). For criticism, see Stephen Bainbridge, 'Comity and Sovereign Debt Litigation: A Bankruptcy Analogy' (1986) 10 Md J Intl L 1, 33–39.

51 757 F 2d 516 (2d Cir 1985). See also *Braka v Bancomer*, 762 F 2d 222 (2d Cir 1985) (holding that the *situs* was in Mexico since the deposits and the place of payment were located in Mexico); *Callejo v Bancomer, S.A.*, 764 F 2d 1101 (5th Cir 1985); *Lloyds Bank Plc v The Republic of Ecuador*, 1998 US Dist LEXIS 3065, 34–36 (SDNY 1998).

52 22 USC §2370(e)(2).

53 For an application, see *West v Multibanco Comermex*, 807 F 2d 820 (9th Cir 1987) (holding that the Act of State doctrine does not apply to a claim for expropriation of certificates of deposits by Mexico).

54 Eric Robert, 'Rééchelonnement de la dette ou règlement judiciaire' in D Carreau and M Shaw, *La Dette extérieure: The External Debt* (1995) 641. However, the court failed to do so in the recent *pari passu* litigation, discussed in Chapter 7.

executive branches is a particularity of the doctrine of separation of powers in the United States. It is redolent of the governmental interests doctrine commonly used in the US conflict of laws analysis, particularly in the weighing of the factors present in the application of the doctrine of *forum non conveniens*.[55]

6.52 It is doubtful that the English courts will defer to the UK's official governmental policy in the same way that the US courts have.[56] It is indicative that Lord Collins, commenting extrajudicially upon the *Allied* case, affirmed that the US courts could have taken an alternative route to weighing US governmental interests against the interests of Costa Rica, and instead held that US law governed the loan transactions and therefore Costa Rican decrees were not applicable *in casu*.[57] Applying the governing law to questions of discharge is the well-established position in English law.[58] The House of Lords in a case about personal injuries of South African workers incurred as the result of exposure to asbestos stressed that public interest considerations not related to the private interests of the parties and the ends of justice would have no bearing on its decision.[59] Lord Hope expressly refused 'to follow those judges in the United States who would decide issues as to where a case ought to be tried on broad grounds of public policy'.[60]

3. Prescription

6.53 A tale of caution for all bondholders, especially those active on secondary markets, is well illustrated by the recent developments in the Argentine saga. In 2016, Argentina, following a change of government, announced its intention to settle its outstanding claims with the holdout bondholders. However, later on, it reserved its right not to pay those bondholders whose claims are barred under the Argentine statute of limitations.[61] The very same issue is bound to arise in the recovery of other historic debts.

6.54 The expiry of the limitation period is a ground for striking out the claim of holdout litigants. The expiry of a limitation period bars any judicial

[55] On which see Symeon Symeonides, *The American Choice-of-Law Revolution: Past, Present and Future* (2006) 13–24, 71–81; Friedrich Juenger, 'Conflict of Laws: A Critique of Interest Analysis' (1984) 32 Am J Comp L 1.

[56] FA Mann, 'Judiciary and Executive in Foreign Affairs' in FA Mann, *Studies in International Law* (2008) 394–95, 400–01, 418–19; FA Mann, 'The Judicial Recognition of an Unrecognised State' in FA Mann, *Further Studies in International Law* (2008) 386–88; Lawrence Collins, 'Foreign Relations and the Conflict of Laws' (1995–1996) 6 KCLJ 20, 37.

[57] Collins (n 56) 32.

[58] *Wight v Eckhardt Marine GmbH* [2003] UKPC 37, para 15.

[59] *Lubbe v Cape* [2000] 1 WLR 1545, 1561.

[60] Ibid 1566.

[61] *Arag-A Ltd v Argentine Republic*, No 16-cv-2238 (TPG) (2016).

remedies, with the overriding aim of ensuring predictability and putting an end to legal controversies. Limitation periods pursue the policy of protecting people from being perpetually at risk of litigation and preventing situations where evidence is lost or witness memories have been contaminated over time.

It is well established that limitation periods apply both to actions on the merits to recover the *debt* and to the enforcement of the ensuing *judgment*.[62] In both cases, as a matter of English law, the limitation period is set at six years. In setting the limitation period for the enforcement of judgments, English law (and, for that matter other, jurisdictions) draws a distinction between suing for recognition and enforcement of a judgment (obtaining an exequatur) to which the limitation period applies, and actually executing the judgment.[63] The latter is a procedural matter on which the limitation period should have no bearing.[64] What this means in practice is that once the bondholder brings an action to recognise and enforce the judgment against the judgment debtor, the limitation period stops. Once this first step is completed, the creditor may take as much time as necessary to execute the judgment against the assets of the sovereign debtor.[65] **6.55**

The limitation period in New York is similar. New York's CPLR §213 stipulates a six-year statute of limitations for 'an action upon a contractual obligation or liability, express or implied'. An exception is set out in CPLR §211(a) which extends the limitation period to twenty years for claims on certain bonds. The exception is engaged when the bonds (i) are 'indebtedness of the State of New York or of any person, association or public or private corporation'; (ii) were 'originally sold by the issuer after publication of an advertisement for bids for the issue in a newspaper of general circulation'; and (iii) were 'secured only by a pledge of faith and credit of the issuer'. However, the District Court found that the exception does not apply to foreign States because they are not 'persons' within the meaning of CPLR §211(a).[66] **6.56**

Another preliminary point that needs to be clarified at the outset is that limitation periods are determined by the governing law of the contract.[67] It is up to the governing law of sovereign bonds to determine how long **6.57**

62 Or indeed an arbitral award (*The Amazon Reefer* [2009] EWCA Civ 1330).

63 Limitation periods do not apply to judgments emanating from EU Member States.

64 *Lowsley v Forbes* [1999] AC 329.

65 See, however, s 24(2) of the Limitation Act (1980). See also *Duer v Frazer* [2001] 1 WLR 919, para 25.

66 *White Hawthorne v Republic of Argentina*, 2016 US Dist LEXIS 177895 (SDNY 2016).

67 Rome I Regulation on the Law Applicable to Contractual Obligations, Art 12(1)(d); Foreign Limitation Periods Act 1984.

the limitation period is and in what circumstances, if at all, it applies. In principle, in so far as limitation periods are a function of the governing law of the contract, they should not vary depending on the jurisdiction where the action is brought.

6.58 Although the limitation period is a question of substance and thus falls to be determined by the governing law of bonds, it may not be stopped by bringing proceedings in a single jurisdiction with universal effect across other jurisdictions. An action, either on the merits or on a judgment, is required in any jurisdiction where execution will be sought.

The Limitation Act of 1980

6.59 In English law, limitation periods are regulated by the Limitation Act of 1980. The Act consolidates previous law, and the case law decided prior to 1980 is not overridden. For defaults preceding the entry into force of the Limitation Act of 1980, the parties would be required to consult the precursor statutes. These statutes go back as early as 1623 and the transitional provisions in respective statutes would delineate the temporal scope of application of each of these statutes.

6.60 Some relevant key limitation periods, as articulated in the 1980 Act, are set out below:

- simple contract—six years from the date of breach;[68]
- specialty actions/contracts executed as a deed—twelve years from the date of breach;[69]
- tort—six years from the date of damage,[70] or
  - three years from the date of discovery of the damage;
  - specific torts such as personal injury, and defamation have their own time limits;
- breach of trust—six years;[71]
- fraudulent breach of trust—unlimited;[72]
- recovery of money secured by mortgage— twelve years;[73]
- equitable remedies—inapplicable.[74]

6.61 The most relevant provision in the context of sovereign debt disputes is s 5 of the 1980 Act, which stipulates that for simple contracts (including loans), the limitation period is six years since the date of breach of the

[68] Limitation Act of 1980, s 5. [69] Ibid s 8.

[70] Ibid s 2. With regard to tort, many contract claims can be litigated as tort claims where negligence is an element of a cause of action. However, this is unlikely to be the case in a sovereign debt dispute.

[71] Ibid s 21(3). [72] Ibid s 21(1). [73] Ibid s 20. [74] Ibid s 36.

contract.[75] The limitation period runs from the day following the day on which the cause of action arose, ie, breach of contract.[76] When the State has defaulted both on the principal and interest, the analysis of both needs to be disentangled. In other words, the limitation periods run separately for each of the claims, and different rules may apply to the repayment of the principal and interest payments. The limitation period for the payment of the principal starts from the maturity date or when the repayment becomes due following an event of default. Gulati suggests that, in addition to the default on sovereign bonds, each breach of the *pari passu* clause is a fresh violation of a financial covenant and the statute of limitations should be reset each time a breach of the *pari passu* clause occurs.[77] Under this regime, the prospects of recovering historic claims against sovereign debtors seem rather bleak if the action for one reason or another has not been brought within six years since the date of default or maturity. A number of doctrines can be advanced to circumvent the short limitation periods.

Acknowledgement and Part Payments

Limitation periods can be reset in a number of ways. The first means of resetting is through acknowledgement and part payments (s 29 of the 1980 Act). Section 30 of the 1980 Act requires the acknowledgement to be in writing and signed by the person liable or his agent.[78] **6.62**

The peculiarity of these two methods of extending the prescription period is that if the six-year limitation period has expired, acknowledgements/part payments are not capable of reviving the limitation period. They only act before the limitation period has expired (s 29(7)). **6.63**

The part payment of a debt acknowledges the existence of the debt and thus extends the limitation period. Under s 29(6) of the Limitation Act of 1980, the payment of interest sets the limitation period for the recovery of the principal afresh. In *International Finance Corporation v Utexafrica Sprl*, the recovery of debt should have been time-barred by 15 December 1994, however the part payment of *interest* on 29 July 1992 sought to reset the **6.64**

[75] See, eg, *JJ Metcalfe v Dennison* [2013] QBD (TCC) (holding that the claim for unpaid sums under the construction contract time accrued at the date of completion of works).

[76] *Marren v Dawson Bentley and Co Ltd* [1961] 2 QB 135.

[77] Mitu Gulati, 'Has the Second Circuit (Unwittingly) Breathed Life into the Nostrils of Imperial Chinese Government Bonds?' (2013) 6. For the contrary, see *Ajdler v Province of Mendoza*, 2017 US Dist LEXIS 122659 (SDNY 2017).

[78] Financial statements sent to the claimant may amount to acknowledgement of debt if they recognise the existence of debt (*International Finance Corporation v Utexafrica Sprl* (2001) LTL 9/5/01).

limitation period for the *principal* afresh.[79] The utility of this provision, when applied in the context of historic debts, should not be underestimated since as long as the sovereign debtor continues to repay interest, it resets the limitation period for the principal (but not for the remainder of interest payments then due).

The Exception of Loan Contracts

6.65 The Limitation Act of 1980 sets out an exception from the general rule of limitation period for loans of a rather peculiar character. This section only applies to 'certain loans' which:

- do not provide for repayment of debt on or before a fixed or determinable date;
- do not effectively (whether or not it purports to do so) make the obligation to repay the debt conditional on demand for repayment made by or on behalf of the creditor or on any other matter.[80]

6.66 Principally, when the loan does not provide for repayment of the debt on or before a fixed or determinable date, the limitation period begins its course only after the demand to repay the debt has been made (s 6(3)). However, s 6, as interpreted by the courts, applies primarily to loans of informal character where the loan is silent on the date of repayment (eg, loans extended within the family).[81] Sovereign bonds would ubiquitously provide a fixed or a determinable date of repayment, either through the maturity (repayment date) or upon an event of default.

Limitation Period Renewed Each Time the Bonds Pass Hands

6.67 Further, the sovereign bondholder may argue that limitation periods start anew each time the bonds pass hands, ie, when the bond is sold to a new bondholder. This is especially so since in sovereign debt markets, the bonds pass hands without the old and new owners knowing each other. Should we wipe the slate clean for each new bondholder? The rather convincing riposte to this would be that the assignee of sovereign bonds steps into the shoes of the previous bondholder and cannot benefit from an extended limitation period.

[79] (2001) LTL 9/5/01. [80] S 6 (2) (a), (b)

[81] Andrew McGee, *Limitation Periods* (2015), para 10.043, p 200.

A Claim of Expropriation of Debt

6.68 There are no common law rules on limitation beyond the Limitation Act of 1980.[82] The implication is that if a certain cause of action is not regulated in the Limitation Act of 1980, the statutory regime of limitation periods does not apply to it. It is often the case that behind the non-payment of sovereign debt stands the expropriation of the rights of private bondholders. The sovereign may take actions which are tantamount to expropriation of the entitlements of private bondholders. Potentially, such an action might be couched in terms different from a contractual claim for repayment (eg, infringement of property rights), and fall outside the ambit of the Limitation Act of 1980.

Regulation of Prescription in Sovereign Bonds

6.69 English law recognises the capacity of parties to contract out of the statutory limitation periods. The parties may either extend or decrease the limitation periods. Parties may also agree to a standstill or denounce their right to bring a claim entirely.

6.70 What distinguishes prescription clauses from limitation periods is that the failure to bring the action within the period provided within the prescription clause renders the claims extinguished or void,[83] whereas the limitation period, as set out in the 1980 Act, simply seeks to bar judicial remedies.

6.71 The implications arising from this distinction are twofold: first, the expiry of a limitation period is a procedural defence, which needs to be specified in the defence,[84] ie the court will not apply limitation periods of its own motion. The defendant has to raise the limitation period so as to bar the remedy, and may decide not to do so.

6.72 And, second, limitation periods seek to bar judicial remedies, which means the extrajudicial methods of enforcing contractual rights remain open to the creditor.[85] An example of such an extrajudicial remedy is set-off. By contrast, if the bonds are void following the failure to comply with

[82] Subject, of course, to the equitable doctrine of laches, and acquiescence, which apply to equitable remedies.

[83] Republic of Austria, Medium-Term Note Programme, 16 September 2003, p 25; Republic of Iceland, US$2,000,000,000, Euro Medium Term Note Programme, p 34.

[84] CPR PD 16.13.1.

[85] McGee (n 81) para 2.029 (citing *C. & M. Matthews Ltd v Marsden Building Society* [1951] Ch 758).

the prescription clause, the claims of the creditor will be extinguished and that will prevent the use of extrajudicial methods.

6.73 A quick perusal of sovereign bond documentation demonstrates that prescription clauses are common in sovereign bonds. As an illustration, the Austrian Medium-Term Note Programme, subject to English law, provides for the prescription of the principal after thirty years and the prescription of the interest after three years:

> Claims against the Republic for payment in respect of the Notes, Receipts and Coupons (which, for this purpose shall not include Talons) shall be prescribed and become void unless made within 30 years (in the case of principal) and 3 years (in the case of interest) from the appropriate Relevant Date in respect thereof.[86]

6.74 Similarly, English law governed Greek bonds provide the prescription for the payment of principal after ten years:

> Claims for payment of principal in respect of the Notes shall be prescribed upon the expiry of ten years, and claims for payment of interest in respect of the Notes shall be prescribed upon the expiry of five years.[87]

6.75 Other bonds provide for a shorter prescription:

> Claims for principal and interest on the bonds shall become void unless made within the period of five years from the Relevant Date.[88]

Adjudication in Alternative Forums

6.76 The rules on prescription and limitation periods are strict. One way to circumvent the rather stringent rules on limitation periods is to seek redress before an international investment tribunal. International investment law sets out a much more lax regime, if any, of prescription (limitation periods) at the international level. Bilateral investment treaties are commonly silent on limitation periods and the limitation periods at municipal level are inapposite at the international level.[89]

6.77 Two caveats need to be mentioned. First, international law may recognise the doctrine of equitable prescription. That said, investment tribunals are divided as to the existence of the doctrine and its actual content.[90]

[86] Republic of Austria, Medium-Term Note Programme, 16 September 2003, p 25.

[87] The Hellenic Republic, Offering Circular, Euro 130,000,000 Fixed to CMS Spread Linked Notes due 2026, p 12.

[88] The Hellenic Republic, Invitation Memorandum, 24 February 2012, p 45.

[89] *Link-Trading Joint Stock Company v Department for Customs Control of the Republic of Moldova*, UNCITRAL, Final Award, 18 April 2002, para 62.

[90] See, for example, *H&H Enterprises Investments, Inc v Arab Republic of Egypt*, ICSID Case No ARB/09/15, Decision on Respondent's Objections to Jurisdiction, 5 June 2012, para 87

Second, if the bonds contain a prescription clause, with the effect of voiding claims, it may well be arguable that no claim will lie under a bilateral investment treaty.

4. Champerty

6.78 In principle, sovereign debt is assignable, both in the form of bonds and in the form of judgments and awards upon such bonds.[91] In the market of syndicated loans, no-assignability clauses were commonplace. Under these clauses, the creditor might not assign its rights under the contract to third parties without the debtor's prior consent. If the creditor failed to comply with said clauses, no rights would pass to him and he would have no right to sue under the loan agreements.[92]

6.79 The right to litigate to enforce assigned obligations was historically precluded by the champerty defence. Under the law of New York, the champerty defence is, however, no longer a real threat to the distressed debt purchasers. In *Elliott v Peru*, the District Court found that Elliott purchased Peru's debt with the intention to bring a suit thereon, thus infringing NY Judiciary Law §489, and denied recovery on that basis. The Second Circuit reversed the finding and held that buying debt with the purpose of collecting it did not infringe §489, even though litigation might be a necessary step in the process; §489 would only be engaged when litigation is the 'primary' purpose, which was not Elliott's intent.[93]

6.80 The originally harsh position of English law with respect to champerty has also undergone dramatic changes. The Court of Appeal in *Camdex International Ltd v Bank of Zambia*, relying upon section 136 of the Law of Property Act 1925 and earlier cases, ruled that, like other species of property, debts may be transferred to another. And the legal rights which are incidents of that property may be exercised by the new owner of the property.[94] When trading on the secondary markets, one bondholder is selling his bonds to another person, with the concomitant right to sue on

(refusing to recognise the existence of equitable prescription); *Nordzucker AG v Republic of Poland*, UNCITRAL, Partial Award (Jurisdiction), 10 December 2008, para 221 (recognising a general principle that a claimant shall not unreasonably delay the pursuit of its claim).

91 See, eg, *Blue Ridge Investments LLC v Republic of Argentina*, 902 F Supp 2d 367, 381 (SDNY 2012) (in respect of an assignment of arbitration awards).

92 *Barbados Trust Co Ltd v Bank of Zambia* [2007] EWCA Civ 148.

93 *Elliott Associates LP v Banco de la Nacion and Republic of Peru*, 194 F 3d 363, 374–81 (2d Cir 1999).

94 [1998] QB 22, 32.

the bonds. The doctrine of champerty may engage only in the exceptional cases when the claim only is assigned.[95]

5. Odious Debt

6.81 The doctrine of odious debt is more a creature of academic literature than positive law. The doctrine refers to the funds borrowed by illegitimate governments or for illegitimate purposes (war, apartheid, etc). Given their parochial nature, such funds, it is said, do not bind the new government which succeeds the illegitimate government.

6.82 The leading authority on odious debt is the award in *Tinoco* (1928).[96] There, the Costa Rican dictator Tinoco borrowed funds from the Royal Bank of Canada. Although Tinoco was an illegitimate ruler, the arbitrator Taft found that he was the de facto government at the time in Costa Rica and a State is bound by the obligations of its previous governments. More importantly, it was established that payments, fraught with irregularities, were paid for the use of the then president Tinoco for his personal support after he had taken refuge in a foreign country. The other part of the funds was paid to his brother as a salary for four years in advance. The borrowed funds were thus not for 'legitimate government purposes'. In both instances, the arbitrator Taft was convinced that the bank knew or must have known about the final destination of the funds provided.[97] Waibel notes:

> But the holding is narrow. The reason why Costa Rica did not need to repay the loans was not the illegitimacy of Tinoco's government under international law. Rather, it was because of the lending bank's knowledge that the sole purpose of the loans was personal. Without such knowledge, Costa Rica would have been under an obligation to service the loans.[98]

6.83 Wider interpretations of the doctrine of odious debt may not find support in current international law. The Iran–US Claims Tribunal held that whatever the merits of the doctrine in cases of State succession, at least in cases of government continuity the doctrine of odious debt has no merit.[99]

[95] For a recent application, see *JEB Recoveries LLP v Binstock* [2015] EWHC 1063 (Ch).

[96] For more historical examples, see Jeff King, *The Doctrine of Odious Debt in International Law: A Restatement* (2016); Waibel, *Sovereign Defaults* (n 9) 136–43, 180.

[97] *Tinoco Arbitration (Great Britain v Costa Rica)*, 18 October 1923, 1 UNRIIA 369.

[98] Waibel, *Sovereign Defaults* (n 9) 137–38.

[99] *USA v Iran, Iran–United States Claims Tribunal*, Case no B36, (1996) 32 CTR 162, paras 54–55. On the effects of State succession on public debt, see James Crawford, *Brownlie's Principles of Public International Law* (2012) 431–33.

In this sense, the doctrine of odious debt may better be treated as an 'umbrella' doctrine, which unifies various legal justifications for challenging what may seem as odious debt. Gulati, Buchheit, and Thompson seek to unfold the meaning of odious debt by reference to and by analogy with a cluster of national doctrines: considerations of public policy, unclean hands, agency, disregarding entity separateness in corporate law.[100] Other legal rules may provide substance to the doctrine of odious debt. Thus, if the facts permit, the State may argue that the bonds were ultra vires in so far as they were issued in breach of its constitution and statutes.[101] If the place of payment of bonds is in the territory of the State, the State may also seek to rely on its mandatory provisions relating to the ruling of the illegitimate government.[102] **6.84**

6. Usury and Penal Clauses

It is possible to dispense with the doctrine of usury summarily since it has no application to sovereign debt. English law does not recognise a separate doctrine of usury.[103] The court enjoys a general discretion under ss 19–22 of the Consumer Credit Act 2006 to strike down a consumer credit if it is unfair. However, this power applies only to credit agreements entered into by an individual. In New York, the statutory provisions on usury do not apply to loans in excess of $2.5 million (NY Gen Oblig Law para 5-526(6)(a)). **6.85**

Nonetheless, the doctrine may persist in other jurisdictions—perhaps the jurisdiction of the sovereign debtor. This may in itself incite the sovereign debtor to engage in 'forum shopping' in the jurisdiction which may strike down the interest rate as usurious. **6.86**

States may also argue that the contractual provisions, including the interest rate, are penal and therefore should not be enforced. In *Donegal International v Republic of Zambia*,[104] Romania assigned to a distressed debt investor, Donegal, the debt owed to it by Zambia. Following the assignment, Donegal entered into a settlement agreement with Zambia. When **6.87**

[100] Mitu Gulati, Lee Buchheit, and Robert Thompson, 'The Dilemma of Odious Debts' (2007) 56 Duke LJ 1201.

[101] Ukraine did not seek to rely on the doctrine in the litigation involving the debt owed to the Russian Federation but instead invoked the doctrine of capacity, even though Ukrainian officials suggested at various points in time that the bonds were a bribe by Russia to the then current regime so as to avoid the European Association Agreement (discussed in paras 6.89–6.108 below).

[102] On mandatory rules, see Chapter 4.

[103] An Act to repeal the Laws relating to Usury and to the Enrolment of Annuities 1854.

[104] [2007] EWHC 197 (Comm).

Zambia failed to pay, Donegal initiated proceedings in England. Among other things, Zambia contended that Donegal bribed two former Zambian officials to obtain more information on the validity of the debt and that the Minister of Finance who signed the settlement agreement did not have authority to do so. Smith J rejected these allegations.

6.88 Zambia further contended that the interest rate provisions in the settlement agreement were penal since the sum payable on breach was not a genuine pre-estimate of the loss that the innocent party was likely to suffer as a result of the breach. The settlement agreement provided that on default, Zambia will pay a higher and compounded interest rate. Smith J considered, on a summary judgment application, that Zambia had a real prospect of defending the claim on the ground that the interest rate was penal and invited further submissions on the precise relief.[105] The case never proceeded to full trial. In any case, this decision in respect of penal interest rate may not stand in light of the recalibration of the law on penalties by the Supreme Court in *Cavendish Square Holdings BV v Makdessi*.[106]

7. Capacity to Issue Bonds

6.89 The issue of the capacity of the State to enter into loan agreements or issue bonds is truly a legal minefield. A State's constitutional law may contain various requirements of form, authorisation and substance that need to be fulfilled to issue valid debt.[107] The consequences for non-compliance with these provisions are uncertain.

6.90 The issue of capacity to issue bonds was canvassed in great detail in *Law Debenture Trust Corporation plc v Ukraine*,[108] which arose on the footing of and as a corollary to the Russian–Ukrainian conflict. In late 2013, Ukraine borrowed $3bn from the Russian Federation through an issuance of bonds. The sole subscriber of the bonds was the Russian Federation. When the revolution in Ukraine unfolded in 2014, Mr Yanukovich fled the country and the next Ukrainian government issued a moratorium and refused to pay the debt upon maturation, although they paid some of the interest payments in the meantime. Instructed by the Russian government, the Law Debenture Trust Corporation brought an action against the

[105] Ibid paras 509, 523–24. [106] [2015] UKSC 67.

[107] For the examination of the Argentine constitutional rules on the issuance of bonds, see Hector Mairal, 'Issues Arising from the Legal and Constitutional Validity of the Debt under the Debtor's Own Law' in David Sassoon and Daniel Bradlow (eds), *Judicial Enforcement of International Debt Obligations* (1987) 147.

[108] *Law Debenture Trust Corporation plc v Ukraine* [2017] EWHC 655 (Comm).

Ukrainian government pursuant to an English choice of court agreement in the bonds.

The Trustee alleged that the debt was 'a simple English law debt obligation' and any claims based on political aggression or breaches of international law had no part to play in considering the creation of obligations or their repayment. Ukraine contended that the claim was part of a broader strategy of unlawful and illegitimate economic, political, and military aggression by Russia against Ukraine and should be treated thus. Ukraine also contested that the bonds were not a private arrangement but rather a bilateral loan in disguise, however, it did not ask for legal recharacterisation of the bonds as a bilateral loan. Nor did it seek to rely on the law on the moratorium given that the governing law was English. **6.91**

Among other things, Ukraine raised a defence that because it was acting through its CMU (Cabinet of Ministers of Ukraine), it lacked capacity to issue the Notes.[109] Ukraine's capacity defence was based on two strands: (a) the bonds breached the limit set out in the Budget Law and accordingly the CMU could not authorise any borrowing beyond that limit; and (b) the decree authorising the issuance breached constitutional principles, namely, the CMU did not receive an expert opinion on the Decree and it was not aware of the terms of the bonds. **6.92**

In the absence of legal authority on the capacity of States to enter into transactions, there were two alternative routes pursued by the parties: (1) either to treat the capacity of States in a manner analogous to the capacity of individuals which is unlimited; (2) or to approximate the State's capacity to the capacity of corporations which is subject to limitations (mostly under the local law of the corporation). Arguing for the former proposition, the Trustee claimed that Ukraine had unlimited capacity and hence could not rely on its internal law to invalidate the bonds. The Trustee contended that at most, this could be an issue of authority in so far as the CMU did not exercise its powers correctly. **6.93**

Blair J first confirmed the general understanding that unlike issues of capacity, issues of authority can be mitigated by the doctrines of usual or ostensible authority. If treated as an issue of authority, the questions of usual or ostensible authority are governed by English law, the putative governing law of the contracts, rather than by Ukrainian law. If, by contrast, this matter were treated as an issue of capacity, Ukrainian law would be the governing law. **6.94**

[109] The second defence contended that the contractual arrangements were procured by duress exercised by Russia. Blair J, however, held the matter non-justiciable as it involved adjudication of the law on the use of force and breach of the international law of trade.

6.95 Blair J first distinguished *Haugesund Kommune v DEPFA ACS Bank*, where the Court of Appeal found that the contracts entered into by Norwegian local authorities in defiance of their capacity were void.[110] *Haugesund* was concerned with local authorities and drew analogies from the law on the capacity of corporations. Blair J considered that the analogy with the capacity of corporations did not apply to States, not least because the State might change its own law (which governs issues of capacity) unilaterally. Blair J then discarded the analogy with individuals proffered by the Trustee.

6.96 Instead, Blair J adopted the Trustee's argument based on the Lotus principle, set out in the landmark *S.S. Lotus* case,[111] namely that States have unlimited capacity and, in this context, unlimited capacity to borrow. In light of this, the State's internal laws as to borrowing cannot operate to restrict the unlimited capacity of the State.

6.97 Taking the matter to its logical conclusion, Blair J considered that compliance with Ukrainian law was a question of authority and not capacity. The Minister of Finance enjoyed the requisite power but that power was not exercised as required by the law. Given that this was an issue of authority, the court considered whether the Minister had usual or ostensible authority. Applying English law to this issue, Blair J found that the Minister of Finance had usual and even ostensible authority to sign the bonds on behalf of Ukraine.

6.98 A number of points can be raised. First, the court refused to approximate State capacity with the capacity of corporations since the State could change its capacity unilaterally. On the facts, the issue of capacity existed at the time of issuance of bonds. There is no reason why separate rules could not be designed for unilateral changes of capacity introduced after the contract had been concluded.[112]

6.99 Second, the Lotus principle was concerned with the powers of the State exercised at the international level. The Lotus principle may not be entirely apposite in the context of the capacity of a State to enter into a commercial transaction governed by English law and the treatment thereof by English conflict of laws.

[110] [2010] EWCA Civ 579. See also *Dexia Crediop SPA v Comune di Prato* [2017] EWCA Civ 428 (where it was common ground that Italian law applied to the issue of capacity of an Italian municipality). A similar decision but in respect of State-controlled enterprises was rendered in *Banco Santander Totta SA v Companhia de Carris de Ferro de Lisboa SA* [2016] EWHC 465 (Comm), paras 254, 323 (applying Portuguese law to the capacity of Portuguese public enterprises).

[111] *S.S. Lotus (France v Turkey)*, (1927) PCIJ Series A No 10.

[112] On which see Chapter 5.

Third, an alternative interpretation of the Lotus principles might cautiously be suggested. First, the Lotus principle is in no sense absolute and many reservations have been expressed in respect of the principle. Judges Higgins, Kooijmans, and Buergenthal in the *Arrest Warrant Case* stated that 'the dictum [in the *S.S. Lotus* case] represents the high water mark of laissez-faire in international relations, and an era that has been significantly overtaken by other tendencies'.[113] **6.100**

Further, and more importantly, the *S.S. Lotus* case could have led to the opposite conclusion. The Permanent Court of International Justice held in *S.S. Lotus* that: **6.101**

> Far from laying down a general prohibition to the effect that States may not extend the application of their laws and the jurisdiction of their courts to persons, property and acts outside their territory, it leaves them in this respect a wide measure of discretion which is only limited in certain cases by prohibitive rules; as regards other cases, every State remains free to adopt the principles which it regards as best and most suitable.[114]

What the famous *obiter* from *S.S. Lotus* thus stands for is the freedom of the State to apply its own law without incurring international responsibility, unless prohibited from doing so. The implication of the decision of Blair J was to limit the power of the State in holding that it could not rely on its internal law as a question of capacity. On the contrary, the Lotus principle allows for the application of the rules on the capacity to borrow unless prohibited to do so by international law. The Lotus principle stands for empowering the State and not for constraining it. **6.102**

Furthermore, international tribunals never recognised full and unlimited capacity of States. Thus, in the *Aboilard Case (France v Haiti)*, the concessions entered into by Haiti were in breach of its constitutional requirements since, under the constitution of Haiti, the transactions had to receive the authorisation of the Haitian parliament. The interstate arbitral tribunal confirmed that the transactions were 'null and without effect'.[115] **6.103**

Of course, the Tribunal then went on to find Haiti liable under international law for frustrating the expectations of the investor. Other tribunals have also found States liable for entering into ultra vires transactions.[116] Article 7 **6.104**

[113] *Case Concerning the Arrest Warrant (Democratic Republic of the Congo v Belgium), Joint Separate Opinion of Judges Higgin, Kooijmans and Buergenthal* [2002] ICJ 1, para 51.

[114] *S.S. Lotus (France v Turkey)*, (1927) PCIJ Series A No 10, pp 18–19.

[115] *Affaire Aboilard (France v Haiti)*, Volume XI Reports of International Arbitral Awards 71, 80 (1905). However, then the Tribunal held Haiti liable in damages for entering into contracts in breach of its own constitution and thus breaching the legitimate expectations of the private contractors.

[116] For other cases, finding the State liable in similar circumstances, see Theodor Meron, 'Repudiation of ultra vires State Contracts and the International Responsibility of States'

of the ILC Articles on the Responsibility of States for Internationally Wrongful Acts stipulates that the conduct of an organ of a State or of a person or entity empowered to exercise elements of the governmental authority shall be considered an act of the State under international law if the organ, person or entity acts in that capacity, even if it exceeds its authority or contravenes instructions.[117] Further, in cases when the State has relied on its local law to avoid an arguably ultra vires choice of forum agreement, international tribunals have found ways to give effect to such agreements.[118]

6.105 However, the tribunals in *Aboilard* and other cases were competent under international law to find the State in breach of international law. English courts cannot so easily sit in judgment of a foreign State's acts allegedly in breach of international law and hold a State liable for a breach of international law. Article 7 of the ILC Articles only deals with issues of attribution and therefore a separate finding of breach of international law is necessary.

6.106 If one thus recognises the possibility that a State may lack capacity, it may be appropriate to draw a line between lack of capacity properly speaking and mere procedural defects. The lack of parliamentary approval of the acts of the executive or States (provinces) is a valid example of the lack of capacity, however, the failure to obtain an expert opinion may be better treated as a procedural defect.

6.107 Other examples may be less straightforward. In *Dexia Crediop SPA v Comune di Prato*, the Italian municipality of Prato raised two arguments to substantiate its claim that it lacked capacity to enter into swap agreements. The first was based on Art 119 of the Italian Constitution, which provided that municipalities may resort to 'indebtedness only as a means of funding investments'. It was common ground that this was an issue of capacity and any indebtedness in breach of the provision would be null and void. The second argument was grounded in Art 41 of Law 448/ 2001, which imposed the financial advantage test (*convenienza economica*)

(1957) 6(2) ICLQ 273; *Southern Pacific Properties (Middle East) Ltd v Arab Republic of Egypt*, ICSID Case No ARB/84/3, Award, 19 May 1992, para 85. See, however, *Tinoco Arbitration (Great Britain v Costa Rica)*, 18 October 1923, 1 UNRIIA 369, 397–99 (holding that inasmuch as the concession was entered into in breach of the rules on the separation of powers under the Costa Rican constitution, it was invalid and Costa Rica could have defeated the concession).

117 Supplement No 10 (A/56/10).

118 See, eg, Jan Paulsson, 'May a State Invoke its Internal Law to Repudiate Consent to International Commercial Arbitration?' (1986) 2 Arb Intl 90. Whether the arbitration agreement complies with local constitutional requirements may not be an issue of capacity but rather an issue of subjective arbitrability: Tai-Heng Cheng and Ivo Entchev, 'State Incapacity and Sovereign Immunity in International Arbitration' (2014) 26 SAcLJ 942, 946–47, 954.

of restructuring transactions, namely whether the transaction allows for 'a reduction of the financial value of the total liabilities'. Both arguments failed and on that ground, the court did not determine whether the second ground—financial advantage—constituted a case of lack of capacity.[119] In all likelihood, it would, or at least should, have been treated as an issue of lack of capacity since the financial advantage test, if found applicable, was a condition antecedent to entering into the transaction.

In any case, if the court came to the conclusion that the contract was null and void on the ground of the lack of capacity, the funds could be subject to an order of restitution back to the bondholder. According to the majority in *Haugesund*, the consequences of lack of capacity are to be determined by reference to English law.[120] Under English law, the restitution will be 'unaffected by any of the contractual terms governing the borrowing'. However, it will be subject to any applicable restitutionary defences,[121] including the doctrine of clean hands. **6.108**

8. Capacity to Repay/Debt 'Overhang'

A theoretically distinct, but practically interconnected question, is how should the court address the defence of debt 'overhang' that a State may raise in commercial litigation. As a general rule, the State in default is in financial distress and in a legal action, relies on the unsustainably high level of its debt. Economists suggest that when the debt burden of a sovereign reaches a certain level, the State is locked in a self-fuelling debt trap. Locked in such a trap, the sovereign debtor may no longer repay its debt in full, unless it resorts to a debt restructuring (debt 'overhang'). **6.109**

By diverting the available revenues to the service of the debt, the excessive level of debt impedes the economic growth of the sovereign State and undermines the incentives to invest in such an economy. Further borrowing may only exacerbate the situation by crowding out private spending and investment. Often only substantial debt reduction will lead to the revival of the national economy.[122] Once the debt has reached the unsustainable level, austerity measures and additional borrowing—commonly available at prohibitive interest rates—will not realistically offer the debtor the chance **6.110**

[119] [2017] EWCA Civ 428, para 32.

[120] *Haugesund Kommune v DEPFA ACS Bank* [2010] EWCA Civ 579, para 60. See, however, the convincing dissent of Etherton LJ, characterising the result as 'bizarre' (ibid para 144).

[121] *Westdeutsche Landesbank Girozentrale v Islington London Borough Council* [1996] AC 669, 688 (per Lord Goff).

[122] Nouriel Roubini, 'Debt Sustainability: How to Assess Whether a Country Is Insolvent' (2001) 9–10. On the effect of high debt on growth see Carmen Reinhart, Vincent Reinhart, and Kenneth Rogoff, 'Debt Overhang: Past and Present' (2012) NBER Working Paper 18015, 16.

to escape the vicious circle of unsustainable debt. Putting aside the cases of opportunistic default, one may sympathise with the sovereign debtors who lack the wherewithal to pay the excessive debt they have incurred—taking a pound of flesh would also shed drops of blood.

6.111 The preliminary question that a court would be confronted with is whether the courts have the power to assess the payment capacity of the State. The issue, albeit rare, may arise in sovereign debt litigation.[123] The Second Circuit in *NML v Argentina* positively affirmed that:

> The district court found that the Republic had sufficient funds, including over $40 billion in foreign currency reserves, to pay plaintiffs the judgments they are due … (concluding that Argentina 'has the financial wherewithal to meet its commitment of providing equal treatment to [plaintiffs] and [the exchange bondholders]'). Aside from merely observing that these funds are dedicated to maintaining its currency, Argentina makes no real argument that, to avoid defaulting on its other debt, it cannot afford to service the defaulted debt.[124]

6.112 In those cases where the determination of the payment capacity is at stake, the courts (and parties) are well advised to seek expert opinions. The concept of debt 'overhang' does not have the requisite legal precision to be susceptible to straightforward application in judicial proceedings. The level of debt sustainability is on its terms an arbitrary concept and is generally defined rather randomly.[125] To this, one might retort that the IMF and rating agencies routinely conduct debt sustainability studies. However, as one distinguished economist correctly points out, the reliability of their methodologies is often far from perfect and they failed on numerous occasions.[126]

6.113 The conventional thinking is that the debt sustainability may be measured as the ratio of the government debt to the GDP of the country or goods exported,[127] although other financial ratios are also used, such as debt

[123] In Chapter 7, this issue appears twice—first, in respect of the payment capacity and the 'credibility' of alternatives to a restructuring, and, second, in addressing the extent of a permissible debt 'haircut'.

[124] *NML Capital Limited v Republic of Argentina*, 699 F 3d 246, 263 (2d Cir, 2012). See also *Société Commerciale de Belgique (Belgium v Greece)*, (1939) PCIJ Series A/B, 160, discussed in Waibel, *Sovereign Defaults* (n 9) 96.

[125] Arturo Porzecanski, 'Behind the 2012 Greek Sovereign Debt Restructuring' in Eugenio Bruno, *Sovereign Debt and Debt Restructuring: Legal, Financial and Regulatory Aspects* (2013) 45–47.

[126] Arturo Porzecanski, 'Borrowing and Debt: How Do Sovereigns Get into Trouble' in Lee Buchheit and Rosa Lastra (eds), *Sovereign Debt Management* (2014) 322–27.

[127] For instance, the threshold at which the State qualifies as a heavily indebted poor country is set at 150% of exports or, in some cases, 250% of fiscal revenues (David Andrews, Anthony Boote, Syed Rizavi, and Sukhwinder Singh, 'Debt Relief for Low-Income Countries: The Enhanced HIPC Initiative' (1999) IMF Pamphlet Series No 51).

service to government revenue and debt service to GDP.[128] The orthodoxy posits that the higher the debt/GDP ratio is, the more likely it is that the sovereign debt is unsustainable. Among the variations of ratios, it seems that the ratio of government revenues/total debt service is able to catch the payment capacity more aptly. It shifts the focus to the cash-flow capacity of the State, measured through its income, to service the debt falling due in a definite year.

The use of financial ratios for determining the debt unsustainability is, however, imperfect.[129] Financial ratios of the sort described are too simplistic a measure and do not account for a whole range of various factors conditioning the State's capacity to pay, especially in the long run. Such factors are: culture, record of previous debt restructurings, contingent liabilities, currency or maturity mismatches, the nature of the investor base, macroeconomic stability, market sentiment, professionalism of the State's institutions, the level of development, the amount of government revenues, and so forth, which are not always susceptible to easy quantification in advance.[130] So, too, the internal political situation of the State and its internal political support will be hugely relevant in determining the acceptable size of taxes and austerity measures.[131] **6.114**

To make matters worse, the insolvency of a State depends to a large extent upon the saturation of financial markets and the markets' perceptions of the State's capacity to repay.[132] The Japanese governmental debt is very much a case in point. With a debt/GDP ratio of 224%—a higher ratio than that of Greece at the peak of its recent debt crisis—Japan's debt is prima facie extremely high. Yet its debt portfolio is manageable, mainly due to the 'home bias' of local investors.[133] Additional factors reflecting the market confidence in the financial sanity of the debtor should be considered, such as the pricing of sovereign bonds on the primary and secondary **6.115**

[128] Robert Lee, *Public Budgeting Systems* (2013) 523–24; Roubini, 'Debt Sustainability: How to Assess Whether a Country Is Insolvent' 11.

[129] Mark Walker, Barthélemy Faye, 'Sovereign Debt Renegotiation: Restructuring the Commercial Debt of HIPC Debtor Countries' (2010) 73 L & Contemp Probs 317, 322–23.

[130] Porzecanski (n 126) 322–27; Carmen Reinhart, Kenneth Rogoff, and Miguel Savastano, 'Debt Intolerance' (2003) NBER Working Paper 9908.

[131] Stephen Choi, Mitu Gulati, and Eric Posner, 'The Evolution of Contractual Terms in Sovereign Bonds' (2012) 4 J Leg Anal 131, 138.

[132] Michael Waibel, 'La faillite souveraine en droit: Un État peut-il faire faillite?' in Mathias Audit (ed), *Insolvabilité des états et dettes souveraines* (2011) 55.

[133] Naoyuki Yoshino and Uwe Vollmer, 'The Sovereign Debt Crisis: Why Greece, But Not Japan?' (2014) 12 Asia Eur J 325.

markets, ratings of the sovereign debtor by rating agencies,[134] and credit default swaps (CDS) prices.

6.116 A more holistic analysis of the sustainability of the sovereign's debt is called for. In light of this, the court should invite expert evidence (akin to valuers in corporate reorganisations) for assistance. It is worth stressing that the use of experts will only be necessary when the applicable legal rules require assessment of the payment capacity of the State.[135] In such cases, the court may well find on the facts of the case before it that the sovereign debtor is not afflicted by severe financial plight and decide accordingly.[136] This will act as a check upon opportunistic defaults by financially healthy States. Of course, there are rare instances in practice where the State would default out of mere unwillingness to pay and regardless of financial capacity to pay (so-called opportunistic defaults). A 1993 Salomon Brothers report found only 11% of sovereign defaults were opportunistic.[137] That said, in rare cases where the court is called to decide on the sustainability of the debt level and the payment capacity of the State, it will not shy away from the conclusion that the sovereign debtor has sufficient funds to make good on its debts in spite of its claims to the contrary.[138] Of course, the court may also come to the conclusion that the sovereign debtor lacks the wherewithal to meet its contractual obligations.[139]

6.117 Without prejudice to those cases where legal rules require an enquiry into the payment capacity of the sovereign debtor, a finding that the State is incapable of paying will not, at least under English (and New York) law, be dispositive of the dispute. The court may face a State that is clearly overburdened by unsustainable debt under any conceivable benchmark of debt sustainability (heavily indebted poor countries are a pertinent example). Even in such clear-cut situations, the debt 'overhang' cannot be used as a catch-all argument in the litigation of sovereign debt disputes.

[134] Yaron Nili, 'An Economist's View of Market Evidence in Valuation and Bankruptcy Litigation' *Harvard Law Blog* (28 June 2014).

[135] See Chapter 7.

[136] Again, see Chapter 7. In pre-Chapter 9 cases, US courts found the restructuring of the debt not to be 'in the best interests of the creditors' in light of the adequate taxing power still available to the municipality allegedly in distress (Michael McConnell and Randal Picker, 'When Cities Go Broke: A Conceptual Introduction to Municipal Bankruptcy' (1993) 60 U Chi L Rev 425, 465–66).

[137] John Purcell and Jeffrey Kaufmann, 'The Risks of Sovereign Lending: Lessons from History' (1993) Salomon Brothers.

[138] *Kensington International Ltd v Republic of Congo*, Docket No 05-1988-cv, 14–15 (2d Cir 2006).

[139] See, eg, *Camdex International Ltd v Bank of Zambia (No 2)* [1997] 1 WLR 632 (discussed in detail in Chapter 3).

In sovereign debt litigation, courts simply are called to confirm the debt due through the issuance of binding judgments: the serious financial predicament of the sovereign debtor was judged on many occasions not to constitute a bar to obtaining a judgment.[140]

In any event, if that is of any conciliation, creditors will most likely face serious obstacles to full recovery of money at the stage of enforcement of the judgment. The strong shield of State immunity from enforcement affords the necessary protection to those States with excessive debt levels. If the debt 'overhang' argument were to be used to prevent issuance of a judgment, it would prevent any recovery whatsoever and any disciplining effect that sovereign debt litigation might have upon the sovereign debtor. **6.118**

In this context, Scott, questioning the mainstream approach, argues that: **6.119**

> The root of the sovereign debt problem is that sovereigns overborrow.... Overborrowing results from the fact that sovereigns face few consequences as a result of default.... The default does not impede their access to future credit because creditors have short memories. The only effective remedy against sovereign overborrowing is to allow creditors to enforce their contract rights effectively against sovereigns in default.[141]

Irrespective of the stance one takes on who is to blame for the unsustainability of sovereign debt,[142] the sovereign debtor in financial distress does not have carte blanche to restructure the debt or refuse to pay those who did not partake in the reduction of the sovereign debt burden. Of course, the sovereign debtor may take whatever legal measures it has at hand to bring its debt to a sustainable path, but it cannot flex legal rules by reliance on the unsustainable level of its debt. The unsustainability of the debt is **6.120**

[140] See Chapter 1. See also *Red Mountain Finance Inc v Democratic Republic of Congo and another*, All England Official Transcripts (1997–2008), para 15 (the Court of Appeal not swayed by the difficult position of an extremely poor country which has been in the throes of civil war for many years and had a change of government as a good defence to the award of a summary judgment); ICC award n 6219, (1990) 117(4) JDI 1047, 1051–53 (in the context of arbitration).

[141] Hal Scott, 'Sovereign Debt Default: Cry for the United States, Not Argentina' (2006) Washington Legal Foundation, Working Paper Series No 140, 1.

[142] See, eg, Federico Sturzenegger and Jeromin Zettelmeyer, *Debt Defaults and Lessons from a Decade of Crises* (2006) 3–6, 41–42 (sovereign debt defaults may be triggered by an array of factors, including by overborrowing); Waibel (n 132) 63 (giving the debtor a fresh start irrespective of the fault in the unsustainable level of the debt); Klaus Armingeon and Lucio Baccaro, 'Political Economy of the Sovereign Debt Crisis: The Limits of Internal Devaluation' (2012) 41(3) Industrial LJ 254 (the eurozone debt crisis is not only about irresponsible governments, but also the result of the decision to create a currency union and the latter's ineffective economic policies).

already catered for by the contractual provisions,[143] considerations of payment incapacity in the context of challenges to the conduct of sovereign debt restructurings built into English law[144] and wide-ranging restructuring practices at the service of States (whether such practices are efficacious and cost-effective is a question in its own right). Stretching the debt unsustainability argument further to defend abusive practices or ignore valid contractual claims is not a valid extension of the debt 'overhang' defence.

9. Frustration

6.121 This defence does not require much examination. English courts have discarded financial crises as a ground for frustration of a commercial contract.[145] English courts held in the aftermath of the 2008 financial crisis that 'a change in economic/market circumstances, affecting the profitability of a contract or the ease with which the parties' obligations can be performed, is not regarded as being a force majeure event'.[146]

10. Counterclaims

6.122 Rarely, sovereign bonds may contain language to prohibit the use of set-off[147] or even set-off and counterclaims.[148] More commonly, the sovereign debtor will recognise the possibility of set-off by waiving immunity against set-off.[149]

6.123 In *Law Debenture Trust Corporation plc v Ukraine*, Ukraine argued a term was to be implied into the Trust Deed whereby Russia would be prohibited from: (i) deliberately interfering with or hindering Ukraine's ability to repay; or (ii) demanding repayment if it was in breach of its obligations towards Ukraine under public international law. Blair J, while accepting the general proposition that a term may readily be implied into a contract

143 Among others, majority action clauses which inflict a majority-approved debt restructuring on minority bondholders on which see Chapter 2.

144 On which see Chapter 7.

145 *Tandrin Aviation Holdings v Aero Toy Store LLC* [2010] EWHC 40; *Gold Group Properties Ltd v BDW Trading Ltd* [2010] EWHC 323. For an in-depth discussion, see Thomas Wälde, 'The Sanctity of Debt and Insolvent Countries: Defenses of Debtors in International Loan Agreements' in David Sassoon and Daniel Bradlow (eds), *Judicial Enforcement of International Debt Obligations* (1987) 119, 130–44.

146 *Tandrin Aviation Holdings v Aero Toy Store LLC* [2010] EWHC 40, para 40.

147 Republic of Ukraine, US$1,984,838,000 5.00 per cent Notes due 2015, p 28.

148 Republic of Austria, Australian Dollar Medium Term Note Programme, 3 May 2004, p 21.

149 See, eg, Bolivarian Republic of Venezuela, Prospectus Supplement to Prospectus Dated 11 February 2004, s-34.

whereby a party will not seek to prevent contractual performance, refused to imply it on the facts. He substantiated the refusal to imply by saying that in so far as the bonds were transferable, potential transferees, who had to be able to ascertain the nature of the obligation they were acquiring, could not do so through implied terms. The implication of such terms would make the bonds 'unworkable and untransferable'. It could perhaps be suggested that any reasonable person should anticipate implied obligations which, by definition, go without saying, including the terms put forward by Ukraine.

The last defence that Ukraine raised was that it was entitled to decline to make payments to Russia as a 'countermeasure' under public international law. The judge held that this matter was non-justiciable. **6.124**

7

A Taxonomy of Challenges to Sovereign Debt Restructurings

I. INTRODUCTION

Currently, the impecunious sovereign debtor does not enjoy the benefit of a bankruptcy regime proper akin to the insolvency statutes for companies or individuals. Rather, the sovereign debtor restructures its debt through an often disordered process of consensual exchange offers and debt restructurings. What is characteristic to this process is that the State enjoys strong bargaining power which, in the throes of a financial crisis, it might be tempted to abuse. **7.01**

Generally speaking, courts proceed with caution when asked to rule on the legality of the arguably abusive exercise of sovereign powers in a sovereign debt restructuring. Yet, the deference given to the restructuring process and the manner in which it is conducted is by no means absolute. The restructuring process may on occasions be characterised by the use of coercive and expropriatory measures. **7.02**

The *prise de conscience* of the harsh impact that such measures might have on the rights of creditors requires addressing the circumstances in which sovereign bondholders can *ex post* challenge the results and the conduct of sovereign debt restructurings. The non-recognition of sovereign debt restructurings acts as a *post factum* control over sovereign debt restructuring lest the borrowing States abuse their sovereign powers. While this is a meritorious endeavour, the devil is in the detail: the courts need to walk a fine line between ensuring a meaningful protection to creditors and not intruding into the conduct of sovereign debt restructurings. **7.03**

Courts may be called to intervene when the sovereign debtor restructures its debt through an arguably invalid or objectionable application of collective action clauses (CACs)[1] and the disgruntled creditor argues that such an application of CACs was invalid, perhaps because the restructuring was exorbitant, discriminatory, or abusive. The analysis of this scenario has **7.04**

[1] Discussed in detail in Chapter 2.

Sovereign Defaults Before Domestic Courts. First Edition. Hayk Kupelyants. Published 2018 by Oxford University Press.

been chosen as the cornerstone for this chapter for the very simple reason that in modern sovereign debt restructurings, CACs are the essential toolbox for the sovereign debtor in distress to structure a smooth sovereign debt reduction. CACs permit the majority of bondholders in agreement with the State to bind the minority. Conducive to an orderly debt restructuring and barely objectionable in and of themselves, CACs may, however, give rise to abuses or oppressions of the minority of bondholders.

7.05 The common theme in the discussion below is the extent to which the courts are ready to constrain the powers the majority enjoys in the application of CACs, and thus limit the abuse of the rights of minority creditors. Sovereign bond contracts, although usually lengthy in other respects, do not address the challenges that the minority bondholder may mount against abusive exercise of majority powers. Instead, they are regulated by the common law rules (discussed below), which are convoluted and labyrinthine.

7.06 Drawing on the rich repository of the common law, this chapter presents a systematic taxonomy of the challenges that the minority of bondholders can initiate against the majority of bondholders. Such actions are brought on the basis that through the abusive exercise of collective decision-making powers, the majority has engaged its responsibility towards the minority of bondholders by aiding the sovereign debtor to coercively restructure the debt. Such intercreditor actions test the outer limits of majority powers.

7.07 The chapter will treat various CACs separately, conscious that each variation of CACs may call for a different level of judicial scrutiny. The taxonomy of legal actions open to disgruntled creditors might serve as a cautionary tale for sovereign debtors engaged in sovereign debt restructurings, and at the same time, for litigious minority creditors.

II. GENERAL PRINCIPLES OF THE JUDICIAL SCRUTINY OF MAJORITY POWERS

1. The Proper Respondent

7.08 In a typical sovereign debt restructuring, the majority of bondholders, solicited by the sovereign debtor, restructures the sovereign's obligations through the exercise of majority powers under various CACs, mostly majority action clauses and exit consents.[2] In the application of powers

[2] See Chapter 2.

available under CACs, the majority of bondholders undeniably exercises a wide-ranging contractual discretion. It implicitly assesses the financial stability and health of the debtor, the chances of recovering the debt through litigation, and the extent of financial concessions to be accorded to the debtor.

The exercise of this discretion can have prejudicial repercussions for the rights of minority bondholders. Typically, the majority of bondholders triggers the operation of CACs so as to restrain the substantive or procedural rights of the minority. Thus, the disgruntled minority bondholder may see its contractual entitlement reduced (either the principal or interest rate payments), its remedial rights under the sovereign bond documentation denied, and so on. The broader question at stake is thus that of intercreditor relationships (or, what may be called, intercreditor equity) between the disgruntled minority creditor and the majority of creditors. This is a dilemma that is aptly described to require a balancing of 'tyrannical minorities' and 'oppressive majorities'.[3] The review of contractual discretion of the majority of bondholders is in a sense unique, given the *sui generis* interrelation between the minority and majority of bondholders. **7.09**

This subsection addresses the preliminary point of exactly who the respondent in challenges to sovereign debt restructurings should be—the majority of bondholders or the sovereign debtor. As explained, the majority of bondholders trigger CACs in a manner prejudicial to the minority. That said, the sovereign debtor is the one putting the restructuring in motion by soliciting the creditors to accept the exchange offer. In this triangular relationship, depicted in Figure 7.1, the disgruntled minority faces the dilemma of suing either the debtor or the majority bondholders. **7.10**

English and (some) US cases take contrasting positions as to who is the proper respondent in *ex post* challenges to sovereign debt restructurings. Under English law, actions are commonly framed against the majority of bondholders who ultimately make the decision whether or not to restructure the sovereign's debt.[4] In the United States, good-faith claims—when and if raised—are usually couched against the debtor in distress who purports to restructure its debt.[5] **7.11**

[3] Lee Buchheit and Mitu Gulati, 'Sovereign Bonds and the Collective Will' (2004) 51 Emory LJ 1317, 1338.

[4] See, eg, *Northern Assurance Company, Ltd v Farnham United Breweries, Ltd* [1912] 2 Ch 125, 131.

[5] See, eg, *Katz v Oak Industries Inc*, 508 A.2d 873 (Del Ch 1986). One noticeable exception is *Hackettstown National Bank v DG Yuengling Brewing Co*, 74 F 110, 112 (2d Cir 1896) (holding fellow bondholders to a good-faith obligation towards minority bondholders).

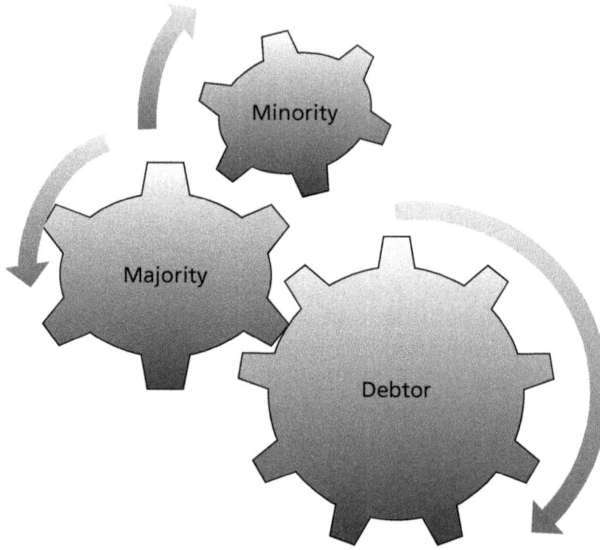

Figure 7.1: The actors and victims of the abuse of powers in a sovereign debt restructuring

7.12 Channelling the action against majority bondholders may seem justifiable in two ways. First, there is a perception under English law that the liability of the debtor cannot be engaged. Only fellow creditors can wield the coercive power of CACs (exit consents or majority action clauses), not the issuer who lacks any power to bring about an expropriatory amendment to the terms of the obligation.[6] Finding the State in breach of some good-faith obligation is controversial. The sovereign is the party on the other side of the negotiating table, and the causation link between its acts and the damage sustained by disgruntled bondholders is only indirect. Due to the proximity between majority and minority bondholders, English law imposes good-faith obligations on the majority of bondholders who eventually engaged the CACs. Second, the action against fellow bondholders removes the element of sovereignty and obviates the need for the disgruntled creditor to counter all sorts of (legal and extralegal) arguments available to shield the State from a finding of contractual liability.

7.13 While these two points are compelling, there is an inherent drawback in designing an action against majority bondholders when they do nothing but follow the course prescribed by the sovereign debtor in

[6] *Assénagon Asset Management SA v Irish Bank Resolution Corporation Limited* [2012] EWHC 2090 (Ch), para 75.

a take-it-or-leave-it exchange offer. In *Redwood Master Fund v TD Bank Europe Ltd*, the debt restructuring, as put forward by the debtor, imposed a discriminatory financial burden on one of the two groups of lenders. The funds which the disadvantaged group was requested to advance were to be used to repay the other group of lenders. The majority of lenders assented to such discriminatory treatment and accordingly triggered the CAC under the syndicated loan documentation. To uphold the tenet of fairness, the majority (or the debtor) could have distributed the financial burden between the two groups of lenders more or less equally. However, the court found, among other things, that the majority was unable to act in the interest of the whole mass of lenders since the allocation of the burden came unilaterally from the debtor.[7] By this, the court shielded the majority from liability given the extraneous source of the pressure to restructure, while at the same time leaving the minority creditors without any efficient remedies against the debtor.

This leads to a paradox: the disgruntled creditor is unable to hold the majority of bondholders liable for operating the CAC since the majority simply follows the restructuring plan as composed by the sovereign debtor. Yet, the sovereign debtor also cannot be held liable given that it is at the other side of the negotiating table. The court in *Redwood Master* found itself in this uncomfortable position—while recognising the unfairness of the debt restructuring, it did not and could not provide an effective remedy. **7.14**

This state of affairs renders it necessary to consider whether the remedy available to the minority lenders should lie against the majority of bondholders—which might be a mere pawn in the hands of the debtor—or, rather, against the debtor who plays the key role in designing the restructuring of sovereign debt. Often, the majority of bondholders would have little say in the design of the exchange offer put forward by the sovereign debtor (and more often than not does not have much of a choice). The better option is to invest the bondholders/lenders with a direct action against the debtor in cases where the majority of bondholders cannot be blamed for the inherently unfair design of the restructuring. **7.15**

The obvious counterargument is on what ground? Despite some recent judicial pronouncements,[8] English law generally does not countenance obligations of good faith in contract law,[9] and an argument against the **7.16**

[7] *Redwood Master Fund v TD Bank Europe Ltd* [2002] EWHC 2703 (Ch), paras 94, 110–12.

[8] *Yam Seng v International Trade Corporation* 2013 EWHC 111 (QB), paras 137–41 (interpreting good faith as honesty and fidelity to the parties' bargain).

[9] *Walford v Miles* [1992] 1 All ER 453; *Banque Financiere de la Cite v Westgate Insurance Co* [1990] 1 QB 665; *TSG Building Services PLC v South Anglia Housing Limited* [2013] EWHC 1151 (TCC), para 46 (distinguishing *Yam Seng*).

debtor predicated upon this ground is likely to face a legal dead end. Seeking to impose a fiduciary duty on the debtor to protect the interests of the bondholders is equally ill-conceived.[10] Similarly, it is unlikely that a tortious interference claim against the debtor will succeed.[11] A likely avenue might be a claim for fraud by the debtor[12] which would be extremely hard to substantiate in sovereign debt restructurings.

7.17 To the extent that this situation might lead to the erosion of contractual rights, it is proposed, at least *de lege ferenda*, to treat the sovereign debtor and majority bondholders as acting jointly in consortium and hence jointly liable for a defective debt restructuring.[13] This would allow the court to treat the prejudicial course of conduct between the majority and the debtor as constituting one complete multipartite design and derive legal repercussions from such a construction. In actions designed in this fashion, the majority of bondholders would not be able to avoid the rescission of the debt restructuring by claiming that the restructuring was imposed on it by the debtor. The liability of the sovereign debtor, albeit the opposing contractual party in a debt restructuring, can and shall be amalgamated with that of the majority of bondholders if the sovereign is imposing in practical terms its will upon the majority of bondholders.

7.18 It goes without saying that the determination of the joint liability of the debtor and majority bondholders will be a fact-specific enquiry, and will largely depend upon the degree of complicity between the two respondent actors. The extent of negotiations and freedom to modify the terms and conditions of the restructuring is a factor that the court would need to take into account in its finding. In negotiated exchange offers, the majority

[10] *Katz v Oak Industries Inc*, 508 A2d 873, 879 (Del Ch 1986); *Simons v Cogan*, 549 A2d 300, 302 (Del 1988). See also Nicholas Saggese, Gregg Noel, and Michael Mohr, 'A Practitioner's Guide to Exchange Offers and Consent Solicitations' (1991) 24 Loy LA L Rev 527, 594–95, fn 323; Marcel Kahan, 'The Qualified Case against Mandatory Terms in Bonds' (1995) 89 Nw U L Rev 565, 587–88, fn 90, 612–17; William Bratton, 'The Economics and Jurisprudence of Convertible Bonds' (1984) Wis L Rev 667, 738–79. See, on the other side of spectrum, Morey McDaniel, 'Bondholders and Corporate Governance' (1986) 41 Bus Law 413, 442–50; Lawrence Mitchell, 'The Fairness Rights of Corporate Bondholders' (1990) 65 NYU L Rev 1165, 1165–1213 (making a case for fiduciary duties of debtors to bondholders).

[11] *Yucyco, Ltd v Republic of Slovenia*, 984 F. Supp. 209, 221 (SDNY 1997) (rejecting the argument that the defendant debtors tortiously interfered with the majority of creditors which relieved the defendant debtors of the joint and several liability for the loans contracted); *Elliott Associates, LP v The Republic of Panama*, 975 F Supp 332, 341–42 (SDNY 1997) (rejecting the counterclaim of tortious interference)

[12] *Metropolitan Life Ins Co v RJR Nabisco, Inc*, 716 F Supp 1504, 1524 (SDNY 1989); *Hartford Fire Insurance Company v Federated Department Stores*, 723 F Supp 976, 994–95 (SDNY 1989).

[13] Some US cases have indeed named both the debtor and the majority bondholders as respondents (*Aladdin Hotel Co v Bloom*, 200 F 2d 627, 628 (8th Cir 1953)).

of bondholders may not shift the blame completely to the debtor given the role it plays in the approval of the exchange offer. Conversely, in take-it-or-leave-it debt restructurings, more sympathy may be felt for the majority of bondholders who, to some extent, felt constrained by the terms put forward by the debtor.

2. The Standard of Scrutiny

Should the minority wish to contest the outcome of the debt restructuring, the starting point under English law is that the interests of bondholders may and in practice do often vary significantly. The bondholders cannot thus be blamed for voting in their own interests or in the direction they wish to the detriment of other bondholders.[14] So too, it is beyond doubt that the majority of bondholders, in the exercise of their contractual powers, is not bound by fiduciary duties of any kind towards the minority of bondholders.[15] Few would argue against the logic of this reasoning—the majority of bondholders ought not be compelled to give weight to the interests of the minority of bondholders at the expense of their own interests or predilections. **7.19**

Buttressing this proposition is that sovereign bonds are silent on the limits of the contractual discretion that the majority of bondholders enjoys. This could be read as providing almost unfettered discretion to the majority wielding their powers under CACs. The enforceability of the bonds in accordance with the plain reading of their terms is thought to be the norm in sovereign debt litigation,[16] and courts are generally reluctant to imply extensive obligations on the side of the majority of bondholders. A bondholder is taken to have been conscious of the risk that the terms of the bond issue may be modified when subscribing to a bond issue containing a CAC.[17] **7.20**

[14] *Goodfellow v Nelson Line (Liverpool) Ltd* [1912] 2 Ch 324, 333 (holding that the guarantor of the debtor was entitled to vote in favour of a scheme that would release its guarantee); *Re Astec* [1998] 2 BCLC 556, 584 (by analogy, in the context of shareholder voting).

[15] Buchheit and Gulati (n 3) 1340; William Bratton and Mitu Gulati, 'Sovereign Debt Reform and the Best Interest of Creditors' (2004) 57(1) Vand L Rev 1, 65–69. In the particular context of syndicated loans, the agents and the managers of the syndicate, might, given the particular facts of the case and the sophistication of lenders, hold a fiduciary duty towards lenders (Padazis Karamanolis, *The Legal Implications of Sovereign Lending through Syndicated Loan Agreements* (1992) 141–77, 253–78). See also *Torre Asset Funding Limited v The Royal Bank of Scotland plc* [2013] EWHC 2670 (Ch) (narrowly circumscribing the duties of the agent toward lenders).

[16] Carmine Boccuzzi, Michael Brennan, and Jacob Johnston, 'Defences' in Rosa Lastra and Lee Buchheit (eds), *Sovereign Debt Management* (2014) 111–13.

[17] *Allen v Gold Reefs of West Africa* [1900] 1 Ch 656, 678.

7.21 That said, it is revealing that in certain circumstances, courts feel compelled to overlook the plain meaning of a clause, or, more precisely, the silence of bonds in an effort to protect the disgruntled lender.[18] As this chapter elucidates, since at least the late nineteenth century, English courts have come down in favour of the proposition that the majority of bondholders does not enjoy unfettered discretion. The courts may intervene on occasion to rein in the majority power and inhibit the abusive exercise of majority powers that is harmful to the rights of minority creditors.

7.22 Quite how extensive this judicial scrutiny is and quite where the source of such judicial power stems from is somewhat obscure. There are three possible explanations for the source of such judicial scrutiny. First, the plain language of the bonds almost invariably dictates that the majority of bondholders are empowered to 'modify' (and amend, supplement) the rights and obligations of all bondholders. The textual argument would suggest that the power of the majority to '*modify*' the debt could not extend to *confiscations* or *destructions* of sovereign debt holding and a confiscation of the rights of creditors is not a 'modification' properly so called. Modifying implies some degree of adaptation of the existing provision rather than a complete overhaul.[19] As a result, the overhaul of sovereign debt might not fall within the contractual powers which the majority of bondholders possesses. Indeed, the occasions in which English courts intervened to rescind the restructurings were characterised as 'extinguishing'[20] or 'destroying the rights rather than modifying them'.[21] That said, the instances where this textual argument would succeed are few far and between.[22]

7.23 Second, some courts may imply a term in fact that will seek to constrain the abusive exercise of majority powers.[23] The difficulty of this approach lies in establishing the necessity of implication under the English law on implied terms in fact. Third, and more convincingly, English courts imply a term in law to scrutinise the exercise of majority powers by reference to

[18] William Bratton, 'The Interpretation of Contracts Governing Corporate Debt Relationships' (1983–84) 5 Cardozo L Rev 371, 400–06 (discussing the tension between plain reading and purposive interpretation of debt contracts).

[19] See by analogy a similar interpretation of the words 'compromise or arrangement' in *Re NFU Development Trust Ltd* [1973] 1 All ER 135, 140. See also Lord Millett (ed), *Gore-Browne on Companies*, vol II (2004), para 29[8].

[20] *Mercantile Investment and General Trust Co v International Company of Mexico* [1893] 1 Ch 484, 489 (in the context of a debt-equity swap).

[21] *Northern Assurance Company, Ltd v Farnham United Breweries, Ltd* [1912] 2 Ch 125, 134 (in the context of the extension of maturities).

[22] For a recent application, see *Myers v Kestrel Acquisitions Ltd (Kestrel)* [2015] EWCH 916 (Ch), paras 66–74 and the authorities discussed therein.

[23] See below for the discussion and criticism of the holding in *Katz v Oak Industries Inc*, 508 A 2d 873, 880 (1986).

the common law rules that require the majority to act in good faith in the best interests of the company/bondholders.

7.24 Deriving the judicial power from this latter ground, the tenor of English judge-made law is broadly in favour of holding the majority of bondholders to a good-faith obligation in respect of the minority. The overarching principle is that the majority's power should not be abused and should be exercised bona fide for the benefit of the entire company, or in the case of bond restructurings, for the benefit of all the bondholders.[24] This principle will appear time and time again in this chapter and will be used as a general benchmark for judging the legality of the powers the majority of bondholders may wield.

7.25 As is the case with other open-ended and deliberately imprecise standards, the expression 'in good faith for the benefit of the company' (or for the benefit of bondholders) is an elusive concept. Its application strongly depends upon the infinitely varied circumstances of each case.[25] In assessing the benefit for and interests of the company, courts are likely to consider the overall context of the transaction, the circumstances in which it was taken,[26] the overall rate of bondholders supportive of the restructuring,[27] and, last but not least, the extent of the reduction of creditor rights.

7.26 Although this principle may resonate with the proponents of extensive bondholder rights, the obligation to exercise power in the interests of the company/bondholders should not be taken literally—the majority of bondholders cannot consider and give effect to the interests of all the bondholders, especially since they are often conflicting. A certain prejudice to the rights and interests of the minority of bondholders is unavoidable when the debt of a sovereign is held by various groups of creditors.[28] The majority of bondholders ought not be precluded from taking actions that might ultimately affect the rights of minority creditors if they are

[24] *British America Nickel Corporation Ltd v O'Brien* [1927] AC 369, 373; *Assénagon Asset Management SA v Irish Bank Resolution Corporation Limited* [2012] EWHC 2090 (Ch), para 72; *Greenhalgh v Arderne Cinemas* [1951] Ch 286, 291.

[25] *Clemens v Clemens Bros Ltd* [1976] 2 All ER 268, 282.

[26] *Rights & Issues Investment Trust Ltd v Stylo Shoes Ltd* [1965] Ch 250 (holding that the increase of voting shares of the management was valid as it was aimed at ensuring the continuity of the management in the context of an upcoming merger of companies).

[27] See, eg, *In Re Empire Mining Company* (1890) 44 Ch D 402, 410–11; *Re Alabama Co* [1891] 1 Ch 213, 227. Bab suggested that the court should also consider the degree of sophistication of the bondholder (Andrew Bab, 'Debt Tender Offer Techniques and the Problem of Coercion' (1991) 91 Colum L Rev 846, 889).

[28] *Peters American Delicacy Company Limited v Heath and others* (1938–39) 61 CLR 457, 511–13 (approved by *Redwood Master Fund v TD Bank Europe* [2002] EWHC 2703 (Ch), para 103); *Sidebottom v Kershaw, Leese and Company, Ltd* [1920] 1 Ch 154, 164–65.

taken for the benefit of the entire group of bondholders. Holding otherwise is to insist that a minority may jeopardise a sovereign debt restructuring that is conducive to the financial recovery of the debtor and brings long-term benefits to creditors.

7.27 One thing that is clear and needs to be stressed at the onset is that the courts will not embark on an analysis of the reasonableness (or proportionality) of sovereign debt restructurings, and rightly so. It is up to the creditors to make the business assessment of the financial situation of the sovereign and the degree of concessions they are willing to make.[29]

7.28 The flip side of the same question is to which standard should the court judge the exercise of the majority power? The subjective good faith, ie, what the majority believed to be fair,[30] or the objective test, ie, whether the use of majority powers was genuinely for the benefit of the entire group of bondholders?[31] Following the argument to its logical conclusion, the courts are likely to adopt the standard of subjective good faith and defer to the business assessment of the majority power. This is, however, subject to (objective) equitable constraints.[32] English courts have shown little hesitation in reversing the presumption of the subjective good faith when the oppression of the minority was overwhelming:

> The alteration may be so oppressive as to cast suspicion on the honesty of the persons responsible for it, or so extravagant that no reasonable men could really consider it for the benefit of the company.[33] [*mutatis mutandis* all the bondholders]

7.29 The conventional interpretation of the standard of 'good faith in the best interests of all the bondholders' is that it is an overarching principle from which more specific standards derive. While those standards, as applied

[29] *Socimer International Bank Ltd v Standard Bank London Ltd* [2008] EWCA Civ 116, para 66; *Lymington Marina v Macnamara* [2007] EWCA Civ 151, para 43; *Shuttleworth v Cox Brothers and Company (Maidenhead) Ltd* [1927] 2 KB 9, 23. See, however, *Walker v Elmore's German and Austro-Hungarian Metal Co* (1901) 85 LT 767, 770–72 (taking a close look at the purpose behind the modification of the rights of debenture-holders and enquiring whether the proposed amendment of the rights of debenture-holders pursued the function of alleviating the financial predicament of the debtor).

[30] *Greenhalgh v Arderne Cinemas* [1951] Ch 286, 291; *Shuttleworth v Cox Brothers and Company (Maidenhead) Ltd* [1927] 2 KB 9, 18–19; John Machell and Jennifer Haywood, 'Discretionary Decision Making in a Commercial Context' (2013) 4 JIBFL 195, 197–98.

[31] *Dafen Tinplate Company, Ltd v Llanelly Steel Company Ltd* [1920] 2 Ch 124, 140 (discarded by the Privy Council in *Citco Banking v Pusser's Ltd* [2007] BCC 205, paras 15, 24); *Brown v British Abrasive Wheel* [1919] 1 Ch 290, 295–96; *Lymington Marina v Macnamara* [2007] EWCA Civ 151, paras 59, 61.

[32] *Citco Banking v Pusser's Ltd* [2007] BCC 205, paras 15–18; *Rights & Issues Investment Trust Ltd v Stylo Shoes Ltd* [1965] Ch 250, 256.

[33] *Shuttleworth v Cox Brothers and Company (Maidenhead), Ltd* [1927] 2 KB 9, 18.

by English and US cases, are impervious to easy categorisation, Wood has identified the following four specific principles underpinning the valid exercise of majority powers, the breach of any one of which might result in a successful challenge to the majority decision:

(1) the decision was clearly within the terms of the power,
(2) the majority were in good faith, i.e. not motivated solely by malice or vindictiveness,
(3) there were no secret advantages to some creditors to procure their votes, e.g. bribes, and
(4) most difficult of all, there was no unjust oppression of the minority so as to constitute a fraud on the minority, e.g. by a discriminatory decision denying the minority an advantage granted to the majority.[34]

As for the first principle, it is premised on the undeniable proposition that majority powers under CACs have to be exercised within the express limits of the contract and comply with any express limitations set on the majority power.[35] The ultra vires exercise of majority powers will never be recognised.[36] **7.30**

Under a typical English law governed majority action clause, the majority enjoys a wide-ranging power to modify the provisions as set out in an extensive list of matters. Those broad powers, although interpreted extensively,[37] are in principle subject to judicial scrutiny, and so are the powers that are comprehensively regulated in the contract.[38] That said, in the face of an express stipulation prescribing the precise content of a power (eg, haircut or sale *at a specified amount*), courts are reluctant to interfere with the decision of the majority of bondholders taken in compliance with such a clause. Thus, English and US courts typically do not rewrite the parties' agreement by implying an obligation to act in good faith when the bonds expressly cater for the contested issue.[39] Conversely, when the intention **7.31**

[34] Philip Wood, 'Syndicated Credit Agreement: Majority Voting' (2003) 62(2) CLJ 261, 261–262.

[35] *Dunham v Omaha & C.B. ST RY CO*, 25 F Supp 287, 291–92 (SDNY 1938).

[36] *Assénagon Asset Management SA v Irish Bank Resolution Corporation Limited* [2012] EWHC 2090 (Ch), para 51; *Follit v Eddystone Granite Quarries* [1892] 3 Ch 75, 81–82.

[37] *Reineccius et al v Bank for International Settlements*, Partial Award, 22 November 2002, paras 143–44 (expansively construing, under public international law, an article of the constituent document of the Bank for International Settlements that provided the majority with open-ended powers).

[38] *Blisset v Daniel* (1853) 10 Hare 493.

[39] *Phillips v Manufacturers' Securities Ltd* [1917] 86 LJ Ch 305, 316 (per Lush LJ); *SNCB Holding v UBS AG* [2012] EWHC 2044 (Comm), para 108; *Hartford Fire Insurance Company v Federated Department Stores*, 723 F Supp 976, 991–93 (SDNY 1989). But see *Marblegate Asset Management v Education Management Corp*, 75 F Supp 3d 592 (SDNY 2014).

of the parties to subject the minority rights to the will of the majority was unclear, courts have construed majority action clauses rather cautiously.[40]

7.32 As for the second and fourth principles, one cannot fail to notice their clear overlap in that they provide differing standards for the review of the majority decision-making—good faith, on the one hand, and oppression of the minority, on the other. Hollington, relying on the authority of the Privy Council in *Citco Banking v Pusser's Ltd*,[41] explains that these two standards of judicial scrutiny regulate two distinct categories of cases. The first category comprises cases where the company as a corporate entity (or all the bondholders in their totality) has an interest in the restructuring, so that such cases should be assessed as against the benefit for the entire company. That is where the standard of the action 'in good faith for the benefit of the company' applies. The second category covers cases where the restructuring causes the interests of one group of shareholders/bondholders to conflict with those of another group of shareholders/bondholders. In this category of cases, the applicable test is that of the 'fraud on the minority'.[42] In other words, when facing a clash of interests between various bondholders, the applicable test is that of fraud on the minority.[43] Meeting this test can be a more burdensome exercise than the breach of the duty of 'good faith for the benefit of the company'.

7.33 Finally, the review of sovereign debt restructurings is not a mechanical exercise. To prevail, the creditor might wish to show two additional factors: the payment capacity of the sovereign debtor and the credible alternatives to the sovereign debt restructuring as conducted and completed. First, there is some authority to argue that the payment capacity is a precondition for triggering majority action clauses. Thus, the court in *Mercantile* held that the debt-equity swap, to which the majority consented, should

[40] *Hay v The Swedish and Norwegian Railway Co Ltd* (1889) 5 TLR 460 (deciding in respect of a majority action clause that omitted a reference to the matters that the majority could modify that the majority had no power to modify the rights of the minority); *Mercantile Investment and General Trust Co v International Company of Mexico* [1893] 1 Ch 484, 489 (holding that the power to release a security does not include the power to release the debtor from the obligations secured by such security); *Enoch v Brandon* 128 Misc 695 (1927) (holding that, when the majority action clause was contained in a trust deed, a less obvious location for the bondholder than the terms of the bonds themselves, the minority bondholder could prevent the attempt to modify the principal and the interest of the bonds if it was able show that the bonds contained an unqualified promise to pay).

[41] [2007] BCC 205, para 18.

[42] Robin Hollington, *Shareholder Rights* (2013) 135–145. See also David Chivers and Ben Shaw (eds), *The Law of Majority Shareholder Power: Use and Abuse* (2008) 10–12 (stressing that the test of the interests of creditors is unsuitable for the clashes of interests between shareholders).

[43] *Redwood Master Fund v TD Bank Europe Ltd* [2002] EWHC 2703 (Ch), para 105.

not bind the minority of creditors, if and in so far as the debtor had the capacity to pay and the debt was undisputed.[44] The subsequent decision in *Northern Assurance* refused to imply such a condition into the review of debt restructurings.[45] Yet, the 'sequel' to *Mercantile*, followed by other cases,[46] reiterated this condition by deciding that the debt-equity swap was binding on the minority because the debtor had difficulties in paying and the prospects of the recovery did not look promising.[47] Incorporating the enquiry into the payment capacity of the debtor within the scrutiny of sovereign debt restructurings presupposes that the court is equipped with capacity to calculate the debt burden of the State, distinguish a simple 'rollover' crisis from a genuine insolvency of the State, and assess the economic development of the sovereign debtor over the following decades. That said, the examination of the financial predicament of the State is necessary to avoid unjust attempts to alleviate the financial burden of a State with a healthy national economy and sustainable debt level (the so-called opportunistic defaults).

Of course, the authorities on payment capacity as a precondition for valid restructurings date back to the early twentieth century and may be a relic of the past. It would be too far-fetched to allow the court to review the payment capacity of the sovereign debtor in every sovereign debt restructuring. That would be beyond the current understanding of the role of the judiciary in the review of sovereign debt restructurings. Nevertheless, the requirement may reappear in certain extreme cases perhaps where the court hesitates as to whether it should uphold or quash the restructuring or where the default and restructuring is on the balance of probabilities opportunistic.[48] **7.34**

Second, for a challenge to be cogent and compelling, the disgruntled creditor would be well advised (note the optional character) to provide, as it were, an account of credible alternatives to the debt restructuring. These **7.35**

[44] *Mercantile Investment and General Trust Co v International Company of Mexico* [1893] 1 Ch 484, 489.

[45] *Northern Assurance Company, Ltd v Farnham United Breweries, Ltd* [1912] 2 Ch 125, 133–34; *Meade-King v Usher's Wiltshire Brewery Ltd* (1928) 44 TLR 298, 299. Neither would such a condition be implied into the schemes of arrangement (although it might play a role in the discretionary approval of the scheme—Geoff O'Dea, Julian Long, and Alexandra Smyth, *Schemes of Arrangement: Law and Practice* (2012) 132–35).

[46] *Sneather v Valley Gold Ltd* [1893] 1 Ch 477, 493–94; *Walker v Elmore's German and Austro-Hungarian Metal Co* (1901) 85 LT 767, 770–71.

[47] *Mercantile Investment and General Trust Co v River Plate Trust, Loan & Agency Co* [1894] 1 Ch 578, 586–98.

[48] See below where payment capacity may be used to review a haircut of 80–90% of the original value of bonds.

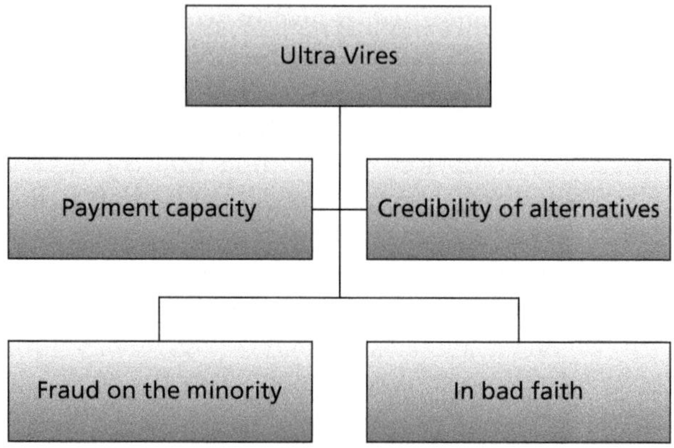

FIGURE 7.2: Structure of challenges to a sovereign debt restructuring

might include an assessment of the debtor's payment capacity, the feasibility of the restructuring, and alternative modes of restructuring/financing that the State was able to resort to, but chose not to.

7.36 The need to show these two factors—payment capacity and credible alternatives—is strong when the minority creditor seeks to challenge the size of the restructuring. If the creditor seeks to dismantle the process of the restructuring (eg, excessive level of coercion), the need to ascertain the payment capacity or the credible alternatives is only peripheral since the claimant's task is to satisfy the court that the restructuring has not been conducted in accordance with the procedural standards of a restructuring. In other words, the absence of a credible alternative does not obviate the need to respect the minimum fairness in the restructuring.[49]

7.37 The complex line of reasoning and standards, as it has gradually emerged from this discussion, is presented in Figure 7.2.

7.38 As explained, not all the conditions will be relevant in a typical action for judicial scrutiny of sovereign debt restructurings. Payment capacity and credibility of alternatives will reappear only in extreme cases.

3. TIMING OF THE CHALLENGE

7.39 As a rule, creditors will mount a challenge against the outcome of a sovereign debt workout after it has been consummated. This does not necessarily limit the right of creditors to request a court to assess the fairness

[49] See the section Coda on this.

of an exchange offer before the exchange offer is consummated, even if the court might be more reluctant to conduct a review of the terms pending the completion of the restructuring. Thus, in *Urban GmbH v Republic of Argentina*, the court refused to review the upcoming sovereign debt restructuring in part because the judicial scrutiny of the exchange offer might deprive the bondholders 'of whatever opportunity the exchange offer affords with no assurances that a so-called "improved" offer would ever be made'.[50] Similarly, the District Court in *Marblegate Asset Management v Education Management Corp*[51] refused to award a preliminary injunction even though the restructuring was likely to impair the rights of the minority. The balance of equities, and in particular the risk of imperilling the negotiations and pushing the debtor to the brink of insolvency, tipped against the grant of an injunction. By contrast, the US District Court for the District of Puerto Rico found that (some of) the claims to review a statute establishing a regime for the restructuring of the debt of Puerto Rican public corporations were ripe for review even though the statute was yet to be applied.[52]

4. Remedies

So far as the legal consequences of judicial scrutiny are concerned, the court has the power to declare restructuring invalid following a successful challenge by a minority creditor.[53] The decision to invalidate would not affect the majority which would remain subject to the terms of the restructuring rescinded, for, as principle suggests, the majority cannot evade the restructuring which it has previously consented to. The minority is no exception to this principle if it has subsequently ratified the outcomes of the restructuring and would thus be estopped from challenging its validity.[54] In addition to the declaration of invalidity, nothing in principle prevents the minority creditor from claiming damages if the minority is able to adduce necessary evidence to that effect. **7.40**

With these generalisations in mind, the remainder of this chapter reviews the case law on the challenges to the exercise of majority powers under various CACs. Assuming that the exercise of powers is intra vires, the **7.41**

[50] *Urban GmbH v Republic of Argentina*, 2010 US Dist LEXIS 40580, 5 (SDNY 2010).

[51] 75 F Supp 3d 592 (SDNY 2014).

[52] *Franklin California Tax-Free Trust et al v Commonwealth of Puerto Rico*, 2015 US Dist LEXIS 14855, 19 (DPR 2015).

[53] *Assénagon Asset Management SA v Irish Bank Resolution Corporation Limited* [2012] EWHC 2090 (Ch), paras 39, 87.

[54] *Goodfellow v Nelson Line (Liverpool) Ltd* [1912] 2 Ch 324, 334; *Aladdin Hotel Co v Bloom* 200 F 2d 627, 632–33 (8th Cir 1953).

fundamental question underpinning this analysis is in which circumstances are the English courts prepared to circumscribe the abusive exercise of majority powers?

7.42 The law on judicial scrutiny of CACs has been in a state of arrested development for a considerable period of time given that the fairness review was eclipsed by statutory law. For this reason, this chapter draws sparingly on the case law on the review of schemes of arrangement (under Part 26 of the Companies Act 2006) and company voluntary arrangements (CVAs) (under Part 1 of the Insolvency Act 1986), as well as the decisions of majority shareholders (when they affect minority shareholders). The former two—schemes of arrangement and CVAs—are statutory procedures that allow creditors to be 'crammed down', overriding the votes of the minority in a manner akin to the operation of majority action clauses. The case law under these mechanisms is in principle transposable to bond restructurings, although caution is warranted since the standard of judicial scrutiny under statutory procedures is generally more extensive. Further thoughts on the criticism of the English position are offered in the last section of this chapter.[55]

7.43 Finally, to draw a comparison with the position under English law, this chapter also relies on the case law from US courts with the caveat that no equivalent doctrine of good-faith exercise of majority powers exists on the other side of the Atlantic. While the court in *Hackettstown National Bank v DG Yuengling Brewing Co* departed from this general rule and held the majority to a good-faith obligation,[56] it is nevertheless a doubtful authority given its age and the dearth of cases citing it. [57] That said, the duty of good faith reappears in certain cases.[58]

7.44 It is seemly to divide the discussion of exit consents and majority action clauses into the separate treatment of payment-related modifications and payment-unrelated modifications. It is true that the modifications through exit consents and majority action clauses vary in many respects. In the restructurings carried out through exit consents, the majority of bondholders exiting old bonds is left with better terms, either financial or non-financial, and receives a bigger slice of the pie than the more persevering minority of bondholders. By contrast, in respect of majority action clauses, the whole class (class being defined as a group of bondholders holding the same issue of bonds) of sovereign bondholders stands on the same line in respect of the amount of compensation. It is unrealistic that the

[55] See the section Coda. [56] 74 F 110, 112 (2d Cir 1896). [57] Bab (n 27) 873.

[58] See, eg, *MeehanCombs Global Credit Opportunities Funds, LP v Caesars Entertainment Corp*, 80 F Supp 3d 507 (SDNY 2015), as well as other cases discussed in this chapter.

supermajority would subject itself to so deep a haircut to give an actionable claim to the minority of bondholders, unless the excessive pressure of the sovereign State has forced it to incapacitate itself.[59] The restructuring through an exit consent is therefore more unfair to the minority and thus, one may argue, the latter should make a more convincing case for the challenge of a sovereign debt restructuring.

But the two restructuring techniques also share many commonalities—in both cases modifications to bonds are introduced through clauses that foist the consent of the majority on the minority. One might query whether it really makes a difference whether the bond modification will affect all the bondholders, as in the case of a majority action clause, or non-consenting bondholders only, as in the case of exit consents. It is of little or no interest to the disgruntled minority shareholder whether the majority is better or worse off after the restructuring. What the minority is concerned with is the fate of its personal investment. **7.45**

5. Payment-Related Modifications

In a leading case *Assénagon Asset Management SA v Irish Bank Resolution Corporation Limited*,[60] arising out of the restructuring of the obligations of Anglo Irish Bank Corporation Limited, the majority of bondholders, solicited by Anglo Irish, consented to exchange the notes it held in return for new notes at a ratio of 20 cents per euro. Yet the restructuring was conditional upon the provision of an exit consent, whereupon the majority of bondholders voted, through a proxy, to include a call option in the old bonds so as to permit the debtor to redeem the debt of any holdout creditor for a pittance. The debtor eventually redeemed the old bonds of a holdout creditor for a mere 0.00001, which led the afflicted creditor to challenge the arguably abusive exercise of the exit consent technique. **7.46**

Briggs J sitting in the Chancery Division started by reiterating the settled law that the majority ought to exercise its powers for the benefit of the whole class of noteholders. Under this rule, as understood by English courts, the majority of noteholders would be liable whenever the exercise of its powers was unfair and oppressive, and used in bad faith. On **7.47**

[59] In (what is) an unfair prejudice case, the majority shareholder decided to raze to the ground its subsidiary company after it had served its purpose. The minority shareholder in the subsidiary company claimed that such conduct was oppressive and obtained an order from the court compelling the majority to purchase the shares of the minority (*Scottish Co-Operative Wholesale Society Ltd v Meyer* [1958] 3 All ER 66, 71–72). This is indicative of the possibility that the courts might be willing to rescue the minority bondholder from the shared vessel that the majority has decided to vacate.

[60] [2012] EWHC 2090 (Ch).

the facts of the case, the court considered that the majority of bondholders, by way of coercion, abusively permitted the debtor to expropriate the minority's rights under the bonds. This was indeed the case, given that the exercise of the call option substantially destroyed the value of the rights arising from the bonds. It was a straightforward conclusion in light of the exorbitant loss that the minority noteholder suffered (a mere €170 received for €17m face value debt).

7.48 The size of the loss suffered by the minority was not the only determinative point in the decision of Briggs J. What was distinctive in *Assénagon* was that the exit consent was designed in a way to retract the exchange offer of 20 cents per euro from any bondholder who failed to accept the offer once initially placed. This lack of forgiveness meant that any bondholder, who had second thoughts about the offer, faced a particularly compelling dilemma—either to accept the 'haircut' or have the bonds redeemed, without the option to subsequently change their mind.

7.49 The counsel for the claimant acknowledged that the result of the challenge could have differed had the offer to exchange the bonds been available for acceptance even after the passing of the resolution, so that any dissenting minority could then avail itself of that which had been offered to the majority.[61] While it goes without saying that these sorts of 'forgiving' schemes are less persuasive and efficient than the 'unforgiving', two-tier schemes, leaving the door open to recalcitrant holdouts would mitigate most of the objectionable features in coercive restructuring techniques, such as exit consents.[62] In any event, in the sovereign debt practice holdout creditors are more often than not afforded the opportunity to have a change of heart,[63] and in the past, contractual provisions were designed to ensure equal treatment for non-consenting bondholders.[64]

7.50 This procedural element is a feature peculiar to exit consents, where the minority has the choice between old and new bonds. In majority action

[61] See similarly *Katz v Oak Industries Inc*, 508 A 2d 873, 881 (Del Ch 1986). For criticism of such exit consents, see Victor Brudney, 'Corporate Bondholders and Debtor Opportunism: In Bad Times and Good' (1992) 105 Harv L Rev 1821, 1834–35.

[62] John Coffee and William Klein, 'Bondholder Coercion: The Problem of Constrained Choice in Debt Tender Offers and Recapitalizations' (1991) 58(4) Uni Chi L Rev 1207, 1244–46. See arguing otherwise Lewis Peterson, 'Who's Being Greedy? A Theoretical and Empirical Examination of Holdouts and Coercion in Debt Tender and Exchange Offers' (1993) 103 Yale LJ 505, 534–35.

[63] See, eg, Lee Buchheit and Elizabeth Karpinski, 'Belize's Innovations' (2007) 22 JIBFL 278, 280.

[64] For examples of such clauses, see *Yucyco, Ltd v Slovenia*, 1999 WL 169530, 2 (SDNY 1999); Lee Buchheit and Mitu Gulati, 'Drafting a Model Collective Action Clause for Eurozone Sovereign Bonds' (2011) 6(3) CMLJ 317, 324.

clauses, the matters are more straightforward: if the majority inflicts a potentially exorbitant haircut, it is binding on the minority against its will and the issue of 'forgiveness' just does not arise. Hence, in scrutinising majority action clauses, the only benchmark is that of exorbitant character of the modification.

Although the parties settled before the judgment reached the Court of Appeal, *Assénagon* is a leading authority on the review of exit consents (and majority action clauses) in that it outlaws overt expropriations of the property of the minority of bondholders. Of course, the exorbitant character of the debt write-off in *Assénagon* makes it an aberration unlikely to occur in practice with recurrent periodicity. **7.51**

Again, walking a thin line between preserving the discretionary power to modify and preventing excessive modifications, the Court of Appeal in *Nash v Paragon Finance* read an implied term into the contract that would limit the otherwise unfettered discretion that the lender enjoyed under the loan contract to vary interest rates. The implied term sought to outlaw the variations of interest rate to exorbitant levels or variations exercised dishonestly—for an improper purpose, capriciously, or arbitrarily (ie, for reasons related to the identity of the borrower or to oust the borrower). However, in principle, the lender was able to vary interest rates to a merely unreasonable level.[65] **7.52**

It is somewhat unclear quite how wide-reaching the holding in *Assénagon* is. In a rather obvious situation, a haircut as low as 20% was judged not to be 'so unreasonable as to call for the intervention of the court'.[66] The Debt Relief (Developing Countries) Act 2010 imposes a 67% haircut on the debt of HIPC countries. In a more complex situation, the Second Circuit decided that due to the total estimate of the assets remaining on the bankruptcy of the debtor company, a settlement assuring the unsecured creditors of 19 cents on the dollar could hardly be regarded as unreasonable.[67] One would expect that the State would be walking a tightrope should it effectuate a haircut north of 80–90%.[68] It is suggested that in this grey area **7.53**

[65] *Nash v Paragon Finance* [2001] EWCA CIV 1466, paras 30–36, 41–42.

[66] *Meade-King v Usher's Wiltshire Brewery Ltd* (1928) 44 TLR 298, 299.

[67] *Re W.T. Grant Co*, 699 F. 2d 599, 613–14 (2d Cir 1983). See also *Chalmers v Nederlandsch Amerikaansche Stoomvaart Maatschappij*, 36 NYS 2d 717, 727–28 (NY City Ct 1942) (upholding a reduction of 72% of the principal).

[68] Sovereign debt restructurings rarely exceed this threshold; cf 20–47% haircut in Moldova's restructuring of 2002 and 10% in Uruguay's 2003 restructuring (Federico Sturzenegger and Jeromin Zettelmeyer, *Debt Defaults and Lessons from a Decade of Crises*, 61, 62, 207, 216, 220); cf the net present value haircut in the Greek debt restructuring of 79%, which is an outlier.

of a haircut of 80% and above, the court should supplement a quantitative analysis of the size of haircut with other, qualitative factors: the extent and good-faith nature of debtor–creditor dialogue, the level of unsustainably high debt held by the State, the recognition of the restructuring by multinational institutions, alternatives available to the debtor, the price at which the bonds were purchased on the secondary market, and so on.

7.54 A conceptual problem arises here. If the supermajority decides that a 90% haircut is necessary, why would this amount to an exorbitant loss? Can a majority of creditors ever 'expropriate'? If they agree to so large a haircut as 80–90% of debt reduction to their own bondholding, how can they be found not to be acting for the benefit of the minority?

7.55 One way of responding is to say that so extensive a haircut may not be considered as 'modification' under the textual interpretation of majority action clauses. However true it might be, the majority of creditors may still foist exorbitant loss on minority creditors and be liable for it for the same reason as someone sinking a ship he is travelling in may be held liable for damage to others in the same ship. In the absolutely prevailing number of cases courts will accept the restructuring to be in the best interests of creditors. However, in principle, the fact that the majority accepts a haircut to its own bondholding does not mean to say that it may not be acting in breach of its duty to act for the benefit of all bondholders.

7.56 The majority might have other, ulterior motives in accepting the exorbitant loss to its bondholding, for instance preserving the long-term relations with the debtor, local bias, quid pro quo for another debt restructuring or transaction. In such cases, it may be argued that the majority's power to inflict so large a haircut should be reined in in spite of the majority's right to act in its own interests. In cases involving 80–90% haircut to the interests of the minority, and only in those cases, the disgruntled creditor may be able to bring expert evidence as to the sustainability of the debt reduction and convince the court of the inequitable nature of the restructuring.

7.57 Some commentators have argued that by invalidating the operation of the exit consent in *Assénagon* Briggs J indubitably deviated from the more orthodox position of US courts which have consistently upheld the use of exit consents. As such, the decision presents excessive risk to the usage of exit consents under English law governed bonds.[69] The reality is more complex. In the judgment, Briggs J considered US decisions that upheld the technique of exit consents. He made a crucial caveat that those cases

[69] Apostolos Gkoutzinis, *Law and Practice of Liability Management: Debt Tender Offers, Exchange Offers, Bond Buybacks and Consent Solicitations in International Capital Markets* (2014) 295.

fell 'short of expropriation'.[70] As the below section elucidates, US courts have equally frowned upon the exorbitant application of exit consents although there is a certain feeling that the English courts, influenced by *Assénagon*, might be more protective of bondholders.[71] It is for future case law to reinforce or dissuade the practical reality of this sentiment. However, one thing that is clear is that both US and English courts adopt in principle a deferential stance towards (sovereign) debt restructurings. Only in extreme cases would they be tempted to police the conduct of the insolvent debtor and the majority bondholders.

For payment-related modifications other than the reduction of the principal, the courts have consistently upheld exchange offers to extend maturities, going as far as converting debentures redeemable on a precise date into irredeemable (perpetual) debentures.[72] As for debt-equity swaps to which sovereigns do resort at times,[73] the dominant case law, with some exceptions,[74] has upheld them.[75] **7.58**

6. Payment-Unrelated Modifications

The precise ambit of the *Assénagon*-like judicial scrutiny of the modification of non-financial provisions is rather uncertain. Assuming that the same principles of good-faith exercise of majority powers, as applied in *Assénagon*, do in principle govern the modification of non-financial terms of bonds, the difficulty remains: where does the line run between acceptable and unacceptable modifications of non-financial terms of the bonds? **7.59**

[70] *Assénagon Asset Management SA v Irish Bank Resolution Corporation Limited* [2012] EWHC 2090 (Ch), para 5.

[71] Dominic McCahill and Jamie Baron, 'Bond Exit Consents: US Courts Offer Pragmatic Approach' (2013) 24(6) PLC 17, 18.

[72] *Assurance Company, Ltd v Farnham United Breweries, Ltd* [1912] 2 Ch 125; *In Re Joseph Stocks & Co, Ltd* [1912] 2 Ch 134. See also *Pepe v City and Suburban Permanent Building Society* [1893] 2 Ch 311, 313; *Walker v Elmore's German and Austro-Hungarian Metal Co* (1901) 85 LT 767, 770–71 (extension of three years); *Aladdin Hotel Co v Bloom*, 200 F.2d 627, 632–33 (8th Cir 1953) (extension of ten years).

[73] IMF, 'Involve the Private Sector in the Resolution of Financial Crises—Restructuring International Sovereign Bonds' (2001) 7.

[74] *Mercantile Investment and General Trust Co v International Company of Mexico* [1893] 1 Ch 484, 489–91 (holding that the power to modify the rights of debenture-holders did not include the power to extinguish them and that a debt-equity swap amounted to an extinction of rights).

[75] *Sneather v Valley Gold Ltd* [1893] 1 Ch 477; *Dey v Rubber* [1923] 2 Ch 528 (the restructuring unchallenged); *Chalmers v Nederlandsch Amerikaansche Stoomvaart Maatschappij*, 36 NY S 2d 717, 727–28 (NY City Ct 1942) (upholding a debt-equity swap).

7.60 The prima facie answer is that English courts would endorse modifications of non-financial terms of the bonds unless they amount to an exorbitant modification of the non-financial terms contained in the bonds. Clarifying precisely what exactly is an exorbitant modification will be an intricate enquiry. Arguably, the outcome of the challenge would often turn on the extent to which the claimant would effectively be prevented from recovering under its contractual entitlements following the modification of the non-financial clauses of the bonds. That is, when the removal of protective covenants reaches a certain threshold where the recovery of the rights under the bonds is no longer practical, the court might be willing to intervene and rescind the restructuring.

7.61 In the following instances, derived from English (and US) case law, the courts determined that the modification of non-financial terms of the bonds was objectionable and did not bind the aggrieved minority:

Divesting Itself of Assets and Stripping the Bonds from Various Protective Covenants.

7.62 A striking example of an objectionable modification is the restructuring in *Federated Strategic Income Fund v Mechala Group Jamaica*,[76] where the debtor sought to strip the contract from the waiver of immunities, choice of forum agreement and other protective covenants, as well as divest itself of all its assets through a corporate reorganisation. The District Court found that such a stratagem amounted to an overt violation of the rights of bondholders to recover the payment due, protected under s 316(b) of the Trust Indenture Act. The court did not indicate what it would have decided had the covenants only been abrogated, without the accompanying divestiture of assets.

7.63 The District Court in *Marblegate Asset Management v Education Management Corp*[77] dealt with a comparably questionable restructuring where the majority of bondholders agreed: (a) to release the guarantor from its obligation to guarantee the payments to minority creditors; and (b) to foreclose 'substantially all' the assets of the debtor and then to resell them to another, interrelated corporate entity, with the effect of completely impairing the minority's right to payment. The judge held that this restructuring amounted to a breach of s 316(b) of the Trust Indenture Act which consecrates the 'right ... to receive payment' of bondholders. The District Court held that depriving the creditor of the guarantee may impair the right to payment in certain contexts and would not in others, without necessarily explaining what those precise contexts are.[78] A similar conclusion was

[76] 1999 US Dist LEXIS 16996 (SDNY 1999).

[77] 75 F Supp 3d 592 (SDNY 2014).

[78] In this case, the guarantee which the majority agreed to release was conferred upon them only two months prior to the litigation, which is a rather peculiar situation and does not shed light on other contexts.

reached in *MeehanCombs Global Credit Opportunities Funds, LP v Caesars Entertainment Corp*, where the restructuring removed the guarantees and the parent company of the debtor was accorded the right to divest itself of its assets. Not only did it breach s 316(b) of the Trust Indenture Act but also the implied duty of good faith and fair dealing.[79]

On appeal to the decision of the first instance judge in *Marblegate*, the Second Circuit reversed the judgment (and, accidentally, the related case law) on the technical ground that s 316(b) applies only to the modification of core payment terms.[80] The court considered that the non-consensual modifications obtained in the course of the restructuring did not violate the *right* to receive payment under s 316(b). Section 316(b) cannot be read to protect the bondholders from modifications which merely affect the practical *ability* to collect payment. The court's form-over-substance analysis is at first sight striking in that it provides carte blanche to the debtors to design as extreme a restructuring as possible so long as it does not directly violate the right to payment terms under the bonds. The decision was accompanied by a strong dissent which underscored that s 316(b) protects the right to receive payment from being 'impaired or affected' and the ordinary meaning of such a broad phrase is to protect the minority's right to collect payment. On the facts, he considered that the terms of the restructuring not only impaired or affected the right to payment but 'annihilated' it. **7.64**

This is not necessarily bad news for the creditors in sovereign debt restructurings. The Second Circuit held that its decision does not prejudice actions brought under other federal or State laws. More importantly, it is worth recalling that the Trust Indenture Act, and s 316(b) in particular, do not apply to sovereign debt restructurings. Possibly, in the face of an excessive sovereign debt restructuring, the actions based on the implied duty of good faith and fair dealing may still be brought. **7.65**

English courts are unlikely to be constrained to the legal straitjacket as are the US courts by s 316(b). The restructurings of the kind in *Federated Income* and *Marblegate* may well be breaches of the duty to act in the best interests of the bondholders and amount to an unfair and oppressive exercise of majority powers. Of course, a sovereign may not undergo a corporate reorganisation. What it might do, though, is devise a series of transactions to avoid the attachment of its assets through the transfer of such assets to **7.66**

[79] 80 F Supp 3d 507 (SDNY 2015).

[80] *Marblegate Asset Management v Education Management Corp*, 2017 US App LEXIS 782 (2d Cir 2017).

a controlled entity. English courts might find this course of action to trespass the boundaries of fairness.[81]

Depriving the Creditor of the Guarantees Attached to its Bondholding even in Exchange for an Increase in the Interest Rate.[82]

7.67 The authority in *Goodfellow v Nelson Line (Liverpool) Ltd* suggests that releasing the bondholder from the benefit of a guarantee is in principle unfair and oppressive.[83] The same would perhaps be equally true of releasing a security (the Brady bonds being the most prominent example of using securities in a sovereign debt).

7.68 Conversely, it is likely that courts would tolerate replacing one security with a better type of security,[84] releasing the security held for the benefit of debenture-holders in the context of a debt-equity swap[85] and disclaiming the security on payment of less than what was actually due.[86]

Vesting in a Third Party of the Power to Modify the Rights under the Bonds without the Consent of Bondholders.[87]

7.69 This would give rise to a substantial modification of the restructuring process. Vesting in a third party the majority powers under the bonds

[81] *Kensington International Ltd v Congo* [2005] EWHC 2684 (Comm), paras 186–87; cf *Kensington International Ltd v Republic of Congo*, 2007 US Dist LEXIS 25282 (SDNY 2007). See also *Walker International Holdings Limited v Republique Populaire du Congo and others* [2005] EWHC 2813 (Comm), para 107. The Privy Council considered that the facts in *Kensington v Congo* were 'extreme' (*La Générale des Carrières et des Mines v F.G. Hemisphere Associates LLC* [2012] UKPC 27, para 48).

[82] Guaranteed sovereign debt is not unheard of in the sovereign debt market (see, eg, Andrew Yianni and Lauren Malek, 'Seychelles Debt Restructuring: Restoring the Viability of the Public Finances' (2010) 25(7) JIBLR 330, 336).

[83] [1912] 2 Ch 324, 333–34 (although the beneficiaries of the guarantees voted in favour of releasing it which estopped them from challenging the restructuring). *Shaw v Royce Ltd* [1911] 1 Ch 138 came to a diametrically opposed position holding that an arrangement depriving the debenture-holders of a guarantee constitutes a valid exercise of the majority power. Note that an abuse of majority power was not argued there, and the claimant contended that an arrangement between the debtor and debenture-holders cannot bind a somewhat separate agreement which is the guarantee agreement.

[84] *I. Kelheimer v Consolidated Tobacco Co*, 59 Atl 363, 366 (N J Eq 1904).

[85] *In Re Empire Mining Company* (1890) 44 Ch D 402; *Re Labuan & Borneo Ltd* (1901) 18 TLR 216.

[86] *Re Madras Irrigation Company* (1888) (referred to in *Re Alabama Co* [1891] 1 Ch 213, 228, 246 (per Fry LJ)). For a more detailed coverage, see Mary Arden et al (eds), *Buckley on the Companies Act*, vol II (2010), para 425.21. See also *In re MPM Silicones, LLC*, Case No 14-22503 (Bankr SDNY 2014).

[87] *British America Nickel Corporation Ltd v O'Brien* [1927] AC 369.

would not, however, attract judicial opprobrium should sovereign bonds expressly provide that the supermajority of bondholders may confer their powers to a committee of bondholders as some bonds do.[88] By contrast, appointing a committee to simply represent bondholders in the sovereign debt workout would hardly be objectionable.

Limiting the Free Transferability of Bonds on the Secondary Market

Typically, sovereign bonds would grant an unfettered right to the bondholder to freely transfer its bondholding to a third party.[89] In times of severe financial crises, the debtor might be tempted to divest the bondholders of their right to assign its bonds freely on the secondary market. A modification of this sort, if enforced from the time of the consent solicited from the majority bondholders, would constitute a powerful sword to prevent the acquisition of sovereign bonds by aggressively oriented specialised creditors on the secondary market. Primary holders of sovereign debt instruments—deprived of the opportunity to transfer their title to parties with necessary litigation skills and readiness to engage in costly proceedings—would be more submissive to the exchange offers of a sovereign. While there is no authority on this scenario, such a ploy may be held to be abusive. To draw an analogy with corporate reorganisations, in a situation where a company is reregistered as a private company and a minority shareholder is unable to dispose of his share in the company, the court will exercise its power to procure the sale of the shares of a discontent minority.[90] **7.70**

Of course, the rescission of the modification is an exception to the general rule of non-interference. A perusal of related case law suggests that the following kinds of majority-imposed contractual modifications, among others, are likely to withstand attacks before the English or US judiciary. **7.71**

Removing All Protective Financial Covenants

In *Katz v Oak Industries Inc*, the debtor sought to strip from the old debt all protective financial covenants by soliciting the majority to employ the exit consent technique and remove the covenants from old bonds. Although recognising in principle that the debtor owed a contractual duty of good faith and fair dealing to bondholders, albeit remote in its breadth from **7.72**

[88] See Art. 12(c)(xiii), The Republic of Azerbaijan, US$1,250,000,000 4.75 per cent Notes due 2024, 13 March 2014; s 8, United Kingdom, US$3,000,000,000 2.25 per cent Notes due 2008, 4 July 2003.

[89] See, eg, Cl 10, EUR 300,000,000 2.75% Fixed Rate Bonds due on 20 August 2043, Grand Duchy of Luxembourg.

[90] *Re a company (No 005685 of 1988), ex parte Schwarcz (No 2)* [1989] BCLC 427, 437–38.

fiduciary duties, the Court of Chancery of Delaware found no breach of such duty for the removal of all protective financial covenants.

7.73 The way the court came to this conclusion is somewhat perplexing. Chancellor Allen stated that the enquiry to locate the obligation to act in good faith and to deal fairly was an enquiry to gauge an implied obligation agreed to by the parties. The threshold question was whether it was 'clear from what was expressly agreed upon that the parties who negotiated the express terms of the contract would have agreed to proscribe the act later complained of as a breach of the implied covenant of good faith—had they thought to negotiate with respect to that matter'.[91] By focusing the enquiry on the express terms of the contract and the intention of the parties to the contract, the enquiry is very reminiscent of the method of implying a term in fact (recall the second ground for judicial power of scrutiny).

7.74 To locate the implied good-faith obligation thus defined, Chancellor Allen analysed the contractual clauses of the bonds, which were unsurprisingly silent on the issue of coercive exchange offers. Masking its enquiry as a search for an implied term, in reality, the court constrained its analysis to an analysis of the express terms of the bonds. The interpretation in *Katz* suffers from an obvious deficiency—it purports to define the *implied* covenant through *express* terms of the contract.

7.75 What is all the more striking about the court's enquiry was that it was rather narrowly circumscribed—to locate the implied consent of the parties 'to proscribe the act later complained of'—the specificity of which is likely to exclude any finding in the affirmative, and excludes any reliance on wider considerations, such as those that an English court would resort to in implying terms in law. As explained above, English courts locate the source of the scrutiny of coercive and abusive debt restructurings in the rules of the common law which obviates the need to search for an implied term in fact.

7.76 In light of this seemingly significant difference, would English courts uphold an extensive overhaul of the contractual bargain between parties à la *Katz v Oak Industries*? The water has not yet been tested, but it might be argued with caution that the elimination of all protective covenants

[91] 508 A 2d 873, 880 (1986) (referred to by the court in *Assénagon Asset Management SA v Irish Bank Resolution Corporation Limited* [2012] EWHC 2090 (Ch), para 5). The holding in *Katz* as to the existence of good-faith obligations was narrowly defined in the subsequent case law (*Cincinnati SMSA Ltd Partnership v Cincinnati Bell Cellular Systems Co*, 708 A 2d 989, 992–93 (Del 1998)).

is tantamount to expropriation in the context of payment-unrelated modifications.

In any event, the court in *Katz* did not in fact face a fully unreasonable modification of the financial indentures since the debtor advanced a cash payment over the market price of the bonds exchanged.[92] **7.77**

Modifying Waivers of Sovereign Immunity

The US courts have upheld, although with reservations, the practice of exit consents which purported to modify the sovereign immunity waivers contained in old, exchanged bonds. In *Greylock v Province of Mendoza*, the debtor, the Argentine province of Mendoza, sought to amend the sovereign immunity waiver contained in the bond documentation by reimmunising the sums that the province of Mendoza would pay under the new bonds. This left untouched all other assets originally contemplated by the waiver. The bondholder contended that the modification of the sovereign immunity waiver in the bonds violated the 'unconditional' right of the bondholder, as entrenched in the bonds, to receive the payment. The Second Circuit disagreed on the grounds that such an 'unconditional' right did tolerate an alteration of the bondholder's ability to recover payment.[93] **7.78**

A word of caution is due here: the sovereign immunity waiver was affected rather mildly in *Greylock v Province of Mendoza* in that it reimmunised only a particular category of assets. The District Court distinguished *Federated Strategic Income Fund*—the case discussed above on the divesting of assets—on its facts, given that the claimant in *Greylock v Mendoza* could still attach all the property of the defendant to the exclusion of the class of assets reimmunised.[94] In light of the decision of the Second Circuit in *Marblegate*,[95] even a full cancellation of the waiver of sovereign immunity may not amount to a breach of s 316(b) of the Trust Indenture Act and, possibly, a contractual clause protecting the 'unconditional' or 'absolute' right to payment. Moreover, many jurisdictions ascribe to the relative theory of sovereign immunity and the aggrieved creditor could attach the commercial property of the sovereign under the default rules on State immunity even in spite of the relative or absolute revocation of the waiver clause.[96] **7.79**

[92] Gkoutzinis (n 69) 290.

[93] *Greylock Global Opportunity Master Fund Ltd v Province of Mendoza*, 2006 WL 140576 (2d Cir 2006).

[94] *Greylock Global Opportunity Master Fund Ltd v Province of Mendoza*, 2005 US Dist LEXIS 1742, 15 (SDNY 2005).

[95] *Marblegate Asset Management v Education Management Corp*, 2017 US App LEXIS 782 (2d Cir 2017).

[96] *Greylock Global Opportunity Master Fund Ltd* (n 94) 16–18.

Modifying the Priorities of Charges in Favour of New Lenders Ready to Lend into Arrears,[97] or Watering Down the Security by Issuing New Bonds that Will Rank *pari passu*.[98]

7.80 These two are intended to ensure access to new funding for the sovereign in distress.

Introducing Provisions that Will Allow Compulsory Buy-Back of Bonds

7.81 In the context of purchase of shares, the Privy Council[99] discarded the uncompromising authority of *Dafen Tinplate Company, Ltd v Llanelly Steel Company Ltd*,[100] namely that the inclusion by the majority of a provision allowing the compulsory purchase of the shares of a minority was not in the interests of a company.

Modifying a Right in the Bonds that Is also Comprised in Another Contract Binding upon the Majority of Bondholders

7.82 The majority of shareholders has no power to modify the articles of association when that would result in a breach of contract.[101] This would imply, by analogy, an inability on the part of bondholders to modify a minority right embedded both in the bonds, and in a separate contract, such as a trust deed over which the majority does not possess powers to modify.

Modifying of Choice of Law and Jurisdiction Clauses

7.83 Colman J sitting in the Commercial Court held that the unilateral variation of the proper law of the contract, when permitted by the terms of the contract, would be valid if exercised in good faith in commercial interests.[102] This is a rather broad and deferential test. A pertinent example of a bad faith modification of choice of law clauses (or choice of forum clauses) would be if such a modification were to avoid an already pending litigation and shift the focal point of the sovereign debt payments to a more favourable jurisdiction. This was arguably the intention of Argentina in the recent *pari passu* litigation.[103]

[97] *Follit v Eddystone Granite Quarries* [1892] 3 Ch 75; *Re The Dominion of Canada Freehold Estate and Timber Co Ltd* (1886) 55 LT 347, 350–51.

[98] *Walker v Elmore's German and Austro-Hungarian Metal Co* (1901) 85 LT 767, 770–71.

[99] *Citco Banking v Pusser's Ltd* [2007] BCC 205, paras 15, 24.

[100] [1920] 2 Ch 124, 140.

[101] *British Murac Syndicate Ltd v Alperton Rubber Company Ltd* [1915] 2 Ch 186.

[102] *BP v National Fire Insurance Co* [2004] EWHC (1132) (Comm), para 35.

[103] Sarah Marsh and Walter Bianchi, 'Argentina Aims to Skirt U.S. Court, Bring Debt under National Law' *Reuters* (20 August 2014).

7.84 To rebut such a deferential standard of judicial scrutiny, it could be said that if the right to modify the applicable law of bonds was not expressly stipulated in the sovereign bonds, the market and bondholders might perceive choice of law and jurisdiction clauses to be quintessential to a fair restructuring. This is because they establish a mechanism for the vindication of rights or, at the very least, the background against which the negotiations are held. To this end, some recent bonds issues contain a unanimity requirement ('entrenched provisions') for the amendment of clauses related to the right of action of bondholders (choice of law, choice of jurisdiction, sovereign immunity waiver).[104]

7.85 In terms of choice of forum clauses, the sovereign debtor may, in a fashion similar to the modification of immunity waivers, argue that a creditor deprived of a choice of forum clause may still persuade a foreign court to assume jurisdiction over a dispute between the sovereign debtor and the bondholder. However, this argument sounds more artificial in the context of choice of forum agreement since the bondholder would have to establish a sufficient ground of jurisdiction and overcome the *forum non conveniens* hurdle, if applicable.

7. Unfair Discrimination

7.86 Sovereign debt restructurings lack an established priority structure to determine the order in which the claims of unsecured creditors are to be satisfied.[105] It is for this reason that sovereign debtors enjoy considerable leeway in according preferences to different groups of creditors for various reasons of political economy and commercial sense. For one, international financial institutions are afforded de facto preference in the treatment of their credit entitlements, similarly short-term and trade credits are almost invariably left out of the restructuring. The State-to-State debt may also be treated preferentially—by way of example, Argentina in May 2014 agreed to repay the Paris club (the State-to-State debt) on terms much more favourable than the terms offered to its private creditors.

7.87 The general thrust of English law is that attacking a sovereign debt restructuring on the grounds that a certain group of creditors was accorded preferential treatment would go against the grain of the existing perceptions. Customarily, English courts afford a wide-ranging discretion to the debtor in designing the scheme of the restructuring. That being the default

104 Anna Gelpern and Mitu Gulati, 'Innovation after the Revolution: Foreign Sovereign Bond Contracts since 2003' (2009) 4(1) Cap Mark LJ 85, 99–100.

105 Anna Gelpern, 'Building a Better Seating Chart for Sovereign Restructurings' (2004) 53 Emory LJ 1115.

position, English courts would, however, chastise preferential treatment that gives rise to unfair discrimination between bondholders. The court would only do so if it was truly satisfied that the discrimination was unfair on its terms.[106]

7.88 Quite when discrimination would cross the line and be unfair was rather obscure until the landmark case of *Redwood Master Fund v TD Bank Europe Ltd*.[107] Sitting in the Chancery Division, Rimer J faced a variation of loan terms exercised through an arguably discriminatory operation of a 'modified waiver letter'—a contractual mechanism much like the majority action clauses—by virtue of which a majority of creditors could amend the obligations of the borrower. The syndicated loan was composed of three facilities (tranches)—A, B, and C, of which lenders A and B tranches had clashing interests. B lenders had previously extended further loans to the debtor and were interested in according additional funds to the debtor by further drawing down the A tranche. By contrast, A lenders, including the claimants in the case, did not want to see the A tranche further drawn down by the debtor—a highly distressed company. Through a modified waiver letter, the majority of lenders (81.76%) was able to force the holders of facility A, alongside a write-off to their debt, to advance an additional sum to the borrowers by drawing down the A tranche. This was eventually used to repay the debt obligations owed to B lenders. The claimants, composed of A facility lenders, contended that the majority did not act bona fide in that it discriminated against A facility lenders as a class, and enriched themselves through the funds of A class lenders.

7.89 The court rejected the challenge. First, Rimer J dismissed the argument that the majority of lenders were motivated by considerations of subjective bad faith towards the minority of lenders ('subjective discrimination or oppression'). Nothing indicated that the exercise of the majority power was manifestly disadvantageous, discriminatory, or oppressive. Rather, the majority of lenders were guided by the objective of attaining a successful debt renegotiation and rescuing the syndicate.

7.90 Second, and this is the focal point of the case, the court examined the claim of discrimination or unfairness viewed objectively ('objective discrimination or oppression'). In so doing, Rimer J noted that the syndicated loan was a commercial contract that had been professionally drafted. It expressly provided for the right of the two-thirds of the lenders to modify the lending agreement.

[106] *Greenhalgh v Arderne Cinemas* [1951] Ch 286, 292.
[107] [2002] EWHC 2703 (Ch).

Furthermore, Rimer J found that he could not imply a term whereby the majority of bondholders were to act for the benefit of all the lenders because the lenders did not constitute one unified class of lenders and as a result had no duty to act for the best interests of all bondholders.[108] For Rimer J, there was no doubt that various classes of lenders had different, perhaps conflicting, interests that were hard to reconcile. Rimer J considered that the majority action clause was designed 'to enable the majority of lenders to make decisions binding on all three classes, even though it might perhaps be capable of being said by one class that the decision could not be said to be for its benefit'.[109] *Redwood* thus gives a green light to those bondholders who, backing two horses, would not need to sacrifice their interests in one issue (tranche) of bonds so as to protect the interests of a group of bondholders in another issue (tranche) of bonds. For comparison, the US courts are not preoccupied with the rather formalistic question of class and seem to take a more pragmatic approach.[110] **7.91**

It is true that the syndicated loan in *Redwood* was truncated into three separate classes. Nevertheless, the judge would have reached the same decision had the majority of creditors constituted a unified class together with the minority creditors.[111] Rimer J was of the view that, assuming the majority of creditors were part of the same group and the majority did not act for the benefit of the whole syndicate, '[t]he agreement of the majority lenders to this particular disparity as part of the means of achieving the overall reduction was, in my view, a commercial decision to which they were perfectly entitled to come'.[112] **7.92**

This deferential view is corroborated by other judicial authorities which confirm the general proposition that in situations of conflict between various stakeholders or creditors, the courts should not interfere with the **7.93**

108 For a similar conclusion involving a rather unusual modification clause, see *Myers v Kestrel Acquisitions Ltd (Kestrel)* [2015] EWCH 916 (Ch), para 55 (where the majority and the minority were not even part of 'some wider class').

109 In a similar vein see *Bank of New York Mellon (London Branch) v Truvo N.V. and others* [2013] EWHC 136 (Comm), para 85 (finding that the construction of a contract under which one group of lenders may modify the contract to the detriment of the other group is not 'commercially unreasonable').

110 *Marblegate Asset Management v Education Management Corp*, 75 F Supp 3d 592 (SDNY 2014), reversed on other grounds No 15-2124-cv(L), (2d Cir 2017).

111 Philip Rawlings, 'The Management of Loan Syndicates and the Rights of Individual Lenders' (2009) 24(4) JIBLR 179, 181; Richard Hooley, 'Release Provisions in Intercreditor Agreements' (2012) 3 J Bus L 213, 225–26; Edwin Cheyney, 'Syndicated Loans—Position of Minority Lenders' (2003) 3 JIBFL 88, 89

112 *Redwood Master Fund v TD Bank Europe Ltd* [2002] EWHC 2703 (Ch), para 107, 111.

decision of the majority.[113] In its highly deferential attitude, *Redwood* broke the line of those English authorities that were grounded on the principle of equal treatment of bondholders, and thus were more inclined to find discrimination to the prejudice of the minority when the scheme excluded certain bondholders from the restructuring.[114]

7.94 While the court in *Redwood* recognised that the majority could vote in its interests to the detriment of the minority, it still held that the discretion of the majority could not be left unconstrained. Rather, it should be subject to a higher, more deferential standard of 'manifestly disadvantageous, discriminatory or oppressive' conduct that leads to the inference that the modification was 'motivated by dishonest considerations inconsistent with a proper exercise of the power for the purpose for which it was intended'.[115] This accords with the distinction drawn by Hollington.[116] In his view, the actions affecting the conflicting interests of shareholders/ bondholders are subject to the higher standard of the fraud on the minority.

7.95 It would be rare for the courts to face an instance of 'manifestly disadvantageous, discriminatory or oppressive' conduct, egregious enough to trigger the judicial opprobrium. Rimer J provided the following examples that are at best unclear: if the majority purports to confer special collateral benefits on itself (how is this different from the preference received by Tranche B creditors?)[117] or if the majority power was motivated by the malicious wish to damage or oppress the interests of the minority.[118]

[113] *Peters' American Delicacy Co Ltd v Heath* (1939) 61 CLR 457, 511–13; *Howard Smith Ltd v Ampol Petroleum Ltd* [1974] AC 821, 834–35. Both cases were approvingly cited in *F&C Alternative Investments (Holdings) Ltd v Francois Barthelemy, Anthony Culligan* [2011] EWHC 1731 (Ch), paras 231–35.

[114] *Re German Potash Syndicate's Trust Deed* (1955) The Times, 25 March (finding objectionable that the majority purported to exclude from the restructuring those bonds that have not passed through the validation process set by a German statute of 1952, aimed at preventing payments under the bonds that were stolen or looted by Nazis or Russians in the Second World War); *Re Holders Investment Trust Ltd* [1971] 2 All ER 289 (holding that preference shareholders, who were also ordinary shareholders, ought to disregard their private interests as ordinary shareholders). Wood argues the latter case is doubtful following *Redwood* (Philip Wood, *International Loans, Bonds, Guarantees and Legal Opinions* (2007) para 16-047).

[115] *Redwood Master Fund v TD Bank Europe Ltd* [2002] EWHC 2703 (Ch), para 93; cf *Northern Assurance Company, Ltd v Farnham United Breweries, Ltd* [1912] 2 Ch 134 ('fraudulent'); *Yucyco, Ltd v Slovenia*, 1999 WL 169530, 4 (SDNY 1999) ('malice, fraud, or illegality').

[116] Hollington (n 42) 135–45.

[117] Some cases found that the appropriation by the majority of bondholders of the assets which were to be used to satisfy the claims of all the bondholders was a dishonest exercise of majority powers (*Menier v Hooper's Telegraph Works* (1873–74) LR 9 Ch App 350; *Vogelstein v Athletic Mining Co*, 192 S W 760, 763 (Mo 1917)).

[118] *Redwood Master Fund v TD Bank Europe Ltd* [2002] EWHC 2703 (Ch), para 105. See also *Blisset v Daniel* (1853) 10 Hare 493, 534–36.

So, when does a legitimate preference cross the line and become unjust discrimination? Although the below examples are not taken from the context of majority modifications, they still represent the common patterns of differential treatment in the course of sovereign debt restructurings. Among various forms of differential treatment, it is not unheard of for States to accord preferences to local over foreign banks. This is a commercially sound course of action (as the failure of the former might have repercussions for the national economy)[119] and is extremely likely to survive attacks predicated on the intercreditor fairness under the deferential test set out in *Redwood*. The same can be said for according preference to long-term creditors, those creditors inclined to provide further funding[120] and trade creditors. To preserve access to financial markets, Ecuador[121] and Russia[122] sought to exclude the bulk of Eurobonds from the operation of their restructurings. **7.96**

Many have contested the justification for according preference to the debt held by the official sector, including the IMF and EU institutions, and the State-to-State debt.[123] Yet, whether the de facto preference accorded to IMF and other official sectors is a proportional or necessary step would be a non sequitur before English courts. English courts are unlikely to entertain an action against the sovereign debtor on the ground of unfair preferential treatment. As mentioned, the sovereign debtor does not in principle owe a duty of good faith/equal treatment to other creditors. **7.97**

Issues of intercreditor fairness and unfair discrimination have recently been singled out in the context of single series or enhanced aggregation clauses.[124] As explained in Chapter 2, these types of clauses merely require the consent of an aggregate number of bondholders across all bond issues, **7.98**

119 Anna Gelpern and Brad Setser, 'Domestic and External Debt: The Doomed Quest for Equal Treatment' (2004) 35 Geo J Intl L 795, 796–97.

120 *West Coast Life Ins Co v Merced Irrigation Dist*, 114 F.2d 654, 677 (9th Cir 1940); In *Re Cancol Ltd* [1995] BCC 1133, 1147–49 (holding that to discriminate between those whose cooperation is needed for the business and those whose are not, is not unfair and such distinction is 'realistic and commercially sensible').

121 IMF (n 73) 2.

122 Sturzenegger and Zettelmeyer (n 68) 109.

123 Kunibert Raffer, 'In the Case of Sovereigns, Should Official Sector Debt Be Subordinated to Private Sector Debt?' (2013) IFLR 20; Anna Viterbo, 'Supranational Creditors: A Threat to the Equal Status of Bondholders?' (2015) 10(2) CMLJ 193, 204–05 (contesting the de facto priority of multinational institutions when they purchase sovereign bonds on capital markets as an ordinary investor, as contrasted to the provision of finance in times of criseis); Melissa Boudreau and Mitu Gulati, 'The IMF's Imperiled Priority' (2014) (available at http://scholarship.law.duke.edu/faculty_scholarship/3331).

124 IMF, 'The Restructuring of Sovereign Debt—Assessing the Benefits, Risks and Feasibility of Aggregating Claims' (2003) 5; Philip Wood, 'The Origins and Future of Non-Discrimination in Sovereign Bankruptcies: A Comment' (2014) 9(3) CMLJ 293, 298.

obviating the need to obtain consent from individual bond series. To illustrate, assume that the sovereign has cajoled the aggregate majority of bondholders across all sovereign bond issuances into extending the maturities of a sovereign bond issue A for ten years and the maturity of a sovereign bond issue B for twenty years. Under the highly deferential test in *Redwood*, courts would not penalise such instances of discrimination given that they are not motivated by dishonest considerations inconsistent with a proper exercise of the power for the purpose for which it was intended (recall that *Redwood* dealt precisely with different tranches of debt in a way similar to a single series aggregation clause).

7.99 In any case, the use of single series aggregation clauses in the Greek debt restructuring has ensured[125] and the single series aggregation clause proposed by ICMA[126] and IMF[127] will ensure equality of treatment to all bondholders by extending the same offer to all creditors subject to aggregation. Thus, under the ICMA Model Clauses, single-limb aggregation clauses have to satisfy the Uniformly Applicable condition. That is, the debtor has to offer an identical exchange offer to all bondholders subject to the single-limb vote.

7.100 That said, one may doubt the utility of conveying the same identical offer to all sovereign bondholders. The ICMA did not 'seek to benchmark or equalise a similar form of NPV [net present value] loss across the different series of bonds being restructured' for reasons of complexity of developing and applying such an NPV loss benchmark.[128] Thus, if the sovereign debtor offers an instrument with a 5% interest rate, bondholders who have held a bond with 6% interest rate would suffer less damage than the bondholders whose bonds had an interest rate of 7%. By contrast, history is replete with the examples of sovereign bond exchanges which took account of such differences by tailoring the offers for different bondholders so as to approximate the NPV losses that bondholders suffer.[129] One may wonder whether it is not more optimal to leave the sovereign debtor with the freedom of devising exchange offers fit for each class of bondholders.[130] It is conceived that in practice the sovereign debtor may resort

[125] Jeromin Zettelmeyer, Christoph Trebesch, and Mitu Gulati, 'The Greek Debt Exchange: An Autopsy' (2013) 28 Econ Pol 513, 532.

[126] ICMA, 'Sovereign Bond Consultation Paper Supplement' (2014) 12–14.

[127] IMF, 'Strengthening the Contractual Framework to Address Collective Action Problems in Sovereign Debt Restructuring' (2014) 21, 30.

[128] ICMA (n 126) para 9.

[129] See for instance the Naples terms of the HIPC initiative based on the NPV reduction (David Andrews, Anthony Boote, Syed Rizavi, and Sukhwinder Singh, 'Debt Relief for Low-Income Countries: The Enhanced HIPC Initiative' (1999) IMF Pamphlet Series No 51).

[130] For the criticism of conducting separate votes for different groups of bondholders so as to ensure flexibility for the sovereign debtor as bringing back the risk of blocking positions,

to sub-aggregation, that is to say, make a separate offer to one or more series, without infringing the Uniformly Applicable condition.[131]

Unfair Discrimination in Breach of *Pari Passu* Clauses

The foregoing analysis evidenced a highly docile approach of English courts to the examination of the fairness of debt restructurings. English courts may be more eager to strike down an instance of unfair discrimination if it has been conducted in breach of an explicit provision that sought to ensure parity of treatment.[132] It is not uncommon for sovereign bonds offered in an exchange to include provisions that would guarantee the equal treatment of sovereign creditors at various stages of a restructuring. Such clauses may take the form of a 'comparable treatment' provision, typically found in exchange offers, which explicitly forbids the sovereign debtor from granting additional offers to any other creditor or provides assurances that no special deals will be made.[133] Similarly, some variants of the mandatory prepayment clause contained in bank loans require parity of the reduction of the bank debt with the reduction of the debt owed to third-party creditors.[134] **7.101**

The promise of equal treatment might be more subdued in sovereign bond documentation. It will be argued here that *pari passu* clauses, almost ubiquitous in sovereign bond documentation, may be construed as requiring reinforced fairness in the restructuring of sovereign debt. *Pari passu* clauses remain perhaps the most nebulous clauses found in sovereign bonds. Among varying iterations, the clause in its simplest form provides that the bonds will rank *pari passu* (ie, on equal footing). The clause has puzzled many academics primarily because the State is not subject to a bankruptcy regime where the *pari passu* is naturally well suited. Gulati and Scott extensively researched the origins of the *pari passu* clause trying to unearth its origins and meaning. In their words, they ended 'with more questions than answers'.[135] **7.102**

see IMF, 'Strengthening the Contractual Framework to Address Collective Action Problems in Sovereign Debt Restructuring' (2 September 2014) 22–23.

[131] Deborah Zandstra, 'New Aggregated Collective Action Clauses and Evolution in the Restructuring of Sovereign Debt Securities' (2017) 12(2) CMLJ 180, 196.

[132] *Finlay v The Mexican Investment Corporation* [1897] 1 QB 517.

[133] Lee Buchheit and Elena Daly, 'Minimizing Holdout Creditors: Carrots' in Lastra and Buchheit (n 16) 9–10; Lee Buchheit, 'The Search for Intercreditor Parity' (2002) 8 Law & Bus Rev Am 73, 76–77; Eugenio Bruno, 'Argentina Debt—The Settlement Clause' (2013) (available at http://papers.ssrn.com/sol3/papers.cfm?abstract_id=2456055).

[134] Keith Clark, 'Sovereign Debt Restructurings: Parity of Treatment between Equivalent Creditors in Relation to Comparable Debts' (1986) 20 Intl L 857, 863.

[135] Mitu Gulati and Robert Scott, *The Three and a Half Minute Transaction: Boilerplate and the Limits of the Contract Design* (2013) 138. There might be room for construing negative pledge

7.103 Two interpretations (in addition to the one advanced here) have been offered to demystify the function of the *pari passu* clause in sovereign bonds. The most controversial of these argues that the clause requires equal, rateable *payment* to all, even holdout, bondholders. [136] The Second Circuit in *NML v Argentina* famously endorsed the 'equal payment' interpretation of the clause.[137] The way the injunction was designed was to force Argentina to pay the entire amount of debt due to the holdout creditors upon the next full payment of accrued interest to exchange bondholders. The injunction was ordered to bind third parties, namely the indenture trustee, the registered owners, and the clearing system, but the claimants sought a carve-out for the intermediary banks involved in the payment to exchange bondholders.[138]

7.104 In response to this judgment, certain issuers altered the language of the *pari passu* clause in a direction opposite the decision in *NML v Argentina*, clarifying that the clause merely requires 'equal ranking',[139] although this is not perhaps conclusive of the market's general attitude. Notably, an increased number of bonds contain language referring to 'payment' in *pari passu* clauses and require a supermajority to remove them.[140] Additionally, there are historical antecedents to this interpretation. Following the Iranian revolution of 1979, lenders used this clause against Iran to impose a rateable payment under a syndicated loan. Furthermore, Gelpern documents

clauses whereby the debtor agrees not to subject the debt 'to any preferential arrangement' as not being far from the obligations arising from the *pari passu* clause (Joseph Cotterill, 'The Negative Pledge Saga' *FT Alphaville* (27 June 2013)).

136 In *Re New York Taxicab Co* [1913] 1 Ch 1, unnoticed by academics, the court ruled out the use of a majority action clause that had the effect of distributing the assets of the company among those creditors that consented to the lowest haircut of their debt instruments, and not rateably among all the lenders. Although the court did not expressly refer to the role of the *pari passu* clause in its judgment, *Re New York Taxicab Co* may be read as implying that a payment under bonds ought to comply with the *pari passu* clause. The authority of the case might be doubtful in light of *Redwood's* high standard of 'commercial sensibleness'.

137 *NML Capital Ltd v Republic of Argentina*, 699 F 3d 246 (2d Cir 2012), cert denied 573 US (2014). See also *NML Capital Ltd v Republic of Argentina*, No 14-cv-8601, 2015 US Dist LEXIS 73521 (SDNY 2015); *Trinity Investments Ltd v Republic of Argentina*, No 15-cv-2611, 2015 US Dist LEXIS 147701 (SDNY 2015); *Red Mount v Democratic Republic of Congo*, No CV 00-0164 R (BQRx), 2000 WL 34479543 (CD Cal 2002).

138 *NML Capital Ltd v Republic of Argentina*, 2012 US Dist LEXIS 167272 (SDNY 2012).

139 See, eg, Lee Buchheit and Sofia Martos, 'What to Do about Pari Passu' (2014) 8 JIBFL 491, 493; Georges Affaki, 'Revisiting the *Pari Passu* Clause' in Lastra and Buchheit (n 16) 47; Joseph Cotterill, 'I Can't Belize It's Not Ratable Payment [Updated]' *FT Alphaville* (25 February 2013); Chanda DeLong and Nikita Aggarwal, 'Strengthening the Contractual Framework for Sovereign Debt Restructuring—the IMF's Perspective' (2016) 11 CMLJ 25, 28.

140 Anna Gelpern, 'Contract Hope and Sovereign Redemption' (2013) 8(2) CMLJ 132, 146.

three Swiss cases from the 1930s which endorse the rateable interpretation of the *pari passu* clause.[141]

The bottom line to this interpretation of the clause is that it may become a powerful tool in the hands of holdout creditors. Claiming that it has not been paid rateably, the holdout creditor may seek an injunction to halt payments to consenting creditors—those creditors that have been paid—on the basis that the State has acted in breach of the *pari passu* clause by refusing to pay to the holdout creditors too, subject of course to the discretionary decision-making of the court. Halting payments to other creditors might lead to the default of the State with ensuing acceleration of the debt and cross-default. Such a stratagem would leave little alternative to the sovereign debtor but to settle with the holdout creditor. **7.105**

A recent decision of the District Court narrowly read the holding in *NML v Argentina* where the Second Circuit endorsed this interpretation of the *pari passu* clause on the basis that the Argentine State passed legislative enactments and executive declarations that seriously affected the entitlements of creditors, in particular, but not limited to, the Lock Law that prohibited the opening of negotiations with holdout creditors. This stood in contrast to the less harsh case before the District Court where Grenada simply refused to pay non-consenting bondholders 'unless resources become available to do so'.[142] Although some doubts still remain,[143] it seems that this ruling has allayed the fears of collateral damage, of the kind mentioned in the previous paragraph, arising from the decision in *NML v Argentina*.[144] A general sense is that the judgment of the Second Circuit in *NML v Argentina* was largely predicated upon the uniquely recalcitrant character of Argentina.[145] This seems to be confirmed by the recent decision in *Hawthorne*.[146] **7.106**

141 Anna Gelpern, 'Courts and Sovereigns in the *Pari Passu* Goldmines' (2016) 11(2) CMLJ 251.

142 *Export–Import Bank of the Republic of China v Grenada*, 2013 WL 4414875, 4 (SDNY 2013); cf Rodrigo Olivares-Caminal, 'To Rank *Pari Passu* or Not to Rank *Pari Passu*' (2009) 15(4) L & Bus Rev Am 745, 775–77.

143 Joseph Cotterill, 'Sovereign Pari Passu and the Litigators of the Lost Cause' (2013) 9(1) CMLJ 18, 21; Cheng-Yun Tsang, '*Ex-Im Bank v Grenada*: Adding Clarity or Confusion?' (2015) 10(2) CMLJ 142. But see the reassuring case *Ajdler v Province of Mendoza*, 2017 US Dist LEXIS 122659 (SDNY 2017) (adopting a narrow view of *NML v Argentina*).

144 Anna Gelpern, 'Sovereign Damage Control' (2013) Policy Brief PB13-12 Peterson Institute for International Economics, 1–2.

145 Mark Weidemaier and Ryan McCarl, 'Creditors' Remedies' in Lastra and Buchheit (n 16) 146–50.

146 *White Hawthorne v Republic of Argentina*, 2016 US Dist LEXIS 177895 (SDNY 2016).

7.107 Following the election of the new president, Mauricio Macri, who was inclined to settle the debt with the holdout creditors, the District Court expressed the willingness to vacate the injunctions[147] and eventually did so.[148] It found that the new Argentine government expressed a good-faith willingness to negotiate with holdout creditors and expressed the desire to repeal the Lock Law (and Sovereign Payments Law). Moreover, some (but not necessarily all) holdout creditors agreed to settle the dispute with Argentina. 'The Republic's self-imposed conditions—repealing legislative obstacles and paying settlements in full—represent a "dramatic shift in … policy" that justified vacating the injunctions.'[149] Vacating the injunctions would also serve the public interest and the 'health of the nation', as the court confirmed.

7.108 A cluster of disgruntled bondholders who failed to accept the Standard Proposal of Argentina appealed on the ground that there had been no willingness to negotiate with them regardless of any discussions which may have occurred between Argentina and the creditors who settled the dispute. The Second Circuit held:

> That certain Individual Bondholders have not had the opportunity to fully engage in or complete settlement negotiations does not negate Argentina's willingness to resolve these long-standing disputes. And while Argentina has offered a Standard Proposal for settlement open to all bondholders, Individual Bondholders are not required to accept this proposal, and may continue in their efforts to negotiate different settlement terms.[150]

7.109 Thus, merely paying some creditors but failing to pay others would not result in the breach of the *pari passu* clause.[151] The entire *pari passu* saga may turn out to be an isolated incident grounded in the extreme reluctance of the Argentine government to pay. On a more principled ground, however, many have robustly argued that the equal payment interpretation is too far-fetched, at least for the *pari passu* clauses that do not expressly refer to 'payment' in their wording.[152] The argument is that *pari passu* clauses merely seek to ensure equal legal ranking, whereas the payment under the bonds is a question of factual performance of the contract

[147] *NML Limited Ltd v Republic of Argentina*, 2016 US Dist LEXIS 20633 (SDNY 2016).

[148] *NML Limited Ltd v Republic of Argentina*, 2016 US Dist LEXIS 26355 (SDNY 2016).

[149] *NML Limited Ltd v Republic of Argentina*, 2016 US Dist LEXIS 20633, 44 (SDNY 2016), affd 644 Fed Appx 98, 107 (2d Cir 2016).

[150] *NML Limited Ltd v Republic of Argentina*, 644 Fed Appx 98 (2d Cir 2016).

[151] See also *White Hawthorne v Republic of Argentina*, 2016 US Dist LEXIS 177895 (SDNY 2016).

[152] See contra Financial Markets Law Committee, 'Pari Passu Clauses' (2005) 19–21 (the reference to 'payment' in the *pari passu* clause would not in principle require rateable payment).

and not a question of priorities or ranking, however defined.[153] A number of English and US authorities have been cited as rejecting the equal payment interpretation of the clause.[154] By reference to the (in)famous litigation against Peru[155] and Argentina,[156] the proponents of this view claim that construing the clause as requiring the equal payment to all creditors presents a serious risk in that the holdout creditor might manipulate the *pari passu* clause to thwart sovereign debt restructurings.

Partly in reaction to this criticism of the rateable payment interpretation, the second and conventional interpretation contends that the *pari passu* clause merely ensures equal legal ranking, and concomitantly no factual equality in terms of payment. Under this interpretation, the sovereign debtor would be under no obligation to pay all bondholders. **7.110**

This interpretation is open to two counterarguments. First, the fundamental problem with the argument of legal ranking is that the State is not subject to any sort of insolvency regime, nor can one think of any established legal rankings of sovereign bondholders (other than the de facto priority status of multinational lenders (IMF)). In modern times, sovereign debtors do not pass legislation that legally subordinates a group of bondholders to another group.[157] The *pari passu* clause, as construed to be limited to legal ranking only, would thus carry no practical sense in the modern world. The *pari passu* clause would be, in the words of leading experts, 'emphatic chest-beating'[158] or a 'credibility signal'.[159] **7.111**

Second, the conventional interpretation of the clause tends to locate the origins of the clause in some historical incidents and claim that the clause has been dragged along for decades by inertia or mistake into modern **7.112**

153 Wood (n 114) para 5-027. For a supportive view of the rateable payment interpretation, see Hal Scott, 'Sovereign Debt Default: Cry for the United States, Not Argentina' (2006) Washington Legal Foundation, Working Paper Series No 140, 25–27.

154 *Kensington International Ltd v Republic of the Congo*, unreported, approved by CA at [2003] EWCA Civ 709; *Nacional Financiera SNC v Chase Manhattan Bank NA*, 2003 WL 1878415 (SDNY 2003).

155 *Elliott Associates v Peru*, Cour d'Appel of Brussels, 26 September 2000 (relying on the rateable interpretation of the *pari passu* clause, awarded an injunction to prevent any payments to those creditors who agreed to the debt restructuring). But see *Republic of Nicaragua v LNC Investments LLC*, Cour d'Appel of Brussels, 19 March 2004 (refusing to enjoin Euroclear from making payments to third-party creditors).

156 *NML Capital Limited v Republic of Argentina*, 699 F 3d 246 (2d Cir 2012).

157 For historical examples of such laws, see Lee Buchheit and Jeremiah Pam, 'The Pari Passu Clause in Sovereign Debt Instruments' (2004) 53 Emory LJ 869, 894–900.

158 Philip Wood, 'Bondholders and Banks—Why the Difference in Protections?' (2011) 6(2) CMLJ 188, 192; Philip Wood, 'Pari Passu Clauses—What Do They Mean?' (2003) 10 JIBFL 371, 373–74.

159 Gulati and Scott (n 135) 138.

sovereign bond contracts.[160] With the disappearance of the historical necessities that prompted the insertion of *pari passu* clauses, the clauses would have no practical application in the modern world. Such historical interpretations reduce the *pari passu* clause to nothing more than an archaic, irrational, and intuitively nonsensical clause.

7.113 A commercial judge may not be convinced by a historical interpretation of a clause that does not purport to clarify its modern meaning.[161] This phenomenon might explain the readiness of the Second Circuit in *NML v Argentina* to subscribe to the 'equal payment' interpretation of the clause which affords at least some sense to a contractual clause found in complex commercial transactions which the sovereign bonds undoubtedly are. Courts are not, as a general matter, inclined to recognise the unreasonableness of markets in blindly following a clause that does not serve any purpose and bears no contemporary meaning.[162] Courts would feel the need to rationalise a clause that seemingly rational market players have constantly included in sovereign bonds.

7.114 Consequently, some reasonable interpretation is to be offered to the judge. This monograph offers a third and alternative interpretation. It is suggested here that the *pari passu* clause introduces reinforced protection against unfair discrimination in the *process* of debt restructuring. Under this understanding of the clause, the *pari passu* clause would prohibit unfair discrimination between bondholders at the stage of sovereign debt restructuring and would require the State to treat its bondholders even-handedly. The sovereign debtor that differentiated between creditors without a defensible reason would be acting in breach of the *pari passu* treatment. To illustrate the point, a State that solicits a debt reduction of 50% from group A of bondholders and a reduction of 70% from group B of bondholders, or excludes a certain category of debt from the debt restructuring, might be acting in breach of the *pari passu* clause. Equal 'ranking' would thus imply the existence of a 'level playing field'. This interpretation ensures more protection for bondholders against discriminatory actions of the State, without imposing a burdensome obligation of equal payment on sovereign debtors.

7.115 This view, however, recognises that the promise of equal treatment can never be absolute.[163] It is suggested here that, to constitute a breach of

[160] Ibid 112–35; Buchheit and Pam (n 157) 869.

[161] See in this sense Mark Weidemaier, 'Indiana Jones, Contracts Originalist' (2014) 9(3) CMLJ 255, 257.

[162] For a similar argumentation, see Benjamin Chabot and Mitu Gulati, 'Santa Anna and his Black Eagle: The Origins of Pari Passu' (2014) 9(3) CMLJ 216, 221.

[163] For exceptions to the *pari passu* clause in corporate insolvency scenario, see Vanessa Finch, *Corporate Insolvency Law: Perspectives and Principles* (2009) 602–74. The Swiss Court of

the *pari passu* clause, the de facto discrimination would still have to be unfair. The lesson learned from *Redwood* and preceding English authorities is that the courts are leery of interfering with the State's value judgement. To cite a few examples, the preference given to domestic banks to preserve the national economy is reasonable, as is the according of preference to trade creditors[164] and those creditors inclined to provide further funding over the rest of creditors. In a similar manner, the exclusion of the European Central Bank (ECB) from the Greek restructuring may also be reasonable. By contradistinction, a restructuring that differentiates between two groups of creditors without a defensible reason, as was the case in *Redwood*, is likely to be in breach of the *pari passu* clause. It is arguable that it would breach the *pari passu* clause to exclude from a sovereign debt restructuring the debt owed to State-owned enterprises to ensure that they are paid in full.

This sort of enquiry is reminiscent of the 'like circumstances' standard **7.116** applied in WTO cases and investment arbitration jurisprudence.[165] Under this standard, an adjudicator would assess whether creditors/investors in 'like circumstances' were treated differently. Discrimination would be tolerable when the creditors in different circumstances were treated differently. Nonetheless, it remains true that in practice, bondholders may endlessly justify their preferential status by adducing a myriad of reasons that might eventually forestall an effective review of the fairness of sovereign debt restructurings.[166]

Contrary to what the Second Circuit decided in *NML v Argentina*, under **7.117** this interpretation, the *pari passu* clause would not require rateable payment to all creditors. Unless the bondholders were not presented equal exchange offers at the stage of the restructuring of the bond, they cannot complain of not being paid up. Equally, the proposed interpretation goes further than the traditional interpretation argued by Argentina in *NML v Argentina* by requiring fair treatment as a matter of fact and not merely as a question of legal priorities.

Appeal considered that the instructions given by Germany to the trustee under the bonds in breach of the *pari passu* clause could be disregarded if they were 'on manifestly untenable grounds' (Gelpern (n 141) 263).

164 Netanella Zahavi, 'Sovereign Default: Analyses and Remedies' (PhD thesis, Yale University 2005) 291 (the *pari passu* clause does not cover payments to international financial institutions and trade creditors).

165 See, eg, Jürgen Kurtz, 'The Use and Abuse of WTO Law in Investor–State Arbitration: Competition and its Discontents' (2009) 20 EJIL 749.

166 Lee Buchheit, 'The Search for Intercreditor Parity' (2002) 8 Law & Bus Rev Am 73, 77.

7.118 The third, alternative construction is a more reasonable construction of the clause. It ensures a certain practical meaning to the clause, avoiding the apparent objections to the other two interpretations of the clause mooted to date. Equally, it is not too intrusive of sovereign debt restructurings, nor does it leave the bondholders empty-handed.

7.119 The first historical account of the appearance of the *pari passu* clause in an 1843 Mexico bond, whatever its weight might be, supports this interpretation of the *pari passu* clause. Chabot and Gulati chronicle that Mexico might have inserted the clause to forestall the British diplomatic protection in respect of the Mexican public debt that had been discharged in a discriminatory manner. When, following the introduction of the *pari passu* clause, the UK government complained that various British bondholders had not been paid, the Mexican ambassador to the United Kingdom parried that Mexico offered 'to all creditors' the same exchange offer, and British subjects were not unfairly treated.[167]

8. Disenfranchisement

The Implication of Disenfranchisement Provisions in Payment-Related and Unrelated Modifications

7.120 The debt reduction generously granted to the sovereign debtor theoretically presupposes a transaction at arm's length between the debtor and its creditors. Yet, it may transpire that certain bondholders (eg, central banks, State-owned enterprises) are in practice controlled by the debtor, the mere occurrence of which will cast serious doubts on the impartiality of their voting.

7.121 With disenfranchisement provisions embedded into sovereign bond contracts, the voting configuration will be a matter of contractual construction of the disenfranchisement provision. As of 2010, only around 50% of sovereign bonds contained disenfranchisement provisions.[168] For the remainder of sovereign bonds that are silent on the issue of disenfranchisement, the pertinent question is whether the courts would be inclined to imply a disenfranchisement rule to prevent the voting by the State-controlled bondholders. In principle, nothing prevents the application of the overarching principle of the bona fide exercise of majority powers for the benefit of bondholders, discussed above, so as to disenfranchise entities controlled by the sovereign debtor.

[167] Chabot and Gulati (n 162) 235.

[168] Michael Bradley and Mitu Gulati, 'Collective Action Clauses for the Eurozone' (2014) 18(6) Rev Fin 2045, 2067.

In the US the leading authority is *Hackettstown National Bank v DG Yuengling Brewing Co*,[169] where the majority of bondholders through the exercise of majority powers extended the maturities of the bonds for five years. What was unusual about this otherwise routine restructuring was that the majority bondholder was in fact holding the bonds as an agent for the debtor company: following the default of the debtor, the majority stockholder of the company entered into agreement with a third person, whereby the latter agreed to acquire the majority of outstanding bonds and, as a corollary, the decisive vote at the restructuring. **7.122**

The Second Circuit, drawing on earlier English authorities, first affirmed the general principle that the majority power must be exercised in good faith. On the facts of the case, the court came to the conclusion that the majority of bondholders did not act 'in the exercise of an honest discretion in the general interest' and acted collusively to defeat the legal remedy available to the minority of bondholders. Had it not been for the collusion between the majority bondholder and the debtor, the restructuring would have been upheld. **7.123**

On facts similar to *Hackettstown* in the English case *Punt v Symons & Co Ltd*, the directors, who were also shareholders of the company, had authorised an issuance of shares not for the general benefit of the company, but for the purpose of securing decisive voting rights. The Chancery Division judge granted a robust injunction to restrain the convening of a meeting where such shares could be voted upon.[170] **7.124**

In the cases of collusion, the point of departure is to determine what needs to be established to prove collusion and the intention to defraud the minority. The indices would appear to be: **7.125**

(a) the surreptitious nature of the beneficial holding of bonds,
(b) the acquisition of bonds on the secondary market (not in the capacity of initial bondholders), and
(c) some evidence as to the improper purpose of the acquisition of bonds.

It is not claimed that specific evidence would need to be adduced to prove collusion as that would render the enquiry impractical, but something going beyond the mere purchase of the bonds is needed. As a matter of procedure, plaintiffs in English proceedings may request an order of disclosure, which might shed light on the existence of collusion (or control). Simply incentivising a party to purchase the bonds on the secondary **7.126**

[169] 74 F 110, 112 (2d Cir 1896).

[170] [1903] 2 Ch 506.

market (through, eg, banking regulations) is not enough to trigger the judicial sanction of disenfranchising.

7.127 Addressing the risk of collusion, the Uruguay aggregation clause of 2003 included an anti-manipulation clause preventing the issuer from placing additional bonds with the bondholders expected to vote in its favour.[171] Placing additional bonds with carefully picked bondholders would constitute a clear example of collusion, and should not be upheld by courts.

7.128 As a separate point, it is questionable whether something less than collusion (eg, mere control) would suffice to trigger the implied term of disenfranchisement. A case in point is *CIBC v Brazil*, where a dispute arose between minority and majority bondholders over the acceleration of payments owed by Brazil under a lending agreement (MYDFA). Following a debt restructuring whereupon all but two lenders agreed to a restructuring and exited MYDFA, the majority chunk of Brazilian bonds remained with one of the lenders—a State-owned enterprise, Banco do Brazil (BdB). The acceleration of the principal under the lending agreement could only be sanctioned by 50% of lenders, and BdB, majority-owned by Brazil, refused to accelerate the Brazilian sovereign debt. The other holdout bondholder—CIBC—argued that BdB had not exited MYDFA for the sole purpose of blocking CIBC's acceleration efforts, and that such conduct breached the implied covenant of good faith and fair dealing under the New York law. CIBC claimed that it had the authority to declare an acceleration of the principal under MYDFA, and BdB's holding of bonds should be disregarded for the purposes of calculating the necessary threshold of 50% of creditors.

7.129 The parties' silence as to the disenfranchisement was, in the eyes of the court, qualified silence. The implied covenants of the type adduced by the CIBC could not override explicit contractual provisions. The clear language of MYDFA vested in the majority the discretionary and exclusive power to accelerate the debt once the debtor was in default.

7.130 Further, on the point of disenfranchisement, the court distinguished *Hackettstown* on two grounds. First, it considered that in *Hackettstown*, the stockholder who voted in favour of the debtor acquired the property interest in the bonds after the bonds had been subscribed to, whereas in *CIBC*, BdB was a party to the initial offering from the very moment that the debt agreement had been consummated. Furthermore, it had been represented

[171] David Billington, 'European Collective Action Clauses' in Lastra and Buchheit (n 16) 409. See to the same effect Offering Memorandum, The Dominican Republic, 20 April 2005.

to all the bondholders that a bank might have an existing relationship with Brazil.[172] Implied was that *CIBC* did not discern any trace of collusion.

Second, the court noted that in *Hackettstown*, the majority by its tainted voting affected the right to payment under the bonds. The court described this as defining the debtor–creditor relationship itself.[173] By contrast in *CIBC*, BdB affected what was only an incidental matter (acceleration of the debt). In support of its proposition that the rules on disenfranchisement should apply with equal force to acceleration, the claimant also relied on four areas of law: the New York common law of compositions, the federal Bankruptcy Code, the federal Trust Indenture Act of 1939, and the New York Business Corporation Law. Applying the same reasoning, the court discarded these references as irrelevant on the basis that they all defined the debtor–creditor relationship and did not concern the acceleration of the debt. **7.131**

Arguably, the court in *CIBC* took the view that the comparison lay between matters defining debtor–creditor relations—which would serve as stand-alone grounds for disenfranchising without the plaintiff having to show collusion—and those matters which fell outside the core of debtor–creditor relations (as it were, incidental matters). The judge did not stop at determining that no apparent collusion was present in the case before him. He went further in discarding the claimant's references to disenfranchisement in other areas of law as inapplicable in the case before it for the sole reason that the acceleration of the debt did not define the debtor–creditor relationship. This might be construed as going beyond what the court decided in *Hackettstown* and might be justifiable in light of the abundance of sources, cited by the claimant in *CIBC*, that denounce the biased voting of affiliated entities. **7.132**

Now, if one accepts the premise that collusion should not be the sole ground for the disenfranchisement of the entities controlled by the sovereign debtor and voting by such entities on matters defining debtor–creditor relations should be avoided, the whole distinction between matters that define the debtor–creditor relationship and those that do not seems to be an artificial and unprincipled distinction. Thus, the acceleration of the debt cannot be discarded as not pertaining to the matters defining the debtor–creditor relationship as ultimately the acceleration defines the amount that a debtor can recover. **7.133**

[172] *CIBC Bank and Trust Company (Cayman) Ltd v Banco Central do Brasil*, 886 F Supp 1105, 1115 (SDNY 1995).

[173] Ibid.

7.134 In *Whitridge v Mt Vernon Woodbury Cotton Duck Co*,[174] the court disenfranchised a majority bondholder's vote so that the minority bondholder could avail itself of the 'protective privileges of the mortgage as may be exercised by not less than 25 per cent. of the bonds'. A straightforward reason was given: unless disenfranchised, 'the situation will be very different from that which was originally contemplated by any of the parties to the mortgage'.

7.135 Turning to the position under English law, courts, as discussed above, have held that collusion renders the voting on the debt restructuring ineffective.[175] Going a step further, in the context of schemes of arrangement, English courts have consistently disenfranchised those entities or persons that are fully controlled by the debtor[176] even though no particular statutory provision contemplates such a result.

7.136 Now, if one accepts the premise that the entities controlled by the State should in principle be disenfranchised from voting on the debt restructuring, it is a minor step to admit that the sovereign debtor should also be disenfranchised in apposite circumstances. It is not uncommon for sovereign bonds to appear in the hands of the State that has issued them through debt repurchases on the secondary market.[177] To cater for this risk, the bonds often, but by no means always, provide that the bonds held by the issuing State do not entitle it to vote under the bonds.[178]

7.137 Open questions remain. Should the court disenfranchise financial institutions that act seemingly independently from their government shareholder, such as central banks?[179] Should the courts disenfranchise bondholders that are not fully controlled by the State (although one might be pardoned for thinking that control is either present or not)? A complete

[174] 210 Fed 302, 316–17 (D Md 1913).

[175] *Punt v Symons & Co Ltd* [1903] 2 Ch 506.

[176] O'Dea et al (n 45) 54, 136–37, 146–47. More precisely, they will summon a separate meeting for the minority creditors so as to prevent the controlled entities from imposing their will upon minority creditors (see the discussion of the Court of Final Appeal in Hong Kong in *UDL Argos Engineering & Heavy Industries Co Ltd v Li Oi Lin* [2001] HKEC 1440 paras 21–24 (per Lord Millett), cited approvingly in *PrimaCom* v *A Group of the Senior Lenders & Credit Agricole* [2011] EWHC 3746 (Ch), para 46).

[177] The issue is not always raised in litigation. See *Beck v Manufacturers Hanover Trust Co*, 632 NYS 2d 520, 522–23 (Sup Ct NY 1995) (where Mexico purchased 95% of outstanding bonds).

[178] See Cl 6(2), Republic of Bulgaria, EUR 950,000,000, 4.25 per cent Notes due 2017 ('The Issuer may at its option retain such Notes [acquired by the Issuer in the open market] for its own account and/or resell or cancel or otherwise deal with such Notes at its discretion').

[179] David Billington, 'European Collective Action Clauses' in Lastra and Buchheit (n 16), 412; Art 2.7(c)(iii) of Common Terms of Reference of Model Eurozone CACs (no disenfranchisement for the government-owned enterprises that enjoy 'autonomy of decision').

disenfranchisement might be too draconian in all scenarios, and a golden middle way would need to be found in such cases.

Economic or Other Interests in a Debt Restructuring

By contrast to the preceding discussion, it would be too far-fetched a claim to disenfranchise those parties that have a mere economic or other interest in the (un)successful outcome of the sovereign debt workout. Two examples will be provided. First, it has been suggested that disenfranchisement of those bondholders (such as other eurozone Member States, ECB) that will be inclined to vote with the primary purpose of safeguarding the eurozone, and as a consequence, in a way prejudicial to private bondholders.[180] Notwithstanding the peculiar and accentuated interests of eurozone stakeholders, they are free to vote in their best interests so long as it is not in bad faith.[181] Such voting should not trigger the operation of the common law rule on disenfranchisement (or, for that matter, the disenfranchisement clause). As Smith J wisely noted, '[t]he expression "economic interest" is too vague and will give great hostages to fortune and lead to uncertainty'.[182] The same logic would apply to the question of disenfranchisement of bonds held by the issuer's domestic banks and nationals.[183] **7.138**

The court in *Assénagon* has, rather unconvincingly, extended a disenfranchisement clause to cover not only the beneficial holding of the bonds in a proprietary sense, but also in an economic sense.[184] In the event, Briggs J considered that the majority of bondholders who, by having offered their bonds for exchange and signed a contract of sale, irrevocably committed itself to vote by proxy for the restructuring, and, as a result of this, the **7.139**

180 Lachlan Burn, 'Bondholder Resolutions in the Courtroom' in Patrick Kenadjian, Klaus-Albert Bauer, and Andreas Cahn (eds), *Collective Action Clauses and the Restructuring of Sovereign Debt* (2013) 80; Keegan Drake, 'Disenfranchisement Provisions' in Christoph Paulus (ed), *A Debt Restructuring Mechanism for Sovereigns: Do We Need a Legal Procedure?* (2014) 155–57, 161.

181 *Goodfellow v Nelson Line (Liverpool) Ltd* [1912] 2 Ch 324, 333.

182 *Citicorp Trustee Company Ltd v Barclays Bank plc* [2013] EWHC 2608 (Ch), para 114. See in the similar sense Viterbo, 'Supranational Creditors: A Threat to the Equal Status of Bondholders?' 210–11.

183 Nouriel Roubini and Brad Setser, 'Improving the Sovereign Debt Restructuring Process: Problems in Restructuring, Proposed Solutions, and a Roadmap for Reform' (2003) unpublished paper, 21 (available at http://www.iie.com/publications/papers/roubini-setser0303.pdf). For a contrary view proposing to disenfranchise domestic creditors, see Scott (n 153) 40; Ignacio Tirado, 'Annual Review of Insolvency Law' (2012) 735–37.

184 *Assénagon Asset Management SA v Irish Bank Resolution Corporation Limited* [2012] EWHC 2090 (Ch), paras 56–68.

debtor became the beneficial owner of such bonds prior to the meeting of bondholders. This prevented the bondholders from voting in favour of the restructuring. This interpretation risks undermining the smooth operation of exit consents, but such practice where the debtor accepts the bonds prior to the meeting is not conventional.[185]

7.140 Second, a situation may arise where the private bondholder might have an economic interest in the unsuccessful conclusion of the sovereign debt restructuring. A bondholder might, in another capacity, be the counter-party to a hedging agreement, particularly credit default swaps, in respect of the bonds it has subscribed to.[186] In that capacity, the bondholder would have an indirect financial interest in the default of the State which would result in payments to the bondholder under the hedging agreement. In this very context, Smith J saw no reason why the party be prohibited from exercising rights it had in respect of assets or contractual rights it owns so as to ensure a maximum return in the absence of an express contractual obligation or fiduciary or other obligations.[187]

7.141 One may doubt the soundness of this non-interventionist approach. It could be rebutted that the voting by a directly interested bondholder in a manner prejudicial to the sovereign debt restructuring and purely to secure a windfall under a related contract may be treated as voting for an 'improper purpose'. Yet, how can one ever possibly draw a line between, on the one hand, the rejection of a restructuring for the purpose of securing a windfall, and, on the other hand, the rejection because of a simple disagreement with its substance? Another consideration lurking in the background would be to what extent allowing the parties with a hedge agreement to vote against the restructuring might fuel the escalation of the sovereign's financial crisis.

7.142 While this might be true, there is a consideration that might have prevented the whole discussion of disenfranchisement in the context of hedging, namely to whom does the benefit of disenfranchisement accrue? Mostly, the rule on disenfranchisement that flows from the obligation to act in good faith for the benefit of bondholders protects minority creditors since the creditor-to-disenfranchise tends to be in some sort of tacit agreement with the debtor. But, in the context of hedge agreements, the one seeking to profit from disenfranchisement is the State. Should the standard of good faith protect the debtor State too? The response might consist

[185] Stewart Dunlop, 'Liability Management: Exit Consents and Oppression of the Minority' (2012) *Clifford Chance Briefings* 4.

[186] On which see Michael Waibel, 'Steering Sovereign Debt Restructurings through the CDS Quicksand' (2014) 15 Journal of Banking Regulation 14.

[187] *Citicorp Trustee Company Ltd v Barclays Bank plc* [2013] EWHC 2608 (Ch), paras 56–57.

in saying that by preventing the voting for improper purpose to subvert a debt restructuring, the disenfranchisement also protects the bondholders that have an interest in the successful conclusion of the debt restructuring.

9. Consent Payments and Other Sweeteners

To placate the recalcitrant bondholders, it is not uncommon for the debtor to offer and make cash payments to those bondholders who are willing to place their votes in favour of the restructuring (a technique known as 'consent payments'). Minority bondholders have attempted to challenge this technique on two main grounds: (1) the consent payment is properly speaking a bribe or amounts to vote-buying; (2) the technique is in breach of the implied obligation of good faith and fair dealing. **7.143**

Both arguments have failed before English and US courts. In *Azevedo v Imcopa*, the debtor solicited the consent of noteholders on a number of occasions to postpone the payment of interest. The Court of Appeal, relying on the authority of *Goodfellow v Nelson Line (Liverpool) Ltd*,[188] decided that consent payments openly communicated to creditors were not bribes and were not contrary to English company law.[189] So, too, the US courts have ruled that consent payments proposed to the entire class of bondholders did not constitute vote-buying, did not defy any public policy principles, nor did they breach the implied good-faith obligations.[190] **7.144**

Smith and Sharpe claim that the failure on the part of the court in *Azevedo* even to engage in a reasoning in terms of minority oppression is unjustified given that consent payments are in principle no different from exit consents in terms of their coercion. Thus, the same reasoning in terms of oppression of the minority needs to be applied when scrutinising the legality of consent payments.[191] **7.145**

The reasoning is somewhat speculative, because, as we have seen in the discussion of *Asségnagon*, only exorbitant losses will trigger the judicial intervention into the legality of exit consents. This would hardly be the case for consent payments and it is yet to be seen whether excessive consent fees **7.146**

[188] [1912] 2 Ch 324.

[189] [2013] EWCA Civ 364. Consent payments are not an unusual mechanism in the design of schemes of arrangement (*Primacom Holding GmbH v A Group of the Senior Lenders & Credit Agricole* [2012] EWHC 164 (Ch), para 57).

[190] *Kass v Eastern Air Lines*, 12 Del J Corp L 1074 (Del Ch 1986); *Pisik v BCI Holdings Corp*, No 14593/87, slip op (NY Sup 1987) (cited in Gkoutzinis (n 69) 292).

[191] Stephen Moverley Smith and Harry Sharpe, 'An Offer You Can't Refuse: When Does Coercion of a Group to Accept a Proposal Constitute Oppression of the Minority?' (2014) 5 JIBFL 288, 288–90.

can ever give rise to an actionable claim in unfairness or oppression.[192] Further, as Kahan and Tuckman suggest, consent payments might be a way of sharing gains arising from a beneficial debt restructuring of a company rather than a coercive technique. Thus, large consent payments simply reflect proportionally large positive returns for the debtor.[193]

7.147 Unobjectionable in themselves, the well-established position is that consent payments when secretly communicated to one or more bondholders will be in breach of the duty of good faith and fair dealing.[194] The secretly communicated sweetener does not necessarily have to be a payment of cash. The concept of a sweetener is large enough to embrace various types of quid pro quo: promising unrelated deals, providing valuable information, etc.[195]

10. No-Action Clauses and Trust Deeds

No-Action Clauses

7.148 In English law governed bonds, trust deeds often, but by no means always, go hand in hand with so-called no-action clauses. [196] Pursuant to these clauses, the trustee has the exclusive power to litigate on behalf of all the bondholders. No bondholder is entitled to proceed against the debtor in recovery of its entitlement under the bonds unless the trustee, bound to proceed in accordance with the terms and conditions of the bond (generally when requested by the requisite percentage of bondholders), has failed to do so within a reasonable time and such failure is continuing.[197] This mechanism unifies the power to litigate in the hands of the trustee and inhibits individual actions of holdout creditors unless they manage to

[192] Stewart Dunlop, Simon Sinclair, Paul Deakins, and Kate Vyvyan, 'Noteholder Meetings: Paying the Price for Change?' (2012) *Clifford Chance Briefings* 2–3. Ukraine has offered a consent payment equal to the interest accrued (IMF (n 73) 6). In *MeehanCombs Global Credit Opportunities Funds, LP v Caesars Entertainment Corp*, 80 F Supp 3d 507 (SDNY 2015), the debtor paid to the bondholders a 100% premium over market value for their notes, as a sweetener designed to induce consent to the restructuring, without apparent judicial opprobrium.

[193] Marcel Kahan and Bruce Tuckman, 'Do Bondholders Lose from Junk Bond Covenant Changes?' (1993) 66(4) J Bus 499, 510–11.

[194] *Kass v Eastern Air Lines*, 12 Del J Corp L 1074, 1082 (Del Ch 1986); *Goodfellow v Nelson Line (Liverpool) Ltd* [1912] 2 Ch 324, 333; *British America Nickel Corporation Ltd v O'Brien* [1927] AC 369, 378–79 (inducements not forming part of the scheme to be voted for).

[195] Mark Roe, 'The Voting Prohibition in Bond Workouts' (1987) 97(2) Yale LJ 232, 262.

[196] For statistics see Bradley and Gulati (n 168) 2095–96 (five out of eleven restructured bonds after 2002 contained prohibition on suing).

[197] See, eg, Art 3 of the EU Supplemental Provisions (2012).

accumulate the requisite percentage of bondholders (usually 25% of outstanding bonds) necessary to require the trustee to litigate.

The English and US courts have found the no-action clauses unobjectionable, and strictly held the bondholder to the prohibition to institute individual court proceedings in breach of the no-action clause.[198] Good reasons justify the inclusion of such clauses—they prevent a race to court and avert the duplication of suits.[199] Moreover, English courts have issued anti-suit injunctions against the claimants acting in breach of no-action clauses,[200] assuming the individual action at issue falls within the scope of coverage of the no-action clause. 7.149

When determining the scope of coverage of no-action clauses, the first step is to examine the wording of the clause. No-action clauses may be drafted in various ways: barring any remedy in respect of the bonds, barring the enforcement of the bonds or proceeding against the State in recovery (as per corporate bonds). Depending on how broad the wording of the clause is, a certain range of actions may not fall within the net of the no-action clause—declaratory judgments, actions short of enforcement of the ensuing judgment, etc. Thus, it was held that a narrowly drafted no-action clause that bars actions for the enforcement of 'covenants' does not extend to the recovery of the principal obligation after maturity.[201] However, in sovereign bonds, no-action clauses generally cover 'a suit, action or proceeding with respect to the debt securities of a series'.[202] This is as wide and encompassing a provision as it gets and may even cover actions in other forums, such as investment arbitration. 7.150

The literal interpretation of no-action clauses is not the end of the matter. Jacob J in *Re Colt Telecom* emphasised that no-action clauses should be construed purposively and in a commercially sensible manner that is conscious of the purpose of such clauses, namely to prevent minority 7.151

[198] *Re Colt Telecom Group* [2002] EWHC 2815, paras 62–77. For other US cases, see the cases cited in CT Foster, 'Validity, Construction, and Application of Express Restrictions on Right of Action by Individual Holder of One or More of a Series of Corporate Bonds or Other Obligations' (originally published in 1948) 174 ALR 435, 8; PV Smith, 'Validity, Construction, and Application of Express Restrictions on Right of Action by Individual Holder of One or More of a Series of Corporate Bonds or Other Obligations' (originally published in 1937) 108 ALR 88, 11–16. No-action clauses were also mentioned, without a sign of disapprobation, in *Belgium v Spain (Barcelona Traction Case)*, 1970 ICJ Rep 3, 104–05 (per Judge Sir Gerald Fitzmaurice).

[199] Wood (n 114) para 16-025.

[200] *Elektrim SA v Vivendi Holdings 1 Corp* [2008] EWCA Civ 1178, para 122.

[201] *Hirschfield v Astoria Associates*, 139 NYS 2d 519 (Sup Ct 1955).

[202] See, eg, Debt Securities and Warrants, Prospectus, United Mexican States, 10 November 2014, 7.

litigation.[203] Lewison J, approved on appeal by Collins LJ (as he then was),[204] held that the test of what claims were caught by the no-action clause should be purposive and substantive, and not procedural. It should be construed as including any claim designed to vindicate the rights of a bondholder in his capacity as such.[205] The discourse of US courts has been more cautiously articulated so as to construe no-action clauses strictly,[206] and apply them in strict accordance with their terms.[207] Thus, while the courts from both jurisdictions have held on several occasions that the no-action clause extends to non-contractual claims,[208] the application of no-action clauses to causes of action arising out of the acts preceding the event of default has divided the two jurisdictions.[209]

7.152 In the absence of an express no-action clause, some courts have—rather controversially—implied a clause to that effect. The Supreme Court of New York in *Crédit Français v Sociedad* found that a loan secured by a consortium of banks, designating one of them as an agent, would imply a restriction upon the individual right of lenders to bring proceedings, vesting such right in the agent or the majority of the consortium.[210] But the court in *A.I. v Jamaica* distinguished *Crédit Français v Sociedad* and came to the conclusion that the bondholder had individual standing in light of the clear terms of the loan agreement that provided the creditor with the individual right of action.[211] Older US cases are equally disparate in terms of implying a no-action clause into the bonds issued with a trust indenture.[212] The common view seems to be that the implication of a no-action clause, if ever justified, is limited to syndicated loans, as only they possess

[203] *Re Colt Telecom Group* [2002] EWHC 2815, para 56.

[204] *Elektrim SA v Vivendi Holdings 1 Corp* [2008] EWCA Civ 1178, paras 100–07.

[205] *Law Debenture Trust Corporation Plc v Concord Trust* [2007] EWHC 2255 (Ch), paras 51–56.

[206] *Cruden v Bank of New York*, 957 F 2d 961, 968 (2d Cir 1992).

[207] *Howe v Bank of New York Mellon*, 783 F Supp 2d 466, 473 (SDNY 2011).

[208] *Law Debenture Trust Corporation Plc v Concord Trust* [2007] EWHC 2255 (Ch), paras 51–56; *Re Colt Telecom Group* [2002] EWHC 2815, para 56 (applying New York law to corporate bonds); Marcel Kahan, 'Rethinking Corporate Bonds: The Trade-Off between Individual and Collective Rights' (2002) 77 NYU L Rev 1040, 1050–51.

[209] *Howe v Bank of New York Mellon*, 783 F Supp 2d 466, 473–74 (SDNY 2011) (no-action clause restrained to events of default); *Re Colt Telecom Group* [2002] EWHC 2815, para 56 (applying an identically drafted no-action clause, held that giving freedom to act to individual bondholders in respect of pre-event-of-default claims 'makes no commercial sense').

[210] *Crédit Français International SA v Sociedad Financiera de Comercio*, 490 NYS 2d 670 (Sup Ct NY 1985). One should not lay too much emphasis on this decision (Lee Buchheit and Ralph Reisner, 'The Effect of the Sovereign Debt Restructuring Process on Inter-Creditor Relationships' (1988) 2 U Ill L Rev 493, 503–04).

[211] *A.I. Credit Corp v Government of Jamaica*, 666 F Supp 629, 631–32 (SDNY 1987).

[212] Note, 'The Rights and Remedies of the Bondholder under Corporate Bonds and Indentures' (1927) 27 Colum L Rev 579, 580–82.

a certain communal character. The courts would be vigilant to ensure the right of action in bond disputes.[213]

In practice, no-action clauses present an almost insurmountable difficulty for minority bondholders who do not possess the requisite percentage of bondholding. Lewison J regarded as fanciful the suggestion that a minority bondholder had the means of knowing who the other bondholders were and 'could have whipped up support from 30 per cent of the bondholders'.[214] Generally, the information on entitlements under global bonds held through clearing systems is confidential. In light of this, Kahan suggests the mechanism of supertrustee who will be able to monitor the debtor, take decisions to modify bonds and sue under the bonds.[215] However, in practice bondholders are often able to locate other fellow bondholders—they can publicise online, in newspapers, vehicles may be established to locate and consolidate bondholders. Another mechanism is to insert a clause into sovereign bonds whereby the State will be forced to deliver a list of names and addresses of all bondholders of the given issue upon request by a certain, generally lower percentage of bondholders.[216] **7.153**

Grounds for lifting the no-action clause. Although the inclusion of no-action clauses is legitimate in and of itself, it is suggested that in certain (rare) circumstances, courts might have few qualms about disregarding such clauses. First, there is a suggestion in some US cases that the no-action clause would not bar actions by a minority bondholder against the trustee[217] or the majority bondholders (a clearer language would be necessary to that effect). Further, no-action clauses would not prevent actions alleging fraud or conspiracy between the debtor and the trustee/majority bondholders,[218] or else unequal treatment of the minority bondholder.[219] **7.154**

[213] See Chapter 1.

[214] *Law Debenture Trust Corporation Plc v Concord Trust* [2007] EWHC 2255 (Ch), para 43.

[215] Marcel Kahan, Yakov Amihud, and Kenneth Garbade, 'A New Governance Structure for Corporate Bonds' (1999) 51 Stan L Rev 447.

[216] See, eg, *Hirschfield v Astoria Associates Inc*, 139 NYS 2d 519 (Sup Ct 1955) (where the clause provided that '[t]he Company agrees that upon the written demand of the Registered Holders of twenty per cent (20%) in principal amount of the bonds of this issue outstanding at the time of such written demand, it will deliver a list of names and addresses of all bondholders of this issue').

[217] *Metropolitan West Asset Management v Magnus Funding, Ltd*, 2004 US Dist LEXIS 11761, 10–15 (SDNY 2004); *Cruden v Bank of New York*, 957 F 2d 961, 968 (2d Cir 1992); *Feldbaum v McCrory Co*, 1992 Del Ch LEXIS 113, 23–24 (Del Ch 1992); Philip Rawlings, 'Reinforcing Collectivity: The Liability of Trustees and the Power of Investors in Finance Transactions' (2009) 23(1) Tru L I 14, 22.

[218] Foster (n 198) 9.

[219] *Crosthwaite v Moline Plow Co*, 298 Fed 466, 469 (SDNY 1924); *Whitebox Convertible Arbitrage Partners, LP v World Airways, Inc*, 2006 WL 358270 (ND Ga 2006). See Kahan (n 208)

7.155 What unites these instances is the impossibility (or futility)[220] of requiring the minority bondholder to comply with the no-action clause. It would be futile to vest the majority of bondholders or the trustee with the right to assert a cause of action based on their own misconduct. While it might be argued that these grounds of impossibility flow from the general obligation of the majority to act in good faith for the benefit of bondholders, the correlation between the two is somewhat artificial and the correct view seems to be that impossibility and futility are stand-alone grounds for overriding the no-action clause. Caution is necessary, however, in applying the grounds of impossibility (or futility) as they need to be more than clear to trump the no-action clause.

7.156 Second, and more importantly, a case might be made for the proposition that the repudiatory breach of the contract by the sovereign debtor would unshackle the bondholders from the grip of no-action clauses. The parties in *Azevedo v Imcopa* had agreed that, in principle, a repudiatory breach of contract would bring to an end the no-action clause, thus re-vesting the claimant with the individual right of action. Hamlen J in the Commercial Court accepted this position (although the point was not fully pleaded before him),[221] but found no repudiation on the merits of the case.[222] On appeal, Lloyd LJ accepted that there were reasonable grounds to argue that a demonstration of repudiation would allow the claimant to proceed against the debtor without complying with the no-action clause. But, again, he found no such repudiation.[223]

7.157 It remains rather mysterious why the defendant in *Azevedo* agreed to this position given that such an interpretation did not fall within the plain meaning of the contract. There are two possible justifications. First, one may justify this interpretation by implying a term into no-action clauses to the effect that when and if the debtor repudiates the contract, the repudiation liberates the ties that unite the bondholders and prevent individual litigation. Such an implied term would fly, however, in the face of the clear language of no-action clauses that does not distinguish between the two eventualities.

7.158 Second, it could be argued that the concession made by the parties in *Azevedo* might fit into the doctrine of repudiation. If so, it is contended here that this concession was not rightly made. The construction of no-action

1075 (making a general proposition that holding a minority bondholder who has been unfairly treated by the debtor to the no-action clause is illogical).

[220] See *Re Dura Automotive Systems, Inc*, 379 BR 257, 263–64 (SDNY 2007) (futility of barring the action of the noteholder).

[221] *Azevedo v Imcopa* [2012] EWHC 1849 (Comm), para 38.

[222] Ibid para 67.

[223] *Azevedo v Imcopa* [2013] EWCA Civ 364, para 73.

clauses along these lines asks the wrong question and therefore receives the wrong answer. The proper question is who is to decide whether the State has repudiated the debt. If the doctrine of repudiation were accepted as trumping the no-action clause, then the court would have to review the substance of the contractual performance and decide whether the sovereign had indeed repudiated the debt. This is exactly the right that the no-action clause vests in the majority of bondholders.

On a more technical level, an idea that reappears in different contexts is **7.159** that not every contractual provision is terminated upon the acceptance of the repudiation. The clauses, which have a contractual function that is ancillary or collateral to the subject matter of the contract[224] or are designed to address the change of contractual circumstances[225] are commonly held to survive the discharge of the contract. A whole array of ancillary clauses, including arbitration clauses, liquidated damages clauses, and exclusion clauses, were held to survive the contractual repudiation,[226] and so should no-action clauses.

On a more abstract level, no-action clauses do not operate in the exclusive **7.160** interest of the debtor. They also benefit the majority of bondholders in that they preclude opportunistic behaviour by the minority bondholder.[227] Opportunistic bondholders draw funds down from the State's treasury at the expense of the proportionate payment to majority bondholders.

Quite unusually, the US courts have recognised a wider defence to the no- **7.161** action clause. Under the defence, the minority creditor may bring an action against the debtor in apparent circumvention of the no-action clause, provided the action is for the payment of principal and interest. The defence stems from s 316(b) of the Trust Indenture Act which embodies the right to payment of principal and interest and which trumps contractual provisions, including the no-action clause.[228] Ostensibly, the defence does not apply to sovereign debt, which does not fall within the ambit of the Trust Indenture Act.

224 *Yasuda Fire & Marine Insurance Co of Europe Ltd v Orion Marine Insurance Underwriting Agency Ltd* [1995] QB 174, 190.

225 *B.P. Exploration Co (Libya) Ltd v Hunt (No 2)* [1979] 1 WLR 783, 829 (per Goff J).

226 Neil Andrews, Malcolm Clarke, Andrew Tetternborn, and Graham Virgo, *Contractual Duties: Performance, Breach, Termination and Remedies* (2012) 246.

227 *Feldbaum v McCrory Co*, 1992 Del Ch LEXIS 113, 18–19 (Del Ch 1992).

228 For a recent application extending it to contractual clauses which track the language of s 316(b) of the Trust Indenture Act, see *MeehanCombs Global Credit Opportunities Funds, LP v Caesars Entertainment Corp*, 80 F Supp 3d 507 (SDNY 2015).

Trust Deeds

7.162 Trust deeds and no-action clauses, taken in conjunction, shift the right of bringing legal action from the individual bondholders to the trustee who is purportedly acting for the entire group of bondholders. Among its powers, the trustee has generally the (exclusive) right of initiating proceedings against the sovereign debtor either upon the request of at least 25% of bondholders, or of its own discretion. In practice, the trustee is also occasionally joined in court proceedings brought by an individual bondholder to convey the views of the group of bondholders through a unified channel.

7.163 While the trustee has the power to initiate proceedings of its own discretion, such proceedings are rarely, if ever, seen in practice. In general, it would be incumbent upon 25% of bondholders to give directions to the trustee to bring a legal claim. Should the trustee fail to comply with the direction given by the requisite percentage of bondholders, the right to recover reverts to the creditors.[229] Additionally, the requisite percentage of bondholders may judicially compel the trustee to take legal action.

7.164 In cases when the minority of bondholders does not reach the threshold required for requesting an action of the trustee (25% of bondholders), courts would be slow to interfere with the discretionary exercise of the trustee's powers. The parameters of the review of the discretionary power to bring an action against the debtor are narrowly defined and the standard of review is set very high. The courts would only intrude into the discretionary exercise of the power, if the trust power is 'exercised for a purpose, or with an intention, beyond the scope of or not justified by the instrument creating the power'.[230] The refusal to initiate proceedings against the State falls squarely within the scope of the power conferred by the trust instrument. The party contesting the decision of the trustee would have to meet the high standard of proving that the trustee acted 'unreasonably, perversely or in bad faith'.[231] There is also room to argue that the trustee in sovereign bonds is strictly limited to his functions described in the trust deed and is not the 'guardian of the bondholder in a general sense'.[232] In this sense, US cases recognise that an indenture trustee for a bond is not

[229] Lee Buchheit and Elizabeth Karpinski, 'Grenada's Innovations' (2006) 21 J Intl Bank Regul 227, 230.

[230] *F&C Alternative Investments (Holdings) Ltd v Francois Barthelemy, Anthony Culligan* [2011] EWHC 1731 (Ch), para 229.

[231] *Law Debenture Trust Corporation v Elektrim Finance* [2005] EWHC 1999 (Ch), para 20.

[232] League of Nations, *Report of the Committee for the Study of International Loan Contracts* (1939a), paras 53–56.

subject to the ordinary rules governing the trustee's duty of undivided loyalty.[233]

11. Acceleration and Reverse Acceleration Clauses

Upon the occurrence of an event of default (non-payment, cross-default, and so forth), the bondholders may accelerate the debt, that is, to declare the bonds immediately due and payable. Requesting the payment to be made forthwith allows the bondholder to claim the payment of the principal and interest accrued, without necessarily following the payment schedule as provided for in the bond. It is in principle open to the debtor to challenge the acceleration of the debt on the ground that an Event of Default—the usual trigger of the acceleration clause—has not occurred,[234] but successful challenges on this ground are rare. **7.165**

Acceleration clauses vest the exclusive right of acceleration into 25% of bondholders. When embedded in the bonds, this provision would frustrate the aggressive litigation strategy of a bondholder who, without securing the consent of 25% of bondholders, would be unable to recover the principal and would be limited in its litigation endeavours to the accrued and payable interest only. **7.166**

The US courts have been faithful to the plain meaning interpretation of these clauses, rejecting attempts to accelerate the debt without the requisite consent of bondholders.[235] In principle, given the functional similarity between acceleration and no-action clauses, most principles governing no-action clauses may equally be applied to acceleration clauses. These principles, discussed in the preceding section, are designed to preclude tactical attacks by the minority bondholder to surpass the restrictions contained in no-action clauses and initiate individual proceedings. **7.167**

As is the case with no-action clauses, minority bondholders may attempt to invoke the doctrine of repudiation to accelerate the debt as of right without complying with the acceleration clause, which arguably has been put to an end by the repudiation of the State's financial obligations. The Foreign Claims Settlement Commission in the *Zentler Claim* held that the **7.168**

[233] *Elliott Associates v Henry Schroder Bank & Trust Co*, 655 F Supp 1281, 1288–89 (SDNY 1987), affd, 838 F 2d 66 (2d Cir 1988); *Hazzard* v *Chase Nat Bank of City of New York*, 287 NYS 541, 566 (Sup Ct NY 1936).

[234] *Concord Trust v Law Debenture Trust Corporation Plc* [2005] UKHL 27, paras 24–26.

[235] *Yucyco, Ltd v Republic of Slovenia*, 984 F Supp 209, 221 (SDNY 1997) (rejecting the argument that getting the consent of the majority of bondholders was 'futile'); *New Bank of New England v Toronto-Dominion Bank*, 768 F Supp 1017, 1021–22 (SDNY 1991) (rejecting an action by minority lenders to compel majority lenders to accelerate the debt).

acceleration was not 'a mere formality', and in the absence of the proof of acceleration by 25% of bondholders, the claimant was necessarily limited in its recovery to the interest accrued.[236] Commissioner Clay in his dissenting opinion took the view that when the sovereign debtor had de facto repudiated the debt, denied justice to the bondholder in its national courts and had not displayed any willingness to repay the debt upon its maturity, the Commission could award the claimant the principal, bypassing the no-action clause.[237] For the reasons expressed above in respect of no-action clauses, it is maintained here again that the doctrine of repudiation is not a good attack against the plain meaning reading of acceleration clauses.

7.169 By virtue of reverse acceleration clauses, which mostly go together with acceleration clauses, a qualified majority of bondholders may overturn (rescind) the minority's decision to accelerate the payment of the principal. Generally, 25% of bondholders of an issue of bonds would have the power to accelerate the debt, and, in turn, a majority of 50% or 66⅔% could rescind such acceleration.[238]

7.170 It is to be recalled here that the statement in *Allen v Gold Reefs* was very broad in providing that 'all powers conferred on majorities and enabling them to bind minorities' should be exercised in good faith for the benefit of the company. The reference to 'all powers' implies that the same overarching principle may apply in respect of other CACs, including reverse acceleration clauses.

7.171 While that is in principle true, such claims would rarely, if ever, succeed. Under the overwhelming majority of sovereign bonds, the majority of bondholders will have the power to rescind the acceleration of the principal in two situations: (1) when the event of default has been cured (eg, the State has paid up under the bonds); (2) when the State's default has been waived.[239] It would be hardly imaginable for an English or New York court to review the decision of the majority of bondholders to rescind the acceleration of the bonds taken in pursuance of a reverse acceleration clause that expressly sets out the two situations when the majority have the power to rescind the acceleration of the debt.[240]

[236] *Zentler Claim* (1958-II) 26 ILR 258. [237] Ibid 260–62.

[238] IMF 'Progress Report to the International Monetary and Financial Committee on Crisis Resolution' (2005) 7–9.

[239] See, eg, Offering Memorandum, Plurinational State of Bolivia, US$500,000,000 5.950% Notes Due 2023, 22 August 2013, 128.

[240] As discussed above, courts would be reluctant to review the exercise of the powers taken in pursuance of a specifically drafted majority power.

Rarely, some bonds vest the supermajority of bondholders (75%) with the power to rescind the declaration of acceleration with no conditions attached to such reversal.[241] The supermajority is not bound to waive the default in order to overturn the declaration of acceleration, and neither is the State required to cure its default. In this situation, the supermajority of bondholders enjoys discretion and the doors for the review of discretion are not in principle foreclosed. 7.172

12. Contractual Limitation of the Judicial Scrutiny

Briggs J in *Assénagon* noted that the prohibition on abusing majority powers in debt restructurings was an implied term of contract and thus could be opted out of or strictly constrained.[242] US courts have equally recognised the liberty of parties to waive the protection afforded by the implied duty of good-faith covenants in financial transactions.[243] 7.173

Assuming that the power to modify the intercreditor good-faith obligation is established, the judicial scrutiny may be tipped in favour of either the minority or the majority bondholders, depending upon the negotiating powers and the shifts in market practice. Thus, to ensure reinforced protection for minority bondholders, sovereign debt issuers can amend the modification clauses to include an explicit reference to the 'utmost good exercise of majority powers'.[244] 7.174

Circumscribing the full extent of judicial scrutiny is possible, but completely eliminating it is not. Contractual references to 'absolute' or 'sole' discretion of one contracting party have not had the desired effect of preventing courts from making a judgment upon the discretionary exercise of contractual powers.[245] This is so because English courts consider it repellent to public policy to allow the exercise of discretion in a dishonest or irrational manner whatever the contractual qualification of such power 7.175

[241] See, eg, Listing Prospectus, Republic of Côte d'Ivoire, New US Dollar Denominated Step-Up Bonds due 2032, 30 November 2012, 9.

[242] *Assénagon Asset Management SA v Irish Bank Resolution Corporation Limited* [2012] EWHC 2090 (Ch), para 46.

[243] *New Bank of New England v Toronto-Dominion Bank*, 768 F Supp 1017, 1021–22 (SDNY 1991); *Banco Espanol de Credito v Security Pacific National Bank* 763 F Supp 36, 44–45 (SDNY 1991).

[244] For the distinction between 'good faith' and 'utmost good faith' see *SNCB Holding v UBS AG* [2012] EWHC 2044 (Comm), para 72.

[245] Christopher Hare, 'The Expanding Judicial Review of Contractual Discretion: *Carte Blanche* or *Carton Rouge*' (2013) JIBFL 269, 270–71; *Law Debenture Trust Corporation v Elektrim Finance* [2005] EWHC 1999 (Ch), paras 62, 71 (apprehending the opportunity to review, in spite of Trustee's 'absolute and uncontrolled discretion', the reasonableness of the costs incurred by the Trustee).

is.[246] The courts have stated that the widely drafted contractual discretion ('in its absolute discretion') may not be exercised capriciously, irrationally, or arbitrarily.[247] That said, the parties may provide that the payment obligations may not only be modified but 'cancelled', too. This may have the effect of avoiding any attacks to the fairness of payment modifications.

13. Coda: Criticism and Comparison with other Regimes

7.176 The English courts' approach to the judicial scrutiny of contractual discretion has invited favourable and unfavourable opinions alike. Some commentators argue that in commercial cases, the courts should give up the jurisdiction to review contractual discretion altogether, for the uncertainty of judicial scrutiny creates opportunism and increase in costs, and leave the regulation of abuses of contractual discretion to markets.[248] This is indeed the quintessential approach to good faith under English law according to which courts are most leery to modify mercantile arrangements between the parties. The District Court has gone so far as to deny the existence of any good-faith obligation in the relations between the minority and majority bondholders.[249]

7.177 Indeed, like in any system of democracy, including 'financial democracy', the minority should not easily, if ever, be able to undermine a majority-approved restructuring by bringing an action for judicial scrutiny. CACs have been extensively debated, and to the extent that no protections have been built into the text of CACs, why should minority creditors be able to escape the terms of the restructuring binding on all creditors?

7.178 That said, the peculiar nature of sovereign debt restructurings, whereby the majority may effectively bind in a minority, might justify at least a *de minimis* review of the exercise of majority powers. The reality of sovereign debt restructurings is that the rights of creditors may effectively be destroyed by the exercise of majority powers. The resolution of the dispute cannot be left to the contract alone, as sovereign debt markets are

[246] Richard Hooley, 'Controlling Contractual Discretion' (2013) 72(1) CLJ 65, 81–82.

[247] *Lombard Tricity Finance Ltd v Martin Shaun Paton* [1989] 1 All ER 918, 923; *Automotive Latch Systems Ltd v Honeywell International Inc* [2008] EWHC 2171, para 711; Hare (n 245) 271–72. For US case law references, see Corey Chivers, '"Contracting Around" the Good Faith Covenant to Avoid Lender Liability' (1991) Colum Bus L Rev 359, 377.

[248] Jonathan Morgan, 'Against Judicial Review of Discretionary Contractual Powers' [2008] 2 LMCLQ 230, 236–238; Keegan Drake, 'The Fall and Rise of the Exit Consent' (2014) 63 Duke LJ 1589, 1622–23.

[249] *Yucyco, Ltd v Slovenia*, 1999 WL 169530, 3 (SDNY 1999) (where the majority released the obligors from the joint and several liability thus affecting the chances of the minority to recover its debt).

remarkably short-memoried.[250] Codes of good conduct strongly advocate fairness in sovereign debt restructurings,[251] yet such soft codes, devoid of mandatory character, are unable to resolve the unfairness in sovereign debt restructurings.

Gloster LJ, speaking extrajudicially, disapproved of the overturning of the exit consent in *Assénagon*, arguing that without the benefit of exit consents the debtor would have gone broke, leaving the claimant creditor with no recourse against the assets of the debtor.[252] The argument has some indirect support in the law of schemes of arrangement where the courts, while acknowledging that the bonds may have a substantial face value and that they may be traded on the secondary market, accept that in some cases a bondholder would receive nothing upon the winding up of the debtor company. In such a case, that bondholder would not have any economic interest in the debtor and his votes may be ignored in the calculation of the votes necessary for the approval of the scheme of arrangement.[253] **7.179**

The unease associated with her ladyship's argument is that the fairness of a restructuring, as it is understood and applied in CVAs)[254] is to be assessed not only vertically (the comparison between the terms of restructuring and no restructuring, as her ladyship has suggested), but also horizontally (comparison with the treatment of other creditors affected). Under the last strand of comparison, the disgruntled bondholder in *Assénagon* was clearly much worse off than other bondholders. The bottom line to this argument is that certain minimum standards of treatment cannot be dispensed with simply because the debtor lacks the wherewithal to pay. **7.180**

Although many of the cases cited in this chapter on the *de minimis* protection of creditors date back to the late nineteenth and early twentieth **7.181**

250 Udaibir Das, Michael Papaioannou, and Christoph Trebesch, 'Sovereign Debt Restructurings 1950–2010: Literature Survey, Data, and Stylized Facts' (2012) IMF Working Paper WP/12/203, 60.

251 Principles 3 and 4 of IIF Principles for Stable Capital Flows and Fair Debt Restructuring (2012); Principles 7 and 15 of UNCTAD Principles on Promoting Responsible Sovereign Lending and Borrowing (2012).

252 Elizabeth Gloster, 'Derivative Delights and Oligarch Feuds—What Contribution Is English Law Making to our Post-Modern Financial World?' Public Lecture, 27 November 2013, Cambridge (available at http://www.privatelaw.law.cam.ac.uk/news/allen-overy-lecture-2013-derivative-delights-and-oligarch-feuds-2013-what-contribution-is-english-law-making-to-our-post2013modern-financial-world).

253 *Re British & Commonwealth Holdings (No 3)* [1992] 1 WLR 672; *Re Tea Corporation* [1904] 1 Ch 12; *Re Bluebrook Ltd* [2009] EWHC 2114 (Ch). But see *Re My Travel Group* [2004] EWHC 1734. See also 'no-creditor-worse-off' principle in bank resolutions (Phoebus Athanassiou, 'Valuation in Resolution and the "No-Creditor-Worse-Off Principle' (2014) 1 JIBFL 16).

254 See, eg, *Prudential Assurance v PRG Powerhouse* [2007] EWHC 1002, para 75; *Re a debtor (No 101 of 1999)* [2001] 1 BCLC 54.

centuries when English courts were more generous in the application of equity powers, many (but not all) of the principles received endorsement in the recent case of *Assénagon*. Still, one may wonder whether the tenure of older cases has not dwindled in relevance since the early twentieth century with the retreat of the law of equity over the twentieth century, or even if it has become a relic of the past.

7.182 Another powerful critique against the law of judicial scrutiny of debt restructurings asserts that many of the cases on majority powers are drawn from disputes between shareholders and the company, and not necessarily a group of bondholders. Arguably, the ties that unite shareholders are stronger than those uniting bondholders who may purchase the bonds without prior knowledge of or contact with one another.[255] Twisting the same argument in the completely opposite direction, Smith and Sharpe argue that the outcome in *Redwood* may well be explained by the fact that the debt, modified through the exercise of majority powers, was in the form of syndicated loans where the members of the syndicate could collaborate more easily to increase their bargaining power.[256] This suggests that the highly deferential bar for finding oppression of the minority might not apply with equal rigour to bondholders who are more dispersed and less prone to consolidation.

7.183 On the other side, a camp of authoritative scholars supports broader, or at least minimal, judicial control of contractual discretion.[257] For example, Buchheit and Gulati are in favour of broader judicial control of the actions of the majority so as to control abuses of majority powers and overturn commercially non-justified modifications of the principal or payment dates, or when the changes are impermissibly severe.[258] Branton and Gulati, relying on the case law pre-dating the US federal statutory reorganisation regime, robustly argue that in the sovereign debt context, a more extensive judicial

[255] See Chapter 1 which draws a similar distinction between syndicate loans and bonds in respect of the right to bring individual actions.

[256] Moverley Smith and Sharpe (n 191) 288–290.

[257] See, eg, Hooley (n 246) 65; Hugh Collins, 'Discretionary Powers in Contracts' in David Campbell, Hugh Collins, and John Wightman (eds), *Implicit Dimensions of Contract: Discrete, Relational and Network Contracts* (2003) 219–54; John Coffee and William Klein, 'Bondholder Coercion: The Problem of Constrained Choice in Debt Tender Offers and Recapitalizations' (1991) 58(4) Uni Chi L Rev 1207, 1263 (distinguishing between 'benign' and 'pernicious' uses of exit consents); Victor Brudney, 'Corporate Bondholders and Debtor Opportunism: In Bad Times and Good' (1992) 105 Harv L Rev 1821, 1834, 1853 (proposing to ban exit consents given that the strategic behaviour of the debtor to induce consent of dispersed bondholders taints the volitional character of consent and exerts pressure upon bondholders).

[258] Buchheit and Gulati (n 3) 1341, 1346.

scrutiny of CACs is needed. They assert that corporate debt restructuring cases, where the judicial scrutiny is strictly circumscribed, are not a suitable analogy for sovereign debt restructurings. In the former category of cases, the creditors enjoy, in addition to the abuse of rights review of the courts, a second layer of protection, namely the bankruptcy regime with the judicial scrutiny of the cram down on minority creditors. By contrast, in sovereign debt restructurings, minority creditors are left at the mercy of the majority of bondholders.[259]

In support of their argument, Branton and Gulati also rely on Chapter 9 insolvencies (US municipalities) under which US courts review the reorganisation plan of a municipality, already approved by the supermajority of the municipality's creditors, against the benchmark of the 'best interests of creditors', set out in 11 USC §943(b)(7). In this context, the US courts undertake a rather substantive enquiry into the debt burden of a municipality and the fairness of the debt restructuring.[260] **7.184**

There is no denying that a certain degree of bondholder protection is required and that is indeed the position under English law. However, the Chapter 9-like extensive review may be too far-fetched in sovereign debt restructurings on three grounds. First, such an extensive inquiry is unforeseen by either the creditors or the debtor—no one appointed the English courts to sit as an international bankruptcy court with extensive powers bordering on the review of the reasonableness of the restructuring. Examining the merits of a restructuring process would amount to second-guessing the challenges that the sovereign debtor faced at the time and the judgement calls it had to make. **7.185**

Second, the fairness review in Chapter 9 insolvencies (and other statutory mechanisms) hinges upon the statutory prescription of such extensive powers. Absent such a statutory regime of judicial scrutiny, the common law rules on the review of CACs ought to prevail. Parties prescribing the use of CACs are presumed to act within the zone of freedom they enjoy. Deriving an extensive judicial scrutiny might upset the delicate contractual balance put in place. **7.186**

Third, although the argument of the additional layer of protection might seem welcome in other respects, it is still very deferential in nature when applied by bankruptcy courts. In a recent Detroit Chapter 9 judgment, Judge Rhodes was asked to assess whether the adjustment plan **7.187**

[259] Buchheit and Gulati (n 15) 69–70, 78.

[260] See, eg, *Kelley v Everglades Drainage Dist*, 319 US 415, 419–22 (1943); *West Coast Life Ins Co v Merced Irrigation Dist*, 114 F 2d 654, 674 (9th Cir 1940).

unfairly discriminated against dissenting creditors. He adopted a rather deferential standard by enquiring whether the settlements with the groups of creditors that allegedly received a preferential treatment were reasonable.[261]

7.188 Similarly, while it is true that English schemes of arrangement vest the court with sufficiently broad discretion to sanction the schemes of arrangement as against the standard of 'an intelligent and honest person, a member of the class concerned and acting in respect of his own interest' who 'might reasonably approve the scheme',[262] courts are reluctant to interfere with the reasonableness of schemes of arrangement[263] (save for procedural irregularities). No English court has so far overturned the decision of the majority on the ground of fairness.[264] In the context of CVAs, the courts have stated that:

> It is not for the court to speculate whether the terms of the proposed compromise were the best that could have been obtained; or whether the proposed compromise would have been better if it did not contain all the terms that it does contain.... the court will give weight to the wishes of creditors and contributories whose interests it has to consider, for the reason that creditors and contributories, if uninfluenced by extraneous considerations, are likely to be good judges of where their own best interests lie.[265]

7.189 So far as unjust discrimination is concerned, the review of fairness under statutory procedures, such as CVAs, stands in sharp contrast to the highly deferential review in *Redwood*. In statutory procedures, English courts might be more eager to strike down debt restructurings when a group of creditors would be disadvantaged by the design of the restructuring.[266] However, even with the judicial scrutiny of CVAs, the threshold is set very high: what is necessary to challenge a CVA is 'a disproportionate prejudice

[261] *In re City of Detroit*, Case No 13-53846 (Bankr ED Mich 2014), paras 25–28.

[262] O'Dea et al (n 45) 53–58. For the US law on the matter, see Buchheit and Gulati (n 15) 40–41.

[263] *Re English, Scottish and Australian Chartered Bank* [1893] 3 Ch 385, 409 ('creditors are ... much better judges of what is to their commercial advantage than the Court can be').

[264] O'Dea et al (n 45) 145. On occasions, courts have come close to striking down CVAs (see, eg, *Prudential Assurance v PRG Powerhouse* [2007] EWHC 1002). See also Christian Pilkington, *Schemes of Arrangement* (2013) 102–04. For a more intrusive analysis in Australia, see *Gambotto v WCP Ltd* (1995) 13 ACLC 342.

[265] Edward Bailey and Hugo Groves, *Corporate Insolvency: Law and Practice* (2007) 284–85 (referring to *Re Greenhaven Motors Ltd* [1999] 1 BCLC 635, 643). See also *Sisu Capital Fund v Tucker* [2005] EWHC 2170, para 73.

[266] See, eg, *Prudential Assurance v PRG Powerhouse* [2007] EWHC 1002, para 75; *Re a debtor (No 101 of 1999)* [2001] 1 BCLC 54.

to one class of creditors, which cannot be justified, for example as necessary for the continuation of the debtor company's business'.[267]

From a policy perspective, the test set out in *Redwood* provides the ultimate, albeit deferential, standard of review of unfair discriminations. Courts and international tribunals are ill-positioned to look over the shoulders of a sovereign debtor in distress through the application of broader standards of judicial scrutiny of debt restructurings. Even though some may be tempted by the idea of establishing an order of preferences *ex ante*,[268] the search for the holy grail of efficient intercreditor equality in the courts is parochial. **7.190**

An idea that has permeated the discussion in this chapter was that there is a discrepancy between the review of CACs in sovereign debt restructurings and the extent of scrutiny of statutory mechanisms, such as schemes of arrangement in the UK or Chapter 9 bankruptcies in the US. One may question how principled this discrepancy is. In other words, does something inherent justify the extended review of the fairness of statutory procedures, on the one hand, and on the other, the *de minimis* review of CACs? **7.191**

Both statutory procedures and contractually enhanced debt restructurings are in essence a means for the distressed debtor to obtain financial relief. But the apparent discrepancy in the treatment of the schemes of arrangement and CACs lies in the source of the power to restructure: statute in the case of schemes of arrangement, and contract in the case of CACs. In the case of schemes of arrangement, minority creditors do not explicitly consent to being bound by the will of the majority, while in the case of CACs, the majority powers are part and parcel of the contractual bargain between the parties. Having consented to the 'financial democracy' in CACs, the creditors have less room to complain. This explains why courts are more willing to scrutinise the former, but less so the latter. **7.192**

Further, English courts enjoy a heightened level of scrutiny in cross-border insolvencies. By subscribing to the theory of modified universalism and accepting the need to recognise and provide assistance to foreign insolvency proceedings, English courts condition their support by their **7.193**

267 Gabriel Moss, Daniel Bayfield, Adam Al-Attar, Howard Seife, and Seven Rivera, 'Giving Effect to Debt Compromise Arrangements—Binding the Minority or Out of the Money Classes of Creditors' in C Mallon and S Waisman (eds), *The Law and Practice of Restructurings in the UK and US* (2011) 175 (citing *Doorbar v Alltime Securities Ltd (No 2)* [1996] BPIR 128, 132 and *SISU Capital Fund Ltd v Tucker* [2006] BPIR 154, para 69).

268 Gelpern (n 105) 1119, 1140–55.

review of fairness of bankruptcy proceedings. Lord Hoffmann was adamant in expressing this position in *Cambridge Gas*:

> The protection for the shareholders is that the court will not sanction a scheme, even if adopted by the statutory majority, if it appears unfair. And no doubt the discretion to refuse assistance in the implementation of an equivalent plan which has been confirmed in a foreign jurisdiction would be exercised on similar lines.[269]

7.194 Fletcher demonstrates that the English courts would not recognise and enforce foreign corporate insolvencies, including schemes of arrangement, without the safeguards deemed necessary for the protection of local (English) interests. Broad discretion is vested in the courts when awarding recognition and enforcement: the foreign reorganisation plan should not be such as to offer a disproportionately unfair compensation to the local creditor.[270] It should 'satisfy certain minimum standards of integrity and due process, including adequate protection for individual creditors, … to safeguard them against unfairly prejudicial treatment'.[271] The public policy defence acts as a broad-ranging shield against the recognition of unfair institutional restructurings.[272]

7.195 In *Central Hanover Bank & Trust Co v Siemens & Halske Aktien-Gesellschaft*, German bond laws, adopted after the bonds had been subscribed, forbade German and only German debtors from paying under the bonds. The German debtor, in a case brought against it for repayment of the debt in the US courts, raised the defence that German bond laws had excused its non-performance. The argument received short shrift from the District Court given that the bonds were governed by US law. In the alternative, German bondholders sought to rely on the authority in *Gebhard* to which the court responded that:

> [T]he German law invoked by the defendants is not an insolvency law applicable alike to all creditors but is rather a law that discriminates against nonresident creditors. It is safe to say that the Gebhard Case would not have been decided as it was if the Canadian reorganization had provided that one treatment should be given to Canadian creditors and another and less favorable one to all other creditors. It is true that in the Gebhard Case broad language was used as to the extent to which creditors of foreign corporations submit themselves to the laws of the

[269] *Cambridge Gas Transport Corporation v The Official Committee of Unsecured Creditors* [2006] UKPC 26, para 26.

[270] Citing *Felixstowe Dock and Railway Co v US Lines Inc* [1989] QB 360. For the position in the US, see *In the Matter of Banque de Financement, SA*, 568 F 2d 911 (2d Cir 1987).

[271] Ian Fletcher, *Insolvency in Private International Law* (2005) 220–22.

[272] See also John Briggs, 'Bars to Common Law Recognition' in R Sheldon (ed), *Cross-Border Insolvency* (2015) 447.

foreign government. But even in the broadest passages the submission was said to be to 'such laws of the foreign government, affecting the powers and obligations of the corporation with which he voluntarily contracts, as the known and established policy of that government authorizes'.... It certainly will not be claimed in this case that in 1925 there was a 'known and established policy' of the German government to prohibit German corporations from paying their debts to creditors abroad.[273]

The analysis in terms of modified universalism grants considerable leeway to the court to assess the fairness of the domestic debt restructuring. Thus defined, such judicial scrutiny is certainly more extensive than the judicial scrutiny of CACs under English contract law. **7.196**

[273] 15 F Supp 927, 930 (SDNY 1936).

8

Enforcement of Sovereign Debt

I. INTRODUCTION

In the litigation before the English and New York courts, bondholders are commonly able to obtain summary judgments against sovereign debtors.[1] The ease of receiving the judgment stands in sharp contrast with the hurdles that a creditor faces to successfully enforce the judgment. Sovereign immunity, which has seen its scope of application severely curtailed in the twentieth century, still remains the last bastion of protection available to the sovereign debtor. While on occasions claimants have been successful in attaching the property of the State,[2] enforcing judgments against States and State-owned enterprises has generally proved to be an exceedingly uphill struggle. **8.01**

There is no silver bullet in the quest for the enforcement of sovereign debt judgments. Creditors need to engage the entire armoury of remedies and mechanisms available under national law. The attempts to attach the property of the sovereign debtor are costly for the debtor who, to evade the risk of attachment, must conduct its trade in roundabout ways.[3] This pressure partly explains why some sovereign debt disputes do not result in a final court judgment but end up being settled by the parties. Attaching some assets may force the State to repay the rest. **8.02**

The range of remedies that a national court enjoys to compel the performance of the State's pecuniary obligations is limited. None of the remedies commonly available in corporate insolvency, such as the appointment of an insolvency receiver with all its extensive powers, is beyond the ambit of a foreign court selected to adjudicate a commercial claim between the sovereign and its private creditors. The almost exclusive method of securing repayment is the enforcement of judgments. **8.03**

[1] For defences, see Chapter 6.

[2] Rodrigo Olivares-Caminal, *Legal Aspects of Sovereign Debt Restructuring* (2009) 39–99.

[3] William Bratton and Mitu Gulati, 'Sovereign Debt Reform and the Best Interest of Creditors' (2004) 57(1) Vand L Rev 1, 16. One of the explanations among many for why Venezuela did not default on its bonds was the fear, perhaps justified, that if it defaults, the export of oil to the United States will be seised by aggressive litigators (see John Dizard, '"Complete Chaos in Caracas" Invites Vulture Fest' *Financial Times* (2 September 2016) 3).

8.04 The process of enforcement of a valid judgment is customarily composed of two stages: obtaining an enforceable title followed by enforcing the judgment by attaching property. It is noteworthy that to obtain an enforceable title in England and the US the judgment creditor might not need even to show assets located within the jurisdiction.[4] However, the property that is being attached needs to be situated within the territory of the State.[5]

8.05 In the UK, the regime for the enforcement of foreign judgments depends on the origin of the given foreign judgment. Judgments from EU Member States are enforceable without an *exequatur* pursuant to the Brussels I Regulation. Judgments from other jurisdiction, notably the United States, are enforceable at common law. At common law, a foreign judgment creates a debt that is enforceable in England: the judgment creditor may bring an action for the enforcement of such debt, the evidence of such debt being the foreign judgment itself. An English judgment (usually, but not necessarily, secured by way of application for summary judgment) will be given in respect of such debt.

8.06 Judgments from Commonwealth countries (Australia, Canada, India, Pakistan), and Israel and Suriname, are enforced under the statutory registration schemes which mirror the common law rules (Administration of Justice Act 1920 and Foreign Judgments (Reciprocal Enforcement) Act 1933). The details of these enforcement regimes are set out extensively in leading practitioner titles.[6]

8.07 In what follows, this chapter examines the law of State immunities both at the level of assumption of jurisdiction and attachment of State property. The chapter also considers State immunity in respect of disclosure of information, interim measures, contempt of court, third-party debt orders and assets of State-owned enterprises. State immunity is of course a subject on its own and for a more extensive discussion of the subject the reader is referred to leading titles.[7] What this chapter attempts to do, however, is to

[4] Hayk Kupelyants, 'Recognition and Enforcement of Foreign Judgments in the Absence of the Debtor and his Assets within the Jurisdiction: Reversing the Burden of Proof' (forthcoming JPIL); Linda Silberman and Aaron Simowitz, 'Recognition and Enforcement of Foreign Judgments and Awards: What Hath *Daimler* Wrought?' (2016) 91 NYUL Rev 344.

[5] See, eg, in the US, 28 USCS §1609; *Aurelius Capital Partners Ltd v Republic of Argentina*, 584 F 3d 120, 130 (2d Cir 2009).

[6] Lord Collins of Mapesbury et al (eds), *Dicey, Morris & Collins on the Conflict of Laws*, vol 1 (2012) ch 14; Richard Fentiman, *International Commercial Litigation* (2015) ch 18.

[7] Hazel Fox and Philippa Webb, *The Law of State Immunity* (2015); Xiaodong Yang, *State Immunity in International Law* (2012); Andrew Dickinson, Rae Lindsay, and James Loonam, *State Immunity: Selected Materials and Commentary* (2004).

focus the discussion on financial litigation, in general, and on sovereign bond litigation, in particular.

II. IMMUNITY

State immunity is a cardinal principle of both public international law and municipal law. It insulates foreign States from the litigation in the domestic courts of another sovereign. The underlying rationale is that States are equal, and no State may sit in judgment of another State. In essence, State immunity is a procedural bar which helps determine whether or not the courts of one State may exercise jurisdiction in respect of another State and attach its assets. **8.08**

In so far as immunity is a procedural matter, issues of immunity are determined by the law as it stands at the time of court proceedings.[8] This has enormous importance for historic debts entered into in the era of absolute immunity but for which enforcement is sought in the modern times when the restrictive theory of immunity prevails. In other words, those debts would benefit from the more beneficial current regime of sovereign immunity. **8.09**

Rules of sovereign immunity act to prevent assumption of jurisdiction under the Brussels I Regulation. Tugendhat J in *Grovit v Netherlands De Nederlandsche Bank* held that the Brussels Regulation 'is to be read subject to the international law of state immunity, and not as precluding reliance upon state immunity'.[9] Article 71 of the Brussels Regulation preserves the application of conventions to which EU Members are party and this shall include the European Convention on State Immunity pursuant to which the UK State Immunity Act (SIA) was adopted.[10] **8.10**

In principle, State immunity is reserved to States and their various emanations (heads of the State, diplomatic missions, and so on). Separate State-owned entities do not in principle enjoy State immunity (s 14(1) of **8.11**

[8] *Republic of Austria v Altmann*, 541 US 677, 696 (2004); *Mortimer Off Shore Services Ltd v Germany*, 615 F 3d 97 (2d Cir 2010) (applying the commercial exception to acts taken in 1953, pre-dating the adoption of the FSIA); Trib de Grande Instance, *Association Fédérative Internationale des Porteurs d'Emprunts Russes v La Fédération de Russie*, 4 novembre 2015. See, however, *Carl Marks & Co v Union of Soviet Socialist Republics*, 665 F Supp 323 (SDNY 1987) (finding that the FSIA did not apply retrospectively to the Russian empire's debt).

[9] [2005] EWHC 2944 (QB), para 47.

[10] Adrian Briggs, *Civil Jurisdiction and Judgments* (2015) 389.

the SIA), unless they exercise sovereign authority (s 14(2) of the SIA).[11] The immunity of the Central Bank calls for different treatment and is addressed below.

8.12 Until recent times, State immunity has been absolute and there were no, or almost no, exceptions to the rule of State immunity.[12] However, over time, with the expansion of the cross-border activities of States, the absolute principle of State immunity has been tempered in the UK and the US. In 1976, the US adopted the Foreign Sovereign Immunities Act (FSIA) and two years later, in 1978, the UK adopted the SIA. Both statutes recognised a whole range of exceptions to the operation of the rule of State immunity. Satisfying any one of these exceptions is in principle sufficient to raise the procedural bar of State immunity and establish the jurisdiction of English courts over the foreign State. That said, there still remain jurisdictions which subscribe to the absolute immunity of States.[13]

8.13 At the outset, one needs to distinguish between two types of immunity: immunity from jurisdiction (adjudicative immunity) and immunity from enforcement. Immunity from jurisdiction establishes the immunity in respect of civil actions against the State in the courts of other States. By contrast, immunity from enforcement shields from attachment the assets of the State located outside its own territory. The extent of the two types of immunity varies and is treated below.

1. Adjudicative Immunity

8.14 The starting premise is that a claimant may not establish the jurisdiction of a national court against a sovereign State in the courts of a foreign State, unless it is able rely on one of the exceptions, set out under the national law of the forum. The exceptions to immunity from jurisdiction, relevant for our purposes, are:

- waiver/consent; and
- commercial transactions.

[11] See the discussion below.

[12] For a historical analysis in respect of public debt, see Edwin Borchard, *State Insolvency and Foreign Bondholders* (1951) 162–71.

[13] Hong Kong being one of them—*Democratic Republic of the Congo v FG Hemisphere Associates LLC*, FACV 5-7/2010 (2010).

Waiver/Consent

It is well established that the State waives[14] its immunity from jurisdiction by consenting to the jurisdiction of a foreign court or taking steps inconsistent with the availability of State immunity.[15] Section 2 of the SIA recognises four ways in which a State may waive its immunity before the English courts: **8.15**

(i) by submission after the dispute (s 2(1));[16]
(ii) by prior written agreement (s 2(2));
(iii) by institution of proceedings (s 2(3));
(iv) by intervening or taking any step in the proceedings other than to claim immunity or assert an interest in property in certain cases (s 2(4)).

The most common form of waiver is through a choice of court agreement. By contrast, the choice of English law is not to be regarded as a waiver of sovereign immunity.[17] As a matter of contractual construction, an agreement to litigate in the courts of one jurisdiction does not imply waiver of immunity for the courts of another jurisdiction, including at the place of enforcement of an ensuing judgment.[18] It is not clear whether a nationalised entity would be considered to have waived sovereign immunity on the basis that its private predecessor has entered into a jurisdiction agreement prior to the nationalisation.[19] **8.16**

Section 2(7) stipulates that any person who has entered into a contract on behalf of and with the authority of a State shall be deemed to have authority to submit on its behalf in respect of proceedings arising out of the contract. This is designed to prevent any arguments of lack of authority to submit to the jurisdiction of English courts and waive immunity thereby. **8.17**

[14] On the intricacies of negotiating a waiver clause, see Lee Buchheit, 'How to Negotiate the Waiver of Immunities Clause' (1993) 12 IFLR 31.

[15] See to a similar extent §1605(a)(1) of the FSIA (explicit or implicit waiver).

[16] Compare with Art 26 of the Brussels Regulation which establishes the jurisdiction by submission.

[17] See, however, the position of the Court of Appeal for the Fifth Circuit in *Af-Cap Inc v Republic of Congo*, 462 F 3d 417, 426–27 (5th Cir 2006).

[18] *SI Group Consort Ltd v Ukraine*, 2017 US Dist LEXIS 12515 (SDNY 2017).

[19] *Fir Tree Capital Opportunity Master Fund v Anglo Irish Bank Corporation Limited*, 2011 US Dist LEXIS 136018, 31 (SDNY 2011) (holding that the nationalised bank was not bound by the waiver of immunity).

Commercial Transactions

8.18 Under English law, foreign States are not immune from jurisdiction for disputes arising out of the commercial transactions they have entered into. The rule, in s 3 of the SIA, draws a distinction between commercial transactions (not covered by immunity, immune-free) and non-commercial transactions which enjoy immunity from jurisdiction. Section 3 cements the distinction between immune-free and immune transactions in the following way:

(1) A State is not immune as respects proceedings relating to—
  i. a commercial transaction entered into by the State; or
  ii. an obligation of the State which by virtue of a contract (whether a commercial transaction or not) falls to be performed wholly or partly in the United Kingdom.

8.19 On proper construction, s 3(1)(a) applies even if there is no jurisdictional connection to the UK. If, for example, a commercial transaction has been entered into in another jurisdiction, the private claimant may rely on s 3(1)(a), assuming, of course, he is able to satisfy the otherwise applicable requirements of service out of the jurisdiction. This is different for s 3(1)(b) which requires the obligation to be performed (wholly or partly) in the United Kingdom.

8.20 Section 3(3) defines commercial transactions as:

(a) any contract for the supply of goods or services;
(b) any loan or other transaction for the provision of finance and any guarantee or indemnity in respect of any such transaction or of any other financial obligation; and
(c) any other transaction or activity (whether of a commercial, industrial, financial, professional or other similar character) into which a State enters or in which it engages otherwise than in the exercise of sovereign authority.

8.21 Under this definition, sovereign bonds fall within subparagraph (b) ('loans or other transaction for the provision of finance'). Subparagraph (c) is a catch-all provision capable of encompassing any type of non-sovereign transaction activity. It seems to be established that subparagraph (c) covers both contractual claims and non-contractual claims so long as they are commercial. So, for instance, the tort of misrepresentation in a commercial context will be caught by paragraph (c). By contrast, the provision of concessions for oil and gas fields is likely to be an exercise of sovereign authority.[20]

[20] *Pearl Petroleum Company Limited v The Kurdistan Regional Government of Iraq* [2015] EWHC 3361 (Comm), para 36; *Svenska Petroleum Exploration AB v Government of the Republic of Lithuania, AB Geonafta* [2006] EWCA Civ 1529, para 133.

The commercial transactions exception is given an increasingly broad scope of application. First, Lord Diplock in *Alcom Ltd v Republic of Colombia* considered that the proviso 'otherwise than in the exercise of sovereign authority' in 3(3)(c) does not apply to the two preceding subparagraphs (a) and (b).[21] This means that contracts for the supply of goods or services and loan contracts are properly characterised as commercial transactions even if entered into in the exercise of sovereign authority.[22] In *Orascom v Chad*, discussed below, a World Bank loan was treated as commercial since, per Lord Diplock in *Alcom*, a loan is commercial, whether or not entered into in the exercise of governmental authority.[23] **8.22**

More generally, it is now commonly recognised that it is the nature of the contract that determines the character of the transaction and not its purpose.[24] So, if for instance, the State has entered into a contract for the purchase of army boots, or cement for the construction of barracks, the purpose of the transaction is public—to supply boots to the army and construct barracks. However, the public purpose is irrelevant in determining immunity of the State: what matters is that the contract for sale is by its nature a commercial transaction, even if the boots are to be used for public purposes.[25] What will be decisive is the character of the transaction. Thus, in *In re Banco Nacional De Cuba*,[26] the transfer of shares for the purpose of a bank reorganisation was held to be commercial in spite of its public purpose and context. **8.23**

Second, the courts have established the principle 'once commercial, always commercial'. This means that if the transaction was commercial at the moment it was entered into, the State's intervention on public grounds or of public character at a later stage will not necessarily modify the commercial character of the transaction.[27] In *I Congreso del Partido*, companies owned by the Republic of Cuba entered into a contract of sale of sugar with a Chilean company. In the course of performance of the contract, the government in Chile was overthrown, and Cuba, unwilling to engage with the new government in Chile, ordered the two vessels which were delivering/unloading the sugar in Chile to return. The intervention of the Cuban government for political reasons raised the question of whether the commercial exception could still be used. The majority decided that an originally commercial transaction remained commercial in character **8.24**

[21] *Alcom Ltd v Republic of Colombia* [1984] 1 AC 580, 586–87.
[22] See also *Orascom Telecom Holdings v Chad* [2008] EWHC 1841 (Comm), para 14.
[23] Ibid. [24] *I Congreso del Partido* [1981] 2 All ER 1064, 1072.
[25] *Trendtex Trading Corpo v Central Bank of Nigeria* [1977] 1 QB 529, 558.
[26] [2001] 1 WLR 2039, para 28.
[27] *I Congreso del Partido* [1981] 2 All ER 1064, 1073.

even if it was terminated for political reasons because the acts complained of—the return of the vessels from Chile—were effected under private law.

8.25 Lord Wilberforce, however, expressed a word of caution against oversimplification. He considered that whether an act is commercial or not will be determined by assessing the whole context and determining what the relevant acts are upon which the claim is based:

> Essentially it amounts to an assertion 'once a trader always a trader'. But this may be an over-simplification. If a trader is always a trader, a state remains a state and is capable at any time of acts of sovereignty. The question arises, therefore, what is the position where the act upon which the claim is founded is quite outside the commercial, or private law, activity in which the state has engaged, and has the character of an act done *jure imperii*. The 'restrictive' theory does not and could not deny capability of a state to resort to sovereign or governmental action: it merely asserts that acts done within the trading or commercial activity are not immune. The inquiry still has to be made whether they were within or outside that activity.... The conclusion which emerges is that in considering, under the 'restrictive' theory whether state immunity should be granted or not, the court must consider the whole context in which the claim against the state is made, with a view to deciding whether the relevant act(s) upon which the claim is based, should, in that context, be considered as fairly within an area of activity, trading or commercial, or otherwise of a private law character, in which the state has chosen to engage, or whether the relevant act(s) should be considered as having been done outside that area, and within the sphere of governmental or sovereign activity.[28]

8.26 The principle 'once commercial, always commercial' was not uniformly applied in sovereign debt disputes. While it is beyond doubt that sovereign bonds are commercial in nature,[29] a number of jurisdictions have found that in the course of sovereign debt restructurings, sovereign bonds metamorphose into public acts. Thus, the Italian Supreme Court in one of the numerous iterations of the Argentine saga held that the Argentine State, in, among other things, declaring a moratorium, had acted in its public capacity and therefore it enjoyed immunity in respect of an otherwise commercial loan agreement.[30] Similarly, the German Federal Supreme Court held that Greece enjoyed immunity in a claim for compensation brought by private creditors for the conversion of bonds following the introduction of CACs. The court considered that the modification of the rights of bondholders by virtue of a legislative amendment is a sovereign measure

[28] Ibid 1071–74. [29] See Chapter 1.

[30] Corte di Cassazione, 27 May 2005, decision No 11225, (2005) RDIPP 1091. See also the decision of Spanish courts (Auto de la Audicencia Provincial de Madrid, Sección 18a, núm 192/2007, de 19 septiembre 2007). For criticism, see Beatrice Bonafé, 'State Immunity and the Protection of Private Investors: The *Argentine Bonds* Case before Italian Courts' (2006) 16 IYBIL 165, 170–76.

which attracts immunity before German courts.[31] The Austrian Supreme Court held that the action to challenge the lawfulness of the State's legislation is covered by immunity, however the claim for contractual repayment can proceed and will not engage the protection of immunity.[32]

As per Lord Wilberforce's statement in *I Congreso del Partido*, the court has to identify the act upon which the claim is based. In many Argentine cases, the claim of bondholders was for repayment under the bonds. Since the bonds were often governed by some foreign law (English or New York laws), the Argentine declaration of moratorium was inapplicable and the creditor did not need to challenge it separately. **8.27**

However, in cases where the bonds are governed by the local law of the sovereign debtor, the creditor may need to challenge the legislative acts of the debtor, as was indeed the case before the German courts above. In such circumstances, the only act upon which the claim is based may be a public act, in which case the State may regain immunity from jurisdiction. However, even in such a situation, the claims may be structured in a manner where the overall context indicates that the act upon which the claim is based is a commercial transaction. Chapter 5 examined the defence of public policy to unilateral modifications of bonds. In such a case, the act upon which the claim is based is the default of the State and the private creditor is raising public policy as a defence against unilateral modifications. It is at least arguable that in such an instance, the whole context would be commercial, notwithstanding the public overtones of the public policy defence. **8.28**

The reverse metamorphosis is possible, too. The House of Lords decided that immunity conferred by reason of the governmental nature of the initial seizure of another State's property may disappear where the subsequent retention and use of the unlawfully obtained property was commercial in nature.[33] By contrast, the Second Circuit added a caveat: to satisfy the 'commercial activity' exception, the subsequent commercial treatment of expropriated property ought not to be sufficiently 'in connection with' the prior expropriation.[34] **8.29**

Section 3(2) provides that: **8.30**

This section does not apply if the parties to the dispute are States or have otherwise agreed in writing; and subsection (1)(b) above does not apply if the contract

[31] Case VI ZR 516/14, Judgment of 8 March 2016.

[32] Austrian Oberste Gerichtshof, 4Ob227/13f, 20.05.2014.

[33] *Kuwait Airways Corporation v Iraqi Airways Co* [1995] 1 WLR 1147, 1163.

[34] *Garb v Republic of Poland*, 440 F 3d 579, 598 (2d Cir 2006). See *Republic of Austria v Altmann*, 541 US 677, 706–07 (2004) (finding that the activity was commercial).

(not being a commercial transaction) was made in the territory of the State concerned and the obligation in question is governed by its administrative law.

8.31 In *Cardinal Financial Investment Corporation v Central Bank of Yemen*,[35] the interpretation of the first part of s 3(2) was at issue. The promissory notes at hand were originally issued by what later became the Central Bank of Yemen and were payable to Czechoslovakia. These promissory notes were in reality a method of payment between Czechoslovakia and what later became the Republic of Yemen. The Czech Republic later assigned the promissory notes to Cardinal, which sought recovery in the English courts.

8.32 The counsel for the Central Bank of Yemen sought reliance on s 3(2) claiming that the original transaction was made between two States, whereby the Republic of Yemen was liable as a principal on the notes. Further, the counsel for the Central Bank submitted that pursuant to s 14 of the SIA the Bank of Yemen was entitled to immunity under s 3 given that it had acted in the exercise of sovereign authority. Longmore J rejected these contentions. First, he held that a promissory note takes effect as a contract between the payee or the endorsee or the holder, as the case might be, and the maker of the note. And on the facts the maker of the promissory notes, the Central Bank of Yemen, was not a State. Of course, it could benefit from immunity if it exercised sovereign authority pursuant to s 14, but Longmore J considered that the issuance of promissory notes was not an exercise of governmental authority. Second, he ruled that s 3(2) is engaged if the parties to the dispute are States, irrespective of the parties to the original transaction. In other words, by assigning the debt to a private person, the parties may circumvent the application of s 3(2).[36]

8.33 The law of the United States, too, recognises the commercial activity exception (§1605(a)(2) of the FSIA). Section 1603(d) of the FSIA stipulates that the commercial character of an activity shall be determined by reference to the nature of the course of conduct or particular transaction or act, rather than by reference to its purpose. The Supreme Court in *Weltover v Republic of Argentina* has unambiguously established that the issuance of sovereign bonds was a commercial activity, even if the bonds were issued to assuage a domestic financial crisis. In a different context, the Second Circuit ruled that Germany's assumption of responsibility for the bonds of Prussian private banks, pursuant to a statute and a treaty, was a commercial act for the

[35] 2000 WL 699384.

[36] The Court of Appeal affirmed the reasoning in *Central Bank of Yemen v Cardinal Financial Investments Corporation* [2001] Lloyd's Rep 1.

purposes of sovereign immunity. However, the automatic assumption of responsibility upon State succession will not constitute a commercial act for the purposes of §1605(a)(2).[37]

Claimants in *EM Ltd v Republic of Argentina* claimed that Banco Central de la República Argentina (BCRA) engaged in commercial activity in the United States. Claimants relied on the following activities to establish the commercial character of BCRA's activities: loans made by BCRA to Argentina, coordination of monetary policy, the appointment and removal of BCRA governors. The Second Circuit found that none of these actions were commercial activities that occurred in the United States.[38] **8.34**

2. Enforcement Immunity

Once the private creditor obtains a judgment against the State, the next hurdle is to overcome immunity from enforcement. As the discussion below will demonstrate, immunity from enforcement is in principle more extensive than immunity from jurisdiction. The reason is that immunity from enforcement seeks to shield State-owned property from attachments. **8.35**

Section 13 of the SIA lists comprehensively all measures of constraint likely to be invoked against a State and shields the State from them subject to two exceptions: **8.36**

- prior written consent of the State (ie, waiver); or
- measures taken in respect of property in use or intended for use for commercial purposes.

In the US, the property of a foreign State can be attached if it is used for a commercial activity at the time of attachment, even if the State has waived its immunity (§1610(a) of the FSIA).[39] In other words, a waiver of immunity is not sufficient in itself—the property has to be in use for commercial purposes. By contrast, under the SIA, English courts may attach State property on the ground that the State waived its immunity, even if the property is not used for commercial purposes (with some exceptions). **8.37**

As an ad hoc exception, Buchheit, Gulati, and Tirado suggest immunising all the property which belongs to a eurozone State involved in sovereign debt restructurings, with the overall aim of reducing the incentives **8.38**

[37] *Mortimer Off Shore Services Ltd v Germany*, 615 F 3d 97 (2d Cir 2010).

[38] 800 F 3d 78, 97 (2d Cir 2015).

[39] *Aurelius Capital Partners v Republic of Argentina*, 584 F 3d 120, 129–30 (2d Cir 2009); *LNC Investments INC v Republic of Nicaragua*, 2000 US Dist LEXIS 7814 (SDNY 2000).

for active holdout litigation.[40] A number of points need to be raised in this respect. First, the drafters of such legislation need to be wary of infringing Art 6 of the European Convention on Human Rights, namely the right to a fair trial,[41] and Art 1 Protocol 1, namely the right to property. Second, curtailing the rights of creditors in this manner will expose them to the almost unrestricted powers of a sovereign.

Waiver

8.39 As a matter of principle, the waiver of immunity from jurisdiction or a submission to the jurisdiction of the English courts is not sufficient to waive immunity from enforcement (s 13(2) of the SIA). Further, in *Orascom v Chad*, Burton J was unconvinced that by consenting to ICC arbitration, including Art 28(6) of the ICC Arbitration Rules which requires the parties to comply with awards and waive the right to any form of recourse, the State has waived its immunity from execution.[42]

8.40 A more specific wording is necessary to that effect. The court in *A Company v Republic of X* construed a general waiver contained in a commercial contract as extending not only to the jurisdiction from immunity but also to enforcement.[43] Although this decision has been criticised as overly liberal and blurring the SIA's requirement that waiver should be separately given in respect of both jurisdiction and enforcement,[44] it should be noted that the reference to property in the immunity waiver clause was an indication of the intent of the parties to extend the waiver to enforcement.

8.41 The waiver clause may waive immunity from execution if the language of the waiver clause is sufficiently specific. Thus, Czech bonds waive not only immunity from jurisdiction but from execution, too:

> To the extent that the Issuer or any of its revenues, assets or properties shall be entitled to any immunity from suit, from the jurisdiction of any such court, from

[40] Lee Buchheit, Mitu Gulati, and Ignacio Tirado, 'The Problem of Holdout Creditors in Eurozone Sovereign Debt Restructurings' (2013) 4 JIBFL 191, 193

[41] For the possibility of breaching Art 6 by extensive rules of sovereign immunity, see *Oleynikov v Russia* (Appl No 36703/04) ECtHR 9 September 2013; *Benkharbouche v Embassy of Sudan* [2015] EWCA Civ 33; *Cudak v Lithuania* (Appl No 15869/02) 23 March 2010. See also *Pringle*, Case C-370/12, EU:C:2012:756 (for the liability of EU institutions for infringing human rights).

[42] *Orascom Telecom Holdings v Chad* [2008] EWHC 1841 (Comm).

[43] *A Company v Republic of X* [1990] 2 Lloyd's Rep 520 (the waiver clause read: 'The Ministry of Finance hereby waives whatever defence it may have of sovereign immunity for itself or its property (present or subsequently acquired)').

[44] Fox and Webb (n 7) 189.

set-off, from attachment prior to judgment, from attachment in aid of execution of judgment, from execution of a judgment or from any other legal or judicial process or remedy, and to the extent that in any such jurisdiction there shall be attributed such an immunity, the Issuer irrevocably waives such immunity to the fullest extent permitted by the laws of such jurisdiction.... The Issuer does not waive any immunity in respect of property which is ambassadorial, consular or defence real property or buildings or the contents thereof, in each case situated outside the Czech Republic.[45]

The Estonian sovereign bonds contain an even wider waiver of immunity, both from jurisdiction and execution: **8.42**

The Issuer hereby irrevocably and unconditionally waives and agrees not to raise ... any right to claim sovereign, diplomatic, or other immunity from jurisdiction or execution and any similar defense, and irrevocably and unconditionally consents to the giving of any relief or the issue of any process, *including, without limitation, the making, enforcement or execution against any property whatsoever (irrespective of its use or intended use)*.[46]

Immunity waivers will in some cases clarify that the waiving of immunity from attachment does not apply in the territory of the sovereign debtor. Thus, the Chilean bonds provide that: **8.43**

Chile will not waive immunity from attachment prior to judgment and attachment in aid of execution under Chilean law with respect to property of Chile located in Chile.[47]

Commercial Use

Section 13(4) of the SIA provides for the second exception to immunity from enforcement: the property of the State in use or intended use for commercial purposes will be non-immune. The private creditor may attach State property which is in use or intended use for commercial purposes. Such property is the main target of attempts to enforce judgments against foreign States, especially given that the SIA does not require that the property to be attached be connected in any way with the subject matter of the claim. **8.44**

Section 17(1) defines commercial purposes through the medium of s 3(3): '"commercial purposes" means purposes of such transactions or **8.45**

[45] Czech Republic, Offering Circular, Euro Medium Term Note Programme, 2 September 2010, p 46.

[46] Republic of Estonia, Offering Circular, 25 June 2002, 5% Notes due in 2007, cited in Mark Weidemaier, 'Disputing Boilerplate' (2009–10) 82 Temp L Rev 1, 36 (emphasis added).

[47] Republic of Chile, Prospectus, Debt Securities and Warranties, 24 September 2012.

activities as are mentioned in section 3(3) above'. However, it is now established that the test of 'use or intended use for commercial purposes' used for immunity from enforcement is a narrower concept than the equivalent test for immunity from adjudication. In *Rafidain*, the Supreme Court held that the origin of assets is irrelevant, what is relevant is their use. Lord Clarke clarified:

> The language of section 13(4) is to be contrasted with other parts of the Act. It is, for example, to be contrasted with section 3(1), which refers to proceedings 'relating to' a commercial transaction, and section 10, which refers to claims 'in connection with' a ship. In enacting section 13(4), Parliament could have referred to property that 'related to' a commercial transaction, or arose 'in connection with' a commercial transaction as being susceptible to enforcement. It chose not to do so, which suggests that it intended a difference in meaning. Property will only be subject to enforcement where it can be established that it is currently 'in use or intended for use' for a commercial transaction.[48]

8.46 On the facts, Iraq's money was to be transferred to the development fund of Iraq and was therefore non-commercial even though it originated from a commercial transaction.[49] In a similar vein, the District Court held that how the funds came into existence was immaterial,[50] what mattered was how the sovereign 'spends' the money.[51] In other words, the destination/purpose of payment is decisive.

8.47 In some cases, establishing the use of assets may not raise many difficulties. Thus, payments to a third party under a commercial contract will constitute commercial use of the property. By contradistinction, payment of taxes or funds into development initiatives will not qualify as commercial. Many other instances will require a more careful enquiry. Thus, in *LR Avionics Technologies Ltd v Nigeria*, the court held that the lease of State-owned premises to a private party for the outsourcing of consular services was not use of property for commercial purposes. The court found that while the contract for the provision of outsourcing might fall within the definition of commercial transactions under s 3(3), the use of such premises was clearly not commercial. The rent of consular premises in *Avionics* was not for a commercial transaction since the property was being used to provide a public function—consular services. Instead of providing the consular services itself, the Nigerian High Commission has chosen to outsource this task.[52]

[48] *SerVaas v Rafidian Bank* [2012] UKSC 40, para 17. [49] Ibid.

[50] *Export–Import Bank of China v Grenada*, 2012 US Dist LEXIS 87079 (SDNY 2012).

[51] *Connecticut v Congo*, 309 F 3d 240, 251 (5th Cir 2002).

[52] *LR Avionics Technologies Ltd v Nigeria* [2016] EWHC 1761 (Comm), para 40.

In *AIG Capital Partners Inc v Republic of Kazakhstan*,[53] the cash and securities of the National Fund of the Republic of Kazakhstan were located in London. Aikens J upheld the sovereign character of the account. He considered that even though the securities were actively traded in London, the aim of the investments was to enhance the value of the Kazakh national fund which was being used to manage Kazakhstan's economy. The trading of funds in *AIG* was necessary to ensure high profitability levels for the funds. The management of the national economy clearly qualified as a sovereign activity. **8.48**

An outlier is the decision in *Orascom v Chad*. There, the Republic of Chad held a bank account in London for two purposes: (a) to receive the proceeds of oil contracts; and (b) to repay World Bank loans. The repayment of World Bank loans was held to be a commercial transaction. Burton J relied on the pronouncement of Lord Diplock in *Amcom Ltd v Republic of Colombia* who drew a distinction between s 3(3)(a)–(b) (contracts for the provision of goods and services and provision of loans and other finance) and s(3)(3)(c) ('any other transaction into which a State enters otherwise than in the exercise of sovereign authority'). The absence of the reference to 'otherwise than in the exercise of sovereign authority' in subparagraphs (a) and (b) meant that those contracts would qualify as commercial transactions, *even* if they are entered into by the State in the exercise of sovereign authority. On this basis, the judge concluded that the payment of loans by the State was commercial within the meaning of s 3(3)(b) even if entered into in the exercise of sovereign authority. The counter-intuitive result was that the bank account used for repayment of what was clearly a public loan was characterised as a commercial transaction and could therefore be attached in England.[54] In clear opposition to this result, the Second Circuit held that repayment of funds to the IMF was not a commercial activity.[55] **8.49**

It is difficult to reconcile the holding in *Orascom* with the line of cases including *Avionics* and *AIG*. In these latter cases, when deciding whether the property was in use for commercial reasons, the courts did not stop at s 3(3). Having determined the commercial character of such transactions, they further enquired into the purpose of the transactions. In *Avionics*, a contract for the provision of services, clearly a commercial transaction within the meaning of s 3(3)(a), was held to be sovereign because of the **8.50**

[53] [2006] 1 WLR 1420.

[54] *Orascom Telecom Holdings v Chad* [2008] EWHC 1841 (Comm). Burton J also seems to have accepted the proposition that the provision of finance within s 3(3)(b) may be both *by* the State and *to* the State.

[55] *EM Ltd v Republic of Argentina*, 473 F.3d 463, 480 (2d Cir 2007).

purpose pursued by the transaction. In *AIG*, the national fund was used to foster Kazakhstan's national economy. By contrast, Burton J in *Orascom* considered that satisfying s 3(3) was 'sufficient' under s 13.[56]

8.51 The unease associated with *Orascom* is that the loans were repaid to an international institution. Burton J sought to distinguish *AIG* on the ground that the monies in the bank account did not belong to the national fund of Chad, but instead were channelled directly to London for direct payment to the World Bank.[57] It is unclear why this mechanism of payment changed the fact the money was paid to an international institution.

8.52 In practice, to establish that a bank account is in use for commercial purposes, the judgment creditor will need to show that 'the bank account was earmarked by the foreign state solely (save for *de minimis* exceptions) for being drawn upon to settle liabilities incurred in commercial transactions'[58] or that the funds from the bank account were recently used in commercial dealings.[59] The SIA establishes a mechanism for determining the commercial use of a bank account: under s 13(5), the head of a State's diplomatic mission in the United Kingdom will issue a certificate to the effect that the property at stake is not in use or intended for use by or on behalf of the State for commercial purposes and that certificate shall be accepted as sufficient evidence of that fact unless the contrary is proved. This establishes a rebuttable presumption that the certificate of the head of a State's diplomatic mission is correct unless proven otherwise and places the burden of proof on the applicant to establish the commercial use of the property sought to be attached. Discharging this burden will be an uphill struggle, since the head of a State's diplomatic mission is shielded from cross-examination by virtue of his diplomatic immunity.[60]

8.53 How can this presumption be rebutted? In *AIC v Nigeria*,[61] Burnton J noted that the evidence of recent use of an account wholly for commercial purposes over a significant period of time may lead to the conclusion that the account is used or intended for use wholly for commercial purposes;[62] but the older the use in evidence, the weaker the inference that may be drawn as to the use or intended use of the account. According to the ambassador's certificate, the relevant bank account had been dormant

56 *Orascom Telecom Holdings v Chad* [2008] EWHC 1841 (Comm), para 24.

57 Ibid para 20.

58 *Alcom Ltd v Republic of Colombia* [1984] 1 AC 580, 604.

59 *AIC Ltd v Federal Government of Nigeria* [2003] EWHC 1357 (QB), paras 56, 58, 59.

60 Fox and Webb (n 7) 216.

61 *AIC Ltd v Federal Government of Nigeria* (n 60) paras 56, 58, 59.

62 This statement may not sit comfortably with the holding of the House of Lords in *Alcom Ltd v Republic of Colombia* [1984] 1 AC 580, 604, whereby only property specifically earmarked for present or future commercial use can be attached.

for at least eighteen months. Given the period of dormancy, Burnton J held that it could not be said that the account was used for commercial purposes. In a similar vein, the US courts hold that the property 'must' be used for commercial purposes, and not merely capable of being used for commercial reasons, [63] or, at least, it should specifically be designated for commercial use.[64]

What happens to mixed bank accounts, used for commercial and public purposes alike? The House of Lords in *Alcom v Republic of Colombia* declared that the current account of a foreign diplomatic mission was not susceptible to anticipatory dissection into the various uses, commercial as well as sovereign.[65] As a result, in a symbiosis of various purposes of the same bank account, the assets in public use would prevail and determine the nature of the bank account, with the result that the parts of the bank account used for commercial use could not be attached. US courts reached broadly similar results.[66] **8.54**

In the United States, the property in commercial use enjoys a stronger protection. To attach property, under §1610(a), the claimant needs to establish two separate elements: first, that the property is used for a commercial activity in the United States, *and*, second, a waiver of immunity *or* that the property upon which the claim is based is or was used for commercial activity.[67] By contrast, under the SIA, establishing the commercial use of property is sufficient on its own. **8.55**

The property of diplomatic representations, including their bank accounts, has a special status in international (and English) law. Such property is governed by the Vienna Convention on Diplomatic Relations, 1961,[68] Arts **8.56**

[63] *Export–Import Bank of China v Grenada* (n 51) and the cases discussed therein.

[64] *EM Ltd v Republic of Argentina* (n 56) 485.

[65] *Alcom v Republic of Colombia* (n 63).

[66] *Export–Import Bank of China v Grenada* (n 51).

[67] §1610 (a): 'The property in the United States of a foreign state, as defined in section 1603(a) of this chapter, used for a commercial activity in the United States, shall not be immune from attachment in aid of execution, or from execution, upon a judgment entered by a court of the United States or of a State after the effective date of this Act, if—

(1) the foreign state has waived its immunity from attachment in aid of execution or from execution either explicitly or by implication, notwithstanding any withdrawal of the waiver the foreign state may purport to effect except in accordance with the terms of the waiver, or
(2) the property is or was used for the commercial activity upon which the claim is based, or
(3) the execution relates to a judgment establishing rights in property which has been taken in violation of international law or which has been exchanged for property taken in violation of international law

[68] The Convention was given effect in the UK by the Diplomatic Privileges Act 1984.

31–32 and the Vienna Convention on Consular Relations, 1963, Arts 43–45.[69] It seems that a generic waiver of immunity from enforcement does not suffice to waive immunity in respect of the assets of a diplomatic or consular mission and an express (and special) waiver, mentioning the assets or the category of assets, is necessary for the purposes of enforcement.[70]

8.57 Given the specific nature of central banks, s 14(4) of the SIA provides heightened immunity from enforcement for the assets of central banks.[71] Central banks, which in many countries are a separate entity, unlike a State, enjoy complete immunity for their property located in the UK, even in respect of assets which are in use or intended for use for commercial purposes.[72] Of course, the Central Bank may engage in commercial transactions and those will not be shielded by immunity from jurisdiction,[73] but its assets are ring-fenced against enforcement. That is so even if the State has beneficial interest in the assets of the central bank.[74] The same regime is stipulated in the US (§1611(b)(1) of the FSIA).

8.58 The waiver of immunity given by the State does not affect the immunities of the central bank, since only a waiver from the central bank itself is capable of depriving the central bank from its immunity from enforcement.[75] By contrast, under §1611(b) of the FSIA, the parent foreign government of the central bank may waive the central bank's immunity from attachment in aid of execution, or from execution. However, such waiver does not establish the central bank's liability for the debts of the government.[76]

7. Enforcement of Foreign Judgments and Awards

8.59 The enforcement of judgments from a third country (country X) against State Y before the English courts is subject to a specific regime. The House of Lords in *NML v Argentina* addressed immunity from jurisdiction of a

[69] The Convention was given effect in the UK by the Consular Relations Act 1968.

[70] Cour de Cassation, La Société NML Capital c La République Argentine, Arrêt n° 394 du 28 mars 2013 (purporting to set out the position in international customary law).

[71] On the immunities of Central Banks, see Thomas Baxter and David Gross, 'Special Immunities: Central Bank Immunity' in Rosa Lastra and Lee Buchheit, *Sovereign Debt Management* (2014) 117. On the immunity of the Bank of International Settlements, see Diego Devos, 'Special Immunities: Bank of International Settlements' (ibid 127).

[72] *AIG Capital Partners Inc v Republic of Kazakhstan* [2006] 1 WLR 1420, paras 50–59.

[73] *Trendtex Trading Corpn v Central Bank of Nigeria* [1977] QB 529.

[74] *Thai-Lao Lignite (Thailand) Co Ltd v The Bank of the Lao People's Democratic Republic* [2013] EWHC 2466 (Comm), para 25.

[75] Ibid para 22.

[76] *LNC Investments INC v Republic of Nicaragua*, 115 F Supp 2d 358, 362–63 (SDNY 2000). On the liability of State entities for the debts of the government, see below.

State in an action to enforce a foreign (US) judgment in the UK.[77] NML first sought to argue that s 3(1) of the SIA engaged since the enforcement of a foreign judgment was an action 'relating to … a commercial transaction'. Undoubtedly, the sovereign debt dispute in the US courts related to a commercial transaction, namely a sovereign bond issuance. However, the majority (Lords Mance, Collins, and Walker) found that the action for enforcement of a judgment did not relate to a commercial transaction. Fox and Webb[78] argue that this pronouncement was overtaken by the decision of the International Court of Justice in the *Jurisdictional Immunities* case.[79]

However, the claimant prevailed on two further grounds. First, the court considered that s 31 of the Civil Jurisdiction and Judgments Act 1981 deprived Argentina of its adjudicatory immunity. Section 31 provides that a foreign judgment against a foreign State shall be recognised and enforced in the United Kingdom if: (a) it would be so recognised and enforced if it had not been given against a State; and (b) that court would have had jurisdiction in the matter if it had applied rules corresponding to those applicable to such matters in the United Kingdom in accordance with ss 2–11 of the SIA 1978. In other words, a judgment from a foreign country, in order to be enforceable, needs to comply with the rules on sovereign immunity as applied by English courts. And the court was convinced that an English court would have assumed jurisdiction since a sovereign debt dispute was clearly commercial. **8.60**

Second, the widely worded waiver of immunities sought to divest Argentina of immunity in respect of the enforcement of foreign judgments. The waiver of immunities clause provided that a judgment against Argentina 'may be enforced … in any … courts to the jurisdiction of which [it] may be subject' and this in the eyes of the House of Lords included the courts of the place of enforcement. **8.61**

In respect of proceedings to enforce arbitral awards, s 9 of the SIA provides that where a State has agreed to an arbitration agreement, it is not immune as respects proceedings in English courts which relate to the arbitration. The court in *Svenska* held that 'proceedings related to arbitration' include proceedings relating to the enforcement of a foreign arbitral award.[80] The same conclusion arises in the US under §1605(a)(6) of the FSIA.[81] That **8.62**

[77] *NML v Argentina* [2011] UKSC 31. [78] Fox and Webb (n 7) 223.

[79] *Jurisdictional Immunities of the State (Germany v Italy)*, ICJ, 3 February 2012.

[80] *Svenska Petroleum Exploration AB v Government of the Republic of Lithuania, AB Geonafta* [2006] EWCA Civ 1529, paras 117–23.

[81] *Blue Ridge Investments LLC v Republic of Argentina*, 735 F 3d 72, 83 (2d Cir 2013) (relying also on implied waiver by virtue of acceding to the ICSID Convention); *Diag Human v Czech Republic—Ministry of Health*, No 14-7142, 2016 US App LEXIS 9770 (DC Cir 2016).

said, prejudgment injunctive relief is not characterised as 'proceedings related to arbitration'.[82]

8. Immunity from Interim Measures

8.63 English courts enjoy wide-ranging powers to issue freezing injunctions in assistance of both English and foreign proceedings.[83] However, States enjoy heightened immunity from interim measures, including freezing orders. First, s 13(2)(a) of the SIA directly prohibits injunctions against States.[84] The implication is that, under s 13(2)(a), *in personam* interim remedies (freezing orders) are precluded.

8.64 Interim measures may only be granted with the consent of the sovereign (s 13(3) of the SIA): property in use for commercial purposes cannot be attached unless the State has agreed to an appropriately worded waiver.[85] The same regime applies in the US (§1610(d) of the FSIA).

8.65 The waiver has expressly to target interim measures and a generic waiver of immunity from jurisdiction is not sufficient to waive immunity from interim measures (s 13(3)). English courts have commonly understood that a reference in the waiver to 'assets' or 'property' is sufficient to imply consent to injunctive relief.[86]

9. Disclosure of Information

8.66 The order for disclosure of information, the ally of freezing orders, is also subject to the rules of State immunity. Section 13(1) of the SIA provides that no penalty by way of committal or fine shall be imposed in respect of any failure or refusal by or on behalf of a State to disclose or produce any document or other information for the purposes of proceedings to which it is a party. That said, the court is not precluded from drawing an adverse inference from the State's failure to comply with a request for discovery in proceedings.[87]

[82] *ETI Euro Telecom International NV v Republic of Bolivia* [2008] EWCA Civ 880, para 113.

[83] Fentiman (n 6) ch 17.

[84] A procedural order requesting payment of security for adjournment of enforcement proceedings does not constitute an injunction within the meaning of s13(2) (*Soleh Boneh International Limited v Government of the Republic of Uganda* [1993] 2 Lloyd's Law Rep 208).

[85] Fox and Webb (n 7) 215.

[86] *A Company v Republic of* X [1990] 2 Lloyd's Rep 520, 523 (in respect of a freezing injunction); *Sabah v Pakistan* [2002] EWCA Civ 1643 (in respect of an anti-suit injunction); *Pearl Petroleum Company Limited v The Kurdistan Regional Government of Iraq* [2015] EWHC 3361 (Comm), para 44 (in respect of an order to resume payments under the contract).

[87] Fox and Webb (n 7) 213.

In one of the many iterations of the NML saga, NML requested a post-judgment discovery order against two banks that had no claim to sovereign immunity. The Second Circuit upheld the orders of disclosures on the basis that, first, sovereign immunity did not apply to third parties that had no claim to sovereign immunity and, second, the order only sought discovery and no attachment.[88] The argument before the Supreme Court concentrated on the latter point, namely the existence of a separate 'discovery immunity' of the State. Adopting a textual interpretation of the FSIA, the Supreme Court put immunity from discovery to bed since no provision in the FSIA acted to forbid or limit discovery. This was so even if the order of discovery was extraterritorial, namely the order sought to identify the whereabouts of Argentina's assets both inside and outside the United States.[89] This decision provides an invaluable asset to bondholders who may seek discovery of the State's assets located outside the United States. **8.67**

10. Contempt of Court

The customary relief for the failure to comply with an interim measure, a disclosure order, or indeed a third-party debt order is the much-feared contempt of court order. However, the contempt of court is likely to be incompatible with the general prohibition of injunctions or orders of specific performance (s 13(2)(a)).[90] For one, it is a criminal sanction that may not be enforced against a foreign sovereign. **8.68**

The US courts have been more open to finding a State in contempt of court. The usual remedy would be the imposition of a monetary fine against the sovereign in contempt of court.[91] The US court in *Hemisphere* held Congo in contempt of court for disobeying a discovery order on the ground that 'there is not a smidgen of indication in the text of the FSIA that Congress intended to limit a federal court's inherent contempt power'.[92] In *Export–Import Bank of the Republic of China v Grenada*,[93] the claimant requested contempt sanctions of $10,000 per day based on Grenada's alleged failure to comply with a court order requiring post-judgment discovery. Grenada sought to resist the contempt sanction on a number of grounds, **8.69**

[88] *EM Ltd v Republic of Argentina*, No 11-4065-cv(L) (2d Cir 2012).

[89] *NML Capital Ltd v Republic of Argentina*, 134 S Ct 2250 (2014).

[90] Fox and Webb (n 7) 213–15.

[91] For examples, see Mark Weidemaier and Anna Gelpern, 'Injunctions in Sovereign Debt Litigation' (2014) 1 Y J on Reg 189, 205, fn 87. See also *Agudas Chasidei Chabad of US v Russian Federation*, 915 F Supp 2d 148 (DDC 2013).

[92] *FG Hemisphere v Congo*, 637 F 3d 373, 378 (DC Cir 2011).

[93] 2010 US Dist LEXIS 137310.

including the allegation that the principle of comity required a balancing of interests and respect of Grenada's laws in compliance with the interests of the US. The argument was rebuffed by the court which held that the United States had an interest in providing a neutral forum for resolution of the dispute between the Export–Import Bank of China and the nation of Grenada, even more so when the parties agreed to the jurisdiction of US courts. Furthermore, the court stated that US policy supported foreign and domestic creditors who sought to enforce sovereign debt when the payment would be made in the United States. By contrast, the US Court of Appeals for the Fifth Circuit held that the FSIA does not contemplate the possibility of contempt of court.[94]

8.70 In the *NML* saga, Judge Griesa was initially reluctant to issue an order of contempt of court,[95] but his position changed when Argentina sought to displace the then current trustee and change the location of payments to Argentina, with a clear intention of avoiding the obligations imposed by the *pari passu* injunction issued by the court. On this ground, Judge Griesa found Argentina in civil contempt for the failure to comply with the *pari passu* clause. Judge Griesa also extended the contempt of court sanction to third parties assisting the State with the breach of interim measures.[96]

8.71 However, pragmatically, the enforcement of a contempt of court order against a State is not without its difficulties in so far as most assets of the State will be shielded by immunities. Nonetheless, the fear of contempt of court will have a strong impact on any third party involved in the exchange or payment mechanisms and may thus deter the conduct of the State in breach of court orders. As a matter of last resort, upon refusal to comply with a disclosure order, the District Court in *NML v Argentina* ordered that 'any property of the Republic of Argentina in the United States except diplomatic or military property is deemed to be used for commercial activity'.[97]

11. Third-Party Debt Orders and Receivership Orders

8.72 Third-party debt orders have become increasingly popular in sovereign debt litigation. As a further weapon in their arsenal of enforcement mechanisms, the bondholders may seek enforcement against a third party who

[94] *Af-Cap Inc v Republic of Congo*, 462 F 3d 417, 428–29 (5th Cir 2006).

[95] For earlier attempts to obtain a contempt of court order, see *Aurelius Capital Partners v Republic of Argentina*, 379 Fed Appx 74 (2d Cir 2010) (vacating contempt sanctions).

[96] *NML Capital Ltd v Republic of Argentina*, 08 Civ 06978 (TPG) (SDNY 2016), affd *Aurelius Capital Ltd v Republic of Argentina*, Case 16-628 (2d Cir 2016).

[97] *NML Capital Ltd v Republic of Argentina*, Case No 08-cv-6978 (SDNY 2015).

owes money to the sovereign debtor by requiring the third party to pay the bondholder directly. By that, the creditor avoids an unnecessary link in the chain of payments and receives the payment from a third-party debtor of the State, and not from a possibly reluctant State.[98] The starting point here is that the contractual right to a debt is a kind of property and therefore a creditor may in principle require the creditors of the State to pay the private creditor directly. As for the third party, the payment to the creditor is a valid discharge of its obligations. Additionally, the third-party debt order may be drafted so as to prohibit the third party from paying and trading with the debtor.[99]

In England, this is achieved through third-party debt orders under CPR Part 72 (previously known as garnishee orders), whereas in New York it is achieved by a garnishment writ or a turnover order under New York Civil Practice Law and Rules §5225(b). Under English law, the third-party debt order is an *in rem* remedy, and it creates an equitable charge over the debt.[100] In the litigation against sovereign debtors, the debt is attached on a 'first come, first served' basis, without regard to apportionment or *pari passu* treatment of creditors.[101] **8.73**

Often, an obligation to transfer money to the State may arise not under a contract but pursuant to a statutory authority or discretion. Thus, in *Camdex v Bank of Zambia*, a Zambian company was required to transfer a portion of its foreign exchange under the directions of the Central Bank of Zambia. As a preliminary issue, reversing the decision of the first instance judge who relied on the views of FA Mann, the Court of Appeal confirmed that payment of money under a foreign exchange contract does indeed give rise to debt (and not damages). As a result, the Court of Appeal ruled that the payment under foreign exchange transactions might in principle be the object of a third-party debt order. However, the Court of Appeal ruled that on the facts before it, the obligation to transfer money under the foreign exchange regulations was not enforceable by way of what is now a third-party debt order. The arrangement at hand between the Central Bank of Zambia and the Zambian company was not a contract and it did not establish a civil cause of action. Further, English courts do not enforce foreign public laws, including foreign exchange regulations.[102] **8.74**

[98] The Court of Appeal held that a paying agent under the bonds did not owe any monies to the State under the rather commonplace contractual documentation (*Merchant International Company Ltd v Natsionalna Aktsionerna Kompaniia Naftogaz Ukrainy* [2014] EWCA Civ 1603).

[99] *Kensington International Ltd v Republic of Congo* [2007] EWCA Civ 1128, paras 24–25.

[100] *F.G. Hemisphere Associates LLC v Republic of Congo* [2005] EWHC 3103 (Comm), para 12.

[101] Ibid.

[102] *Camdex International Ltd v Bank of Zambia, Zambia Consolidated Copper Mines Limited* [1997] EWCA Civ 798.

8.75 Even if the debt is capable of being subject to a third-party debt order, the court needs to be convinced that it has jurisdiction to do so. The House of Lords in *Société Eram Shipping Co Ltd v Cie Internationale de Navigation*[103] held that an English court could not issue what is now a third-party debt order over 'foreign debt', even if it has personal jurisdiction over the third-party payer (in that case, a bank branch located in England). However, the court was divided as to what 'foreign debt' connoted. For Lord Bingham, an order may be made relating to a chose in action sited abroad, unless the making of the order will not discharge the debt of the third party according to the law which governs that debt. Lord Hobhouse, by contrast, spoke in terms of the *situs* of the debt. Lord Hoffmann, too, considered that the discharge was a matter for *lex situs* and not the law governing the contract.[104] Although criticism has been mounted against the use of *lex situs* in contractual disputes, both by courts[105] and academics,[106] the rule still holds ground.

8.76 What is the *situs*, then? In *Taurus Petroleum Limited*,[107] Moore-Bick LJ (with whom Sullivan and Briggs LJJ agreed in principle) referred to the statement in *Dicey, Morris & Collins* that generally choses in action are situated in the country where they are recoverable or can be enforced, which is the place of residence of the debtor. However, he followed the decision in *Power Curber*[108] that letters of credit constitute an exception from this general rule and their *situs* is at the place of their payment. For the debts of banks to its customers, the *situs* is at the location of the bank account[109] and possibly its governing law.[110] In the US, the *situs* of intangible property (right to payment) is also where the debtor is located.[111]

103 [2003] UKHL 30.

104 For a commentary, see Pippa Rogerson, 'Third Party Debt Orders (Garnishee Order)—Foreign Bank Accounts' (2003) 62(3) CLJ 576 (suggesting that the court should apply the law governing the debt); Trevor Hartley, 'Jurisdiction in Conflict of Laws—Disclosure, Third-Party Debt and Freezing Orders' (2010) 126 LQR 194.

105 *Raiffeisen Zentralbank Osterreich AG v An Feng Steel Co Limited* [2001] EWCA CIV 68, para 37.

106 Pippa Rogerson, 'The Situs of Debts in the Conflict of Laws—Illogical, Unnecessary and Misleading' (1990) 49(3) CLJ 441; Aaron Simowitz, 'Siting Intangibles' (2015) 48 NYU J Intl L & Pol 259.

107 *Taurus Petroleum Limited v State Oil Company of the Ministry of Oil, Republic of Iraq* [2015] EWCA Civ 835.

108 *Power Curber International Ltd v National Bank of Kuwait SAK* [1981] 1 WLR 1233.

109 *Société Eram Shipping Co Ltd* v *Cie Internationale de Navigation* [2003] UKHL 30, 73 (per Lord Hobhouse).

110 *Kuwait Oil Tanker Company SAK v UBS AG* [2003] UKHL 31, para 13 (per Lord Hoffmann).

111 *FG Hemisphere Associates, LLC, v UNOCAL Corporation*, No 12-56031 (9th Cir 2014); *Walker v Congo*, 395 F.3d 229, 235 (5th Cir 2004).

In the US, the turnover order is available against the judgment debtor or garnishee (third party) alike. To obtain a turnover order, the court has to undertake a two-step analysis. Under the first step, the court must first find that the debtor 'has an interest' in the property the creditor seeks to obtain. If the court makes that finding, it must then make one of the two additional findings: it must find *either* that the debtor is entitled to possess the property, *or* that the creditor's rights to the property are superior to those of the third party. In *Ladjevardian*, the creditors of Argentina requested a turnover order as to the proceeds from the Argentine bond issuance (not in use for paying the settlements with other bondholders) held by the Bank of New York of MelloAn. Their claim for turnover failed under the first step of analysis since, under the terms of the trust, Argentina assigned all its rights to receive the proceeds to the trustee under the settlement trust. The beneficiary of the trust was the Banco Central de la República Argentina whom the court found to be separate from the Republic of Argentina. The creditors also failed under the second step of the analysis since they were unable to establish that Argentina was entitled to possess the property or that the rights of the creditors were superior to those of the Banco Central.[112] **8.77**

Because the payment of the debt is a kind of property, it is subject to the same requirements of sovereign immunity, so that the payment of debt has to fall within one of the exceptions of sovereign immunity,[113] that is to say, that the payments to the State are used for a commercial activity. Thus, the District Court held that fees paid by airlines to Lao for flying over its territory were not used for a commercial activity but were an instance of sovereign authority.[114] Similarly, the District Court held that the right to receive taxes is not a commercial property.[115] Further, under §1610(a) of the FSIA, the assets which are the object of a turnover order have to be present in the jurisdiction.[116] **8.78**

In addition to third-party debt orders, the arsenal of English courts includes receivership orders. These orders are *in personam* remedies whereby the court appoints a receiver who will receive the money due to the debtor. Accordingly, the debtor is precluded from receiving payment **8.79**

[112] *Mohammad Ladjevardian v Republic of Argentina*, 06-cv-3276 (TPG) (SDNY 2016). See also *Dussault v Republic of Argentina*, 616 Fed Appx 26 (2d Cir 2015).

[113] *SerVaas v Rafidian Bank* [2012] UKSC 40. For a similar position in the US, see *Thai Lao Lignite (Thailand) Co, Ltd v Government of the Lao People's Democratic Republic*, 10 Civ 5256 (SDNY 2013).

[114] *Thai Lao Lignite (Thailand) Co, Ltd v Government of the Lao People's Democratic Republic*, 10 Civ 5256 (SDNY 2013).

[115] *LNC Investments INC v Republic of Nicaragua*, 2000 US Dist LEXIS 7814 (SDNY 2000).

[116] *Allan Applestein v Republic of Argentina*, 2014 US Dist LEXIS 189256 (SDNY 2014).

from the third party. Being *in personam* remedies, receivership orders are not subject to the same limitations as third-party debt orders: the *situs* of the debt does not have to be in England. Nevertheless, Collins LJ recognised the inherent limitations of receivership orders which operate in respect of foreign debts.[117]

12. State Entities/Subnational Authorities

8.80 Over and above the attempts to enforce State property, private creditors have continuously attempted to attach the assets of State-owned enterprises enjoying separate legal personality (referred to as State entities). It is likely that the regime below will apply to entities, which were nationalised after they had entered into a contract which later became the subject of a dispute.[118] The regime outline below will also apply to the constituent territories of a federal State (s 14(5)).

8.81 Section 14(2) of the SIA provides that a separate entity will be immune from the jurisdiction of English courts if:

(a) the proceedings relate to anything done by it in the exercise of sovereign authority; and
(b) the circumstances are such that a State would have been so immune.

8.82 In *Pearl Petroleum Company Limited v The Kurdistan Regional Government of Iraq*, it was accepted that Kurdistan, a regional government in Iraq, was not a State, but rather a separate entity within the meaning of s 14 of the SIA. To enjoy immunity, Kurdistan had to establish that the proceedings related to anything done by it in the exercise of sovereign authority and the circumstances were such that a State would have been so immune (s 14(2)). The court ruled that a concession to operate gas fields was in principle an exercise of governmental authority.[119] By contrast, in *Taurus Petroleum Ltd*,[120] Moore-Bick LJ found that the sale of crude oil was not an exercise of governmental authority, even if it essentially amounted to disposal of the State's natural resources.

[117] *Masri v Consolidated Contractors International (UK) Ltd (No 2)* [2008] EWCA Civ 303, paras 35, 50, 59.

[118] *Fir Tree Capital Opportunity Master Fund v Anglo Irish Bank Corporation Limited*, 2011 US Dist LEXIS 136018 (SDNY 2011) (where the issue was taken as granted).

[119] [2015] EWHC 3361 (Comm), para 36.

[120] *Taurus Petroleum Limited v State Oil Company of the Ministry of Oil, Republic of Iraq* (n 108) paras 46–47.

The FSIA, too, immunises the property of an agency or instrumentality of a State.[121] An 'agency or instrumentality of a foreign state' is defined in §1603(b) as any entity— **8.83**

(1) which is a separate legal person, corporate or otherwise, and
(2) which is an organ of a foreign State or political subdivision thereof, or a majority of whose shares or other ownership interest is owned by a foreign State or political subdivision thereof, and
(3) which is neither a citizen of a State of the United States, nor created under the laws of any third country.

Section 1610(b) accords State agencies or instrumentalities an immunity regime essentially similar to the immunities of the State. What sets the US and UK laws apart on the immunities of State enterprises is that in the US, once the defendant has demonstrated that the defendant is a State instrumentality, the burden shifts to the claimant to establish any of the exceptions to immunity from jurisdiction or enforcement, whereas in English law the defendant entity bears the burden of establishing that it exercises governmental authority under s 14.[122] **8.84**

Apart from establishing immunity of the State entity for governmental acts, the issue which often arises is the State entity's liability for the debts of the State. In *Trendtex Trading Corp v Central Bank of Nigeria*,[123] Lord Denning stated that a State-owned corporation could be equated with the State for enforcement purposes if it is an 'alter ego or organ' of the State. The factors to consider in coming to this conclusion are the functions and control of the corporation. A relevant example would be a State-owned company which promotes the industrial development of a branch of national economy.[124] **8.85**

The test suggested by Lord Denning was discarded as too liberal and too pro-creditor by the Privy Council in *La Générale des Carrières et des Mines v F.G. Hemisphere Associates LLC*. There, a private party sought the enforcement of two arbitral awards against the assets of a government-owned company. The Privy Council first recognised that the same test should govern two conceptually separate issues: (1) whether a separate entity is to be considered to be an organ of the State if it exercises public functions, so as to profit from immunity of the State; and (2) the question of **8.86**

[121] See, eg, *Parex Bank v Russian Savings Bank*, 81 F Supp 2d 506, 508 (SDNY 2000) (finding that the Russian Savings Bank was an instrumentality of the Russian Federation).
[122] Yang (n 7) 277.
[123] [1977] 1 QB 529.
[124] *Mellenger v New Brunswick Development Corp* [1971] 1 WLR 604.

substantive liability, ie, whether a creditor can enforce the debt of the State by attaching the assets of the company. Holding that the State-owned corporation and the State are one and the same would have meant that the State-owned corporation's assets could be used for satisfaction of the State's debts, but also vice versa—the assets of the State could be attached in lieu of the assets of the State-owned company.

8.87 Lord Mance considered that the test in *Trendtex* was too liberal, and that the right test was based on a presumption of separate identity of the State-owned entity. The presumption would apply both in respect of immunities and substantive liability, even where the State entities exercised certain sovereign authority *jure imperii*, providing them in return with a special functional immunity if and so far as they do exercise such sovereign authority. Lord Mance further held:

> [C]onstitutional and factual control and the exercise of sovereign functions do not without more convert a separate entity into an organ of the State. Especially where a separate juridical entity is formed by the State for what are on the face of it commercial or industrial purposes, with its own management and budget, the strong presumption is that its separate corporate status should be respected, and that it and the State forming it should not have to bear each other's liabilities. It will in the Board's view take quite extreme circumstances to displace this presumption. The presumption will be displaced if in fact the entity has, despite its juridical personality, no effective separate existence. But for the two to be assimilated generally, an examination of the relevant constitutional arrangements, as applied in practice, as well as of the State's control exercised over the entity and of the entity's activities and functions would have to justify the conclusion that the affairs of the entity and the State were so closely intertwined and confused that the entity could not properly be regarded for any significant purpose as distinct from the State and vice versa.[125]

8.88 This pronouncement clarifies that the fact that the State is the sole shareholder of an entity is not sufficient to treat them as the same. To displace the presumption of separate personality, the claimant has to adduce 'extreme circumstances', namely that the entity has no 'effective separate existence'. In *Kensington v Congo*, the Commercial Court ruled that Congo has set up a chain of companies and contracts with the object of evading enforcement of a judgment against the sovereign debtor and reducing the risk of attachment. On this basis, Cooke J agreed to pierce the corporate veil and issue a third-party debt order to bind companies in that chain of companies and transactions. On the ground of such fraud, the money

[125] *La Générale des Carrières et des Mines v F.G. Hemisphere Associates LLC* [2012] UKPC 27, para 29.

due from one company to another was considered to be owed in reality to Congo and a third-party order was made available.[126]

The US jurisprudence on this matter has developed along similar lines. The US Supreme Court in *Bancec* confirmed that government instrumentalities established as separate and distinct entities are presumed to be separate from the State. However, it ruled that the presumption can be rebutted if: (1) the government entity is so extensively controlled by its owner that a relationship of principal and agent is created; or (2) recognising a distinction between the government instrumentality and its government will operate as a fraud or injustice against the plaintiff. If the claimant is able to establish any of these grounds, the assets of the government instrumentality can be attached for discharging the debt of the State.[127] **8.89**

Claimants' efforts to establish that central banks or other separate entities were an arm of the State under the test in *Bancec* often received short shrift from the US courts.[128] The claimants in *EM Ltd v Republic of Argentina* failed to attach the property of the Central Bank of Argentina since the assets were immune under the strict provision of §1611(b)(1). In the ensuing litigation, they claimed that the Central Bank was Argentina's alter ego. The Second Circuit found that Argentina's Central Bank is not Argentina's alter ego because Argentina did not: (1) exercise such significant and repeated control over BCRA's day-to-day operations that a principal and agent relationship was created; and (2) recognising BCRA as a separate entity would not give rise to fraud or injustice.[129] **8.90**

Lastly, if the court refuses to pierce the corporate veil, the private creditor may seek to advance the argument that the property held in the hands of a State entity is beneficially owned by the State under s 6(4) of the SIA ('property … in which the State claims an interest'). Confronted with an argument that the State had a beneficial interest in the assets of the Central Bank, Aikens J held in *AIG v Kazakhstan* that in deciding whether the property of the Central Bank is immune from attachment, the court needs to identify whether the Central Bank has any property rights, broadly defined, in said property and such rights are not irreconcilable with the **8.91**

[126] *Kensington International Ltd v Republic of the Congo* [2005] EWHC 2684 (Comm), paras 169, 191, 199–201 (where oil was sold through a number of companies which merely constituted a facade for the transactions of the State). See also *Walker International Holdings Ltd v Republique Populaire du Congo* [2005] EWHC 2813 (Comm).

[127] *First National City Bank v Banco Para el Comercio Exterior de Cuba*, 462 US 611, 629 (1983).

[128] *Letelier v Republic of Chile*, 748 F 2d 790 (2d Cir 1984); *LNC Investments INC v Republic of Nicaragua*, 115 F Supp 2d 358 (SDNY 2000).

[129] 800 F 3d 78 (2d Cir 2015).

State's proprietary interest in the same property.[130] Even if the beneficial ownership is established, the private creditor will still need to establish that the property at hand is non-immune (s 6(4)). In *EM Ltd v Republic of Argentina*,[131] the Second Circuit held that two decrees requesting the Argentine Central Bank to make funds available for repayment of money to the IMF did not result in the transfer of ownership in the funds to the Republic of Argentina.

[130] *AIG Capital Partners Inc v Republic of Kazakhstan* [2006] 1 WLR 1420, paras 60, 89–91.
[131] 473 F 3d 463, 475 (2d Cir 2007).

Bibliography

BOOKS

Allan Trevor, *Constitutional Justice: A Liberal Theory of the Rule of Law* (2003)
Alvik Ivar, *Contracting with Sovereignty: State Contracts and International Arbitration* (2011)
Andrews Neil, *English Civil Procedure: Fundamentals of the New Civil Justice System* (2003)
——, Malcolm Clarke, Tetternborn Andrew, and Virgo Graham, *Contractual Duties: Performance, Breach, Termination and Remedies* (2012)
Arancibia Jaime, *Judicial Review of Commercial Regulation* (2014)
Arden Mary et al (eds), *Buckley on the Companies Act*, vol II (2010)
Bailey Edward and Groves Hugo, *Corporate Insolvency: Law and Practice* (2007)
Barry Christian, Herman Barry, and Tomitova Lydia (eds), *Dealing Fairly with Developing Country Debt* (2007)
Batiffol Henry, *Les Conflits de lois en matière de contrats* (1938)
Borchard Edwin, *State Insolvency and Foreign Bondholders* (1951)
Briggs Adrian, *Agreements on Jurisdiction and Choice of Law* (2008)
—— *Civil Jurisdiction and Judgments* (2015)
Cane Peter, *Introduction to Administrative Law* (2011)
Chivers David and Shaw Ben (eds), *The Law of Majority Shareholder Power: Use and Abuse* (2008)
Chorafas Dimitris, *Sovereign Debt Crisis: The New Normal and the Newly Poor* (2011)
Collins Lawrence et al (eds), *Dicey, Morris & Collins on the Conflict of Laws*, vols 1 and 2 (2012)
Crawford James, *Brownlie's Principles of Public International Law* (2012)
Cresswell Peter, Blair William, and Wood Philip (eds), *Butterworths Encyclopaedia of Banking Law* (2013)
de Haan Jakob, Oosterloo Sander, and Schoenmaker Dirk, *Financial Markets and Institutions: A European Perspective* (2012)
Delaume Georges, *Legal Aspects of International Lending and Economic Development Agreements* (1967)
Dickinson Andrew, Lindsay Rae, and Loonam James, *State Immunity: Selected Materials and Commentary* (2004)
Domke Martin, *La Clause "dollar-or": la non-application de la legislation américaine aux emprunts internationaux* (1935)
—— *International Loans and the Conflict of Laws: A Comparative Survey of Recent Cases* (1937)
Ely James, *The Guardian of Every Other Constitutional Right: A Constitutional History of Property Rights* (1998)
Fentiman Richard, *International Commercial Litigation* (2015)
Finch Vanessa, *Corporate Insolvency Law: Perspectives and Principles* (2009)
Fletcher Ian, *Insolvency in Private International Law* (2005)
Fox Hazel and Webb Philippa, *The Law of State Immunity* (2015)

Fox Justin, *The Myth of the Rational Market: A History of Risk, Reward and Delusion on Wall Street* (2009)
Friedmann Wolfgang, *Law in a Changing Society* (1972)
Gavalda Christian, *Les Conflits dans le temps en droit international privé* (1955)
Gkoutzinis Apostolos, *Law and Practice of Liability Management: Debt Tender Offers, Exchange Offers, Bond Buybacks and Consent Solicitations in International Capital Markets* (2014)
Greer Steven, *The European Convention on Human Rights: Achievements, Problems and Prospects* (2006)
Gulati Mitu and Scott Robert, *The Three and a Half Minute Transaction: Boilerplate and the Limits of the Contract Design* (2013)
Harlow Carol and Rawlings Richard, *Law and Administration* (2009)
Hartley Trevor, *International Commercial Litigation: Text, Cases and Materials on Private International Law* (2015)
Hayek Friedrich, *Law, Legislation and History: Rules and Order* (1973)
Hollington Robin, *Shareholder Rights* (2013)
Hood Parker, *Principles of Lender Liability* (2012)
Jacquemont André, *L'Emission des emprunts euro-obligataires* (1976)
Janis Mark, Kay Richard, and Bradley Anthony, *European Human Rights Law: Text and Materials* (2008)
Juratowitch Ben, *Retroactivity and the Common Law* (2008)
Karamanolis Padazis, *The Legal Implications of Sovereign Lending through Syndicated Loan Agreements* (1992)
Kaye Peter, *The New Private International Law of the European Community* (1993)
King Jeff, *The Doctrine of Odious Debt in International Law: A Restatement* (2016)
Kinsch Patrick, *Le Fait du prince étranger* (1994)
Lauterpacht Hersch, *Private Law Sources and Analogies of International Law* (1927)
Lee Robert, *Public Budgeting Systems* (2013)
Lienau Odette, *Rethinking Sovereign Debt: Politics, Reputation and Legitimacy* (2014)
McGee Andrew, *Limitation Periods* (2015)
McGregor Harvey, *McGregor on Damages* (2016)
McKendrick Ewan, *Contract Law: Text, Cases and Materials* (2014)
McLachlan Campbell, *Foreign Relations Law* (2014)
McParland Michael, *The Rome I Regulation on the Law Applicable to Contractual Obligations* (2015)
Megliani Mauro, *Sovereign Debt: Genesis, Restructuring, Litigation* (2015)
Millett Lord (ed), *Gore-Browne on Companies*, vol II (2004)
Mitchell John, *The Contracts of Public Authorities* (1954)
Morgan Jonathan, *Contract Law Minimalism: A Formalist Restatement of Commercial Contract Law* (2013)
O'Dea Geoff, Long Julian, and Alexandra Smyth, *Schemes of Arrangement: Law and Practice* (2012)
Olivares-Caminal Rodrigo, *Legal Aspects of a Sovereign Debt Restructuring* (2009)
Piketty Thomas, *Capital in the Twenty-First Century* (2014)
Pilkington Christian, *Schemes of Arrangement* (2013)

Plender Richard and Wilderspin Michael, *The European Private International Law of Obligations* (2009)
Proctor Charles, *The Law and Practice of International Banking* (2010)
—— *Mann on the Legal Aspect of Money* (2012)
Ranganathan Surabhi, *Strategically Created Treaty Conflicts and the Politics of International Law* (2014)
Reinhart Carmen and Rogoff Kenneth, *This Time Is Different: Eight Centuries of Financial Folly* (2011)
Rieffel Lex, *Restructuring Sovereign Debt: The Case for Ad Hoc Machinery* (2003)
Rogerson Pippa, *Collier's Conflict of Laws* (2013)
Salomon Margot, *Global Responsibility for Human Rights: World Poverty and the Development of International Law* (2007)
Schier Holger, *Towards a Reorganisation System for Sovereign Debt: An International Law Perspective* (2007)
Schreuer Christoph, *State Immunity: Some Recent Developments* (1988)
Scott Hal and Gelpern Anna, *International Finance: Law and Regulation* (2012)
Skeel David, *Debt's Dominion: A History of Bankruptcy Law in America* (2003)
Smith Adam, *An Enquiry into the Nature and Causes of the Wealth of Nations* (2007)
Snowdon Brian, Howard Vane, and Peter Wynarczyk, *A Modern Guide to Macroeconomics: An Introduction to Competing Schools of Thought* (1994)
Sturzenegger Federico and Zettelmeyer Jeromin, *Debt Defaults and Lessons from a Decade of Crises* (2007)
Symeonides Symeon, *The American Choice-of-Law Revolution: Past, Present and Future* (2006)
Tennekoon Ravi, *The Law and Regulation of International Finance* (1991)
Timberlake Richard, *Constitutional Money: A Review of the Supreme Court's Monetary Decisions* (2013)
Tomz Michael, *Reputation and International Cooperation: Sovereign Debt across Three Centuries* (2007)
van Hecke Georges, *Problèmes juridiques des emprunts internationaux* (1964)
Waibel Michael, *Sovereign Defaults before International Courts and Tribunals* (2011)
Watrin Germain, *Essai de construction d'un contentieux international des dettes publiques* (1929)
Waye Vicki, *Trading in Legal Claims* (2008)
Weigert Julius, *The Abrogation of Gold-Clauses in International Loans and the Conflict of Laws* (1940)
Weller Marc-Philippe, *Die Grenze der Vertragstreue von (Krisen-)Staaten: Zur Einrede des Staatsnotstands gegenüber privaten Anleihegläubigern* (2013)
Wood Philip, *Conflict of Laws and International Finance* (2007)
—— *International Loans, Bonds, Guarantees and Legal Opinions* (2007)
—— *Set-off and Netting, Derivatives, Clearing Systems* (2007)
Wuarin Albert, *Essai sur les emprunts d'Etats et la protéction des droits des porteurs de fonds d'Etats étrangers* (1907)
Yang Xiaodong, *State Immunity in International Law* (2012)

ARTICLES, BOOK CHAPTERS, AND MISCELLANEOUS

Acevedo Paloma, Alberola Enrique, and Broto Carmen, 'Local Debt Expansion and Vulnerability Reduction: An Assessment for Six Crisis-Prone Countries' (2008) BIS Papers No 36

Adam Klaus and Grill Michael, 'Optimal Sovereign Default' (2013) Deutsche Bundesbank No 09/2013

Affaki Georges, 'Revisiting the *Pari Passu* Clause' in Rosa Lastra and Lee Buchheit (eds), *Sovereign Debt Management* (2014) 39–48

Ahdieh Robert, 'Making Markets: Network Effects and the Role of Law in the Creation of Strong Securities Markets' (2003) 76 S Cal L Rev 277–350

Allen & Overy Global Law Intelligence Unit, 'How the Greek Debt Reorganisation of 2012 Changed the Rules of Sovereign Insolvency' (2012)

—— 'Uses and Abuses of Collective Action Clauses in Sovereign Bonds' (2013) 14(3) Bus L Intl 269–94

Amador Garcia, 'Second Report on State Responsibility' (1957) 2 ILC Yearbook 104–30

Andrews David, Boote Anthony, Rizavi Syed, and Singh Sukhwinder, 'Debt Relief for Low-Income Countries: The Enhanced HIPC Initiative' (1999) IMF Pamphlet Series No 51

Armingeon Klaus and Baccaro Lucio, 'Political Economy of the Sovereign Debt Crisis: The Limits of Internal Devaluation' (2012) 41(3) Industrial LJ 254–75

Armour John, Menezes Antonia, Uttamchandani Mahesh, and van Zwieten Kristin, 'How Do Creditor Rights Matter for Debt Finance? A Review of Empirical Evidence' in Frederique Dahan (ed), *Research Handbook on Secured Financing of Commercial Transactions* (2015) 3–25

Athanassiou Phoebus, 'Valuation in Resolution and the "No-Creditor-Worse-Off" Principle' (2014) 1 JIBFL 16–20

Audit Matthias, 'La dette souveraine appelle-t-elle un statut juridique particulier?' in Matthias Audit (ed), *Insolvabilité des Etats et dettes souveraines* (2011) 67–88

Awrey Dan, Blair William, and Kershaw David, 'Between Law and Markets: Is there a Role for Culture and Ethics in Financial Regulation' (2012) LSE Law, Society and Economics Working Papers 14/2012

Bab Andrew, 'Debt Tender Offer Techniques and the Problem of Coercion' (1991) 91 Colum L Rev 846–90

Bainbridge Stephen, 'Comity and Sovereign Debt Litigation: A Bankruptcy Analogy' (1986) 10 Md J Intl L 1–54

Bardozzetti Alfredo and Dottori Davide, 'Collective Action Clauses: How Do They Affect Sovereign Bond Yields?' (2014) 92 J Intl Econ 286–303

Barry Christian and Tomitova Lydia, 'Fairness in Sovereign Debt' in Christian Barry, Barry Herman, and Lidya Tomitova (eds), *Dealing Fairly with Developing Country Debt* (2007) 41–79

Batiffol Henri, 'Subjectivisme et objectivisme dans le droit international privé des contrats' in Henri Batiffol, *Choix d'articles* (1976) 249–63

Baxter Thomas and Gross David, 'Special Immunities: Central Bank Immunity' in Rosa Lastra and Lee Buchheit (eds), *Sovereign Debt Management* (2014) 117–25

Bi Ran, Chamon Marcos, and Zettelmeyer Jeromin, 'The Problem that Wasn't: Coordination Failures in Sovereign Debt Restructurings' (2011) IMF Working Paper WP/11/265

Billington David, 'European Collective Action Clauses' in Rosa Lastra and Lee Buchheit (eds), *Sovereign Debt Management* (2014) 399–416

BIS 'The Development of Bond Markets in Emerging Economies' (2001) BIS Papers No 11

Block-Lieb Susan, 'Austerity, Debt Overhang and the Design of International Standards on Sovereign, Corporate and Consumer Debt Restructuring' 22(2) Ind J Glob L Stud 487–541

Blommestein Hans, 'Responding to the Crisis: Changes in OECD Primary Market Procedures and Portfolio Risk Management' (2009) 2 OECD Journal: Financial Market Trends

Boccuzzi Carmine, Michael Brennan, and Jacob Johnston, 'Defences' in Rosa Lastra and Lee Buchheit (eds), *Sovereign Debt Management* (2014) 103–15

Bohoslavsky Juan Pablo, 'Responsibility for Abusive Granting of Sovereign Loans' (2008) 14 Law & Bus Rev Am 495

—— 'Report on Financial Complicity: Lending to States Engaged in Gross Human Rights Violations' (2015) UN General Assembly A/HRC/28/59

—— and Letnar Cernic Jernej (eds), *Making Sovereign Financing and Human Rights Work* (2014)

——, Li Yuefen, and Sudreau Marie, 'Emerging Customary International Law in Sovereign Debt Governance?' (2014) 9(1) CMLJ 55–72

Bolton Patrick and Skeel David, 'Inside the Black Box: How Should a Sovereign Bankruptcy Framework Be Structured?' (2004) 53 Emory LJ 763–822

Bonafé Beatrice, 'State Immunity and the Protection of Private Investors: The *Argentine Bonds* Case before Italian Courts' (2006) 16 IYBIL 165–85

Bonomi Andrea, 'Article 9' in Ulrich Magnus and Peter Mankowski, *Rome I Regulation: European Commentaries on Private International Law* (2017) 599–661

Borchard Edwin, 'International Loans and International Law' (1932) 26 Proceedings of the American Society of International Law at its Annual Meeting (1921–69) 135–86

Bothe Michael and Brink Josef, 'Public Debt Restructuring—The Case for International Economic Co-operation' (1986) 29 GYIL 86–110

Boudreau Melissa, 'Restructuring Sovereign Debt under Local Law: Are Retrofit Collective Action Clauses Expropriatory?' (2012) 2 HBLR Online 164–86

Boudreau Melissa and Gulati Mitu, 'The IMF's Imperiled Priority' (2014) (available at http://scholarship.law.duke.edu/faculty_scholarship/3331)

Bowett Derek, 'Claims between States and Private Entities: The Twilight Zone of International Law' (1986) 35 (4) Cath Univ L Rev 929–42

—— 'State Contracts with Aliens: Contemporary Developments on Compensation for Termination or Breach' (1988) 59 BYBIL 49–74

Bradley Michael and Gulati Mitu, 'Collective Action Clauses for the Eurozone' (2014) 18(6) Rev Fin 2045–2102

—— and Roberts Michael, 'The Structure and Pricing of Corporate Debt Covenants' (2003) (available at https://papers.ssrn.com/sol3/papers.cfm?abstract_id=466240)

——, Cox James, and Gulati Mitu, 'The Market Reaction to Legal Shocks and their Antidotes' (2010) 39 J Leg Stud 289–324
Bratton William 'The Interpretation of Contracts Governing Corporate Debt Relationships' (1983–84) 5 Cardozo L Rev 371–407
—— 'The Economics and Jurisprudence of Convertible Bonds' (1984) 3 Wis L Rev 667–740
—— and Gulati Mitu, 'Sovereign Debt Reform and the Best Interest of Creditors' (2004) 57(1) Vand L Rev 1–79
Briggs Adrian, 'Principle of Comity in Private International Law' (2012) 354 Recueil des Cours 65
Briggs John, 'Bars to Common Law Recognition' in Richard Sheldon (ed), *Cross-Border Insolvency* (2015) 447–68
Broner Fernando, Martin Alberto, and Ventura Jaume, 'Enforcement Problems and Secondary Markets' (2007) NBER Working Paper 13559
Broomfield Elizabeth, 'Subduing the Vultures: Assessing Government Caps on Recovery in Sovereign Debt Litigation' (2010) 2 Colum Bus L Rev 473
Brudney Victor, 'Corporate Bondholders and Debtor Opportunism: In Bad Times and Good' (1992) 105 Harv L Rev 1821–78
Bruno Eugenio, 'Argentina Debt—The Settlement Clause' (2013) (available at http://papers.ssrn.com/sol3/papers.cfm?abstract_id=2456055)
Buchheit Lee, 'Act of State and Comity: Recent Developments' in David Sassoon and Daniel Bradlow (eds), *Judicial Enforcement of International Debt Obligations* (1987) 95–106
—— 'How to Negotiate the Waiver of Immunities Clause' (1993) 12 IFLR 31–32
—— 'Sovereign Debt Litigation' (1999) Memorandum for the International Monetary Fund
—— 'How Ecuador Escaped the Brady Bond Trap' (2000) 19(12) IFLR 17–20
—— 'The Search for Intercreditor Parity' (2002) 8 Law & Bus Rev Am 73–80
—— 'Supermajority Control Wins Out' (2007) 26 IFLR 21
—— and Daly Elena, 'Minimizing Holdout Creditors: Carrots' in Rosa Lastra and Lee Buchheit (eds), *Sovereign Debt Management* (2014) 3–13
—— and Gulati Mitu, 'Sovereign Bonds and the Collective Will' (2004) 51 Emory LJ 1317–63
—— and Gulati Mitu, 'Restructuring a Nation's Debt' (2010) 29 IFLR 46–49
—— and Gulati Mitu, 'Drafting a Model Collective Action Clause for Eurozone Sovereign Bonds' (2011) 6(3) CMLJ 317–25
—— and Karpinski Elizabeth, 'Grenada's Innovations' (2006) 21 J Intl Bank Regul 227–31
—— and Karpinski Elizabeth, 'Belize's Innovations' (2007) 22 JIBFL 278–80
—— and Martos Sofia, 'What to Do about Pari Passu' (2014) 8 JIBFL 491–93
—— and Pam Jeremiah, 'The Pari Passu Clause in Sovereign Debt Instruments' (2004) 53 Emory LJ 869–922
—— and Pam Jeremiah, 'Uruguay's Innovations' (2004) 19(1) JIBLR 28–31
—— and Reisner Ralph, 'The Effect of the Sovereign Debt Restructuring Process on Inter-Creditor Relationships' (1988) 2 U Ill L Rev 493–517

——, Gulati Mitu, and Tirado Ignacio, 'The Problem of Holdout Creditors in Eurozone Sovereign Debt Restructurings' (2013) 4 JIBFL 191–94

Bulajic Milan, 'Indebtedness of Developing Countries and New International Economic Order' in Detlev Dicke (ed), *Foreign Debts in the Present and a New International Economic Order* (1986) 43–73

Bullow Jeremy and Rogoff Kenneth, 'A Constant Recontracting Model of Sovereign Debt' (1989) 97(1) J Polit Econ 155–78

Burn Lachlan, 'Bondholder Resolutions in the Courtroom' in Patrick Kenadjian, Klaus-Albert Bauer, and Andreas Cahn (eds), *Collective Action Clauses and the Restructuring of Sovereign Debt* (2013) 73–83

Bush Oliver, Farrant Katie, and Weight Michelle, 'Reform of the International Monetary and Financial System' (2011) Bank of England Financial Stability Paper No 13

Carletti Elena, Colla Paolo, Gulati Mitu, and Ongena Steven, 'Pricing Contract Terms in a Crisis: Venezuelan Bonds in 2016' (2016) 11(4) CMLJ 540–55

—— 'The Price of Law: The Case of the Eurozone Collective Action Clauses' (2016) (available at http://scholarship.law.duke.edu/faculty_scholarship/3543)

Carreau Dominique, 'La nouvelle décision américaine Allied Bank International ou un retour ambigu à la protection juridique des créanciers dans la procédure des rééchelonnements de dettes internationales' (1986) 113 JDI 123–25

—— 'Rapport du directeur d'études de la section française du centre' in Dominique Carreau and Malcolm Shaw (eds), *La Dette extérieure: The External Debt* (1995) 3–24

Chabot Benjamin and Gulati Mitu, 'Santa Anna and his Black Eagle: The Origins of Pari Passu' (2014) 9(3) CMLJ 216–41

Chamon Marcos, Schumacher Julian, and Trebesch Christoph, 'Foreign Law Bonds: Can They Reduce Sovereign Borrowing Costs?' (2014) (available at https://www.econstor.eu/bitstream/10419/113199/1/VfS_2015_pid_874.pdf)

Cheng Tai-Heng and Entchev Ivo, 'State Incapacity and Sovereign Immunity in International Arbitration' (2014) 26 Sac LJ 942–74

Cheyney Edwin, 'Syndicated Loans—Position of Minority Lenders' (2003) 3 JIBFL 88–90

Chivers Corey, '"Contracting Around" the Good Faith Covenant to Avoid Lender Liability' (1991) Colum Bus L Rev 359–86

Choi Stephen and Gulati Mitu, 'The Pricing of Non-Price Terms in Sovereign Bonds: The Case of the Greek Guarantees' (2016) JLFA 1

Choi Stephen, Gulati Mitu, and Posner Eric, 'Pricing Terms in Sovereign Debt Contracts: A Greek Case Study with Implications for the European Crisis Resolution Mechanism' (2011) 6(2) CMLJ 163–87

—— 'The Evolution of Contractual Terms in Sovereign Bonds' (2012) 4 J Leg Anal 131–79

—— 'The Dynamics of Contract Evolution' (2013) 88(1) NYU L Rev 1–50

Clare Andrew and Schmidlin Nicolas, 'The Impact of Foreign Governing Law on European Government Bond Yields' (2014) (available at http://papers.ssrn.com/sol3/papers.cfm?abstract_id=2406477)

Clark Keith, 'Sovereign Debt Restructurings: Parity of Treatment between Equivalent Creditors in Relation to Comparable Debts' (1986) 20 Intl L 857, 863

Coffee John and Klein William, 'Bondholder Coercion: The Problem of Constrained Choice in Debt Tender Offers and Recapitalizations' (1991) 58(4) Uni Chi L Rev 1207–73

Collet Stéphanie and Oosterlinck Kim, 'Pricing the Odious in Odious Debts' (2016) Discussion Paper DP11653

Collins Hugh, 'Discretionary Powers in Contracts' in David Campbell, Hugh Collins, and John Wightman (eds), *Implicit Dimensions of Contract: Discrete, Relational and Network Contracts* (2003) 219–54

Collins Lawrence, 'Foreign Relations and the Conflict of Laws' (1995–96) 6 KCLJ 20–37

Cotterill Joseph, 'I Can't Belize It's Not Ratable Payment [Updated]' *FT Alphaville* (25 February 2013)

—— 'The Negative Pledge Saga' *FT Alphaville* (27 June 2013)

—— 'Sovereign Pari Passu and the Litigators of the Lost Cause' (2013) 9(1) CMLJ 18–25

—— 'Ukraine's Bonds: A Little Local Leverage' *FT Alphaville* (26 March 2015)

Cowan Kevin, Levy-Yeyati Eduardo, Panizza Ugo, and Sturzenegger Federico, 'Sovereign Debt in the Americas: New Data and Stylized Facts' (2006) Working Paper of Inter-American Development Bank No 577

Cross Karen, 'Is a Foreign State a "Person"? Does It Matter?: Personal Jurisdiction, Due Process, and the Foreign Sovereign Immunities Act' (2001) 34 NYU J Intl L & Pol 115–87

D'Agostino Antonello and Ehrmann Michael, 'The Pricing of G7 Sovereign Bond Spreads: The Times, They Are a-Changin' (2013) ECB Working Paper Series No 1520

Das Udaibir, Papaioannou Michael, and Trebesch Christoph, 'Sovereign Debt Restructurings 1950–2010: Literature Survey, Data, and Stylized Facts' (2012) IMF Working Paper WP/12/203

Dawson John, 'The Gold Clause Decisions' (1935) 33(5) Mich L Rev 647–84

De Broeck Mark and Guscina Anastasia, 'Government Debt Issuance in the Euro Area: The Impact of the Financial Crisis' (2010) IMF Working Paper WP/11/21

de Luca Anna, 'L'immunità degli stati stranieri dalla giurisdizioni civile' in Natalino Ronzitti and Gabriella Venturini (eds), *Le immunità guirisdizionali degli stati e degli altri enti internazionali* (2008) 15–27

de Szaszy Etienne, 'Les conflits de lois dans le temps' (1934) 47 Recueil des Cours 145

Debt Campaign Jubilee, 'Debt and Public Services' (2007) Briefing

DeLong Chanda and Aggarwal Nikita, 'Strengthening the Contractual Framework for Sovereign Debt Restructuring—the IMF's Perspective (2016) 11 CMLJ 25–37

Devos Diego, 'Special Immunities: Bank of International Settlements' in Rosa Lastra and Lee Buchheit (eds), *Sovereign Debt Management* (2014) 127–37

Diamond Peter, 'National Debt in a Neoclassical Growth Model' (1965) 55(5) Am Econ Rev 1126–50

Dizard John, '"Complete Chaos in Caracas" Invites Vulture Fest' *Financial Times* (2 September 2016)

—— 'Delusional Lawyering Won't Save European Bonds' *Financial Times* (24 February 2017)

Dockray Martin, 'The Inherent Jurisdiction to Regulate Civil Proceedings' (1997) 113 LQR 120–32

Drake Keegan, 'Disenfranchisement Provisions' in Christoph Paulus (ed), *A Debt Restructuring Mechanism for Sovereigns: Do We Need a Legal Procedure?* (2014) 141–62

—— 'The Fall and Rise of the Exit Consent' (2014) 63 Duke LJ 1589–1624

Drazen Allan, 'Towards a Political–Economic Theory of Domestic Debt' (1997) NBER Working Paper 5890

Dunlop Stewart, 'Liability Management: Exit Consents and Oppression of the Minority' (2012) *Clifford Chance Briefings*

Dunlop Stewart, Sinclair Simon, Deakins Paul, and Vyvyan Kate, 'Noteholder Meetings: Paying the Price for Change?' (2012) *Clifford Chance Briefings*

Eaton Jonathan, 'Standstills and an International Bankruptcy Court' (2002) (available at www.researchgate.net/publication/228884996_Standstills_and_an_International_Bankruptcy_Court)

Eaton Jonathan and Gersovitz Mark, 'Debt with Potential Repudiation: Theoretical and Empirical Analysis' (1981) 48(2) Rev Econ Stud 289–309

Economic and Financial Committee, 'Progress Report on Primary Dealership in EU Public Debt Management' (2000), EFC/ECFIN/665/00-En-fin

Eichengreen Barry, 'Can the Moral Hazard Caused by the IMF Bailouts Be Reduced' (2000) Geneva Reports on the World Economy Special Report I

Eichengreen Barry and Hausmann Ricardo, 'Exchange Rates and Financial Fragility' (1999) NBER Working Paper 7418

Eichengreen Barry, Hausmann Ricardo, and Panizza Ugo, 'Original Sin: The Pain, the Mystery, and the Road to Redemption' (2002) Paper prepared for the conference 'Currency and Maturity Matchmaking: Redeeming Debt from Original Sin'

—— 'Currency Mismatches, Debt Intolerance and Original Sin: Why They Are Not the Same and Why It Matters' (2003) NBER Working Paper 10036

EMTA, 'Preliminary Analysis of Creditor Litigation in the Non-HIPC Sovereign Debt Restructuring Context' (2009)

Engelen Christian and Graf Lambsdorff Johann, 'Fairness in Sovereign Debt Restructuring' (2007) Diskussionsbeitrag Nr V-50-07

Erifillidis Yannis, 'Legislative Measures to Prevent Greece's Economic Collapse: A Step Too Far?' (2014) 7 JIBFL 468–69

Euler Dimitrij and Bianco Giuseppe, 'Breaking the Bond: Vulture Funds and Investment Arbitration' (2013) 31(3) ASA Bulletin 558–82

Feliciano Florentino, 'Report of the Director of Studies of the English-speaking Section of the Centre' in Dominique Carreau and Malcolm Shaw (eds), *La Dette extérieure: The External Debt* (1995) 25–52

Fenwick Charles, 'The Gold Clause Decision in Relation to Foreign Bondholders' (1935) 29 AJIL 310–13

Financial Markets Law Committee, 'Pari Passu Clauses' (2005)

Fisch Jill and Gentile Caroline, 'Vultures or Vanguards?: The Role of Litigation in Sovereign Debt Restructuring' (2004) 53 Emory LJ 1043–113

Fischer Williams John, 'Le droit international et les obligations financières internationales qui naissent d'un contrat' (1923) 1 Recueil des Cours 289

Flandreau Marc, 'Do Good Sovereigns Default? Lessons of History' in *Sovereign Risk: A World without Risk-Free Assets?* (2013a) BIS Papers No 72

—— 'Sovereign States, Bondholders Committees, and the London Stock Exchange in the Nineteenth Century (1827–68): New Facts and Old Fictions' (2013b) 29(4) Oxford Rev Econ Policy 668–96

Foster CT, 'Validity, Construction, and Application of Express Restrictions on Right of Action by Individual Holder of One or More of a Series of Corporate Bonds or Other Obligations' (originally published in 1948) 174 ALR 435

Francq Stéphanie, 'Article 45' in Ulrich Magnus and Peter Mankowski, *Brussels I Regulation: European Commentaries on Private International Law* (2012) 858–946

Franzina Pietro, 'Sovereign Bonds and the Conflict of Laws: A European Perspective' in Pasquale Nappi et al (eds), *Studi in onore di Luigi Costato* (2014) 513–36

Garcimartín Alférez Francisco, 'Cross-Border Listed Companies' (2007) 328 Recueil des Cours 9

Gelpern Anna, 'How Collective Action Is Changing Sovereign Debt' (2003) 22(5) IFLR 19–23

—— 'Building a Better Seating Chart for Sovereign Restructurings' (2004) 53 Emory LJ 1115–60

—— 'Domestic Bonds, Credit Derivatives, and the Next Transformation of Sovereign Debt' (2008) 83 Chi-Kent L Rev 101–33

—— 'Contract Hope and Sovereign Redemption' (2013) 8(2) CMLJ 132–48

—— 'Sovereign Damage Control' (2013) Policy Brief PB13-12 Peterson Institute for International Economics

—— 'Courts and Sovereigns in the *Pari Passu* Goldmines' (2016) 11(2) CMLJ 251–77

—— and Gulati Mitu, 'Innovation after the Revolution: Foreign Sovereign Bond Contracts since 2003' (2009) 4(1) Cap Mark LJ 85–103

—— and Setser Brad, 'Domestic and External Debt: The Doomed Quest for Equal Treatment' (2004) 35 Geo J Intl L 795–814

Gianviti François, Krueger Anne, Pisani-Ferry Jean, Sapir André, and Von Hagen Jürgen, 'A European Mechanism for Sovereign Debt Crisis Resolution: A Proposal' (2010) Bruegel Blueprint Series Volume 10

Gillette Clayton, 'What States Can Learn from Municipal Insolvency' in Peter Conti-Brown and David Skeel (eds), *When States Go Broke: The Origins, Context, and Solutions for the American States in Fiscal Crisis* (2012) 99–122

Giuliano–Lagarde Explanatory Report to the Rome Convention on the Law Applicable on Contractual Obligations, [1980] OJ C 282/1

Glinavos Ioannis, 'Casenote: Decision 1116–1117/2014 (21.3.14) of the Greek Council of State (Συμβούλιο της Επικρατείας)' (2014) (available at http://papers.ssrn.com/sol3/papers.cfm?abstract_id=2445568)

—— 'Haircut Undone? The Greek Drama and Prospects for Investment Arbitration' (2014) 5 J Intl Disp Settl 475

Gloster Elizabeth, 'Derivative Delights and Oligarch Feuds—What Contribution Is English Law Making to our Post-Modern Financial World?' Public Lecture, 27

November 2013, Cambridge (available at http://www.privatelaw.law.cam.ac.uk/news/allen-overy-lecture-2013-derivative-delights-and-oligarch-feuds-2013-what-contribution-is-english-law-making-to-our-post2013modern-financial-world)

Goldmann Matthias, 'Sovereign Debt Crises as Threats to the Peace: Restructuring under Chapter VII of the UN Charter?' (2012) 4 Go JIL 153–75

—— 'Good Faith and Transparency in Sovereign Debt Workouts' (2014) (available at http://www.unctad.info/upload/Debt%20Portal/DWM%20Good%20Faith%20and%20Transparency%2020131223.pdf)

—— 'Human Rights and Sovereign Debt Workouts' (2014) (available at http://papers.ssrn.com/sol3/papers.cfm?abstract_id=2330997)

—— 'Necessity and Feasibility of a Standstill Rule for Sovereign Debt Workouts' (2014) (available at http://unctad.org/en/PublicationsLibrary/gdsddf2014misc4_en.pdf)

Goren Jonathan, 'State-to-State Debts: Sovereign Immunity and the "Vulture" Hunt' (2010) 41 Geo Wash Intl L Rev 681–708

Grodecki Jan, 'Conflict of Laws in Time' (1959) 35 BYBIL 58–82

—— 'The Greek Bond Cases' (1961) 24(6) MLR 701–14

Gruson Michael, 'Controlling Choice of Law' in Michael Gruson and Ralph Reisner, *Sovereign Lending: Managing Legal Risk* (1984) 51–67

Guillaume Guilbert, 'La défaillance financière des Etats devant les juges et les arbitres internationaux' (2013) Public Lecture (on file with author)

Gulati Mitu, 'Has the Second Circuit (Unwittingly) Breathed Life into the Nostrils of Imperial Chinese Government Bonds?' (2013) (available at https://papers.ssrn.com/sol3/papers.cfm?abstract_id=2340299)

—— and Zettelmeyer Jeromin, 'Making a Voluntary Greek Debt Exchange Work' (2012) 7(2) CMLJ 169–83

—— 'Engineering an Orderly Greek Debt Restructuring' in Christoph Paulus, *A Debt Restructuring Mechanism for Sovereigns: Do We Need a Legal Procedure?* (2014) 119–28

——, Buchheit Lee, and Thompson Robert, 'The Dilemma of Odious Debts' (2007) 56 Duke LJ 1201–62

——, Trebesch Christoph, and Zettelmeyer Jeromin, 'International Finance and Sovereign Debt' in Francesco Parisi (ed), *Oxford Handbook of Law and Economics: Volume 3* (2017) 482–500

Hagan Sean, 'Debt Restructuring and Economic Recovery' in Lee Buchheit and Rosa Lastra (eds), *Sovereign Debt Management* (2014) 359–85

Harati Southan, 'Loan Rescheduling and Third Parties' (1987) 6 IFLR 44

Hare Christopher, 'The Expanding Judicial Review of Contractual Discretion: *Carte Blanche* or *Carton Rouge*' (2013) 5 JIBFL 269–77

Harris Jonathan, 'Mandatory Rules and Public Policy under the Rome I Regulation' in Franco Ferrari and Stefan Leible (eds), *The Rome I Regulation* (2009) 269–342

Harrison Natasha and Huntriss Fiona, 'Hedge Funds and Litigation: A Brave New World' (2015) 10(2) CMLJ 135–41

Hart Henry, 'The Gold Clause in United States Bonds' (1934–35) 48 Harv L Rev 1057–99

Hartley Trevor, 'Jurisdiction in Conflict of Laws—Disclosure, Third-Party Debt and Freezing Orders' (2010) 126 LQR 194–221

Häseler Sönke, 'Individual versus Collective Enforcement Rights in Sovereign Bonds' (2008) German Working Papers in Law and Economics

—— 'Trustees versus Fiscal Agents and Default Risk in International Sovereign Bonds' (2012) 34 Eur J L & Econ 425–48

Hausmann Ricardo and Panizza Ugo, 'Redemption or Abstinence? Original Sin, Currency Mismatches and Counter-Cyclical Policies in the New Millennium' (2010) CID Working Paper No 194

Herzog Bodo, 'A Behavioural Model of European Bond Markets' (2014) 3(3) J Stock Forex Trad 2014

Higgins Rosalyn, 'The Availability of Damages for Reliance by Government on Executive Necessity' in Werner Flume, Hugo Hahn, Gerhard Kegel, and Kenneth Simmonds (eds), *International Law and Economic Order, Festschrift für F. A. Mann* (1977) 21–33

Hooley Richard, 'Release Provisions in Intercreditor Agreements' (2012) 3 J Bus L 213–34

—— 'Controlling Contractual Discretion' (2013) 72(1) CLJ 65–90

ICMA, 'Sovereign Bond Consultation Paper Supplement' (2014)

IIF, 'Principles for Stable Capital Flows and Fair Debt Restructuring' (2012)

ILA, 'State Insolvency: Options for the Way Forward: Hague Conference Report' (2010a)

—— 'The Hague Conference Report: Sovereign Insolvency Study Group' (2010b) 1–50 (available at https://ila.vettoreweb.com/Storage/Download.aspx?DbStorageId=1451&StorageFileGuid=58bc4db7-4213-440c-93fe-978a0a2896cb)

IMF, 'Involving the Private Sector in the Resolution of Financial Crises—Restructuring International Sovereign Bonds' (2001)

—— 'Sovereign Debt Restructuring Mechanism—Further Considerations' (2002)

—— 'The Design and Effectiveness of Collective Action Clauses' (2002)

—— 'The Design of the Sovereign Debt Restructuring Mechanism—Further Considerations' (2002)

—— 'Collective Action Clauses: Recent Developments and Issues' (2003)

—— 'Local Securities and Derivatives Markets in Emerging Markets: Selected Policy Issues' (2003) IMF Financial Markets Quarterly

—— 'Proposed Features of a Sovereign Debt Restructuring Mechanism' (2003)

—— 'The Restructuring of Sovereign Debt—Assessing the Benefits, Risks and Feasibility of Aggregating Claims' (2003)

—— 'Progress Report to the International Monetary and Financial Committee on Crisis Resolution' (2005)

—— 'A Survey of Experiences with Emerging Market Sovereign Debt Restructurings' (2012)

—— 'Sovereign Debt Restructuring—Recent Developments and Implications for the Fund's Legal and Policy Framework' (2013)

—— 'Strengthening the Contractual Framework to Address Collective Action Problems in Sovereign Debt Restructuring' (2014)

—— 'Second Progress Report in Inclusion of Enhanced Contractual Provisions in International Sovereign Bond Contracts' (2016)

Institut du Droit International, 'The Problem of Choice of Time in Private International Law' (1981)

International Law Association, 'International Monetary Law Committee: Berlin Conference' (2004)

Jeanneret Alexandre, Paget-Blanc Eric, and Souissi Slim, 'Sovereign Defaults by Currency Denomination' (2014) (available at http://papers.ssrn.com/sol3/papers.cfm?abstract_id=2365059)

Jèze Gaston, 'Les défaillances d'Etat' (1935) 53 Recueil des Cours 377

Jenks Wilfred, 'The Authority in English Courts of Decisions of the Permanent Court of International Justice' (1939) 20 BYBIL 1–36

Jolls Christine, 'On Law Enforcement with Boundedly Rational Actors' in Francesco Parisi and Vernon Smith (eds), *The Law and Economics of Irrational Behavior* (2005) 268–86

Juenger Friedrich, 'Conflict of Laws: A Critique of Interest Analysis' (1984) 32 Am J Comp L 1–50

Kahale George III 'State Loan Transactions: Foreign Law Restrictions on Waivers of Immunity and Submissions to Jurisdiction' (1981–82) 37 Bus L 1549–68

Kahan Marcel, 'The Qualified Case against Mandatory Terms in Bonds' (1995) 89 Nw U L Rev 565–622

—— 'Rethinking Corporate Bonds: The Trade-Off between Individual and Collective Rights' (2002) 77 NYU L Rev 1040–89

—— and Tuckman Bruce, 'Do Bondholders Lose from Junk Bond Covenant Changes?' (1993) 66(4) J Bus 499–516

——, Amihud Yakov, and Garbade Kenneth, 'A New Governance Structure for Corporate Bonds' (1999) 51 Stan L Rev 447–92

Kahn-Freund Otto, 'Constitutional Review of Foreign Law?' in Werner Flume, Hugo Hahn, Gerhard Kegel, and Kenneth Simmonds (eds), *International Law and Economic Order, Festschrift für F. A. Mann* (1977) 207–25

Kämmerer Jörn, 'Der Staatsbankrott aus völkerrechtlicher Sicht' (2005) 65 ZaöRV 651–76

Kirchhof Paul, 'The Public Debt, Democratic Principles and the Rules of Law' in Detlev Dicke (ed), *Foreign Debts in the Present and a New International Economic Order* (1986) 339–60

Kissam Leo and Leach Edmond, 'Sovereign Expropriation of Property and Abrogation of Concession Contracts' (1959) 28 Fordham L Rev 177–214

Kremer Josiane and Mnyanda Lukanyo, 'Norway Oil Fund Rejected Greek Debt Swap, CEO Slyngstad Says' *Bloomberg* (16 March 2012)

Kronke Herbert, 'Capital Markets and Conflict of Laws' (2000) 286 Recueil des Cours 245

Krueger Anne, 'New Approaches to Sovereign Debt Restructuring: An Update on our Thinking' (2002) IMF Publication

Kupelyants Hayk, 'The German Taxpayer and the Greek Sovereign Debt' (2015) Lexis PSL

—— 'Recognition and Enforcement of Foreign Judgments in the Absence of the Debtor and his Assets within the Jurisdiction: Reversing the Burden of Proof' (forthcoming JPIL)

Kurtz Jürgen, 'The Use and Abuse of WTO Law in Investor–State Arbitration: Competition and its Discontents' (2009) 20 EJIL 749–71

Lagarde Paul, 'Le nouveau droit international privé des contrats après l'entrée en viguer de la Convention de Rome du 19 juin 1980' (1991) 80(2) Rev Crit 287

Lalive Jean-Flavien, 'Recent Version: Abrogation or Alteration of an Economic Development Agreement between a State and a Private Foreign Party' (1961–62) 17 Bus Law 434–68

—— 'Unilateral Alteration or Abrogation by either Party to a Contract between a State and a Foreign National' in Symposium on the Rights and Duties of Foreigners in the Conduct of Industrial and Commercial Operations Abroad, *Rights and Duties of Private Investors Abroad* (1965) 265–80

Lauterpacht Hersch, 'The Problem of Jurisdictional Immunities of Foreign States' (1951) 28 BYBIL 220

League of Nations, *Report of the Committee for the Study of International Loan Contracts* (1939a)

—— Study Committee Report, II Econ and Finan (1939b) II.A 10

Lehmann Matthias, 'Prospectus Liability and Private International Law—Assessing the Landscape after the CJEU's Kolassa Ruling (Case C-375/13)' (2016) 12 JPIL 318–43

Lein Eva, 'Jurisdiction and Applicable Law in Cross-Border Mass Litigation' in Fausto Pocar, Ilaria Viarengo, and Francesca Clara Villata (eds), *Recasting Brussels I* (2012) 159–72

Levine Matt, 'Argentina's Bond Fight Comes Down to its Worst Bonds' *Bloomberg View* (8 February 2016)

Levy Yeyati Eduardo, 'Dollars, Debt, and International Financial Institutions: Dedollarizing Multilateral Lending' (2007) 21(1) World Bank Economic Review 21–47

Lewyn Marc, 'Foreign Debt—Act of State Doctrine—Unilateral Deferral of Obligations by Debtor Nations Is Inconsistent with United States Law and Policy: Allied Bank International v. Banco Credito Agricola de Cartago' (1985) 15 Ga J Intl & Comp L 657–69

Li Yanying, 'Policy Implication of Poštová Tribunal's Jurisdiction over Sovereign Bonds: Bankruptcy Cram-Down and ICSID Arbitration' (2014) (available at http://papers.ssrn.com/sol3/papers.cfm?abstract_id=2402643)

Li Yuefen and Panizza Ugo, 'The Economic Rationale for the Principles on Promoting Responsible Sovereign Lending and Borrowing' in Carlos Espósito, Yuefen Li, and Juan Pablo Bohoslavsky (eds), *Sovereign Financing and International Law: The UNCTAD Principles on Responsible Sovereign Lending and Borrowing* (2013) 15–38

Lienau Odette, 'Legitimacy and Impartiality in a Sovereign Debt Workout Mechanism' (2006) Cornell Law Faculty Publications, Paper 1110

Lipstein Kurt, 'Conflict of Laws—Debt—Foreign Statute—Proper Law' (1960) 18(2) Camb LJ 169–71

—— 'Proof of Foreign Law: Scrutiny of its Constitutional Validity' (1967) 42 BYBIL 265–70

—— 'The General Principles of Private International Law' (1972) 135 Recueil des Cours 97

Longstaff Francis, Jun Pan, Lasse Pedersen, and Kenneth Singleton, 'How Sovereign Is Sovereign Credit Risk?' (2011) 3(2) Am Econ J 75–103

Lubben Stephen, 'Out of the Past: Railroads and Sovereign Debt Restructuring' (2004) 35 Geo J Intl L 845–57

Lucas Vicente, 'Conflicts of Laws in International Lending Transactions—Governing Law and Choice of Forum' in Dominique Carreau and Malcolm Shaw, *La Dette extérieure: External Debt* (1995) 439–84

McCahill Dominic and Baron Jamie, 'Bond Exit Consents: US Courts Offer Pragmatic Approach' (2013) 24(6) PLC 17–18

McConnell Michael and Picker Randal, 'When Cities Go Broke: A Conceptual Introduction to Municipal Bankruptcy' (1993) 60 U Chi L Rev 425–95

McDaniel Morey, 'Bondholders and Corporate Governance' (1986) 41 Bus Law 413–60

McKinsey & Company, 'McKinsey Global Institute: Debt and (Not Much) Deleveraging' (2015)

McLean Roberto, 'Legal Aspects of the External Debt' (1989) 214 Recueil des Cours 31

McNulty John, 'Corporations and the Intertemporal Conflict of Laws' (1967) 55 Cal L Rev 12–73

Machell John and Haywood Jennifer, 'Discretionary Decision Making in a Commercial Context' (2013) 4 JIBFL 195–98

Mairal Hector, 'Issues Arising from the Legal and Constitutional Validity of the Debt under the Debtor's Own Law' in David Sassoon and Daniel Bradlow (eds), *Judicial Enforcement of International Debt Obligations* (1987) 147

Maniruzzaman Munir, 'State Contracts with Aliens: The Question of Unilateral Change by the State in Contemporary International Law' (1992) 9(4) J Intl Arb 141–72

Mankowski Peter, 'Article 7' in Ulrich Magnus and Peter Mankowski, *Brussels I Regulation: European Commentaries on Private International Law* (2016) 121–369

Mann FA, 'The Law Governing State Contracts' (1944) 21 BYBIL 11–33

—— 'The Time Element in the Conflict of Laws' (1954) 31 BYBIL 217–47

—— 'Sovereign or Fisc?' (1960) 9 ICLQ 691–94

—— 'State Contracts and State Responsibility' (1960) 54 AJIL 572–91

—— 'On the Sacrosanctity of the Foreign Act of State' (1965) 14(3) ICLQ 985–87

—— 'The Proper Law of Contracts Concluded by International Persons' in FA Mann, *Studies in International Law* (1973) 211–40

—— 'Judiciary and Executive in Foreign Affairs' in FA Mann, *Studies in International Law* (2008) 391–419

—— 'The Judicial Recognition of an Unrecognised State' in FA Mann, *Further Studies in International Law* (2008) 386–88

Marsh Sarah and Bianchi Walter, 'Argentina Aims to Skirt U.S. Court, Bring Debt under National Law' *Reuters* (20 August 2014)

Mayer Pierre, 'La neutralisation du pouvoir normatif de l'Etat en matière de contrats d'Etat' (1986) 113 JDI 1–78

—— 'Mandatory Rules of Law in International Arbitration' (1986) 4(2) Arb Intl 274–93

—— 'L'arbitre international et la hiérarchie des normes' (2011) 2 Revue de l'arbitrage 361–84

Meron Theodor, 'Repudiation of ultra vires State Contracts and the International Responsibility of States' (1957) 6(2) ICLQ 273

Metallinos Alexander, 'The Greek Sovereign Debt' in Bruno Eugenio (ed), *Sovereign Debt and Debt Restructuring: Legal, Financial and Regulatory Aspects* (2013) 19–32

Mitchell Lawrence, 'The Fairness Rights of Corporate Bondholders' (1990) 65 NYU L Rev 1165–1229

Miyajima Ken, Mohanty Madhusudan, and Chan Tracy, 'Emerging Market Local Currency Bonds: Diversification and Stability' (2012) BIS Working Papers No 391

Mody Ashoka, 'Sovereign Debt and its Restructuring Framework in the Euro Area' (2013) Bruegel Working Paper 2013/05

Moody's Special Comment, 'The Role of Holdout Creditors and CACs in Sovereign Debt Restructurings' (2013)

Moore Elaine, 'Kazakhstan First to Introduce Post-Argentina Bond Contracts' *Financial Times* (5 October 2014)

Morgan Jonathan, 'Against Judicial Review of Discretionary Contractual Powers' [2008] 2 LMCLQ 230–42

Morris John, 'The Time Factor in the Conflict of Laws' (1966) 15(2–3) ICLQ 422–35

Moss Gabriel, Bayfield Daniel, Al-Attar Adam, Seife Howard, and Rivera Seven, 'Giving Effect to Debt Compromise Arrangements—Binding the Minority or Out of the Money Classes of Creditors' in Christopher Mallon and Shai Waisman (eds), *The Law and Practice of Restructurings in the UK and US* (2011) 163–212

Moverley Smith Stephen and Murphy Heather, 'Sovereign Bond Collective Action Clauses: Issues Arising' [2015] 2 JIBFL 128A, 1–3

—— and Sharpe Harry, 'An Offer You Can't Refuse: When Does Coercion of a Group to Accept a Proposal Constitute Oppression of the Minority?' (2014) 5 JIBFL 288–90

Muir-Watt Horatia, 'Private International Law as Global Governance: Beyond the Schize, from Closet to Planet' (2011) (available at https://works.bepress.com/horatia_muir-watt/1)

Nili Yaron, 'An Economist's View of Market Evidence in Valuation and Bankruptcy Litigation' *Harvard Law Blog* (28 June 2014)

Note, 'Conflict of Laws and the Gold Clause in Foreign Government Bonds' (1937) 46(5) Yale LJ 891–96

Note, 'Decisions of National Tribunals involving Points of Public or Private International Law' (1937) 18 BYBIL 210, 215–21

Note, 'The Rights and Remedies of the Bondholder under Corporate Bonds and Indentures' (1927) 27 Colum L Rev 579–87

Nurick Lester, 'The IMF Articles of Agreement' in David Sassoon and Daniel Bradlow (eds), *Judicial Enforcement of International Debt Obligations* (1987)

Olivares-Caminal Rodrigo, 'To Rank *Pari Passu* or Not to Rank *Pari Passu*' (2009) 15(4) L & Bus Rev Am 745–78

Oliveira Luís, Dias Curto José, and Pedro Nunes João, 'The Determinants of Sovereign Credit Spread Changes in the Euro-Zone' (2012) 22 Int Fin Markets, Inst and Money 278–304

Panizza Ugo, Sturzenegger Federico, and Zettelmeyer Jeromin, 'The Economics and Law of Sovereign Debt and Default' (2009) 47(3) J Econ Lit 651–98

Paulsson Jan, 'May a State Invoke its Internal Law to Repudiate Consent to International Commercial Arbitration?' (1986) 2 Arb Intl 90

Peterson Lewis, 'Who's Being Greedy? A Theoretical and Empirical Examination of Holdouts and Coercion in Debt Tender and Exchange Offers' (1993) 103 Yale LJ 505–34

Piaggio Nicolas, 'Lessons for Europe: The Pre-Emptive Restructuring of Uruguay' in Eugenio Bruno, *Sovereign Debt and Debt Restructuring: Legal, Financial and Regulatory Aspects* (2013) 201–08

Porzecanski Arturo, 'Behind the 2012 Greek Sovereign Debt Restructuring' in Eugenio Bruno, *Sovereign Debt and Debt Restructuring: Legal, Financial and Regulatory Aspects* (2013) 33–50

—— 'Borrowing and Debt: How do Sovereigns Get into Trouble' in Lee Buchheit and Rosa Lastra (eds), *Sovereign Debt Management* (2014) 309–29

Power Philip, 'Sovereign Debt: The Rise of the Secondary Market and its Implications for Future Restructurings' (1995–96) 64 Fordham LR 2701–72

Pryles Michael, 'The Time Factor in Private International Law' (1980) 6 Monash U L Rev 225–43

Purcell John and Kaufmann Jeffrey, 'The Risks of Sovereign Lending: Lessons from History' (1993) Salomon Brothers

Raffer Kunibert, 'What's Good for the United States Must Be Good for the World: Advocating an International Chapter 9 Insolvency' in Bruno Kreisky Forum for International Dialogue (ed), *From Cancún to Vienna: International Development in a New World* (1993) 64–74

—— 'Risks of Lending and Liability of Lending' in Christian Barry, Barry Herman, and Lydia Tomitova (eds), *Dealing Fairly with Developing Country Debt* (2007)

—— 'In the Case of Sovereigns, Should Official Sector Debt Be Subordinated to Private Sector Debt?' (2013) IFLR 20

Rawlings Philip, 'Reinforcing Collectivity: The Liability of Trustees and the Power of Investors in Finance Transactions' (2009) 23(1) Tru L I 14–34

—— 'The Management of Loan Syndicates and the Rights of Individual Lenders' (2009) 24(4) JIBLR 179–85

Ray George, 'Some Reasons for the Binding Force of Development Contracts between States and Foreign Nationals' (1960–61) 16 Bus Law 942–58

Reddell Michael, 'The New Zealand Debt Conversion Act 1933: A Case Study in Coercive Domestic Public Debt Restructuring' (2012) 75 Reserve Bank of New Zealand Bulletin 38–45

Reinhart Carmen and Rogoff Kenneth, 'The Forgotten History of Domestic Debt' (2008) NBER Working Paper 13946

—— 'Financial and Sovereign Debt Crises: Some Lessons Learned and Those Forgotten' (2013) IMF Working Paper WP/13/266

Reinhart Carmen, Rogoff Kenneth, and Savastano Miguel, 'Debt Intolerance' (2003) NBER Working Paper 9908

Reinhart Carmen, Reinhart Vincent, Rogoff Kenneth, 'Debt Overhang: Past and Present' (2012) NBER Working Paper 18015

Reinisch August, 'Debt Restructuring and State Responsibility Issues' in Dominique Carreau and Malcolm Shaw (eds), *La Dette extérieure: The External Debt* (1995) 537–605

—— 'Necessity in Investment Arbitration' (2010) 41 NYIL 137

Reisman Michael, '"Case Specific Mandates" versus 'Systemic Implications': How Should Investment Tribunals Decide?—The Freshfields Arbitration Lecture' (2013) 29(2) Arb Intl 131–52

Report of the IIF Joint Committee on Strengthening the Framework for Sovereign Debt Crisis Prevention and Resolution (2012)

Robert Eric, 'Rééchelonnement de la dette ou règlement judiciaire?' in Dominique Carreau and Malcolm Shaw (eds), *La Dette éxtérieure: The External Debt* (1995) 607–70

Roe Mark, 'The Voting Prohibition in Bond Workouts' (1987) 97(2) Yale LJ 232–79

Rogerson Pippa, 'The Situs of Debts in the Conflict of Laws—Illogical, Unnecessary and Misleading' (1990) 49(3) CLJ 441–60

—— 'Third Party Debt Orders (Garnishee Order)—Foreign Bank Accounts' (2003) 62(3) CLJ 576–80

Rogoff Kenneth and Zettelmeyer Jeromin, 'Bankruptcy Procedures for Sovereigns: A History of Ideas, 1976–2001' (2002) IMF Staff Papers 49

Rose Scott, 'Russia Sees Risks as Foreigners Amass Government Ruble Bonds' *Bloomberg News* (26 July 2013)

Roubini Nouriel, 'Debt Sustainability: How to Assess Whether a Country Is Insolvent' (2001) (available at http://people.stern.nyu.edu/nroubini/papers/debtsustainability.pdf)

Roubini Nouriel and Setser Brad, 'Improving the Sovereign Debt Restructuring Process: Problems in Restructuring, Proposed Solutions, and a Roadmap for Reform' (2003) unpublished paper (available at http://www.iie.com/publications/papers/roubini-setser0303.pdf)

Saggese Nicholas, Noel Gregg, and Mohr Michael, 'A Practitioner's Guide to Exchange Offers and Consent Solicitations' (1991) 24 Loy LA L Rev 527–620

Sausser-Hall George, 'La clause-or dans les contrats publics et privés' (1937) 60 Recueil des Cours, 651

Schlemmer-Schulte Sabine, 'Fragmentation of International Law: The Case of International Finance & Investment Law Versus Human Rights Law' (2012) 25 Pac McGeorge Global Bus & Dev LJ 409–24

Schmitthoff Clive, 'The International Government Loan' (1937) 19(4) J Comp Leg & Int Law 179–96

Schreuer Christoph, 'Unjustified Enrichment in International Law' (1974) 22(2) Am J Comp L 281

Schumacher Julian, Trebesch Christoph, and Enderlein Henrik, 'What Explains Sovereign Debt Litigation?' (2015) CESIFO Working Paper No 5319

Schwarcz Steven, 'Sovereign Debt Restructuring: A Bankruptcy Reorganization Approach' (2000) 85 Cornell L Rev 956–1034

Schwarzenberger Georg, 'State Bankruptcy and International Law' in Wybo Heere, *International Law and its Sources. Liber Amicorum Maarten Bos* (1989) 137–46

Scott Hal, 'Sovereign Debt Default: Cry for the United States, Not Argentina' (2006) Washington Legal Foundation Working Paper Series No 140

Shleifer Andrei, 'Will the Sovereign Debt Market Survive?' (2003) 93(2) Amer Econ Rev 85–90

Silberman Linda, 'The Role of Choice of Law in National Class Actions' (2007–08) 156 U Pa L Rev 2001–34

—— '*Goodyear* and *Nicastro*: Observations from a Transnational and Comparative Perspective' (2012) 63 SCLR 591

—— 'Daimler AG v. Bauman: A New Era for Judicial Jurisdiction in the United States' (2014/15) 16 YPIL 217

—— and Simowitz Aaron, 'Recognition and Enforcement of Foreign Judgments and Awards: What Hath *Daimler* Wrought?' (2016) 91 NYU L Rev 344–95

Simowitz Aaron, 'Siting Intangibles' (2015) 48 NYU J Intl L & Pol 259–324

Singh Manmohan, 'Recovery Rates from Distressed Debt—Empirical Evidence from Chapter 11 Fillings, International Litigation, and Recent Sovereign Debt Restructurings' (2003) IMF Working Paper WP/03/161

Skeel David, 'Can Majority Voting Provisions Do It All?' (2002) 52 Emory LJ 417–25

—— 'State Bankruptcy from the Ground up' in Peter Conti-Brown and David Skeel (eds), *When States Go Broke: The Origins, Context, and Solutions for the American States in Fiscal Crisis* (2012) 191–213

—— 'States of Bankruptcy' (2012) 79 U Chic L Rev 677–735

Sklar Ruben, 'Renegotiation of External Debt: The Allied Bank Case and the Chapter 11 Analogy' (1985) 17 U Miami Inter-Am L Rev 59–90

Smith PV, 'Validity, Construction, and Application of Express Restrictions on Right of Action by Individual Holder of One or More of a Series of Corporate Bonds or Other Obligations' (originally published in 1937) 108 ALR 88

Sommers Davidson, Broches Aaron, and Delaume Georges, 'Conflict Avoidance in International Loans and Monetary Agreements' (1956) 21 L & Contemp Prob 463–82

Spiro Erwin, 'The Incidence of Time in the Conflict of Laws' (1960) 9 ICLQ 357–82

Stadler Astrid, 'Conflicts of Laws in Multinational Collective Actions—A Judicial Nightmare?' in Duncan Fairgrieve and Eva Lein (eds), *Extraterritoriality and Collective Redress* (2012) 191–214

Stiglitz Joseph, 'Sovereign Debt: Notes on Theoretical Framework and Policy Analyses' (2002) Initiative for Public Dialogue Working Paper Series

Strupp Karl, 'L'intervention en matière financière' (1925) 8 Recueil des Cours 1

Tigert Ricki, 'Allied Bank International: A United States Government Perspective' (1985) 17 NYU J Intl L & Pol 511–26

Tirado Ignacio, 'Sovereign Insolvency in the Euro Zone Public and Private Law Remedies' (2012) Annual Review of Insolvency Law 711–46

Torabzadeh Khalil, Roufagalas John, and Woodruff Criss, 'Self-Selection and the Effects of Poison Put/Call Covenants on the Reoffering Yields of Corporate Bonds' (2000) 9 Intl Rev Econ Fin 139–56

Trebesch Christoph, 'Delays in Sovereign Debt Restructurings' (2008), unpublished paper (available at http:\\www.researchgate.net/publication/46457981_Delays_in_Sovereign_Debt_Restructurings_Should_We_Really_Blame_the_Creditors) 1–30

—— 'Debt Restructuring Delays' (2010) (available at https://sites.google.com/site/christophtrebesch/research)

—— 'Debt Restructuring Delays: Measurement and Stylized Facts' in Robert Kolb (ed), *Sovereign Debt: From Safety to Default* (2011) 169–78

Trebesch Christoph, Enderlein Henrik, and von Daniels Laura, 'Sovereign Debt Disputes: A Database of Government Coerciveness in Debt Crises' (2012) 31(2) J Intl Mon & Fin 250–66

Tribe John, 'Discharge in Bankruptcy: An Examination of Personal Insolvency's Fresh Start Function in English Law: Part 2' (2012) 25(8) Insolv Int 117–20

Tsang Cheng-Yun, '*Ex-Im Bank v Grenada*: Adding Clarity or Confusion?' (2015) 10(2) CMLJ 142–61

Tsibanoulis Dimitris and Anagnostopoulos Iakovos, 'The Greek PSI and the Litigation Surrounding It' (2014) 2 Rev Int des serv fin/Intern Rev Fin Serv 18–24

UN General Assembly, 'Towards the Establishment of a Multilateral Legal Framework for Sovereign Debt Restructuring Processes' (2014) UN Doc A/Res/68/304

UNCTAD, 'Domestic and External Public Debt in Developing Countries' (2008) UNCTAD Discussion Papers

—— 'Principles on Promoting Responsible Sovereign Lending and Borrowing' (2012)

Varriale Gemma, 'Basel Plan to Curb Banks' Sovereign Debt Faces Challenges' (3 February 2015) IFLR

Viterbo Anna, 'Supranational Creditors: A Threat to the Equal Status of Bondholders?' (2015) 10(2) CMLJ 193–211

von Bogdandy Armin and Goldmann Mathias, 'Sovereign Debt Restructurings as Exercises of International Public Authority: Towards a Decentralized Sovereign Insolvency Law' in Carlos Espósito, Yuefen Li, and Juan Pablo Bohoslavsky (eds), *Sovereign Financing and International Law: The UNCTAD Principles on Responsible Sovereign Lending and Borrowing* (2013) 39–70

Waibel Michael, 'Opening Pandora's Box: Sovereign Bonds in International Arbitration' (2007) 101 AJIL 711–59

—— 'Two Worlds of Necessity in ICSID Arbitration: *CMS* and *LG&E*' (2007) 20 LJIL 637

—— 'Debt Relief to Poor Countries: Rules v. Discretion' (2010) 25(5) BB & FLR 295

—— 'La faillite souveraine en droit: Un Etat peut-il faire faillite?' in Matthias Audit, *Insolvabilite des Etats* (2011) 41–63

—— 'Staateninsolvenzen in historischer Sicht' in Georg Kodek and August Reinisch (eds), *Staateninsolvenz* (2012) 55–94

—— 'Out of Thin Air? Tracing the Origins of the UNCTAD Principles in State Practice' in Carlos Espósito, Yuefen Li, and Juan Pablo Bohoslavsky (eds), *Sovereign Financing and International Law: The UNCTAD Principles on Responsible Sovereign Lending and Borrowing* (2013) 87–112

—— 'Steering Sovereign Debt Restructurings through the CDS Quicksand' (2014) 15 Journal of Banking Regulation 14–40

Wälde Thomas, 'The Sanctity of Debt and Insolvent Countries: Defenses of Debtors in International Loan Agreements' in David Sassoon and Daniel Bradlow (eds), *Judicial Enforcement of International Debt Obligations* (1987)

Walker Mark and Barthélemy Faye, 'Sovereign Debt Renegotiation: Restructuring the Commercial Debt of HIPC Debtor Countries' (2010) 73 L & Contemp Probs 317–24

Wasserstein Fassberg Celia, 'The Intertemporal Problem in Choice of Law Reconsidered: Israeli Matrimonial Property' (1990) 39 ICLQ 856–80

Wautelet Patrick, 'Les Fonds Vautours—Vulture Funds, Creditors and Sovereign Debtors: How to Find a Balance?' in Mathias Audit (ed), *Insolvabilité des États et dettes souveraines* (2011) 103–64

—— 'The Greek Debt Restructuring and Property Rights: A Greek Tragedy for Investors?' in André Alen, *Liberae Cogitationes: Mélanges Marc Bossuyt* (2013) 903–28

Weber Stefan, 'The Law Applicable to Bonds' in Hans van Houtte (ed), *The Law of Cross-Border Securities Transactions* (1999) 29–45

Weidemaier Mark, 'Disputing Boilerplate' (2009–10) 82 Temp L Rev 1–54

—— 'Indiana Jones, Contracts Originalist' (2014) 9(3) CMLJ 255–58

—— 'Sovereign Immunity and Sovereign Debt' (2014) 1 U Ill L Rev 67–113

Weidemaier Mark and Gelpern Anna, 'Injunctions in Sovereign Debt Litigation' (2014) 1 Y J on Reg 189–218

—— and McCarl Ryan, 'Creditors' Remedies' in Lee Buchheit and Rosa Lastra (eds), *Sovereign Debt Management* (2014) 139–50

—— and Gulati Mitu, 'A People's History of Collective Action Clauses' (2013) 54(1) Va JIL 51–95

Weisz George, Schwarzkopf Nancy, and Panitch Mimi, 'Selected Issues in Sovereign Debt Litigation' (1991) 12(1) U Pa J Intl Bus L 1–49

Witte Andreas, 'The Greek Bond Haircut: Public and Private International Law and European Law Limits to Unilateral Sovereign Debt Restructuring' (2012) 9(2) Manchester J Intl Econ L 307–38

Wolf Martin, 'Holdouts Give Vultures a Bad Name' *Financial Times* (2 September 2014)

Wood Philip, 'Selected Aspects of International Loan Documentation and Rescheduling' in Lars Kalderén and Qamar Siddiqi (eds), Sovereign *Borrowers: Guidelines on Legal Negotiations with Commercial Lenders* (1984) 123–43

—— 'Pari Passu Clauses—What Do They Mean?' (2003) 10 JIBFL 371–74

—— 'Syndicated Credit Agreement: Majority Voting' (2003) 62(2) CLJ 261–63

—— 'Bondholders and Banks—Why the Difference in Protections?' (2011) 6(2) CMLJ 188–96

—— 'The Origins and Future of Non-Discrimination in Sovereign Bankruptcies: A Comment' (2014) 9(3) CMLJ 293–98

Worthington Sarah and Mellon Grainne, 'Statutory Rules, Common Law Rules and Public Policy in the Global Financial Crisis' (2010–11) 29 Penn St Intl L Rev 613–33

Yianni Andrew and Malek Lauren, 'Seychelles Debt Restructuring: Restoring the Viability of the Public Finances' (2010) 25(7) JIBLR 330–36

Yoshino Naoyuki and Vollmer Uwe, 'The Sovereign Debt Crisis: Why Greece, But Not Japan?' (2014) 12 Asia Eur J 325–44

Zahavi Netanella, 'Sovereign Default: Analyses and Remedies' (JSD thesis, Yale Law School 2005)

Zandstra Deborah, 'New Aggregated Collective Action Clauses and Evolution in the Restructuring of Sovereign Debt Securities' (2017) 12(2) CMLJ 180

Zanghirati Bruno, 'Sovereign Indebtedness: The Complex Relations between Banks and States' (1896–97) 7 IYBIL 133–62

Zettelmeyer Jeromin, Trebesch Christoph, and Gulati Mitu, 'The Greek Debt Exchange: An Autopsy' (2013) 28 Econ Pol 513–63

Index